Crime and Canadian Public Policy

James C. Hackler

University of Alberta

Prentice Hall Canada Inc.
Scarborough, Ontario

*To Bunny, who spent many weekends with-
out seeing her husband during the day*

Canadian Cataloguing in Publication Data

Hackler, James C., 1930-
   Crime and Canadian public policy

ISBN 0-13-512429-8

1. Criminology – Canada.   2. Crime – Sociological
aspects.. I. Title.

HV6807.H3 1994   364'.971   C94-930150-7

Prentice-Hall, Inc., Englewood Cliffs, New Jersey
Prentice-Hall International (UK) Limited, London
Prentice-Hall of Australia, Pty. Limited, Sydney
Prentice-Hall Hispanoamericana, S.A., Mexico City
Prentice-Hall of India Private Limited, New Delhi
Prentice-Hall of Japan, Inc., Tokyo
Simon & Schuster Asia Private Limited, Singapore
Editora Prentice-Hall do Brasil, Ltda., Rio de Janeiro

ISBN 0-13-512429-8

Acquisitions Editor: Michael Bickerstaff
Production Editor: Kelly Dickson
Copy Editor: William Booth
Production Coordinator: Deborah Starks
Cover Design: Olena Serbyn
Page Layout: Phyllis Seto

1 2 3 4 5 TG 98 97 96 95 94

Printed and bound in Canada

Every reasonable effort has been made to obtain permissions for all
articles and data used in this edition. If errors or omissions have
occurred, they will be corrected in future editions provided written
notification has been received by the publisher.

Table of Contents

Introduction

This book reviews a number of approaches to crime with the goal of suggesting policies that make sense in terms of what we know. If the reader were to turn to the last two chapters of this book and reflect on the recommendations offered there, she might think I am somewhat radical in my thinking. Similarly the chapter on women's issues (15), responses to drugs (16), family violence (17), and criminalizing sex (19) suggest that the author is clearly to the left of centre. On the other hand, the chapter on scientific theory (4), and those on statistics (5, 6 and 7) suggest an interest in the use of empirical data to understand crime and guide policies. Both images are correct. Of course, a book on crime, and how knowledge about crime could be used to influence public policy, should present a range of perspectives. Thus, one might say that Parts I and II of this book are traditional and Parts III and IV are somewhat radical. This is partially due to the conventional historical sequence used to present a general review of research strategies and theories of crime. Knowing ideas from the past is necessary to understand developments in the present.

The seemingly radical conclusions of this book should not be particularly surprising. Despite differing views among criminologists, the majority would probably agree that major structural changes are needed to reduce crime. Some of the recommendations made in the final chapters fit more than one particular perspective, because they draw on evidence produced by a variety of orientations. Furthermore, the majority of criminologists probably share my feelings that government policies for the past decade-and-a-half have not been enlightened with regard to crime reduction.

The Organization of This Text

In one sense, the first half of this book is "older" in its orientation, while the second half is "newer." Part I: The Criminological Enterprise concentrates on how crime has been studied, the questions that should be asked, and some of the debates over how the research should be done. Part II: Explanations of Crime follows a somewhat historical sequence, starting with explanations of individual behaviour, gradually adding more social psychological elements and then aspects of the larger society. Towards the end of this section, questions are raised about these traditional views by introducing the conflict perspective. Part III: The Shape and Form of Modern Crime Patterns attempts to bridge traditional and conflict thinking. The chapters on women's issues, drug crime, and criminalizing sex emphasize that the traditional questions might not be appropriate, and that criminologists should re-orient some of their thinking. The chapters on violent crime and property crime draw on historical as well as contemporary themes. Part IV: Responding to Crime focuses on the criminal justice system and criminogenic conditions in Canadian society. For those interested in reform, this last section may be of greater interest. Studies of the agencies of control is an area where current criminology can make meaningful contributions, even though we often end criminology courses without spending much time on them, or we postpone the topic to a later, more specialized criminology course.

Acknowledgements

It is very difficult to identify the source of some ideas, but many people have influenced the thoughts expressed in this book. My former professors, Herbert Costner and Clarence Schrag, clearly moulded my thinking. Bob Ratner made me rethink much of my work. Fran Shaver, John Lowman, and Erin Van Brunschot were particularly helpful with the chapter on Criminalizing Sex. Louise Biron, Elizabeth Stanko, Holly Johnson, and Karen Rodgers provided useful feedback for the chapter on Women and Crime. Doug Wahlsten and Don Kuiken helped to summarize biological and psychological factors in a very limited space. Patricia Erickson generously shared her expertise on drug issues. Rick Linden provided useful critiques of social control theories. Bob Silverman was particularly helpful with several of the figures used in the chapters on statistics. Ron Hinch provided a number of insightful and useful suggestions. John Hagan is one of those former students who gives tremendous satisfaction by telling you that he learned something from you as a teacher, and then producing such a wealth of research and ideas that they make a major contribution to your thinking. Staff Sergeant P.J. Duggan has been a thoughtful commentator on many ideas over the years. Gwynne Nettler has tried to keep me from confusing my social-work tendencies with scholarly work, with only partial success.

Louise Bohachyk assisted with the manuscript in many ways: being innovative with tables and figures, helping me to avoid a variety of pitfalls, and constantly maintaining her sense of humour. Jana Grekul read the chapters, searched out information, and helped with numerous details. Laura Hargrave provided editorial assistance on work that went into this book, and rescued me when I had computer problems. There are others who have helped directly and indirectly, including: Edem Frank Avakame, Helen Boritch, Elizabeth Comack, Jim Creechan, Andrew Donohue, Tim Hartnagel, Les Kennedy, Sergeant Colin Milton, Marianne Nielsen, and Sabrina Park.

I must also acknowledge the important impact of the writings of John Kenneth Galbraith on my overall worldview. Such scholars reinforce my view that crime, like so many human activities, is deeply enmeshed in the economic and social structure of a society. This book argues that effective social policies relating to crime cannot be studied intelligently in isolation from this larger social picture.

PART I

THE CRIMINOLOGICAL ENTERPRISE

How do we study crime?

The history of the criminological enterprise in Canada is reviewed in Chapter 1. It is always difficult to decide who are the "founding fathers," but many would agree with my choices. For some disciplines we have "founding mothers" as well, but criminology has been slow to acknowledge female scholars. Chapter 2 asks what sort of things have been studied in the past under the criminology label and what we should study in the future. Our choices are not always based on logical assumptions. People assume they approach things objectively, but in Chapter 3 I argue that scholars operate from certain perspectives that mould their conclusions. Assumptions that are shared with the dominant society often dictate and guide those perspectives. One of those perspectives is the one used by science. The discussion in Chapter 4 acknowledges that the scientific approach may have been oversold at times, but it still has certain merits. Chapter 5, 6, and 7 present warnings about how crime statistics can be used as well as misused.

THE STUDY OF CRIMINOLOGY IN CANADA

It is time you knew of Tagoona, the Eskimo. Last year one of our white men said to him. "We are glad you have been ordained as the first priest of your people. Now you can help us with their problem " Tagoona asked, "what is a problem?" and the white man said, "Togoona, if I held you by your heels from a third story window, you would have a problem." Tagoona considered this long and carefully. Then he said, "I do not think so. If you saved me, all would be well. If you dropped me, nothing would matter. It is you who would have the problem."

Margaret Craven, *I Heard the Owl Call My Name*, p. 60

THE OUTLOOK FOR CRIME IN CANADA

In some respects, this book is pessimistic. Crime in Canada has probably been relatively stable, contrary to media coverage, which gives the impression that there have been dramatic increases. However, crime will probably increase in Canada in the not too distant future. Part of that increase will be the result of ineffective government policies at both the federal and provincial levels. Other increases in crime will be the product of a variety of reactionary tendencies that have been viewed by politicians as acceptable to North Americans in recent times. For example, there has been a tendency for governments to forget that crime is closely tied to a number of other factors that influence the social order.

To illustrate, governments fight recession by stimulating the economy. One strategy is to provide tax incentives to average-income families so that they will spend or invest more. However, those who are paying taxes may grumble during recessions, but they are not suffering the type of damage that actually tears at the social fabric. On the other hand, the unemployed are not as "well connected" with the mainstream of society. People hurt in different ways, and those who hurt because they are left out of the mainstream are more likely to contribute to crime than those who are making adjustments along with others facing similar circumstances. When governments do not systematically attempt to keep marginal people fully integrated into the mainstream of society, criminogenic conditions increase. Thus, when a government provides financial help to a company which then fires a portion of its work force to become "lean and mean" and compete effectively with businesses in other countries, it may be good for stockholders, but those who lose their jobs are at risk of becoming marginal individuals. Some of these economic forces are clearly beyond the control of the federal and provincial governments in Canada, but in some areas, these negative tendencies that undermine the social order could be ameliorated to some degree.

It is also possible, but unlikely, that cooperative efforts among nations might diminish criminogenic conditions in the world. Such thinking is clearly utopian, but these possibilities should be discussed in a general book on criminology. Crime is not a phenomenon that can be understood in isolation from other social forces. There is no special surgery that can be used to cut out crime, if the entire society is sick. Most of this book will attempt to summarize and examine what we know about crime, but I hope that students and others who read this book will share my inclination to apply current knowledge in a way that might actually lead to improvements in society, which would also mean less crime.

Much of our knowledge about human behaviour and socially constructed institutions suggests that societies that create certain types of conditions will also produce crime. Many of these conditions are known. Furthermore, societies that respond to crime using certain methods will probably encourage crime rather than reduce it, just as some localized policies appear to foster the conditions for crime. So, instead of simply trying to summarize the basic findings in the various fields in criminology, I would like to include guidelines for policy-making in many of these sections.

Despite the wide range of criminological theories, there is considerable agreement about some of the causes of crime and substantial agreement about the social structures that increase the likelihood of crime. Unfortunately, much of this knowledge is being ignored by governments. Perhaps this argument is more appropriate for the United States than Canada, but it applies to us as well. In Canada, we could reduce some of the criminogenic factors looming on the horizon. It is not necessary for us to imitate the failures of the United States, in policies related to crime, as we have imitated them in so many other ways. We have a bit more time, our problems are not as severe, and the experiences of the United States should provide us with sufficient warning.

Areas of Agreement in Identifying Causes of Crime

Some would argue that the research that is needed for policy-making is complex, and that the level of agreement in most areas of criminology is not high enough to allow for a distinct policy based on a consensus. Perhaps this is true for some areas, but there is considerable agreement that the quality of family life, inequality of opportunity and racism are all factors that directly or indirectly affect the level of crime.

Many of our theories of crime involve the family. While the arguments differ, there is considerable overlap in these ideas and, frequently, they are compatible with each other in terms of intervention strategies. Almost everyone agrees with strengthening families. Naturally, politicians give lip service to this argument as well. But, in reality, the United States and Canada have taken actions that have harmed families, decreasing their crime-inhibiting potential, and thus increased the criminogenic characteristics of North America.

In addition to the importance of the family, there is growing evidence that inequality in a society is related to crime. This argument will be explored in a later chapter and, admittedly, the implications are not completely clear. However, there is enough evidence to believe that the increased disparities between rich and poor in North America, along with an ideology that professes equality, have been criminogenic and will lead to greater crime in the future. It is not simply the distribution of wealth that is important, but our attitudes towards material wealth and how opportunities are distributed. Inequality within a society can be modified by governmental strategies, thereby reducing criminogenic tendencies.

A third area where government policies can influence crime is racism. Canadians like to point to the U.S. as having problems that are different from ours. Admittedly, there has been significant progress in North America, but progress has slowed and considerable inequities still remain. A recent conversation illustrates one example of racism in Canada. This person was complaining about the number of foreign students being subsidized by our tax dollars. I argued that the percentage of foreign students was very small. He stated that this could not be true, as he was on campus the other day and saw many "brown-skinned" people. I pointed out that most of these young brown-skinned people were Canadians, children of hard-working immigrants who are making a significant contribution to Canada. The response was, "They're still foreigners to me."

These issues of quality of family life, inequality and racism in society are recognized as three fundamental areas that can affect the level of criminogenic tendencies. Obviously there are others. In this book I hope to go beyond merely summarizing our knowledge of crime. Rather, I hope to raise issues that link crime to the larger social order. In addition to becoming more informed about criminological issues, being informed about the link between crime and broader social issues could lead to changed behaviour as citizens, as voters, as participants in organizations and perhaps as professionals working in fields that have some relationship to crime.

The ideas reviewed in this section are part of traditional themes in criminology, and they will be covered in the first half of the book. However, criminology also includes scholars who challenge many basic assumptions. These challenges are not new, but only in the last two decades do we find large numbers of criminologists working almost entirely as "conflict" theorists. These ideas play a major role in many of the chapters making up the last half of this book.

The Conflict (Radical, Critical) Approach in Criminology

Since this chapter is somewhat historical, it touches only briefly on the "conflict," more recently referred to as "critical," criminologists. I prefer the old term, "conflict theorists," because it captures an essential point which cuts through all of these ideas. Society is viewed as different groups in conflict, struggling to gain advantages over others. Naturally, the powerful groups win these struggles. Some scholars see major differences between these conflict theorists and many other perspectives. Many of the ideas originally offered by the conflict theorists are now accepted as part of mainstream criminology, although one might not get that impression from reading some of the debates. Productive discussions often take place among liberal-humanitarian criminologists, who hold less radical views, and those conflict theorists who see the need to be more directly involved in social policy (the left realists). Criminologists with different perspectives often identify similar weaknesses in the way society is organized. This has provided useful guidelines for policy-makers who are willing to accept new ideas and consider major changes in traditional thinking.

In this book, the ideas from the conflict perspective make their contribution in areas that I have arbitrarily grouped into *macro, micro, feminist,* and *left realist* perspectives. The *macro-level* arguments focus on the larger structure of society. The Marxist conflict theorists would fit here, and will be summarized in Chapter 13. Marie-Andrée Bertrand, Ron Hinsch, Brian MacLean, John McMullan, Bob Ratner, Charles Reasons, and W. Gordon West are among those Canadians who have used macro-level arguments in criminology.

Micro-level arguments focus on agencies that define crime, process those defined as criminals, and punish or attempt to rehabilitate them. That is, these researchers critically examine the criminal justice system and other agents of social control. The studies of police activities by Richard Ericson and Patricia Baranek would fit in this category.

Much of the *feminist* literature could be viewed as using the conflict perspective. When Dorothy Chunn and Shelley Gavigan did a chapter on women and crime in *Canadian Criminology,* edited by Margaret Jackson and Curt Griffiths, they explicitly pointed out how the structure of society has disadvantaged women. Elizabeth Comack takes a similar perspective in her chapter in Rick Linden's *Criminology: A Canadian Perspective.* The chapter I have written in this book on Women's Issues and Criminology has a similar orientation. While Comack *is* a conflict scholar in her other writings, my chapter illustrates the *use of* a conflict perspective for this particular topic. Instead of categorizing scholars, we might be wiser to categorize specific articles or works. The conflict perspective certainly characterizes most or all of the work of some individuals, but we must also recognize that these ideas have had an extensive impact on criminologists who work from a variety of perspectives. When Jane Ursel (1992) discussed the development of welfare practices, or Dorothy Chunn (1992) reviewed the history of the Family Court in Ontario, their feminist orientation was informed by conflict arguments. Thus, one can view the contributions of conflict criminology from at least two angles: 1) those who focus specifically on a conflict or critical criminology, and 2) those who *utilize* different conflict perspectives as tools for dealing with a variety of issues.

The *left realist* perspective views conflict criminology from both of the angles noted above. First, these scholars criticize some of their radical colleagues for romanticizing crime and for assuming that the only serious crimes are those committed by the powerful. Using the second angle, the left realist notes that poor people are frequently victimized by other poor people, that women are frequently abused and harassed by poor and marginal men, and the abuse of children is influenced by a complex web of circumstances. When dealing with a number of criminological issues, it may be difficult, as well as unprofitable, to try to distinguish between a conflict perspective and a liberal-reform orientation.

Basically, I wish to argue *against* a tendency to see conflict (radical, critical) criminology as a domain that is distinct from current mainstream criminology. Nor is it necessarily helpful for scholars to remain "pure" in their ideological orientations. Depending on the questions and issues, a criminologist might find it useful to pay more or less attention to different ideological perspectives. John Hagan's work, for example, ranges widely, with some research reflecting a conflict orientation while other work does not. Similarly, Ezzat Fattah takes a very critical view of the powerful in his recent writings, but he has also pointed out that it is not the elite who push for repressive strategies in criminal justice, as many conflict theorists argue, but rather the lower classes. In sum, ideological consistency may not be particularly advantageous for understanding crime.

The Response to Crime by Agents of Social Control

Traditionally, criminologists have focused on factors that are relevant to criminal behaviour, but they have spent less time on the way society responds to behaviour that is perceived to be criminal. Because of space limitations, this book will touch only briefly on the role of agencies of social control and ask to what extent the response of these agencies can amplify deviance, if not actually create it. For years, many people assumed that the police and other agencies merely respond to crime. Criminals do bad things, and the police and courts are simply reacting to these criminal acts in a rational manner. We now know that agencies of social control can do more than just react. As a result, these agencies of social control can affect the level of crime by the actions that they do or do not take.

Social scientists in the U.S. have done more research on the agents of social control than elsewhere in the world. Such work is not as common in Canada, but the principles seem to operate here as well. It is clearly an oversimplification to label all agencies of social control as nasty bureaucracies, or to label the individuals who work in these agencies as selfish bureaucrats. Instead, we find great similarities between individuals who work in agencies of social control and members of other organizations. The fact remains, however, that these agencies can contribute to the crime problem instead of reducing it. On the one hand, these influences may not be as important as the structural features of society mentioned above. On the other hand, changes in these agencies' functioning, and hence, changes in their impact on crime, may be more amenable to rational policy decisions and modification than the major changes needed in the larger society. Even though making changes at the agency level may seem like tinkering rather than basic change, there is no reason to forego gains in this modest manner if they can be accomplished more easily than fundamental changes. Tinkering can proceed while changes are being considered which are more basic to society. Chapter 20 has some specific suggestions for tinkering.

Historical Aspects of Criminology in Canada During the 1960s and 1970s

Most students of criminology are more interested in crime itself and the people who commit crimes than in the history of the discipline. However, the explanations of crime that are produced are a direct result of the way scholars have been trained and the positions that they take. In 1960, sociology was in its infancy in Canada, and criminology has been more closely linked to sociology in North America than to other disciplines. Since then, the social sciences have grown rapidly, with criminology following in the wake. The sociology departments introduced topics such as social problems which, in turn, generated other courses and areas of study such as criminology.

Any review of the teaching of criminology and the development of research in Canada must take into account the differences between anglophone and francophone criminology. To a large degree, work done in anglophone Canada is integrated with the thinking and research done in the United States and in England. Francophone criminologists in Québec, on the other hand, are familiar with the literature in English, but also share the thinking of criminologists in France, Belgium, and other francophone centres of criminology. Regrettably, anglophone scholars in Canada have relatively little knowledge of the literature in French, and frequently overlook important contributions from the French-speaking world.

The centres of criminology across Canada differ in their origins and orientations. L'École de Criminologie at the Université de Montréal pulls together several disciplines to offer a broad base of teaching, academic research, and applied criminology. The University of Toronto, on the other hand, did not begin with a teaching programme but developed a sophisticated interdisciplinary research unit. Their teaching role evolved at a later time.

The department of sociology at the University of Alberta has always had a combined commitment to both teaching and research, but criminology was clearly influenced primarily by American sociology and thus did not develop the interdisciplinary flavour that evolved in Montréal and Toronto. Most criminological research done in Canada during the 1960s and 1970s dealt with broad issues, rather than topics that were particularly "Canadian." For example, studies done by John Hagan (1975) on the criminal justice system in Alberta and by John Hogarth on the provincial courts in Ontario (1971) have become part of a larger body of literature on criminal justice, which is shared with the United States. Similarly, findings in Ontario by Byles and Maurice (1979) and also by Annis (1979), which concluded that different forms of treatment did not have much of an impact on clients, were consistent with similar findings in the United States. Gendreau and Ross (1979) presented a different view, arguing that there has been considerable success in correctional treatment, an argument that they continue to document (Gendreau and Ross, 1987). Lorne Yeudall's (1977) work on brain damage and learning disability was part of a general intellectual debate. Also, studies of the police by Shearing and Leon (1977), Koenig (1975), and Vincent (1979) were illustrations of part of the larger body of literature shared with the United States, as well as England. In other words, much of criminological research of the 1960s and 1970s in Canada was not uniquely Canadian. Today, more research looks at themes that might be more Canadian, such as Native issues, but there is no agreement as to whether this nationalistic and ethnocentric approach to research will be more meaningful than if we used a broader focus.

The debates over the evaluation of crime prevention programmes provide a good illustration of this dilemma. Does Canadian society require different strategies for preventing crime or rehabilitating criminals? The work by Gendreau and Ross (1979, 1987) emphasized areas where psychologists have brought about change in institutional settings. Their work, and also that of Don Andrews and several colleagues (1990), has had a major impact in the U.S. as well as in Canada. On the other hand, the conditions that produce quality evaluations are rare in Canada. They can mislead by showing unjustified support for weak programmes and by making unrealistic demands on innovative ones (Hackler 1978a, 1978b, 1979). Although evaluations are often recommended in Canada, few meet the necessary scientific standards. Roesch favoured more rigorous evaluation of programmes, reflecting a common theme in U.S. writings (1978). Thus, we are faced with a policy decision. Should we launch crime prevention programmes based on U.S. research, or should we attempt more sophisticated programmes in Canada that would lend themselves to systematic but expensive evaluation?

Québec scholars have made more of an impact in francophone circles with projects like the extensive evaluation of the Boscoville project, an attempt to prevent delinquency by building self-esteem in an institutional setting (LeBlanc, 1983). The assessment of the social costs of prisons by Landreville, Menghile, and

Pepin (1974; Landreville, 1974; Landreville, et al., 1979-80) and the extensive work done by LeBlanc and Biron on juvenile delinquency (Biron and LeBlanc, 1976; LeBlanc, 1976; LeBlanc, et al., 1978), are illustrations of Québécois contributions to these particular topics. During these two formative decades of the 1960s and 1970s, this work from Québec was primarily in French, and unfortunately, did not have as much impact on the rest of Canada as it would have had if it had been published in English.

Recently, Canadian criminological research has focused on what might be seen as uniquely Canadian issues, such as Native peoples and new immigrants and conflicts with the law, policing in a "kinder, gentler" society, and the Canadian *Young Offenders Act* of 1984. Should these issues be viewed differently from those in the U.S? Or, instead of looking more closely at the Canadian scene, should we be making more comparisons with Australia, Japan, and northern Europe? It appears that Canadian criminology has expanded in several directions: those doing mainstream criminology which cuts across national borders, others are looking at specific Canadian issues, and still others would have us expand our horizons by looking at societies somewhat different from our own.

Criminological research during this period should also be seen within the context of the larger research picture. Among the Western industrialized nations, Canada was the only one that spent less than 1% of its gross national product on research and development, according to the Sept 3, 1979 *Financial Times* of Canada. A decade later this same pattern prevailed (Grimond, 1991). This lack of research funding may be one of the factors explaining why criminological research in Canada has lagged behind other countries.

This historical period also produced some unique and innovative changes in criminal justice. In 1967, Alberta borrowed the ombudsman system from the Scandinavian countries and applied it to the criminal justice system and other areas of governmental activities. In 1973, a correctional investigator was established for the Canadian penitentiary service. By 1979, provincial ombudsmen were established in all provinces except Prince Edward Island and the Northwest Territories. The ombudsman style of looking into things and calling them to the attention of authorities may be viewed as a less heavy-handed way of bringing about change. The development of the ombudsman role in Canada, which is utilized frequently for matters regarding the police and complaints arising in the criminal justice system, may have contributed to the view that Canadian institutions of social control are a bit "gentler" than those in the United States. This attitude may make us complacent. Such complacency might lead to policies that could lead to more crime in the future. There is a tendency to believe that many of the problems that plague the United States would never develop in Canada.

Increased Diversity: The Growth of Conflict Criminology

Most of the early criminologists were "traditional" in their training and thinking. During the 1970s and 1980s greater diversity began to characterize Canadian criminology. Conflict criminology provides an illustration. Criminologists began looking at the deviance of the powerful and the impact on ordinary people, as, for example, the work by Reasons, Ross and Paterson (1981) on occupational health and safety, by W. Gordon West (1984) on the juvenile justice system, by Gus Brannigan and John Fleischman (1989) and John Lowman (1991) on prostitution, and by Dekeseredy and Hinch (1992), Dawn Currie (1990) and Jane Ursel (1991) on the abuse of women. Although Canadian conflict theorists still pursued macro issues related to the larger structure of Canadian society, recent studies focusing on specific issues and specific agencies are providing building blocks for greater breadth in criminological thinking. Studies of this nature are the source of much of the discussion in the later chapters on women's issues and crime, prostitution, crimes of the powerful, and the criminal justice system.

Many Canadian criminologists studied in the United States. Marie-Andrée Bertrand brought radical ideas back to Montréal after studying at the School of Criminology in Berkeley, California. Austin Turk moved to Toronto from Indiana. A smaller number, such as Lynn McDonald, took degrees in England. Her book on the sociology of law and order (1976) argues that the conflict arguments make sense for Canada, as well as other Western nations. By the 1980s collections pulling together conflict writings appeared. Some favoured a Marxist orientation (MacLean, 1986), others mixed perspectives somewhat (Ratner and McMullan, 1987), and others focused more on law and the criminal justice system (Caputo, et al., 1989; Comack and Brickey, 1991). Ron Hinch has attempted to clarify some of the conflict arguments (1983; 1992).

CENTRES FOR CRIMINOLOGICAL RESEARCH IN CANADA

In conjunction with this historical review of the criminology scene in Canada, it is appropriate to discuss the research centres that focus on criminology. During the 1960s, many social scientists came to Canada from other countries, mainly the United States. Most criminologists did their work in sociology departments; fewer were connected with psychology, law, or social work. The development of centres for criminological research did not necessarily change the nature of criminology in Canada, but it established a more systematic relationship between government agencies and university researchers.

Not surprisingly, most of the early research done at the centres was traditional and often empirically based. The conflict criminologists rarely define their research interests in a way that encourages government funding. However, systematic government funding for research that is critical of government policy is common, necessary, and normal, as illustrated by the Addiction Research Foundation in Toronto.

L'École de Criminologie, Université de Montréal

The first centre for criminological research was established at the University of Montréal in 1960 by Denis Szabo, who attended the University of Budapest, obtained his doctorate in social and political science at the University of Louvain in Belgium, and received a diploma from the Sorbonne in Paris. His extensive international connections helped Québec maintain a constant exchange of scholars with Europe as well as North America. Later directors of the school brought different influences. André Normandeau took his doctorate at the University of Pennsylvania, Jean Trepanier at the London School of Economics. Thus, criminologists at the University of Montréal participate fully in francophone criminology while sharing extensively in anglophone developments. They also represent a broad spectrum of ideological perspectives, from radical to conservative.

By 1980, the School of Criminology had approximately twenty professors and 350 students. L'École de Criminologie in Québec covers several disciplines, to offer a broad base of teaching, academic research, and applied criminology. This interdisciplinary approach leads to the effective training of academics, researchers, and practitioners. The range of activities is probably greater than in any other criminology centre in Canada. A full academic programme offers bachelor's, master's, and doctoral degrees as well as programmes of an applied nature.

The University of Montréal has had a tendency to become "ingrown," due to the limited number of francophone criminologists in North America. In the 1980s, thirteen of the twenty staff members had taken their doctorates at the University of Montréal. Anglophones have been welcome, but only a few have had the necessary language skills.

The School of Criminology at the University of Montréal has two features that need to be examined when assessing criminology in Canada. First, it is a "hands-on" department, very active in the community and influential in terms of policy decisions that have an impact on society. More than any other centre in Canada, the Montréal criminologists have been actively involved in public life. Guy Tardif, after doing his doctorate at the University of Montréal, became a professor in the School of Criminology and wrote a best-selling book from his dissertation on police and politics in Québec (1974). He then ran for the legislative assembly in Québec under the Parti Québécois and, after winning his seat, became the Minister of Urban Affairs under the premiership of René Levesque. André Normandeau has stood as a Parti Québécois candidate in two elections. Marie André Bertrand was active in the LeDain Commission (the Commission of Inquiry into the Nonmedical Use of Drugs), sponsored by the Ministry of National Health and Welfare, and

Maurice Cusson was a member of the Batshaw Committee investigating juvenile institutions. Jean-Paul Brodeur and Jean-Pierre Lussier were active with the Keable Commission, which had a mandate to look into questionable police practices. The Groupe de Recherche sur l'Inadaption Juvenile (GRIJ) was founded in 1973 by Marc LeBlanc to study juvenile delinquency, and their work influenced the direction of legislation in Québec and eventually in all of Canada. This tradition of public involvement makes these scholars some of the most influential when it comes to government initiatives.

Programmes have been developed to meet the needs of the criminal justice systems. Some would argue that this interferes with the independence that university departments require. By contrast, criminologists at the University of Toronto and the University of Alberta were more independent of community needs. Perhaps aloofness and academic purity are virtues, but the compromises made at the Université de Montréal to accommodate governmental needs may have been more than offset by the extensive impact the university has had on government thinking with regard to criminological matters.

The Université de Montréal was the first in Canada to offer degrees in criminology. Is this unjustified overspecialization? Is the quantity and quality of work in criminology great enough to justify such specialization? Should criminology be viewed as a unique discipline? Alberta and Toronto have favoured less criminology and more exposure to other disciplines, such as psychology, sociology, law, and history.

Should courses on behaviour modification, for example, be taught in psychology departments, with criminology students going to those courses? If criminology students took behaviour modification courses from a criminologist with a psychological background, is there a danger that they might accept more readily the assumptions of the criminal control systems? In other words, should behaviour modification be taught as a tool for controlling inmates or in a manner that would make it a constant subject of debate?

The Centre of Criminology, University of Toronto

This centre was first established at the Dalhousie University Law School, and moved to Toronto in 1963 under the leadership of John L. J. Edwards, who came from a law background in England. Unlike the School of Criminology in Montréal, the Toronto centre was initially a sophisticated interdisciplinary research unit with no teaching responsibilities, although there were cross-appointments with teaching departments. A legalistic orientation influenced part of the early research, but links with the Clarke Institute of Psychiatry provided other perspectives, such as work on sexual offenders by Hans J. Mohr, Alex Gigeroff, and R.E. Turner (1969). Other viewpoints were expressed by P.J. Giffen on criminal statistics (1976), Peter McNaughton-Smith on parole (1976), and Irvin Waller on men released from prison (1974). John Hogarth's work on courts illustrated a blend of law and sociology (1971). The Toronto centre made a particular effort to remain politically independent of funding sources.

The centre gradually moved into the teaching area, with students taking courses at Woodsworth College, and now offers an M.A. programme in criminology. In addition, Ph.D. students in other disciplines can be doctoral student fellows at the centre. The University of Toronto's basic approach to the organization of criminology contrasts sharply with the University of Montréal and Simon Fraser University. At the last two, students concentrate on criminology, while at Toronto they have greater opportunities to maintain their ties with other disciplines. The criminology library facilities at Toronto are the best in Canada, at least for materials in English.

The Centre for Criminological Research, University of Alberta

The development of criminology at the University of Alberta differed from Montréal and Toronto, in that it evolved within the Department of Sociology. When Gwynne Nettler, the best-known criminologist at Alberta, arrived at the University of Alberta in 1963, the enrolment in criminology was already growing. His lectures were popular, and by the mid-1970s approximately one thousand students were enrolled in five sections of introductory criminology, and approximately one thousand other students were enrolled in deviance, advanced criminology, and graduate seminars. The programme has remained highly academic, with the emphasis on research rather than applied programmes. Teaching and graduate training played a major role during the 1970s. By 1980, Nettler had supervised the majority of the doctoral dissertations whose authors went on to teach criminology in Canada.

Interest in interdisciplinary study and in applied programmes led to the establishment of an M.A. programme in Corrections in 1975. As with the University of Toronto, the University of Alberta draws on disciplines outside of criminology to broaden the intellectual scope. An undergraduate degree in criminology was introduced in 1982, with a field placement component as a means of qualifying students for such jobs as probation officers.

The Centre for Criminological Research at the University of Alberta was established in 1977, and the Contributions Grant from the Solicitor General of Canada expedited many small-scale research projects. These funds also support the annual Nettler Lecture, when well-known scholars are invited to make presentations in Edmonton.

Department of Criminology, University of Ottawa

The Department of Criminology at the University of Ottawa established a master's programme in 1967 under the leadership of Tadeusz Grygier. Approximately twelve professors, plus part-time staff, offered an interdisciplinary programme in both French and English.

A master of arts in criminology stresses research, while a master's of correctional administration (M.C.A.) concentrates on a hands-on approach. Both degrees include field work. Thus, the programmes at the University of Ottawa tend to be more applied than theoretical in nature. The candidate for the M.A. degree prepares and presents a thesis, while the candidate for the M.C.A. degree obtains more practical training. The department later took over the teaching of a number of undergraduate courses at the University of Ottawa.

The Department of Criminology at Ottawa had a truly multicultural faculty during its formative period. With degrees from Cracow, Warsaw, and London, Grygier had competence in both psychology and law. Cleobis Jayewardene took his first degree in Sri Lanka, was a medical doctor, and then went to the University of Pennsylvania where he did an M.A. and Ph.D. in criminology. Some of the staff provide important links with francophone Canada.

School of Criminology, Simon Fraser University

With no criminology courses or professors in 1973, the School of Criminology at Simon Fraser University grew rapidly to approximately twenty members by 1979, and now has one of the largest enrolments of any department at the university. This dramatic growth was instigated by financial support from the British Columbia government and the exceptional energy of Ezzat Fattah, the first director. This expansion at Simon Fraser includes library facilities, building construction, and a variety of research activities. They now have B. A., M.A. and Ph. D programmes in criminology with both applied and research elements.

Fattah came from the University of Montréal in 1974 to launch the new programme. Simon Fraser then recruited faculty on a worldwide basis. The Australian Duncan Chappell arrived in 1980. Simon Verdun-Jones, a lawyer, has degrees from Cambridge and Yale. Several criminologists at Simon Fraser did their graduate work under Gwynn Nettler at the University of Alberta. Although a relative newcomer, it has rapidly become one of the major centres of criminology. Under the influence of Ezzat Fattah, Simon Fraser, like the University of Montréal, initially viewed criminology as a discipline in itself, as opposed to seeing it as an area of interest that borrows its methodology and principles from the other social sciences. As new faculty were added, a variety of images of criminology were also added. Today, Simon Fraser, Toronto and Montréal would be seen as the three major criminology centres in Canada, in terms of numbers of faculty, research programmes, and degrees specifically related to criminology.

School of Human Justice and Prairie Justice Research Consortium, University of Regina

In 1977, the Solicitor General of Canada provided a grant to initiate a human justice programme at the University of Regina, under the leadership of Otto Driedger. Matching funds came from the province of Saskatchewan. Activities at Regina include: (1) an undergraduate degree programme leading to work in the criminal justice field, (2) contract research within Saskatchewan, and (3) shared communications within the prairie region. The first and second areas of activity are probably parallel to those of other centres and universities in Canada, but the Prairie Justice Research Consortium has attempted to develop a better communication network across the provinces of Alberta, Saskatchewan, and Manitoba. To work towards this goal, the consortium commissioned three state-of-the-art reviews for a workshop in March 1979. The reviews were on mentally disordered offenders (Steve Wormith), policing (Stuart Johnson), and natives and justice (Melanie Lautt). The reviews were published and circulated to interested scholars (Hepworth, 1979).

Much criminological work goes on elsewhere. York University, for example, has large student enrolments and distinguished criminologists on staff, even though there is no distinct centre of criminology. As federal funds for criminology centres only support one such centre per city, universities such as York, McGill, Calgary, and UBC are illustrations of departments that house active criminologists without official criminology centres. Teaching and research programmes emphasizing criminology exist at Carleton, Dalhousie, the University of Windsor, and the University of Manitoba. In addition, a police administration programme was introduced at Saint Mary's University in Halifax.

The Canadian Centre for Justice Statistics

In 1981 the Chief Statistician of Canada and the federal and provincial deputy ministers with responsibility for justice initiated what was to become the Canadian Centre for Justice Statistics. Although created later than the other organizations mentioned above, it will have a major impact on the study of criminology in Canada. The CCJS collects information on policing, corrections, courts, youth justice, and legal aid. In addition to assembling data from a wide range of agencies, the Centre produces special topical reports (Juristats), which are cited in this book. The Centre also undertakes specific studies, particularly with regard to information gathering.

The creation of the CCJS has led to more than just a more effective way of coordinating the gathering of crime statistics; it has led to better quality data. A variety of data are now readily available to criminologists, along with cautions about weaknesses and interpretations. This has led to more frequent analyses of such data, and the production of scholarly work that would hardly have been possible without these services. In addition, the sophisticated knowledge accumulated by the CCJS makes them valuable colleagues for academics attempting to test a variety of ideas. An excellent illustration of the use of these services and cooperation with scholars is *Deadly Deeds: Murder in Canada* by Robert Silverman and Leslie Kennedy (1993).

CONCLUSION: CANADIAN CRIMINOLOGY, CRIMINOLOGICAL RESEARCH, AND THE WORLD STAGE

Is there any criminological specialty where Canada is unique in the world? Canada has clearly provided leadership in drug and alcohol addiction. The Addiction Research Foundation in Ontario has produced internationally significant studies. John Hagan, and his colleagues at the University of Toronto, have earned international reputations. In general, however, we are modest players on the world scene and our research interests cut across borders.

This book is biased towards the work of Canadian criminologists, and this creates a dilemma. It would be possible to favour Canadian authors to the extent that we distort the impression of the impact of Canadian criminologists on the world scene. On the other hand, criminologists repeatedly give credit to the same scholars, mostly American and, as a result, rely heavily on the same type of thinking. This book is a compromise. It favours work done in Canada but borrows from the wealth of American and international material. At the same time I try to avoid the ethnocentrism that characterizes *both* Canadian and American criminology. For example, hundreds of books in Canada and the United States state that the first juvenile court was established in Chicago in 1899. South Australia established one in 1890. The point is that scholars quote previous scholars, and material from the United States naturally dominates Canadian criminology. This book is somewhat schizophrenic. It favours Canadian scholarship but complains that we should be looking outside North America for new ideas.

WHAT IS CRIME?
WHAT IS DEVIANCE?

(British Columbia in the 1880s) A thousand white men lately employed on the railroad rushed out of cars and into the saloons. In two hours the streets were full of lunatics; they roared and raved and attempted to force their way into private homes. Twelve hundred Chinese arrived by the same train and went into the woods and cooked their rice. It is amusing to see the difference between pagans and Christians.

Stevenson, Lingley, Trasov, and Stanfield, *Drug Addiction in British Columbia*, pp. 446-7

THE DISTINCTION BETWEEN CRIME AND DEVIANCE

Use your imagination. Pretend that in your hand you have a glass of water. See how clear it is. It is fresh water from Banff National Park. Sip it. It is cool and refreshing. Now spit into the glass. Spit again. Notice that the saliva has made the water a bit cloudy. Clear your throat. Now spit that phlegm into the glass. The water has lost its clarity; it is no longer very attractive. And now, put the glass to your lips and drink the contents.

When I go through the above exercise in my criminology classes, the expressions of disgust are obvious. But why? Before spitting into the water, the saliva was previously in your mouth. So, why do you object to putting it back into your mouth? The reaction of disgust is not "rational," and yet there is almost universal agreement in the way Canadian students respond to the above situation. Although we find certain things objectionable, it is sometimes difficult to explain just why we feel the way we do. Similarly, our responses to crime and deviance are not always rational, at least based on seemingly objective criteria. On the other hand, much of human behaviour doesn't make a great deal of sense when viewed from a distance. The clothes we wear, the way we prepare our hair, and the cars we drive take on meaning within a social context; so there is no reason to think that our perspectives on crime would use a logic that is not to be found in other aspects of social life.

In addressing the issue of crime and deviance, rationality is not the only problem we face. Crime and deviance overlap, thus making the boundary between the two difficult to draw. As a result, crime and deviance are often falsely treated as one and the same, but they are definitively two distinct terms despite their commonalities. For example, are all deviant acts criminal? The hippie and punk movements are good examples of deviant behaviour, that is, behaviour that deviates from the norm, but they are not classified as criminal. Are all criminal acts deviant? Speeding is defined by law as a crime, but it is seen, at least to some degree, as acceptable by the majority of society. So, speeding would not necessarily be defined as a deviant act.

These are precisely some of the problematic issues that this chapter wishes to address. In order to distinguish between crime and deviance, we will discuss three factors that influence the way society responds to different types of behaviour.

The Role of Norms

All societies develop normative systems. These norms can be viewed as having two parts: *prescriptions* and *expectations*. Prescriptions are the formal rules laid down by society. Although these prescriptions might not necessarily be written down, they do spell out what members of that particular society *should* do. By contrast, expectations are what we anticipate people *will* do.

For example, there are norms regulating a professor and a class. The *prescriptions* indicate that professors as well as students are to arrive on time. When students arrive late, most of them are aware that they are violating the norm and that their late entrances are somewhat disruptive. Thus, most late students slip into their seats quietly. Now imagine that a professor *always* arrives five minutes late. Does she establish new expectations? Does the class adjust, even though she violates the prescriptions? The class might also fall into a predictable pattern of arriving a few minutes late, corresponding to a newly established expectation but contrary to the prescription. What would happen if this same professor arrived *on time* one day and immediately distributed a very brief quiz, telling everyone that they had just five minutes to complete it? In one sense, this action is within the prescriptions, but even so, the *expectations* had developed so that students would anticipate that the class would actually begin five minutes late.

We can see this violation of expectations, as distinct from prescriptions, in many types of behaviour. The corporation that dumps toxic waste into a stream may not be committing a crime according to the formal prescriptions; that is, the laws of the country. However, most people would agree that some of this behaviour violates societal expectations. Often we say, "that is criminal," or "there should be a law." Similarly, some of the wealthiest people in Canada and the United States pay very little income tax. Again we say, "that is criminal."

Why criminal rather than just deviant? Some people might feel the act was so deviant that some form of action must be taken; i.e., sanctions should be imposed. One aspect of "being a crime" usually includes the fact that many people feel that "something should be done." The violation of the *prescriptions* might not trigger such a reaction; but the violation of some *expectations*, including expectations that differed from the prescriptions, could lead to a genuine sense of outrage on the part of those affected.

Incidentally, did I say something unusual in the paragraph preceding the last one? Many readers will notice that I referred to the professor as "she." Clearly I was not violating a norm, but the conventional use of "he" for professors quite often makes people react as though something unusual had happened. Sometimes conventions take on the connotation of being "right." People say, "That is just the way it is."

Later in this book, I will note that crimes, in a formal and legal sense, can only be the violation of prescriptions, not expectations. We can only prosecute people for violating the *law*, those prescriptions that have been formalized in a certain way. Theoretically, the professor who gave the unexpected quiz might not have violated formal rules, and thus it might be difficult to sanction her. But, as criminologists, should we limit our studies to the violation of prescriptions, or is the violation of expectations also within our range? Should we dabble on the fringes?

The Role of Settings

Nudity offers an interesting illustration of the way in which we respond to deviance and crime. In this case, the setting is all-important and the difficulty in defining the borders is apparent. The lack of clarity as to where the borderlines lie makes nudity a useful behaviour pattern to study. There *are* limits, but those limits differ depending on a variety of circumstances.

One summer, my wife and I were walking along English Bay in Vancouver. We were wearing shorts, and I had bathing trunks in my knapsack. As we walked west around the end of the peninsula, we approached Wreck Beach, which is located below the cliffs near the campus of the University of British Columbia. The number of nude bathers gradually increased until we reached Wreck Beach itself, where thousands of naked bodies were sun-bathing or leaping about. Clothing was rare with perhaps only an occasional shirt, but bottoms were virtually non-existent. Clearly, my wife and I were the deviants, and it amused us.

Should these nude bathers be considered criminals? Which is more important, the laws or local tradition? Occasionally, a few traditional citizens object to the nudity on Wreck Beach, by trying to get the police to make arrests and by holding protest marches (by wearing clothes) on the beach. However, those who strive to uphold the law or the prescriptions have been, to date, unsuccessful. It is the *expectations* of nudity that express the true norms on Wreck Beach. Despite this reality, there seems relatively little chance that the law will be changed in order to conform with the actual behaviour in the near future.

Another side of this issue concerns the limits of the expectations. Violating the prescriptions, that is, the laws, is one thing, but how far can one stretch the unwritten expectations? How far along the beach is it acceptable to be nude? Where are the boundaries and where do the police start enforcing the law? A display of nudity in downtown Vancouver is clearly unacceptable, and people who defy this condition are subject to social as well as legal sanctions. Thus, students of crime and deviant behaviour must be alert to different shades of grey, as well as to the borders of acceptability. It is also of interest just how norms are established and how people determine when the line between acceptable and unacceptable behaviour is crossed.

But what has this got to do with crime? Clearly, behaviour by itself is not enough. It must take place within a social context. This social context is a product of a specific culture which has, over the years, developed norms that regulate the behaviour of all its members.

In his novel, *A Single Pebble,* John Hersey described an American who took passage on a Chinese junk going up the Yangtze river some years ago. After depositing two blasts of nasal phlegm into a square of cloth, he hid these excreta in a pocket. This was revolting to the cook who requested that the American be put ashore. Whose behaviour is "superior?" When the British established control over Hong Kong, they were horrified at the Chinese custom of spitting. Instead, Englishmen cherish the custom described above, blowing hard into a handkerchief, driving the germs into the sinus cavities where they will prolong a head cold, then depositing the contaminated cloth in a pocket, usually next to a warm thigh where the bacteria can breed nicely. Hands are rarely washed after such an operation. Handshakes and other practices guarantee the efficient spread of the infection. The Chinese prefer spitting, but medical facts are irrelevant. Those in power choose the customs, and the Chinese in Hong Kong have adjusted to a degree. When the Chinese take over Hong Kong in 1997 it will be interesting to see if they reject the barbarian English customs regarding nose-blowing.

Are Multicultural Settings More Likely to Have Crime?

While spitting or nose-blowing may seem like trivial examples, the modern world is organized into societies where there is diversity in cultural practices. Those practices often come into conflict. One could argue that simple societies have very little crime. Everyone knows the rules, and informal social control keeps people in line. However, the readers of this book are clearly more interested in complex, heterogeneous societies. Canada is typical of modern countries that have a diverse cultural heritage. While such diversity does not necessarily result in crime, it increases the likelihood that some of the cultural conflict will be criminalized. When a dominant culture invades another, the behaviour of the indigenous culture is judged by the rules established by the dominant culture. When there is culture conflict, the behaviour of those conquered can become criminalized.

In Canada, there is much soul-searching and debate regarding multiculturalism. Many would argue for greater tolerance towards other cultures. While this diversity can enrich a nation, there are some areas where conflict is inevitable. What is seen as acceptable in one culture may be sanctioned in another. For example, when Europeans came into contact with Australian Aborigines they had much difficulty understanding, much less appreciating, the latter's value system. For the Aborigines, work was not seen as meritorious in itself. If you had food or material goods, it was expected that you would share with others. As work was seen as a means to an end and not the end in itself, you did minimal work to achieve what you wanted. Since women were the property of men, trading young girls to white men was an easy way to make money. The goods obtained were then shared with others, making it unnecessary for Aborigines to work for Europeans. Thus, they lived in ease and idleness. Whites had to make the aborigines dependent before they would work (Reynolds, 1981).

Such attitudes and values were, and still are, incompatible with mainstream European thinking. The solution is to resocialize these peoples, get them to adopt our values, and of course, destroy their old value system. This is precisely what the Canadian government and the churches set out to do, as they established the system of residential schools for Native children. The people in power felt that by destroying the Native way of life, they could re-socialize the children to accept the norms of the white society. Such practices occur when cultural conflict is prevalent and the culture with the power wishes to weed out the other culture.

When there is culture conflict, the behaviour of those conquered can become criminalized. In general, it is not hard to find illustrations of practices that criminalize Native peoples. For example, the Plains Indians took pride in stealing horses. Young males who excelled in this activity were held in high regard, but how did this go over with the invading Europeans?

In Canada and the U.S. today, Native peoples have higher than average crime rates. To explain this as just the criminalization of a weaker group by a more powerful one does not take into account many other factors, but the generalization is often valid. More vivid examples arise as Third World people immigrate to countries with European cultures. In parts of Africa, conscientious fathers, who were concerned about the morality of their daughters, would use a piece of glass or razor blade to cut out her clitoris. This was to insure that they would not enjoy sex and would therefore grow up to be better wives. After immigrating to Canada the conscientious father might feel that when his daughter becomes a teenager it is time to perform the traditional operation on the kitchen table. The teenager, however, may have become part of the North American culture, and may resist the father's attempt to do what he feels is appropriate. Whose culture should be respected? Should this behaviour be treated as criminal?

In the above case, most of us would not face a serious dilemma. We would insist that the father respect the rules of his new country. But let's change the situation somewhat. Imagine that the father was part of a powerful invading army which had conquered your country and insisted that Canadian fathers followed the more civilized practices of their superiors. (Those who win the battles are obviously superior.) According to the new morality, Canadian fathers should get out their razor blades and do their duty to protect the virtue of their daughters. Since most of the readers of this book have been part of the conquering cultures, it is difficult to even contemplate such a situation; but if you are a Native Indian in Canada or an Aborigine in Australia, you might understand the point more easily.

The Role of Sanctions

Social groups have sanction systems, which they use to punish people who violate their norms. That is, the group exerts social control over its members. However, sanctions are not used every time a rule is violated, as was illustrated by the nude bathing on Wreck Beach in Vancouver. When are sanctions used? Who has the authority (or power) to use them? Do societies sanction everyone?

Some individuals are not sanctioned, even though they violate clear prescriptions. Children, for example, "don't know any better." However, we try to teach them to follow the rules, using mild sanctions such as a frown, a sharp word. In general, we give people a chance to learn, but our tolerance varies considerably.

A friend of mine travelling in rural India was trying to be alert to the customs of the country. He carefully watched what others were doing and tried to imitate that behaviour. When invited to share a meal, he noticed that everyone reached into the common plate with fingers and used pieces of bread to scope up the other food. After watching carefully, he reached into the plate and immediately noticed a shocked reaction on the faces of his hosts. His action lead to a cessation of eating by the others. He did something wrong, but what was it? After a while he discovered his social error. Being left-handed, he naturally reached into the plate with his left hand. However, this was the "unclean" hand. When he used his right hand, things went much better.

When the child, ignorant foreigner, or colleague behaves badly or expresses ideas that are highly divergent, our first efforts are to educate the ignorant individual. If that does not produce the desired effect, more stringent sanctions are imposed. Those who learn quickly are forgiven for their previous mistakes, especially if they are repentant.

Acts of a criminal nature, on the other hand, are sanctioned by a codified set of formal laws. The criminal law differs from other sanctioning systems in that it is *specific*. It spells out who can be sanctioned for what behaviour. The official sanctioning of criminal behaviour is usually delegated to certain people who follow specific rules. While those rules are often written into criminal codes, they may also evolve as part of a common law based on decisions that have been made in the past. In some societies, the rules may never be recorded in written form, but certain individuals are given the responsibility for knowing the rules and enforcing them.

Many centuries ago under English common law, specific categories of people, such as children, the insane, and women, could not be guilty of certain crimes because they lacked the capacity for crime. As all men knew during these past periods, women were not capable of making many types of decisions and hence, like dumb animals, simply lacked the intelligence and initiative to commit most crimes. Despite the fact that rules are violated, the status of the offender will influence the likelihood of sanctions being applied. Some individuals are not sanctioned even though they violate clear prescriptions. Madonna and similar celebrities are prime examples of deviant behaviour, but instead of facing social sanctions from society, they have risen to star status.

WHY STUDY CRIME? WHICH ACTIVITIES REQUIRE OUR ATTENTION?

Judging Crime According to the Economic Costs

It is understandable to ask why we should study crime. It seems to be undesirable and, therefore, we may wish to reduce it. One factor most people would consider is "cost." The argument has been made that crime should be studied so that the most "expensive" crimes could be reduced. Should cost be measured in terms of dollars or in terms of the "harm" done to people? Let us begin with the economic costs of crime.

How much does crime really cost? Think of the way goods are distributed. Does crime redistribute some goods? If my computer were stolen, I would be annoyed. However, the insurance company might replace it. The insurance company hires people, collects premiums and in general contributes to the welfare of the community. The company that makes computers is not hurt by the theft. If the thief sells the computer to a fence who ends up selling it to an unsuspecting college student, it is possible that the student would use the computer more productively than I did. Did the society lose in economic terms? The transfer of goods by theft may represent damage to an individual, but not necessarily to the society.

A safe-cracker once told me that he kept safe companies in business. He specialized in supermarkets, and considered his profession comparable to manufacturers who produced deceptive packaging. He didn't hurt people, the insurance company covered the costs and sold more policies and the safe companies were constantly well funded so they could upgrade their technology. It is difficult to assess the economic impact of the redistribution of wealth through crime.

It may be difficult to envision robbery and burglary as beneficial to the economy, but let us look at a less dramatic example, such as prostitution. We pay entertainers to make us happy. Their salaries and related activities contribute to the Gross National Product. How about prostitutes? Should their earnings be added to the GNP? Many economists feel that this would make good sense. Entertainers buy food and clothing, pay rent, and redistribute the money they earn, thereby stimulating the economy. So do prostitutes. How does one compare the economic worth of prostitution versus other activities? Actually, prostitution is legal in Canada although soliciting is not, but regardless of the specific legislation, most communities make efforts at various times to suppress prostitution.

What about all the services and institutions that are directly linked to crimes? Why are prisons considered burdens? It is not rare for prisons to be located in some area because a local politician saw it as a way of bringing jobs to the community. Building a road to a tar-sands plant in northern Alberta is seen as an "investment," but building a road to a prison is seen as a cost. The prison "industry" however, keeps many people employed. What about the cost of maintaining a police force? Would the economy be better off if these people were working elsewhere? Do the police provide other services in addition to fighting crime? The old saying "crime does not pay" no longer applies. Crime pays — for all the people working in jobs related to the criminal justice system.

If economic cost is the primary concern, one would assume that the police and other agencies would focus on expensive crimes. In the 1980s, about 1000 bank robberies in Canada cost approximately $2.8 million. During the same period the cost of bike theft was about $45 million. Which crime leads to the more vigorous response? In economic terms (not moral terms) crime is similar to other social activities. We can find parallel economic consequences between most legal and illegal activities. It is not reasonable to talk about the economic burden of crime when we fail to calculate the economic cost of other activities in the same manner. Perhaps, we should talk about costs in terms of the *damage* done to the individual or society.

Judging Crime According to the Non-Economic Damage

If damage to the individual or society were the main criterion for assessing crime, we would probably be studying different things in criminology. For example, the use of alcohol and tobacco would be central topics. Our response to damage-producing situations, however, does not always make sense. Imagine a mother and father sitting in front of a TV. Both are smoking and Daddy has a small child on his lap. Mother is pregnant, and each parent is holding a drink. They are watching a TV programme on marijuana, and one asks the other, "What is it that makes kids do such silly things?"

One hopes that the reader will see the irony in the above situation, but many do not. Over twenty years ago I was at a programme on the prevention of drug use, and one of the speakers was a government official from Ottawa. While delivering his talk on the evils of drug use, he puffed on a cigarette and said, "We adults have learned to handle our alcohol and tobacco, but kids don't know how to handle marijuana." Even at that time most people were aware that adults handle alcohol and tobacco very badly, but comments almost as asinine as the one made by this official are common.

When making comparisons between conventional crimes and the tobacco industry, we have trouble estimating non-economic gains and losses. In order to have a measure of social costs, it is convenient to use dollar values. A few years ago Canadians spent over $2 billion a year on cigarettes. It is difficult to estimate medical costs in terms of cancer and heart disease. The Addiction Research Foundation (1989) estimated that the excess social costs for Ontario in 1986-87 was $1.9 billion for illegal drug abuse, $2.9 billion for prescription drug abuse, and $4.3 billion for alcohol abuse. While dollar costs are hard to assign to cigarettes, in 1985 285 Canadians died of drug-related disorders, 2882 of alcohol-related disorders, and 35 000 died from smoking-related disorders (Addiction Research Foundation, 1989). Clearly, "hard drugs" do not do as much damage as alcohol or tobacco.

Tobacco is grown on 120 000 acres of prime agricultural land, primarily in Ontario. Would Canada be better off if this land produced food? According to a 1984 study, the average cigarette smoker cost employers $4600 per year. On the average, the smoker works 30 minutes less each day than the non-smoker, has more absences, and does $600 each year in property damage. Should this expensive behaviour be criminalized?

On the other hand, several hundred million dollars come back to governments in taxes. Society also saves money on smokers; they die early. We save on pension plans. On balance, however, if costs, in terms of economics or health, were the issue, smoking would be very criminal. This example helps to emphasize the point that *damage to society or the individual plays a fairly modest role in terms of selecting behaviour patterns that we wish to define as criminal.*

How, then, do we decide what we should study as crime and who we should study as the criminal? In the next section I review some conventional guidelines that direct our choices, but we have little trouble justifying our concern with crime. It has broad implications for society. If there were less stealing, less violence, less corporate crime, less illegal industrial pollution and so on, we would clearly have a better quality society. Crime, even if we have trouble knowing the borders, tears at the fabric of society. We may not agree on which crimes tear the fabric the most, nor will we all agree which behaviour should be criminalized, but it is reasonable to assume that citizens should be concerned about that fabric.

Different Types of Wrongs — Which Ones Should Be Crimes?

There are many types of "wrongs" in society, but not all of them can be considered crimes. Which ones deserve the special attention that we apply to crimes? If we speak of violations of prescriptions, that is, the violation of rules and expectations, we might be able to group them in the following manner.

Wrongs Against Persons — "Torts"

Some wrongs are against specific individuals. If someone drives an automobile in a negligent fashion and causes you damage, you could try to obtain compensation in the courts. In the case of torts, it is up to the individual to initiate action. The state will not come to your aid automatically. Your quarrel is, in one sense, a personal one. The goal is primarily compensation rather than punishment.

In the past, many wrongs were treated as torts. In some simpler societies, murder was treated as a tort. Individuals or their families responded to the murder themselves. The society as a whole did not intervene. If one of your relatives was murdered, you might respond. The nature of that response would be dictated by other social rules, but the initiative would have to come from your family. The community might support you in your actions, but the conflict was primarily between the family of the victim and the family of the murderer. As societies became more complex, there was an evolution towards having the state take on the responsibility for initiating action against individuals who had committed wrongs. In fact, individuals were no longer allowed to take punitive actions against offenders.

Offenses Against the State

During the early middle ages, kings and others in power were not particularly concerned if a traveller was robbed while passing from one kingdom to the next. However, the king sometimes sent his messenger to the next kingdom, and it was annoying when the messenger was knocked on the head and robbed. Robbers did not always distinguish between ordinary victims and a messenger for the king. Thus, kings proclaimed that anyone committing robbery on the King's Highway would have to answer to the king. Making certain actions offenses against the state was probably pragmatic rather than idealistic. While kings may have been primarily interested in their own mail service, it was more practical to make all forms of theft offenses against the state.

Even during modern times, some serious crimes have led to responses by the family and friends of the victim, so that feuds and revenge murders have taken place. One can see, however, that such activity would create chaos in a modern society. Just as the king found it more practical to deal with all robbers, rather than just those who knocked off his messengers, so other authorities found it more reasonable to define a broader range of wrongful behaviour as requiring state control. Thus, individuals' responses have been repressed by modern states; state agencies have a monopoly on the use of certain types of force (i.e., police, army, courts). To a large extent, then, we can define modern crimes as *offenses against the state, and we expect the state, not individuals, to take the appropriate action.*

Offenses Against God: Sins

At first glance, one might consider this category clearly outside the realm of crime, but it has not been many centuries since witches were burned in North America. More recently, of course, we have had a number of offenses that were related to religion. For example, commercial activity was not allowed on the sabbath. Many offenses have been defined as criminal because they violated specific religious teachings, but many were simply based on the morality of society rather than against a moral code. The point is, we have a number of crimes that are based on religious and moral beliefs. Some of these have the backing of the state, while others do not. Therefore, it is not surprising to note that arguments made in order to define something as a crime frequently have a moral base.

When we mention prostitution or drug use, many people do not think of these as offenses against God. Sometimes we justify laws against these activities using a variety of other arguments, but the morality of the act often plays the dominant role. As times change the morality changes, or at least there is a change in the willingness to criminalize what some people feel is immoral. Thus, the prohibition of alcohol has been abandoned and laws concerning homosexuality have been altered. However, we should never deceive ourselves into thinking that "sin" is not related to crime.

Violations of Regulatory Law

Another area of wrongs that generate considerable debate as to whether or not they should be viewed as crimes would include antitrust legislation, the *Combines Investigation Act*, anti-pollution legislation, and the like. Several decades ago, criminology classes ignored income tax evasion and, in general, the violations of regulatory law. These activities, some of which might be classified as "white collar crimes," were not seen as "real" crimes by many citizens. Today the definitions are broadening. There is greater awareness that these wrongs are very harmful to society. A changing morality is viewing individuals who commit such transgressions as deserving punishment formerly reserved for conventional criminals. Thus, well-known dealers in stocks and bonds who have violated regulations are not simply "cheaters" and immoral persons, they have been redefined as criminals and sometimes even spend some time in prison.

Shifting from One Category to Another

While criminologists concentrate their efforts on offenses against the state, the borderlines between these various types of wrongs can certainly overlap. We saw how torts became crimes as the king expanded his role to protect others. Other powerful groups can have certain behaviour "criminalized" to serve their interests. The *Carrier* case provides an illustration (Chambliss, 1964). During the medieval period, the wool merchants in England hired others to carry their bales of wool. If a carrier decided to run off with a merchant's wool, it was not the problem of the state. The merchant had to deal with the culprit. But, in the famous *Carrier* case, the court ruled that the state would now intervene on behalf of the merchant. Obviously, this decision was of major importance to those in commerce.

Later, we will ask why these criminal laws came into being. Is it because a powerful group, such as the wool merchants, wanted the laws for their own good, or is the overall good of the society the important factor? Although Adler (1989) argues that Chambliss does not clearly establish that the wishes of the ruling elite shaped the development of law, he acknowledges that Chambliss was insightful in showing that laws are rooted in the social setting in which they are framed. This book does not have to resolve this debate, but it is clear that the *Carrier* case and other legislation extended the reach of the criminal law to what had earlier been viewed as a tort. Similarly, wife-beating was formerly a family affair; now it is a crime. Child abuse is no longer seen as outside the jurisdiction of social control agencies operated by the state.

Just as torts can become crimes, so can sins. In the earlier part of the twentieth century, a number of people, including the members of the Women's Christian Temperance Union, considered the use of alcohol a sin. These people were able to convince governments that this behaviour should be criminalized. In a later period, others convinced the government to reverse the ruling prohibiting the use of alcohol. Clearly, there is a shift in both directions between crimes and sins.

Abortion, the use of drugs, and homosexuality are just some of the areas where moral issues, sin, and crime get intertwined. One might argue that criminologists should not deal with behaviour in this area. It isn't "real" crime. But I would argue that, while there is a difference between deviant lifestyles and crime, it isn't the behaviour alone that helps us to define our area of crime. For example, this book is not going to focus on the gay subculture. It is not criminal to be a homosexual. It is a crime, though, to carry on sexual activities in a public restroom at a shopping centre, and people are being arrested, charged, convicted and jailed for such activities in Canada today (Desroches, 1991). If a behaviour can result in such sanctions, it clearly falls within the realm of criminology. However, the modern criminologist might be much more interested in the question "What are the consequences of different types of police responses to certain types of activities?" In the past, many criminologists were only asking "Why do they do it?"

Despite grey areas, we can use some traditional guidelines for determining what we mean by *crime*.
Crime means:

1. *Law enforcement machinery may be used.* We must emphasize the *may*, because for most crimes the law machinery does not come into play. While part of this is due to the fact that much crime is undetected, there are deliberate decisions made at various stages in the process to remove the case from the system. John Braithwaite (1989) and others would argue that there are considerable advantages to *not* using the formal system.

   In the past, criminologists have considered an "enforcement quotient." This quotient was the visibility of the act divided by public tolerance. If the visibility of the crime was high and tolerance was low, such as robbing a bank, the enforcement quotient was high, and the criminal justice system would exert itself to use the enforcement machinery. Other crimes have a low enforcement quotient. Adultery, for example, has been a crime in different parts of North America during the past century, but it isn't very visible and tolerance has been relatively high. Many crimes do not stimulate much of a response from the justice system.

2. *Crimes and criminal court procedures are (supposedly) very explicit.* Some sanctions can be applied somewhat haphazardly, but in principle, crimes are to be handled very explicitly. The crime itself must be clearly defined. In Merry Old England it seems that common law permitted cows to be executed if they damaged property or did some other terrible thing. The story goes that a cow was on trial for something that could lead to death. The jury was not keen on executing the cow, and someone pointed out that this particular cow had never given birth. Thus she was really a heifer and not a cow. The common law applied to cows, not heifers, and thus the heifer was spared.

3. *Intent is usually necessary.* Accidents are usually not crimes, even if they are caused by negligence. There must be *mens rea*, or a guilty mind. However, there can be *transferred intent*. If George has decided to kill William and shoots at him, but misses and kills Robert instead, George cannot plead lack of intent. Similarly, if George shot at Robert thinking he was William, George would still be guilty of murder.

   Other exceptions to the intent rule would include being in possession of tools for burglary. You may claim that you had no intention of using those tools, but the judge would not be very sympathetic. While a criminal lawyer could provide many more variations on the issue of intent, our simplified sociological definition would argue that intent is normally a part of committing a crime.

4. *Criminal laws are general in their applicability.* In principle, criminal law applies to everyone regardless of social status, race, sex, etc. Neither rich people nor

poor people are allowed to sleep under bridges at night, as the old saying goes. In practice, this principle is violated frequently. Those who have lower status in our society are often more subject to criminal laws than those with higher status. This particular bias is one of the factors we must take into account in explanations of crime, and also when we consider any policies that may be relevant to the reduction of crime. While this principle is most often violated by those agencies that make the initial contacts with those who are likely to be identified as criminals, this discretion is not uniformly negative. The village idiot may be treated leniently by the local policeman even when he violates certain rules.

Crime, then, is not just any sort of nasty behaviour. You and I may disagree as to what things should be considered crimes. I think everyone who mows a lawn should compost their lawn clippings instead of putting them in plastic bags to be hauled to a landfill, that power boats should not be allowed on many lakes, and that city and provincial governments should provide their employees with public transit passes instead of parking space; but no matter how strongly I feel about certain behaviours or how harmful they are to society, they are not crimes unless they meet the criteria listed above. On the other hand, if I could get support from enough people to pass certain laws, I might get some of those behaviours, which I feel are "bad," classified as crimes.

Having worked out a rough definition of crime, one might assume that it would be fairly easy to identify those who are criminals. As we attempt to identify criminals, some other factors must also be considered.

PERSPECTIVES ON WHO IS THE CRIMINAL

Thorsten Sellin — The Conflict of Conduct Norms

In 1938, Thorsten Sellin wrote an influential book, which argued that criminal law should be regarded as part of a larger body of rules that (1) prohibit specific forms of conduct and (2) indicate punishment for violations (Sellin, 1938). The character of these rules, the kind or type of conduct they prohibit, and the nature of the sanctions will depend on the character and interests of those groups in the population that influence legislation. The general argument made by Sellin fits into a framework often referred to as "conflict" theory. Using this perspective, we will attempt to identify individuals who are likely to become criminals.

Sellin argues that the social values that receive the protection of the criminal law are ultimately those values cherished by *dominant* interest groups, those who have the power. Notice, it is not the interests of the *majority* of society, but rather those who are dominant. It is possible that the interests of the dominant and those of the majority are similar, but it is not a certainty. Sellin was one of the earlier sociologists to suggest that the values and interests of dominant groups differed from those of the majority. Thus, those with little influence in the society, who might not share the values of the dominant groups, would be more likely to run afoul of the laws passed by the powerful.

In addition, laws tend to change over time. Sellin argued that everything the criminal law of any state prohibits today may not be prohibited at a given time in the future, unless complete social stagnation sets in. While this may be somewhat extreme, it points to changes in societal values as well as changes that can take place in the dominant groups. Sellin feels that criminologists should study *normal* versus *abnormal conduct*, i.e., conduct in accord with or deviating from a conduct norm. Since behaviour is classified as right or wrong depending on the social values of a particular group, conduct norms are found wherever social groups are found. They are not the creation of *one* normative group and they are *not necessarily embodied in law*, as different social groups will have different norms.

While Sellin feels that social scientists cannot really understand crime unless they study the broader concept of conduct norms, and develop theories that explain abnormal conduct, he recognizes that crimes are unique. They are the product of laws whose creation requires explaining as well.

Paul Tappan — The Emphasis on the Justice System

While many social scientists share Sellin's general view that the study of crime should embrace concepts broader than those found in criminal law, Paul Tappan (1947) disagrees and would restrict the study of crime and the criminal to a narrow legal conceptualization. Criminals are those who are arrested, charged, and convicted. Those people found not guilty are not criminals. Although he is not opposed to the study of conduct norms, Tappan believes specific study of the law-violator is needed for social control purposes.

Thus, Tappan has little interest in the study of "white-collar" or upper-world crime. Unless these people are duly convicted, they are not criminal in any meaningful sense. Unconvicted white-collar criminals, violators of conduct norms, and anti-social personalities may be undesirable individuals, but they are not criminals. When it comes to studying, explaining, understanding and controlling criminals, Tappan believes that *adjudicated* offenders represent the closest possible approximation to those who have in fact violated the law. They have been carefully selected by the sieving process of the law. No other area of social control attempts to ascertain the breach of norms with such rigour and precision.

The Debate Over Who Is the Criminal

While Sellin and Tappan may not disagree dramatically on a definition of crime, they would study different populations. These two perspectives set the stage for a continuing debate over who should be considered criminal, who should be studied, and who needs to be controlled.

Don Cormie, the former head of the Principal Group of companies in Alberta, offers a useful illustration. Cormie misled a large number of investors into believing that their deposits were insured by the government. As a result, millions of dollars were lost by many people who had been assured that their funds were secure. After several years Don Cormie was finally convicted of a crime, so that would solve any definitional problem, but in many such situations, there is no conviction.

An inquiry, which cost the Alberta government about five million dollars, showed that Cormie did many things that were unethical. For example, he hired his wife and children at good salaries to perform services that were of little value to his companies. He transferred money in such a way that he and his family accumulated wealth in accounts that are not accessible to the courts of Alberta. One could argue that Don Cormie was deliberately dishonest and stole the money of others, albeit in a complicated manner. People like Don Cormie are identified as criminals even though they do not always meet Tappan's criteria of having been convicted. The question for us is whether or not people like Cormie should be studied in criminology classes. I think they should.

Other unusual situations make the definition of the criminal even harder to determine. A fire chief is interested in the study of arsonists. Naturally, this is a topic of interest to criminologists, but the fire chief has another reason. He was once an arsonist. Even after becoming a fireman, he continued to set fires, a pattern that is evidently not rare among firemen. The question is: should the fire chief be considered a criminal, since he committed 2000 crimes, even though he has been reformed for many years? Do we look at current status or past activity?

Other situations are easier to resolve. During the Second World War, Canadians of Japanese ancestry (as well as Italian) were interned. They have criminal records. One might assume that those records would not be a problem at a later time, but some Japanese-Canadians found that their "criminal records" came back to haunt them. However, as criminologists, it is unlikely that we would find these particular people suitable objects of study as criminals.

Criminologists can study a variety of populations that are defined arbitrarily but with a certain amount of logic. However, a focus on conventional criminals alone yields a limited perspective. Therefore, we must look at borderline groups, not because we wish to see them prosecuted or formally defined as criminals, but because understanding how they behave and how society responds to their behaviour is important in order to understand the larger picture. Just as most of us who are considered non-criminal have, in fact, engaged in crime in one form or another, those who are clearly considered criminals spend the bulk of their time in non-criminal behaviour. Understanding crime requires that we take a reasonably broad look at the people around us, the institutions that influence our lives, and the society in which we live.

CONCLUSION: MUST WE HAVE A CLEAR DEFINITION OF CRIME OR OF THE CRIMINAL?

We can think of some persons as being *more* criminal than others, rather than being a criminal versus a non-criminal. The bulk of the population has committed infractions of the law. The law and the agencies of social control have developed imperfect, and sometimes illogical, strategies for defining crime and the criminal. Some very harmful acts, such as smoking, drinking alcohol, and pollution are legal while behaviours that are less harmful, such as nudity, are illegal. In this book, we will find it useful to include activities on the fringes.

We can also function with contradictions. Law and practice do not always correspond. Some crimes are "popular." For example, drinking during Prohibition was an "acceptable" crime. Laws that do not reflect the will of many people should probably be changed, since having laws on the books that the people do not support leads to corruption. Others argue that the laws reflect principles that should be stated, even if not always upheld in practice. Still others believe that laws represent the will of the powerful and it is naïve to think that they will reflect the will of the majority.

Discussions about crime make some people pessimistic. The world seems to be getting worse, but there may be grounds for optimism. Let us look back to England in 1712. A club of young men of the higher classes were accustomed to sally out each night into the streets to victimize other citizens (Geis, 1965). One of their favourite amusements was to squeeze the nose of their victim flat upon his face and to bore out his eyes with their fingers. Or they would form a circle around their prisoner and prick him with their swords until he fell exhausted. Another game was to set women on their heads and commit a variety of indecencies. Maidservants, as they opened their masters' doors, were waylaid, beaten and their faces cut. Matrons were enclosed in barrels and rolled down steep and stony slopes. Watchmen were beaten unmercifully and their noses slit.

In the past, upper-class people could commit some crimes with relative impunity. Today we may actually be safer. We may have been able to control at least some of the more obvious violence of the upper classes. The current violence that appears to be so rampant, according to the media, is not a recent phenomenon. It has characterized most of history. Even the interest in criminology classes can have mixed interpretations. Is it a morbid fascination with the seamy and vicious side of life? Or is it a genuine concern with deficiencies in our society, with the hope that it can be changed for the better?

PERSPECTIVES FOR THE STUDY OF CRIME

A madman is not less a musician than you or myself; only the instrument on which he plays is a little out of tune.

Kahlil Gibran

THE ASSUMPTIONS WE MIGHT MAKE

None of us approach a topic without preconceived ideas. The assumptions we take for granted influence the perspectives we select in trying to understand a new subject matter. We all make certain assumptions about the nature of human beings. We assume that other animals do not commit crimes, at least in the sense of committing transgressions against a moral code. What is it about *Homo sapiens* that presents the potential for crime? The following opinions on human characteristics will be oversimplified and will not necessarily be shared by all social scientists, but these assumptions can mould the way we regard crime.

Humans differ from other animals in their capacity to learn, although studies with dolphins and other animals may change our thinking in the future. It appears that early humans were able to adapt to a wide range of environmental conditions, even with minimal tools. Crucial to this learning process was intelligence and a variety of conceptual skills. For example, the Bushmen in the southern part of Africa were aware of a variety of techniques for conserving water, a commodity that was very scarce at times. They gathered the bi plant, which had a watery fibrous root, scraped it into pieces, squeezed it, and drank the juice. The scrapings were then placed in a shallow trench. They urinated on those scrapings and, during the heat of the day, would lie on the scrapings to conserve this scarce moisture. In other words, early humans, in a variety of environments and extreme climatic conditions, displayed an extensive knowledge of their resources and developed skills for utilizing these resources, which required intelligence and the understanding of cause and effect. Modern humans share these characteristics: the ability to learn and the flexibility to adapt. This leads to a traditional debate: which is more important, instincts or learning?

Instincts, Learning, and Crime

Some have argued that humans, especially males, are instinctively criminal. Others claim that *some* people are born criminal; i.e., it is in their genes. I argue that learning is the major factor in determining criminal, or any other, behaviour. This is not to say that genetic characteristics do not provide limitations and opportunities, but the very nature of *Homo sapiens* and the characteristics that have led to the extensive variety of societies that have developed would not have been possible without an animal that was first and foremost a learner. Since the very survival of human beings depends on their ability to innovate, a fixed pattern of behaviour to which nothing could be added or modified would be dysfunctional. In other words, innate behaviour; i.e., instincts, would be counterproductive to a creature who must adapt to a variety of situations.

Early humans depended on this ability to learn and to adapt their behaviour to their environmental conditions. This ability allowed early humans to survive while stronger and better-equipped predators have not. One example of this survival involved *Dinofelis*, a cat less agile than a leopard or cheetah but more solidly built. It had a straight, dagger-like killing tooth and was a combination of a sabretooth tiger and a modern one. The bones of this heavily built, extinct tiger were found in the Transvaal where early humans existed.

"Bob" Brain (1981), director of the Transvaal Museum in Pretoria, suggests in *The Hunter or the Hunted?* that *Dinofelis* may have been a specialized cat that killed primates more than other animals. Caves containing the remains of the cat also contained more bones of baboons and hominids, but relatively few antelopes and other creatures. Could it have been that early humans shared their caves with big cats? Without fire and with only primitive weapons, how did they survive against an animal that had powerful jaws and could eat the entire primate skeleton except the skull? Humans clearly won. Was it fire? Was it the use of spears? Was it some action that required planning and concentrated group effort? Instincts would not have enabled humans to succeed. It was not automatic responses that made success over this big cat possible, but the ability to change and to learn, perhaps within a single generation.

Socialization

Obviously, we cannot be sure how the struggle between *Dinofelis* and *Homo sapiens* evolved, but humans clearly had to learn and had to have a mechanism for teaching their children. Humans are not particularly powerful animals compared to others they conquer, and human infants take much longer to become capable of caring for themselves than other animals. Because of this biological weakness in humans, socialization is not only possible but absolutely necessary. Through socialization, we learn a wide range of simple and complex behaviour patterns, some that require subtle cognitive skills and others that allow us to learn to work in groups.

One might use the following simplified model of the learning mechanism:

Tissue needs → drive → activity → response

Let us assume that a woman is shipwrecked on a desert island. She is from Toronto and her outdoor skills are minimal. She has some vague ideas about finding water and food. Thus, as she now begins to get thirsty, she starts to react to that need by trying to find water; she is driven into some sort of activity. She finds a brackish pond. The water is somewhat salty. She moves farther inland and the water gets better. The final response of finding good water satisfies the tissue need. The next time she is thirsty she goes directly to the fresh water; she does not repeat the steps of testing the salty water. She has learned.

Similarly, her hunger leads her to search for clams. Initially, her attempts are not successful, because her knowledge of clams is rather vague from the books she has read. If her abstract knowledge is too minimal, she may starve before finding food; but if her final responses lead to a satisfaction of her needs, she will continue to refine her actions so that her needs are taken care of more efficiently the next time she is hungry. She has learned.

It is important to note the differences between needs and instincts. Needs have no direction. When a salmon swims upstream to lay eggs this is instinct. A pre-programmed pattern of behaviour does more than make the fish restless; it provides direction in a very specific way. The woman on the desert island may be hungry, but she has not been pre-programmed with a complex behaviour pattern to find food. This gives her an advantage over the fish, which cannot adapt to changing situations, assuming that she survives the learning process.

Physiological needs alone, such as drug addiction, do not automatically guide behaviour. Imagine that a patient has been to the hospital and received an opiate to relieve pain. If the doctor simply tells the patient that she is getting "a painkiller," she may not ask for any more specific information about the drug. If the painful condition persists, the continued use of the opiate could lead to physiological addiction. When the patient leaves the hospital, the doctor explains that she is not going to feel very good for a week or so, but that she will feel better the next week. In fact, the patient goes through withdrawal symptoms. However, she does not connect those symptoms with the opiate pain-killer. She does not know that she can stop those symptoms by using the opiates. After a few weeks life returns to normal. Was she addicted?

Physical dependency alone is not sufficient to make a person an addict. One needs to recognize the withdrawal symptoms as being connected to the drug, and be aware that another dose of the drug will relieve those symptoms. Learning is necessary to become addicted. So, addiction can be divided into two parts — physical and psychological, both of which are necessary for a person to be an addict. To become a *criminal* addict, the woman would need still more knowledge. She would have to learn how to purchase the drug from an illegal source.

Learning can be accomplished alone, using conceptual skills borrowed from other situations, or with others as teachers. My point is that almost all behaviour, including criminal behaviour, is heavily influenced by learning.

The Early Search for Instincts and Why It Failed

A number of classic experiments, conducted by psychologists trying to explain instinctual behaviour, actually led most current social scientists to reject the notion of instincts in humans. One experiment placed a baby monkey in a cage with a python that had been fed a pig. Clearly, the python was not interested in eating. It had been assumed that monkeys were instinctively afraid of snakes, but the baby monkey was simply curious. He inspected the python, twisted its tail, and poked at the head. The well-fed python could not be bothered with another potential meal. Then, the mother monkey was placed in the cage. She shrieked at the sight of the python, grabbed the baby monkey, and huddled terrified in the opposite corner. The mother was removed and, when the baby monkey was returned to the cage, *it* now shrieked and huddled in the corner. Socialization and learning provide a better explanation of these events than instincts.

Another experiment involved raising kittens with three different types of mice. The assumption: cats instinctively kill mice. However, kittens who were raised with different types of mice tended *not* to kill that particular species as they grew older. By contrast, kittens who were raised with mothers who killed mice in their presence did kill mice. Again, the type of mouse made a difference. When mothers killed a certain type of mouse, the kittens chose that type of mouse rather than other types. As in the case of the monkey, instincts do not explain the behaviour adequately; the kittens learned from their mothers. With a number of such experiments, psychologists changed their views about instincts as they realized that learning played a more important role than had previously been thought. To simplify, lower animals rely more on instinct, but the higher up the ladder of animal species one goes, the greater the reliance on learning.

How much can we transfer to humans from the study of animal behaviour? We learn that monkeys who are denied mother-love become poor mothers themselves. Among humans, we also find a correlation between children who received little love from parents and their ability to provide affection to their children a generation later. In other words, the study of social behaviour among monkeys and other primates has helped us to understand how humans learn to become normal, non-criminal adults. One concludes that learning rather than instinct provides a better explanation for almost all complex behaviour.

How do we transfer this simplified argument to crime? Basically, we reject the notion of criminal instincts in favour of learned behaviour. This acknowledges, of course, that people can also *fail* to learn pro-social behaviour, and that anti-social behaviour may have been learned haphazardly; but most sociologically oriented criminologists today would not find instincts, or some innate compulsion to commit nasty deeds, adequate to explain criminal behaviour.

In trying to argue the insignificance of instincts for human behaviour, someone will inevitably raise the question of sex. Isn't sex doing what comes naturally? One assumes that most animals do it without any teaching. On the other hand, animals may have more role models than one assumes. In zoos there has been difficulty getting some animals to reproduce, and one zoo manager thought that my idea of showing the larger apes dirty movies might be of some help. However, our interest is primarily in human behaviour, and therefore we might ask how important learning and socialization are to having sex. Some people would argue that simply putting inexperienced young males and females together would lead them to discover sex "naturally."

Even if young people have never seen anyone else have sex, they would be able to manage because of their conceptual skills, which permit them to *imagine* behaviour that is not observed directly. It is a rare juvenile who doesn't have a reasonable idea of how to "do it." Rather than being different from other behaviour, sex is also heavily influenced by learning and socialization. The first attempts are clumsy but usually improve, depending on the nature of later experiences. One should not confuse the tissue needs and drives, which provide an impetus for some sort of action, with the more complex behaviour patterns that evolve to satisfy those needs. Criminologists acknowledge the pressure to do something, but I stand with those who believe that *what* one actually does and *how* it is interpreted by other humans is a socially constructed process.

The Interaction of Social Learning Processes

In this admittedly superficial discussion of socialization, one cannot spend much time on the distinction between instinctive behaviour and reflex actions, such as the automatic contraction of the pupil of the eye. The majority of social scientists, but certainly not all, believe that humans lack instincts. Their behaviour is learned and is a product of needs, experience, and culture. Genetic theories of crime will be discussed later in this book, but while I will try to be fair, I must admit to a sociological bias. While genetic characteristics provide a potential for, as well as limitations on, certain behaviour, the learning process plays a much more important role in explaining behaviour, including criminal behaviour.

While there is considerable agreement on some aspects of learning criminal behaviour, there is a disagreement on how the many factors that influence behaviour interact. When one claims that behaviour is a product of needs, experience, and culture, it does not make it easy to predict specific behavioural outcomes. For example, the cultural setting does not determine behaviour, but it can provide the context in which behaviour is defined as acceptable or not. This can be illustrated by a telephone conversation one of my colleagues had with his baby daughter. "You went to the bathroom by yourself today Shawnee? My, that's being a big girl. Mommy didn't have to help you? Daddy's proud of you. Where did you go? On the sidewalk?!"

Socialization takes time, and children learn imperfectly and at an uneven pace as their experiences unfold. Shawnee was part of a camping and hiking family. Squatting behind trees or by the side of a trail was one of many options that she had learned. However, she had not yet worked out all of the refinements. A few years later, we had another illustration of the complexities of the socialization process.

We were on a camping trip on a beach with several families. As we were setting up the tents, Shawnee, now about five, was fascinated with Thelma, my wife's former roomate who was now visiting us. For Shawnee, the amazing thing about Thelma was her dark skin color. "Why are the palms of your hands a lighter color than the rest of your skin?" Thelma responded, "Because I'm a Negro." (This was back in the days before "black" became fashionable.) Shawnee, with the innocence and energy typical of five-year-olds, relentlessly pursued the topic, with detailed questions that no adult would dare to ask. Fortunately, Thelma, a school teacher, was both more skilled and more at ease coping with the situation than the rest of us. Obviously, Shawnee had lived in a rather segregated and sheltered world, despite our assumptions that we sociologists and our families were relatively sophisticated on racial issues.

The adults in our group were torn between amusement and discomfort, not knowing whether it was best for a child to explore the questions of race at the top of her lungs in a crowded campground, or if she should be diverted to some other topic of inquiry. Finally, the tents were erected and sleeping spots were assigned when Shawnee came bounding down the beach yelling at the top of her voice, "I want to sleep with the Negro! I want to sleep with the Negro!" again making her the focus of attention for the campground.

Why use such illustrations in a criminology text? Learning to behave in a complex social world is difficult, time-consuming and occurs at differing rates. Most children become more skilled with time and, like Shawnee, become normal, gracious adults, while others do not have the opportunity to learn appropriate social behaviour. In addition, there are those who appear to be surrounded by law-abiding adults in normal settings and still become criminals. Other children are raised in criminogenic settings, but manage to grow up to become nondeviant adults. It is clear that socialization is important, but there is considerable debate over which factors are the most important.

Conclusions Regarding These Assumptions

The debate over whether it is the "nature" of the individual that is important or the strength of the "nurturing" is an old one, but this may not be the important question for understanding crime. For the time being, I simply wish to note the assumptions that influence the way criminologists explain criminal behaviour. While criminologists will argue over which social or psychological variables are more important, they agree that the mixture, or interaction, of a variety of such factors is of major importance. *Homo sapiens* evolved as learning creatures. While the process is complex, humans are determined by, and in turn, help to determine their surroundings.

FREE WILL *VERSUS* DETERMINISM

The assumptions we make about humans influence the direction of our thinking and, to some extent, limit the explanations we hold regarding crime. Another perspective that moulds our basic thinking is the way we view the free-will-versus-determinism debate. During the decades following World War II, this discussion engaged the interest of many academics. Although the issue is less prominent today, it is still implicit in much of our thinking about crime. The goal of this book is not to resolve the debate, or even to suggest that it *is* resolvable, but to simply note that where one stands on the free-will-versus-determinism issue can influence how one does criminological research or interprets information.

Most social scientists follow a deterministic model, which presupposes that all human behaviour is determined by antecedent conditions. All events, including all human actions, are the result of preceding causes. Human behaviour is seen as determined by the events of the past, which includes biological heredity as well as the social and cultural environment. *Determinism* rejects the notion of free will or free choice, which assumes that people decide on a course of action of their own accord.

In the literature, one will often see the terms *positivism* and *empiricism* associated with determinism. Positivism is the use of the scientific method to explain crime, and borrows from methods used by the physical and life sciences. Knowledge can be gained only through sensory experience. Positivism emphasizes measurement in contrast to intuition, metaphysical speculation, and pure logic. Early criminologically oriented positivists measured parts of the body, etc. and produced studies that had many weaknesses. Because of these errors, some scholars have assumed that all studies measuring biological characteristics are suspect. However, this approach is not dependent on the type of variable. Biological, psychological, and sociological variables are all potentially useful. In fact, we are even able to use relatively "soft" data; that is, information that is difficult to count or classify precisely. The key factor is that one creates *testable* hypotheses. Ideas are stated in such a way that information can be gathered that could *reject* those ideas. Empiricism holds that generalizations can be held to be valid only when tested by objective techniques and verified by the senses. Although it may be an oversimplification for some specialists, this book will treat positivism and empiricism as equivalents. Both views are compatible with a deterministic view of the world.

A significant minority of criminologists do not share this view. These critics would argue that these "facts," which scientifically oriented criminologists use, are not facts at all, but rather, they are value-loaded concepts which are very subjective. Therefore, even when manipulated in a scientific manner, these facts produce conclusions that are not truly scientific. This perspective seems to have more followers among criminologists in England than in the United States, with Canada being influenced by both streams of thought.

Radicalism and Anti-Positivistic Views

Some people equate many of the radicals with those who oppose positivism. While in certain cases this may be true, there is no inherent reason to automatically link those who favour dramatic social change, or those who are highly critical of the economic structure of capitalism — for example, the Marxists — with one methodology or another. In fact, one of the better-known radical criminologists, David Greenberg, publishes work in mathematical criminology (1979) and applies a scientific logic to his radical criticisms of the social order. Another illustration of a well-known radical criminologist who uses scientific tools is Barry Krisberg, President of the National Council on Crime and Delinquency. Krisberg's position requires that he work with a relatively conservative board of directors on policy issues relevant to the United States. To develop credibility with those who would influence policy, Krisberg and his fellow researchers support their arguments with statistical data and the types of analysis used by positivists.

On the Canadian scene, Marie-Andrée Bertrand has taken radical positions on many issues, arguing, for example, for the legalization of marijuana, but she works within a framework of empirically based knowledge. There are also economists with Marxist orientations who are sophisticated users of empirical data. On the other hand, some radical criminologists have never studied science in a systematic way and simply do not understand it. When I visited a conference of radical criminologists in England in the early 1970s, one of the speakers referred to "that positivistic shit," reflecting a certain bias that was probably shared by others at the same conference.

The Different Types of Determinism

Many years ago, before I studied sociology, I heard a geographer give an impressive lecture, pointing out how power sources determined the ascendancy of nation-states. England had cheap coal, which led to the Industrial Revolution and England's dominant role on the world scene during the nineteenth century. The speaker was convinced that solar power would be the next major factor in determining national influence. Thus, Africa, which has more sunshine than the other continents, would lead the world by the end of the century. Today, I realize that this well-known professor was simply wrong. The nature of social structure and cultural elements enables countries such as Singapore and Japan, with modest natural resources and power sources, to overcome these limitations. Of course, I am convinced of this perspective. I was trained as a sociologist. Is it possible that I tend to be a "social determinist" while geographers tend to be "geographical determinists?"

If we extend this logic somewhat, is it surprising that some geneticists believe that "it is all in the genes?" Is it surprising that psychologists have greater faith in various sorts of counselling than do sociologists? In other words, a general acceptance of a deterministic model of behaviour does not necessarily lead to agreement on the *factors* that are most influential, or what sort of social programmes might bring about desirable changes.

In this chapter, I do not set out to convince the reader that any one specific perspective is correct, but rather that we must be aware that *the way scholars are socialized into various disciplines and perspectives is also a social phenomenon that must be seen as part of the explanatory process.* Students in college and university must be wary of professors who are absolutely convinced that their view of the world is the correct one. As you read vigorous arguments for certain positions, hopefully supported by empirical evidence, consider the impact of intellectual socialization on the author of those ideas. The way we think and the beliefs we hold are socially constructed.

"Soft" Determinism: A Useful Perspective

Instead of deciding that the assumptions behind determinism are more valid than those underlying free will, perhaps we should ask if holding a certain perspective is *useful*. For example, Western medical practitioners have trouble comprehending Chinese medicine, but others might simply ask "does it work?" Thus, some Western-trained doctors acknowledge that acupuncture can be useful. Similarly, we might adopt a position between the hard determinism characteristic of positivists and the complete freedom of will. "Soft" determinism is partly embodied in Matza's (1964: 29) conception of "drift," where juvenile delinquents often stumble into crime in a piecemeal way. They drift gradually into delinquency, being deflected or nudged by numerous events, often following a process unperceived by the people concerned. Similarly, deflection from the criminal route is often accidental and unpredictable. The outcome is only partially determined. However, sometimes a time comes when the human subject must "make up his mind" and actually make a choice.

Richard Ericson suggested that it might be advantageous to treat humans *as if* they had free will (1975: 4-5). *Symbolic interactionists* argue that human behaviour must be interpreted. Until behaviour is interpreted and weighed by thought processes, humans cannot act on it. The notions of structure, system, group, etc. are only meaningful in social settings. "Systems do not behave or act or take decisions or have consciousness except through the minds of men who give them significance" (Brittan, 1973: 86). "Instead of asking how society orders and controls the individual, students of social control might ask how society takes its organization and momentum from behaving individuals" (Lemert, 1964: 90). In this view, humans are socially determined *after* they have helped to determine society.

This perspective recognizes limitations on choice, but it also questions the inevitable cause-and-effect sequences that characterize determinism. A simple illustration of this *interaction* of behaviour and environment might be a study of a troop of monkeys in Japan. It seems that these monkeys living in the wild had discovered a pond that was heated by a hot spring. They displayed curiosity about this pond. At first they put their hands in it, but they did not swim in it. Gradually some of the members would immerse parts of their bodies in the water. As time went on, more adventurous monkeys encouraged others to immerse more of their bodies, until they were bathing. During the winters, this troop of monkeys eventually evolved the practice of visiting the pond regularly and taking hot baths. They had learned a *new* behaviour, and eventually taught this new behaviour to other members of the troop.

It would be difficult to explain this outcome by simple determinism, unless you assume that there will always be some monkeys (or humans) with above-average curiosity. The sequence of events can be modified by a number of chance factors, but the *individual experimentation* comes from within. If monkeys can invent new forms of social behaviour, we should also expect it from humans. Thus, some of the critics of determinism argue that if you rely on natural-science techniques, you will not be able to understand the moral and social life of the people being studied. It is not that one must *accept* the subjects' viewpoints or morality, but these viewpoints must be taken into account. Ericson argues, "the human ability to construct meaning through the conscious mind negates the logic of natural sciences when applied to the study of human social life. Emphasis is on how actors give meaning to their own social world, a meaning that does not have to be true or objectively correct, but does affect the subjects' actions" (1975: 5).

The "human fly" was a burglar who made the newspapers from time to time. He was not particularly successful, as his *modus operandi* was very predictable, and he was regularly arrested and convicted. The "human fly" only burglarized those places that required a spectacular climb on the outside of a building. This small man with modest intellectual skills was not successful. However, he learned that he could climb better than most. His peers encouraged such behaviour and granted him the recognition that he craved. As his career developed the climbs became more sensational, but the material rewards clearly did not explain the behaviour. The police would immediately go to his place of residence, find the stolen loot, and arrest him. The next day, they would bring the newspaper to his cell so he could read the story entitled "The Human Fly Strikes Again." Although he did not actually gain much prestige from these feats of daring, it was his *perception* of the meaning of these acts that helped to explain his behaviour. From his perspective, wealth was not the goal, but rather, his perceived recognition of his feats.

The symbolic interactionists would agree that behaviour is determined to a degree, but they would add that humans play a constructive part in determining the structure that exists and how it is used. This brings us back to the notion of drift or "soft" determinism. Let us consider the situation of a wino who considers stealing a bottle from a liquor store (Ericson, 1975: 49). Of course he is not compelled to do so. His friends on the street-corner have the same craving and would, therefore, define his behaviour as worthwhile (when he shares the bottle, that is). This support may also encourage the theft, but it does not compel him. The fact that he has been convicted thirty-seven times for previous offenses of stealing wine means that another conviction would not damage his moral character any more, so there would be little lost in stealing a bottle, but it does not compel him.

Ericson concludes that, at times, "freedom" becomes synonymous with "nothing left to lose." Some people engage in criminal acts knowing that even if they are imprisoned, they cannot sink any lower. Travis Hirschi (1969) comes to a similar conclusion with his "control theory." Hirschi is a strong advocate of the scientific method and argues that, when a person's ties to society are ruptured, she is free to deviate. Hirschi's deterministic model also concludes that crime is more likely among those who have "nothing left to lose." When studying explanations of crime, we should not be surprised if scholars come to similar conclusions by quite different routes.

Returning to the symbolic interactionist perspective, researchers limit themselves by trying to decide if human actions were due to free will or determinism. A more fruitful strategy might be to instead take *a person's own definitions* in specific situations. How do potential criminals view the surrounding social forces that will influence their course of action?

Seeing the world through the eyes of the potential criminal is not enough. The agents of social control help to determine criminal reality. The views of the police, probation officers, and judges influence outcomes. These agents of social control interpret the *meanings* of actions. A conservative probation officer with a traditional moral view of the world might see the theft of wine as innately evil, requiring a severe, repressive reaction. By contrast, a probation officer with a therapeutic background may see the wino as a victim of a poor family background. A radical probation officer may view the situation as another unjust outcome of a badly flawed capitalist system. The interaction of many different perceptions of reality makes it difficult to say what the *objective* reality actually is, if there even is one, let alone develop a rational response to behaviour that is supposedly clearly defined as criminal.

CONCLUSION: MUST WE SELECT A SPECIFIC PERSPECTIVE?

There is no one correct perspective for the criminologist, the agent of social control, or the criminal; but the perspectives of all the actors in the drama must be treated as real and taken into account. For the criminologist, being explicit about the assumptions being made can reduce the gap between the various perspectives. Researchers do not have to agree on all of these issues. If they can clearly lay out their assumptions, rather than treat them as God-given truths, criminologists can contribute to a sharing of information that enables those with different research strategies to make use of each other's work. In this respect, those who have differing views on the factors that determine behaviour can make use of the scientific method presented in the next chapter.

USING SCIENTIFIC THEORY TO EXPLAIN CRIME

Men occasionally stumble onto knowledge; but most of them pick themselves up and hurry off as if nothing had happened.

Winston Churchill

CREATING KNOWLEDGE

There are many routes to gaining knowledge. Philosophers, artists, and scholars of literature go at the knowledge business differently than social scientists. Historians construct reality using techniques that are quite different from the physicists. In criminology some postmodernist thinkers even raise some doubts about the possibility of knowing what is "the truth." During the last two decades qualitative research within the social sciences has broadened the way criminologists search for knowledge. In my own research on juvenile justice, I began with traditional data-gathering procedures and found that they did not serve me very well, even though I found them useful in other criminological research. Some criminologists begin sociological careers using empirically based procedures, but later argue that objectivity and rationality are not workable strategies of inquiry and that understanding crime today requires compassion and enlightenment (Pepinsky and Quinney, 1991: Ch 1). Should criminologists be philosophers or social scientists? I certainly will not resolve such debates here. However, basic to what many criminologists do is the question: How do we know we know? Which version of reality is the best? There is much to be gained by understanding conventional scientific thinking. Some criminologists understand science but have deliberately abandoned it for alternative strategies. Unfortunately, there are others who reject science without understanding it, cannot pass on the fundamentals to students, and cannot criticize it intelligently. The scientific procedure has certain advantages. It provides clearer guidelines to let you know when you are wrong. It does not necessarily tell you when you are right; but criminology has so much useless baggage that anything that will reduce the garbage is helpful.

THE USE OF SCIENTIFIC THEORY IN CRIMINOLOGY[1]

After the Second World War, the debate over science and the study of human behaviour was in full swing. In a book entitled *Can Science Save Us?*, George Lundberg, one of the staunchest advocates of sociology as a science, argued that the scientific method would enable scholars to provide guidance to policy-makers in a manner that would make it possible to build a better world. The vehemence of this debate has decreased over the years, but it has influenced the way we do criminological research.

Some "scientific" criminology has been clearly misleading. Nobel-Prize-winning economist Gary Becker offered an economic model of crime (1968) based on unrealistic assumptions; i. e., criminals make rational decisions based on the utility of the crime in terms of gains and losses. When applied to most murderers, these assumptions are simply ridiculous. Theories are often based on untested assumptions, but when the assumptions are completely unrealistic, so are the theories. Not all economists sit calmly in crashing airplanes, confident that the demand will produce a supply of parachutes from the marketplace, but Becker's ideas on crime show how social scientists can become detached from the issues they are studying. These types of "explanations" give rise to the criticism that positivist research on crime is crude and heavy-handed, using analyses that "run the world through a meatgrinder, its observations intensely focused but all too often missing the tangled, shimmering reality of what lies before it" (Goode, 1990:10).

While some criticizms of science are appropriate, criminological knowledge is diminished by the "anti-science" phenomenon. Some assert "that science can claim no more than the status of a useful myth ... not to speak of a new wing of sociologists of science, who, going far beyond their reasonable task, wish ... to abolish the distinction between science and fiction" (Holton, 1992:7). The anti-science movement can be incorporated into political movements, as we have seen in "creationist" religious views that have been successfully pushed by popular evangelist preachers. "Their sympathizers included a President of the USA in the 1980s; he is on record as holding to a worldview that has open arms, not only for astrology, but also for UFOs" (Horton, 1992:10; See also Holton, 1993: Chapter 6). Caution about how science is utilized in criminology is proper, but some anti-science views fall in the category of religion, with those who believe the world was created in six days.

Some criminologists have abandoned the use of science altogether, while claiming to do "social science." Some have offered interesting ideas and called attention to neglected areas, but how do we know what is true? As a result, a number of debates in criminology generate more heat than light, if there is no basis

---

[1]The ideas expressed in this section have been influenced extensively by the teachings and ideas of Clarence Schrag.

for determining truth. Science provides criteria for determining what is true. Currently, students can study criminology without being exposed to the scientific method. During the 1980s more people completed PhD programmes related to criminology without the same grounding in scientific theory that was provided thirty years ago. Like so many intellectual movements, graduate studies in criminology have their fads. Graduate training in some universities, and certainly in Canada, went through a period in the 1970s and 1980s where science was de-emphasized in favour of other orientations.

The Distinctions Between Perspectives and Knowledge

Imagine that you have entered a huge diving bell, in order to view life in the ocean. In addition, imagine that some of the windows of this diving bell magnify and others distort in different ways. Furthermore, the glass is also of different colours. People looking out the different windows would see things differently. No one would actually see the truth. However, the view seen through each window has a certain amount of validity. Each person could stand at her window and argue vigorously that sea life is truly represented by her window and that others must be wrong. Many criminologists today recognize that we use different windows, but they somehow assume that everyone must stay at her original window. I prefer a diving bell where people wander from window to window gaining different perspectives. Soon, discussion would arise about the *nature of the windows themselves*, and then we begin to ask just how each window distorts the outside world and how one might best get a better picture of reality, despite the fact that all the windows distort reality. Most criminologists prefer certain types of windows, while others utilize more than one. Gwynne Nettler warns us that a "perspective" is not the same as knowledge (1972), nor is knowledge the same as information. The way information is assembled and interpreted will determine whether or not genuine knowledge has been created.

In this next section, I would like to review an old-fashioned argument. Social scientists have used the scientific method with a certain amount of success. It is certainly not the only way of understanding crime; however, it has particular advantages over other perspectives. While not denying the need for alternate perspectives on human behaviour, particularly in the study of crime, the application of scientific procedures in Canada in the study of crime is not particularly well developed. The student of human behaviour should be aware of different viewpoints and should peer at the world through a variety of distorted windows, but it would be a mistake to ignore the scientific window; its distortions are better understood.

What Is a Scientific Theory?

Many persons think of scientific theory as being terribly complex. Many esoteric books have been written on the topic, but the basic ideas of science are not as complicated as many assume. Imagine sitting in a large classroom. Just beneath the ceiling balloons and sheep's bladders filled with helium are floating. They are connected to one another by a variety of ropes and sticks. However, we cannot see this network of balloons and bladders because of a thick smog, which lies just below the ceiling. In fact, we will never be able to see this framework because the smog is permanent; but we are sure something is up there and that it will remain fairly constant. We will call that network of balloons and sheep's bladders "reality." Since we cannot see it directly, we must look for techniques to help us describe it indirectly. One ingenious student suggests that we tie a string to a ball of tar. By wandering about the room with these balls of tar and by throwing these balls up through the smog, we will occasionally strike a balloon. If we throw the ball and hear a dull thud, we assume that we missed a balloon and hit the ceiling instead. However, if we hear a *boing*, we will assume that we struck a balloon. If we hear a long, deep *boo-wang*, we will assume that we struck a sheep's bladder.

We then tie a small bell to the end of each string that we suspect is attached to a balloon, and a large bell to those suspected of being connected to a sheep's bladder. By examining the location of those strings with bells attached to them, we attempt to draw a "map" of the invisible network. Scientists are continually drawing maps, or models, or theories, which attempt to describe reality.

Testing Theories

Next, we would like to know just how these hidden balloons and sheep's bladders are related to one another. We notice three strings with bells attached hang in a straight line. Therefore, we might hypothesize that the three balloons are attached to each other by means of a piece of rope. If this were true, and we were to pull on the first string, the bell on the second string would jingle fairly vigorously, and the bell attached to the third string would jingle less vigorously. We perform such an experiment and find that the bells jingle as predicted. We have support for our hypothesis.

Since our hypothesis predicts that our three bells are connected in such a way, we can perform another test. If we hold the second string firmly, so that it cannot move, jerking on the first string will not make the third string and its bell jingle, or at least not very much. We have intervened by controlling the movement of the intervening string and bell. In a similar manner, a researcher can statistically "control" for a variable that intervenes between two others.

But another student has drawn another map. Using the same information, he argues that our three bells are connected to each other by a large sheep's bladder located in the centre of the room. If someone were to hold the string attached to the hypothesized sheep's bladder and keep it from moving, then the second and third bells would not ring if the first bell is jingled. As the reader can see, a variety of tests can be made to test the accuracy of our map of "reality." Even after many tests, our map could be quite incorrect. We will never know if we have found all of the balloons. Furthermore, some of our basic assumptions may be wrong. But as we proceed, our ever-improving map helps us to predict what will happen as we jingle one bell after the other.

The above analogy of balloons and sheep's bladders may not satisfy the sophisticated reader. Following Hempel (1952), a scientific theory is a network of concepts and hypotheses. The concepts can be represented by knots and the hypotheses, which link the concepts together, are represented by threads connecting those knots. The network floats above the plane of observation and is anchored to it by rules of interpretation, like strings that link points (concepts) in the network to the plane of observation. The network can then function as a scientific theory; by observations, we ascend, via an interpretive string, to the theoretical network and then proceed, via hypotheses, to other points, and descend, by another interpretive string, to the plane of observation. Stated more simply, theories are created when we link concepts together in some systematic way by means of hypotheses, but they must be tested with observable measures.

At one time physical scientists believed that theories were reasonably accurate and resembled "reality." Few hold that view today. Rather, many theories are good approximations. When the modern physicist jingles his bells, he can chart the jingling of others accurately. His models may not be absolutely correct, but they are surprisingly good for predictive purposes. This is less so in most social sciences, and rather rare in criminology.

The Components of a Theory

Variables

Scientific theories require variables; that is, something that varies. Sex is a variable. We can classify people into either male or female. There is nothing sacred about a variable. It may be oversimplified. The simplification of sex into male or female is not 100% accurate. However, sex is handled conveniently in two categories. Crime is sometimes treated as if it were a two-part variable; that is, criminals and non-criminals. For some explanations, this simple dichotomy may have some utility. However, we find that most of the people who are criminals resemble those who are not criminals. Thus, this simple dichotomy is often inadequate. One response to some of these difficulties is to create a number of categories of criminals. Still another approach has been to treat delinquency in the way physicists measure heat. Something can be hotter or colder. By being able to measure the variable "heat" precisely, the physicist has been able to improve on his predictions. Attempts have been made to measure criminality on a continuum (Sellin and Wolfgang, 1964). Similar studies have been conducted in Canada (Akman and Normandeau, 1967). The problem of classifying criminals or crime, and the variables related to them, is of considerable magnitude; but the logic of the problem is the same as that used by physical sciences.

The variables scientists use do not exist in their own right. They are only abstractions, which we assume are reflections of reality. In the study of crime we have a series of pet variables: the deteriorating family, bad genes, the opportunity structure, etc. Crime might be approached using different variables. People could be classified as those exploited and those who do the exploiting. We could ignore the behaviour of potential criminals and focus instead on the behaviour of social-control agencies. Or, we may wish to focus on the conflict that arises as a result of the interaction between those social-control agencies with authority and those who are subjected to that authority (Turk, 1969). "Conflict," "power," "types of agencies," etc. can all be seen as variables in a scientific theory. They reflect the particular interests of specific criminologists. In order to work with variables, however, we need to break them down into two components: concepts and operational definitions.

Concepts and Operational Definitions

A *concept* could be seen as an attempt to communicate what we mean by a certain variable. For example, when someone says she is going to describe "crime," it is not always clear what she has in mind. The concept *crime* may take on different meanings to different persons. Therefore, a researcher may spend quite a bit of time making it clear what she means when she uses the word *crime*. Simply defining the concept does not designate anything new; it is neither right nor wrong, and it makes no claims. A concept is a word or short phrase that takes the place of a paragraph of discussion and tries to get us to understand what the concept is all about.

An *operational definition* specifies the procedures of observation that are necessary to identify the concept or measure the variable. We might define crime operationally by using "crimes known to the police." If we go back to our models of the balloons, tar balls, and strings, one can see that the balloons are the concepts and the bells are the operational definitions. We have linked the two together. However, we can *only* work at the operational level, that is, we can only use the bells. Reality remains invisible. We have described our concept as a balloon filled with helium. It may be quite different, but the smog will never let us see it (see Figure 4.1).

Scientists must *work* at the level of the operational plane, but they *think* at the level of the conceptual plane. In Figure 4.1, we must work with the operational definitions (jingle the bells, compute our statistics, etc.), but we are concerned with the linkage among the concepts (balloons that we can only imagine). This logic might be understood more easily by using a model from physics, Boyle's Law (See Figure 4.1a)

The model or theory suggests that there is a direct relationship between heat, volume, and pressure. If volume is constant and the heat increased, the pressure will increase. The operational definition of "heat" may be the height of a narrow column of mercury in a glass tube. Today, we have many types of thermometers, but they are all operational measures of the concept "heat."

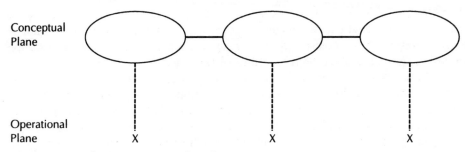

FIGURE 4.1 The Structure of a Theory

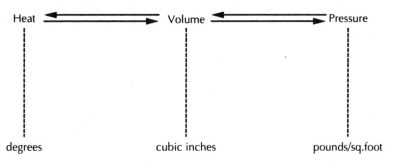

FIGURE 4.1a The Structure of Boyle's Law

Sometimes concepts are understood only partially. For example, heat can be described as the rapid movement of molecules; but if we had a simpler notion of heat, could we still test the theory? Even if I know nothing about the movement of molecules, I know that a fire makes heat. Boyle's Law can be tested with a test tube, a cork, and a fire. By heating the air in a test tube, the pressure builds, and the cork blows off. The test is crude, but we often test theories with crude instruments. In criminology, the instruments are primitive, but other sciences did remarkably well with unsophisticated measuring devices at an earlier time.

Problems Inherent in Using Theories

The Difficulty of Finding Appropriate Operational Definitions

Theories can be used and tested without refined concepts or precise operational definitions. We can make considerable progress even with crude tools. Of course, there can be a variety of problems, both with our measuring devices — that is, our operational definitions — and with our concepts. Let us assume that we measure the concept *crime* as "crimes known to the police." We probably would like to include criminal acts unknown to the police as well, but where can we get such data? Immediately, we can see a dilemma: finding a measuring device, or operational definition that exactly fits our concept will be difficult. Our operational definition may be a poor measure of the concept it attempts to measure. For example, do police statistics reflect what we think of as crime?

In Figure 4.2, we have attempted to draw a diagram that illustrates the relationships that might exist among a concept and operational definitions. The large circle is the concept *delinquency*, but we are aware that arrests by the police account for a relatively small percentage of the juvenile crime that exists. It is also possible that the police arrest a few individuals who have not, in fact, committed a delinquent act, or they have been arrested for acts, such as curfew violation, that we may not wish to count as a crime. The large ellipse represents self-reported delinquency, a device used by criminologists to uncover hidden crime or deviance committed by young people. Note that the two operational definitions also overlap to some degree.

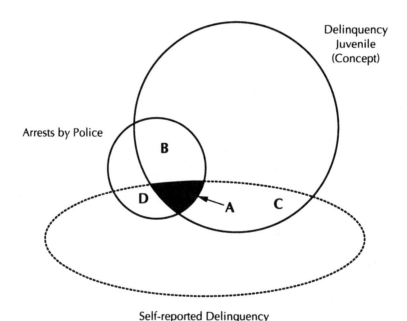

Self-reported Delinquency

FIGURE 4.2 The Overlap of Concept and Operational Definitions

We can understand the problem better if we look at specific sections of the overlapping diagrams. The small area A, with hatched lines, is included in all three circles. This section includes children who commit crimes, are arrested by police, and acknowledge their delinquency on a questionnaire. Unfortunately, this section is rather small. Area B includes those classified as delinquent by the operational definition "arrests by police" but not by the other definition. Similarly, area C indicates those identified by the self-reported measure but not by police arrests. Area D shows places where both operational definitions do not fit the chosen concept. We have a choice between areas A, B, and C or a combination of parts of them. In other words, our measuring devices will be imperfect. Although the overlap between the operational definitions and the concept is rarely 100%, such approximations can and have been used.

Clarifying Concepts

The difficulties in developing clear concepts and appropriate operational definitions are particularly great when one studies crime. While we must be alert to these problems, the scientific method permits one to proceed even though they have only been partially resolved. For example, the Gross National Product has been considered a useful concept in economics for some time. People seem to know what it means. When one looks at it more carefully, however, the concept is really not that clear. There is a temptation to define the concept by simply giving its operational definition. However, describing how a concept is measured is not the same as communicating the essence and meaning of that concept.

Even the operational definition could be questioned. The Gross National Product includes the value of automobiles with defective brakes, breakfast cereals that have no food value, and fees paid for questionable and even dangerous services. Should it also include the fees paid to prostitutes? If we include the fees of other entertainment, why not call girls as well? If a dishonest clerk charges a customer $10.00 but records a sale of $5.00, which figure should be a part of the Gross National Product? If an accountant does a farmer's income tax and accepts a side of beef in payment, does it become part of the GNP? Should it? The point is that the GNP can be somewhat unclear as a concept and imprecise in the way it is measured, but it is still useful. When we begin to treat concepts and operational definitions as sacred, we can be led astray. Unclear concepts and crude measuring techniques can still be useful. Therefore, we should not let such problems paralyse our efforts to understand crime.

The study of crime is not worse off than psychiatry. Concepts such as schizophrenia and other forms of mental disorder are still debated, as are the ways of measuring them. Attempts to diagnose patients in a reliable and consistent manner have been singularly unsuccessful according to some critics, although others would disagree. In order to be useful at all, our concepts must permit us to classify the subjects being studied with at least partial reliability.

Our ability to conceptualize is limited by our experience. Western medicine has developed certain conceptual frameworks for understanding illness. Those who use acupuncture use a different set of concepts, and communication across these two mental sets is not easy. The socialization process experienced by most persons, including those who study crime, limits and moulds the concepts that can be used in developing a theory.

Concepts, then, are not necessarily "true." They are judged by their clarity. Theories may be useful. They are like road maps. They are not necessarily precise, but are designed for utility. If you drive from Vancouver to Montréal, I could provide you with aerial photographs along the Trans-Canada Highway. They would be more precise than the road maps obtained for each province, but the design of the road map makes it more useful than the aerial photograph. Theories, like maps, are creations. Some are more useful than others.

THE UTILITY OF THEORIES

In Boyle's Law, as presented above, we have a parsimonious theory with only three variables; heat, volume, and pressure. However, there are times when our attempts to explain, that is, our untested theories, contain many variables, and we are unable to measure some of them. By systematically linking together those variables that we can measure, we can develop a reasonable explanation even when we only have partial knowledge. Theories can extend the knowledge that is available to us.

Maximizing Partial Knowledge: The Case of the Lobster

Every concept does not have to be measured before progress can be made. I have a theory about lobsters and their gravity organs. I hypothesize that lobsters have a gravity organ in the side of their head, which is something like a small hole lined with a membrane sensitive to pressure. Inside that gravity organ is a piece of sand. The weight of that piece of sand resting against the membrane tells the lobster whether he is right side up or whether he is moving forward or backward. When the lobster sheds his exoskeleton and leaves his old shell behind, the piece of sand in his gravity organ drops out. While the lobster is growing his new shell, he must find a new grain of sand to stick in his gravity organ. After the new exoskeleton has hardened, the lobster has a new grain of sand in his gravity organ and he is able to function as before.

My students don't take me seriously when I describe this theory of the lobster and his gravity organ. However, a clever biologist once placed lobsters in salt water where iron filings replaced the sand. The biologist reasoned that when the lobster shed his exoskeleton he would lose the grain of sand in his gravity organ and would grope around for another one. It is unlikely that the lobster would be able to find the same grain of sand; thus, he would probably pick up one of the small pieces of iron and stick it in his gravity organ. After waiting an appropriate amount of time, the biologist held a magnet above the lobsters. What do you think happened? Soon, there were several confused crustaceans flipping over on their backs. The biologist had made a test of the theory of the lobster and his gravity organ.

Let us look at the logic of the argument more closely. Although the biologist made only one test, he linked many facts and assumptions together. Should the biologist open up the lobster's head to see if a piece of iron was contained inside? This, of course, would be a further test of the theory. It might also be difficult for observers to see whether or not the lobster actually picked up a piece of iron filing in his claws. In other words, the "theory" links together concepts and ideas. In the final test with the magnet, use was made of other knowledge: iron is attracted by magnets. Furthermore, a logical argument is offered that if the iron filing is drawn upwards to the top of the gravity organ, the lobster would confuse the pull of the magnet with normal gravity and would respond accordingly. The credibility of the entire test lies in the fact that the researcher *made his predictions in advance.*

In the study of crime, and in many other disciplines, scholars frequently provide *ex post facto* explanations; that is, explanations after the fact. Admittedly, calling one's shots in advance is difficult; but it lends credibility to one's ideas. If one is attempting to design a crime-prevention programme, a clearly articulated explanatory argument, a "theory," should be spelled out *in advance.* In the social sciences, we are not always careful about making such predictions. After the evidence fails to support our predictions, which is common, *then* we should turn to *ex post facto* interpretations, which are useful in considering new theories for testing. However, we should not fall into the trap of giving these interpretations the credibility of predictions made in advance. In the case of the lobster study described above, a single dramatic test provided credence to the entire linkage of ideas because an integrated theory was developed in advance.

Durkheim's Theory of Deviance

How can stating concepts and linking them together systematically with hypotheses help in the study of crime? A classic work by Émile Durkheim provides a useful illustration. At the end of the nineteenth century, Durkheim studied suicide in France. Our simplified version of the theory contains three concepts: similarity, social cohesion, and deviance. The argument goes as follows: when people live in communities that have a common culture, they share common values and are in agreement on the important issues in life. This similarity in thinking leads to social cohesion. Social cohesion makes people sensitive to the social demands of society and hence leads to the reduction of deviant behaviour.

In Figure 4.3, these three concepts are linked together at the conceptual level. To test the theory, we must work at the operational level. To measure similarity, Durkheim asked what percentage of the population of a community was either Protestant or Catholic. A village with 95% Catholic or 95% Protestant was classified as "similar." A village with 50% Protestant and 50% Catholic was classified as "dissimilar."

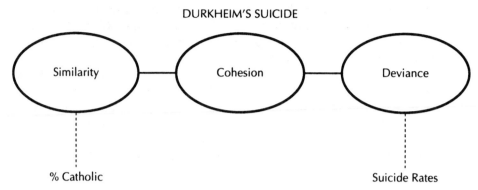

FIGURE 4.3 A Simplified Model of Durkheim's Explanation of Deviance

Durkheim did not use a measure for social cohesion. Today social scientists have measures for social cohesion, but it is important to demonstrate that a scientific theory can be tested even though some of its concepts cannot be measured. If the theory is correct, we would expect similarity to have an impact on social cohesion, and social cohesion would then have an impact on deviance. That is, similarity would have an impact on deviance *via* social cohesion.

Deviance was measured by suicide rates. At the operational level then, we can test the theory by asking if villages with a high concentration of people of the same religion (i.e., they are similar) do in fact have a low suicide rate (i.e., they are less deviant). By the same reasoning, those villages that are half-and-half, or dissimilar, would have a high suicide rate. The data gathered by Durkheim in nineteenth-century France tended to support these ideas.

Using Imperfect Operational Definitions

These ideas are useful, even though there are major weaknesses. The way the concept *similarity* was measured was crude. Obviously "similarity" in culture refers to many things besides religion. In fact, in many parts of the world religious differences would be only one factor, in terms of differing cultural characteristics. For example, we might ask what percentage of a population is francophone or anglophone. In other words, applying the logic of these models, we might predict that communities in Canada that were 99% anglophone or 99% francophone would have lower crime rates than those communities that had 50% in each group. Religious homogeneity, then, is only a *partial* indicator of the concept of similarity.

In a similar manner, suicide may not be a particularly good measure of deviant behaviour in general. In Figure 4.4, it is clear that suicide is a small proportion of the concept *deviance*. There may be other measures of deviance that could be used. Crime, as measured by those known to the police, could provide another test of the theory. A specific type of crime, homicide for example, could be used. Each measure of deviance might be deficient in some ways, but they may still have enough validity to provide a crude test. It is also possible that some suicides would not fit the concept of deviance. A mother, knowing that she had cancer, might commit suicide to avoid being a burden to her family.

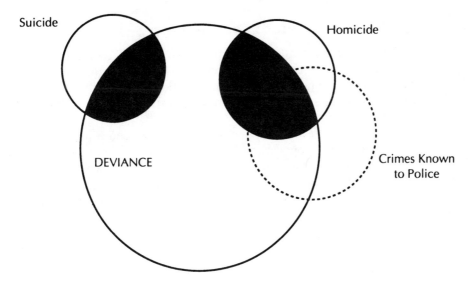

FIGURE 4.4 The Imperfect Fit Among Measures of Deviance

From these illustrations, it is obvious that quite different and imperfect operational definitions can be used, and each one might add a bit more to the test of the overall theory. In fact, criminologists have been using Durkheim's theory in this manner. Treating it as a general explanation of deviance and crime, they have used many different operational definitions. For this reason, Durkheim's initial ideas, even though tested with crude measures, have been very influential.

Choosing Theories to Suit Our Purposes

While Durkheim's ideas may be compatible with the way some people feel the world *is*, these simplifications could make others uncomfortable in terms of the way we feel the world *ought* to be. Durkheim suggests that homogeneous communities have less crime. Does this mean we should all live in ghettos? There are people in Canada who think that everyone should live with people of "their own kind," whatever that means. Theories do not necessarily provide us with clear policy directions. Personally, I believe that Canada has been enriched by its many ethnic groups, and that modern nations must accept the reality of considerable variety in their populations. At the same time, I am also aware that heterogeneity causes strain. Thus, I select theories with certain purposes in mind, and my choices are influenced by personal values. My preference is for theories that tell me how crime can be reduced in *heterogeneous* societies, which I feel are both inevitable and desirable in the modern world.

Applying Theory to Modern Criminology

With many different attempts to explain crime, can we use scientific theory to support one argument or another? Simple debate, without referring to some criteria for truth, may lead nowhere. Those who utilize science state hypotheses so they can be tested. This permits agreement on some points and enables scholars to move to more adequate theories.

Figure 4.5 shows some relationships between social class and crime. In general, those from the middle and upper classes do not get convicted of crimes as often as those in the lower classes. At least two explanations are possible. The first might emphasize the power of the upper classes to manipulate society. The powerful influence legislation so that their values and sense of what is right is written into the laws. In addition, their social clout may make it less likely that they would be arrested, charged, and convicted.

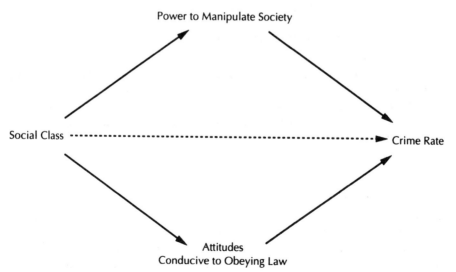

FIGURE 4.5 Simplified Model Explaining Relationship Between Social Class and Crime

The second explanation might argue that upper- and middle-class people are simply more law-abiding, because they have attitudes that are conducive to obeying the law. Lower-class people, this view contends, are not as well socialized, have more delinquent attitudes and, therefore, commit more crimes. Both explanations would suggest that in Figure 4.5, the arrow connecting social class and crime is spurious. That is, there is no real direct link between social class and crime, thus, the link is indicated by a thin, broken line. Instead, the relationship exists due to intervening variables, which translate the meaning of social class into something that leads to crime. The first argument chooses the "power to manipulate society" as that intervening variable, while the second argument chooses "attitudes" as the appropriate intervening variable.

If a researcher were to gather the appropriate data, she could test both ideas at the same time, in order to see which model fits the data best. Unfortunately, many researchers selectively choose data that fit their argument. By utilizing a proposed theory, even a very simple one as used in Figure 4.5, which actually contains two theories, we can clarify the argument and increase the likelihood that our findings can be interpreted in a manner that will actually move knowledge forward. Admittedly, Figure 4.5 oversimplifies the debate and its resolution.

The Advantages of Ideological Inconsistency

Criminologists must attempt to distinguish between their roles as researchers and as socially concerned citizens. Of course, one influences the other. In Figure 4.5 above, those adhering to ideology would use only one of the hypotheses offered. Advancing a theory, on the other hand, would require looking at both. Later in this book, my liberal bias as a citizen influences my social-policy recommendations, but the scholarly enterprise that produces the knowledge used to guide policy recommendations must guard against a tendency to let ideology generate the facts. While the scientific model is not the only way to acquire knowledge, it helps to keep us honest and to restrain us from misusing our position as scholars to push ideological views.

Some of the best illustrations of the use of scientific logic in criminology are provided by John Hagan of the University of Toronto and the many co-researchers who work with him. The range of criminological issues covered has been extensive, and the ideological viewpoint varies. Some criminologists approach issues with a consistent ideological perspective, and as long as this view is acknowledged, it presents few problems. However, there is merit in testing contrasting ideas and trying to let the data guide the conclusions. The role of social class and power is important in many of the articles done by Hagan and his colleagues, but sometimes the discussion leads to radical interpretations (Hagan and Albonetti, 1982; Hagan and Parker, 1985; Hagan, Huxter, and Parker, 1988); at other times, the interpretation is more traditional (Hagan, 1974). In his presidential address to the American

Society of Criminology, Hagan even argued different ideological positions (1992). What is consistent in Hagan's work is the sophisticated use of empirical data. Sometimes the data support Marxist arguments; sometimes they do not. These researchers, who have worked with Hagan at different times since the middle 1970s, would probably not claim to be value-neutral. In fact, they have mixed biases. However, their data guide their conclusions. Thus, they have made a major contribution to criminological research, and, in my mind, provide the best illustration of the effective use of science in criminology in Canada.

If criminologists would be *inconsistent* in their ideology and more *consistent* in their use of science, we would probably create a more reliable knowledge base. In the long run, this could contribute to a better society. At the same time, I would not argue that all criminologists should work the same way. Creative thinking comes in many forms, but the core of criminology as a social science requires strategies that give us criteria for knowing when something has been "explained." We should not use the word *science* to describe much of the interesting and exciting work that scholars do, when it really falls in the area of philosophy. Similarly, some of our useful descriptive work, which can lay the foundation for scientific study, should not be confused with scientific explanations.

Pseudo-Science, Impressive Terminology, and Shamanism in Modern Science

Unfortunately, some academics only sound scientific. Sometimes new concepts require new names, but at times new terminology is a smoke screen. One way for professionals to impress others is to develop a vocabulary that others do not understand (Heather, 1993). Robert Faris tells of a well-known scholar who was losing his hair. The doctor who examined him said, "You have alopecia ariata," and gave him a lotion to put on his head. The hair continued to fall out. Later in France, the sociologist went to a doctor in Paris. After the examination the doctor said, "You have alopecia ariata," and gave him injections of vitamins. The hair continued to fall out. While attending a conference in Italy, the sociologist went to another doctor who said, "You have alopecia ariata," and gave him X-ray treatments.

After he returned to the U.S., the scholar's hair began to grow back in. He thought about his experiences. Each doctor came to the same diagnosis, so they must have had some expertise, but why did they prescribe such varied treatment? Turning to a medical dictionary he looked up *alopecia ariata*. "Latin for falling hair. No known cure. Suggest you give the patient something to rub on his head."

Impressive terminology does not constitute science. Nor do powerful statistics. Computers do not make us scientific. Many of the rituals we follow resemble shamanism as much as science. Admittedly, folklore produces useful knowledge at times and modern practices often use the same type of logic. Criminology often claims to be scientific while engaging in practices that obfuscate the issue. (Instead of *obfuscate*, I could have used *complicate, confuse, muddle* or *distort*, but we professors must impress others with our vocabulary.)

CONCLUSION

After the Second World War, some social scientists who advocated the scientific method felt that this approach would be something of a panacea and would lead to dramatic breakthroughs in the understanding of human behaviour. Criminology was influenced by such thinking. That approach was somewhat oversold. Some of those with this orientation, sometimes referred to as positivists, were unappreciative of contributions from scholars using other strategies. For some criminologists, the pendulum swung the other way during the 1970s with a reaction against empirically based work. Tolerance was sometimes lacking on both sides. Many of the debates were not constructive, because scholars were frequently talking past one another.

Some criminologists are not only critical of the positivistic approach, but have resisted scientific training at the graduate level in universities. In parts of Europe, criminology is characterized by less science and more philosophy. Some French scholars say they cannot be bothered with the trivial type of empirical work done by U.S. criminologists. While creativity and knowledge are certainly possible using a variety of approaches, the neglect of scientific procedures has placed some criminological efforts in the area of ideology and philosophy rather than in the social sciences.

The majority of criminologists, in Canada and the U.S. at least, subscribe to the development of knowledge following the principles used in science. This chapter introduces some of those principles to the beginning student of criminology. It is not the only tool available in the search for knowledge, nor is it infallible, but it is important. The ideas reviewed here are not new, but some Canadian criminologists have neglected them. Criminologists in Canada would probably be more productive if they understood and utilized scientific procedures more than they do at present.

Progress in the explanation of crime depends on contrasting views, contradicting theories, and challenge. Thus, my pleas for science do not imply silencing other approaches to knowledge. It is only one tool in our kit. Many of the critics of empirical research and of positivism have improved it and made the scientific method more flexible and effective. Unfortunately, criminologists are very much like children with a new toy. Give the baby a new hammer and she will pound everything with it. Similarly, some social scientists have one tool that they use for everything. There is certainly room in the discipline to permit those with certain preferences to follow their tastes, but some are always trying to convince others that theirs is *the only* tool. Some tools should be discarded, but it seems unwise to throw away the trusty old saw just because you have a shiny new set of screwdrivers. Despite difficulties in application, traditional scientific procedures have much to offer in the study of crime, such as demolishing false conceptions of social reality, which is of major concern for those of us concerned with intelligent social policy.

GATHERING AND USING CRIME STATISTICS

So . . . per capita GDP is the best over-all measure of standard of living? If Prof Thurow had eaten a healthy meal of home-grown vegetables, gone to bed, and made love to his partner, he would have contributed precisely nothing to GDP.

If, on the other hand, he had driven to a casino, got drunk, crashed his car on the way home and injured himself and passing pedestrians, he would have increased his country's GDP. The fuel, liquor, tow truck, ambulance, car repairs and hospital bills all contribute to GDP and hence to the standard of living.

What nonsensense! The sooner we abandon GDP as a measure of human well-being the sooner we might stop exploiting the environment and fellow citizens.

Bob Lack,, *Auckland, New Zealand, letter to the Guardian*

THE MEANING OF CRIME STATISTICS

We have all heard the cliché about how easy it is to lie with statistics. Like many clichés, this one misses the central issue. The real issue concerns the meaning and interpretation of statistical data. An appropriate interpretation can extend knowledge, and provide a useful tool for making intelligent changes in regard to policies in a complex society. However, statistical data do not interpret themselves, and crime statistics are particularly difficult to interpret.

In the next three chapters, I will explore the utility and limitations of crime statistics. Under some circumstances, crime data can be useful; under others, they can be misleading. For example, crime statistics do not measure criminal behaviour; they measure the *response* of various agencies to their *perception* of crime. Under some circumstances these data may permit estimates of criminal behaviour. However, such situations are uncommon. Crime statistics are a better measure of what social-control agencies do than of what criminals do. Thus, some criminologists claim that crime statistics are invalid and useless. In actuality, many factors influence crime statistics, and it behooves us to sort out those factors to see how these data can be utilized in an intelligent fashion. For example, one study examines the interaction among crime rates, police strength, and the likelihood of the public reporting crime (Koenig, 1991). Koenig concluded that increased numbers of police and greater public concern lead to more crimes being reported and recorded. Another study looked at the dynamics of police work and noted that decisions made by the police influence what gets recorded as crime and what does not (Ericson, 1981). This book can only sensitize the reader to some of these issues. We begin with some common errors that plague everyone who deals with criminological data.

Common Errors in Data Gathering

Errors exist in all data, but some cause more problems than others. *Random* errors can be handled differently than *systematic* ones. Let us assume that the police in Montréal, Toronto, and Vancouver record thefts in the same manner, but they occasionally make mistakes. Assuming that the police in all three cities make mistakes with similar frequency and in a random fashion, and that they make their mistakes about as often in one direction as in another, we can still use the data and compare the three cities. In other words, we can usually handle *random* errors by assuming that they balance each other out. In a similar manner some small detachments of police scattered about a province might over-report certain crimes; other detachments might under-report the same crimes. If we assume that those detachments are similarly distributed in Ontario and in British Columbia, then these errors are *randomized*, and we can still compare Ontario and British Columbia when these statistics are averaged.

Systematic errors present a different problem. When census takers approach a home, they sometimes meet the man of the house at the door. When asked how many children he has, the man might respond "three." Is the wife home? No, she is in the hospital, having a baby. Has the baby been born? Yes, it arrived yesterday. Is that your third child? The husband hesitates. "Oh that's right. I have *four* kids now!" Husbands *systematically* forget their newborn children in counting offspring. This systematic error is not a problem for the census experts in Canada. Sophisticated demographers know how to adjust the number of children reported to get a more accurate count.

A similar systematic error occurs for women aged 39. Every census produces a surplus of women who are 39 and a shortage of woman aged 40 and 41. Our population experts are not fooled, however, and they correct this error with little trouble. While systematic errors that are understood can be handled, there are times when something that appears to be systematic may not be. For example, we might wish to compare crime rates for men and women. If the errors made in recording crime for men and women are random, we have few problems. If the errors are systematic but similar, for example, if we neglect both old women and old men, we might still compare men and women. But if the errors are systematic one way among women but systematic in a different way among men, we would have trouble comparing the sexes. However, we still might be able to make comparisons *within* the sexes.

The Centre for Justice Statistics in Canada deals with many conventional problems that arise with gathering statistics, but this still leaves many other problems that are more difficult to resolve. These next three chapters call attention to issues that place limitations on the use of data. Having data with limitations, of course, is not the same as claiming that such data are useless.

Interpreting Cases, Charges, and Events

Crime statistics sometimes provide data on *charges* and sometimes on *cases*. Researchers who are primarily interested in juveniles favour data on cases, since they are usually interested in the numbers of juveniles involved in crime, rather than the number of offenses. However, some data provide crimes known to the police or the number of criminal charges. If the police have picked up a juvenile who has committed a series of break and enters and also stolen a few cars, they could charge her with many offenses. On the other hand, once having recorded a few offenses, is there much point in adding many more to the list of charges? Thus, a police department that lays many charges, compared to one that lays few, may be dealing with a similar number of juveniles.

Diane Cossins (1991) faced this type of problem when attempting to study the Canadian juvenile justice system. She was really interested in the number of cases, but she only had data on charges. However, for most of Canada, the police laid about two charges per case, with the exception of Québec which laid about three charges per case. In other words, a fairly *systematic* ratio was similar for most of Canada. This enabled her to make comparisons among provinces.

In addition, Cossins knew that the Montréal police screened many juveniles involved in shoplifting, a practice common in some other cities in Québec as well. By handling many of these minor offenses informally, this intelligent strategy meant fewer cases were sent on to the court. These police practices, of course, lowered the recorded crime rate. In other words, knowledge about ratios between charges and cases, and an awareness of some local police practices, enabled Cossins to interpret crime statistics more accurately and make cautious comparisons among the provinces.

Measuring Crime Data at Different Stages

The research done by Cossins (1991) illustrates another characteristic of crime statistics. The activities of the recording agencies at the *early* stages will influence recording activities *later* in the process. If the police screen many minor offenses initially, the remaining cases, which are probably more serious, should result in more charges being laid per case (This appears to be the situation in Québec). The cases sent to court would be more serious and be more likely to receive punitive sanctions in court. By contrast, Youth Courts that receive more trivial offenses should give more lenient sanctions. Thus, *one cannot compare court statistics from place to place without taking into account the nature of police operations or actions of the prosecutor that lead up to cases going to court.* If some of these operations produce *systematic* differences, and we can assess that systematic bias, we can still make intelligent comparisons.

When Hackler and Paranjape (1984) were trying to understand the flow of cases through the juvenile justice system, they used data from the police and from the courts. Since these are two different data sets, one would anticipate some discrepancies. On the other hand, common sense might suggest that the number of charges laid by the police should be very similar to the charges heard by the courts. In fact the police were recording the number of *incidents*, while the courts were using the number of *charges*, so the data were not the same. By limiting the research to a single offense, in this case, theft, Hackler and Paranjape found that, for most of the provinces in Canada, the charge rate in the courts was somewhat less than the rate measured by the police using incidents. This seemed reasonable. Some charges might be eliminated before a court appearance. For example, in Ontario in 1978, the police charged juveniles for theft at the rate of 312 per 100 000 juveniles. For court appearances, the rate was 285. Saskatchewan had a police charge rate of 193, with a court appearance rate of 118. These appeared to be reasonable measures of juveniles passing from the system. However, Alberta recorded a *higher* rate for juveniles appearing in court than the rate for those charged by the police. The discrepancy itself was not surprising, as the two sources of data were different. The problem arises from the fact that nine provinces showed a discrepancy in one direction while Alberta showed a discrepancy in the other direction. This called into question the possibility of using the official data to indicate *systematic* patterns that would help us compare police activities with court activities. We simply do not know if these agencies are *recording* things differently or if they are actually *handling* juveniles differently.

This type of problem is inherent in many official crime statistics. Some criminologists see all these differences as "errors," making it impossible to use official statistics meaningfully, but these differences may be viewed as measures of how systems operate. While these data are inadequate in terms of measuring criminal behaviour, they may be useful indicators of what agencies do. This requires a different perspective on crime statistics. There is a tendency to assume that the system responds in a uniform and rational way; thus, crime rates vary according to the behaviour of criminals. In fact, variation in the systems is inevitable, and we will utilize data more intelligently when we accept this inescapable fact.

Interpreting Data at Different Stages in the System

Does it matter whether statistics are used at the level of police statistics or at a later stage in the system? Usually, there is a loss of cases at each stage. However, that loss differs by offence. Depending on the question being asked, criminologists may select data at different stages.

In terms of studying individuals, most criminologists favour data that are close to the original offense, usually crimes "known to the police." But the types of biases that arise at each stage may *compensate* for the nature of the error that existed at the earlier stage. For example, if not many crimes are recorded, those that do become official either are more serious or have deliberately been recorded because the police feel they are likely to be able to make an arrest. In other words, low recording increases the likelihood of action at the next level. Similarly, if the police arrest selectively, those arrested are more likely to go to court. By contrast, if many arrests are made, the evidence may be weaker on some and prosecutors may feel that they cannot take more of these cases to court. Finally, if the courts receive a relatively small selection of the more serious, more extensively investigated cases, the likelihood of conviction goes up. Thus, each step compensates for the other. Measures at the *end* of the judicial cycle may be more valid measures of crime in terms of regional comparisons.

This argument would be questioned by the majority of criminologists, and there are several flaws in my argument. Differences in the way judges decide may override the other factors. If we assume that judges respond uniformly across Canada, my hypothesis might be reasonable, but the work done by Palys and Divorski (1986) and earlier by Hogarth (1971) suggests that variability in judicial decision-making is the norm rather than the exception.

Another flaw is that instead of *compensating*, certain biases could *accumulate*. Liska and Tausig (1979) found that, in the U.S., the percentage of blacks processed at each level was consistently greater. Although the differences were small at each level, the racial differential accumulated with each decision level. In Canada, Hackler and Paranjape (1984) suggest that this could be happening for Native youngsters and those who are learning-disabled. Note, however, subtle accumulations might occur for certain types of *individuals*, but for a category of *offenses* the system might compensate at each level.

Again, it is important to remember what we are trying to measure. Clearly, the *individuals* who arrive at the conviction stage of the process differ from those who committed the original offenses. The different screens remove different types of people from the process, usually those who are more affluent and influential. Thus, those convicted tend to be the losers in life in a variety of ways. However, if we are asking which city, or province, or region *produces* more losers, then comparing convictions may be appropriate.

The reader should not be dismayed by the type of problems raised above. Although crime statistics as portrayed in the media can be misleading, criminologists who spend time with crime data usually learn to use them cautiously. Some of the problems lie in the lack of clarity and uniformity in procedures and definitions.

The Difficulty of Establishing Uniform Procedures and Definitions

Robert Silverman (Silverman, Teevan, and Sacco, 1991: 59-60) points out that some of the problems with official statistics begin with the definitions. In offenses against persons, one offense is counted per victim, while in property crimes, one offense is counted for every "distinct or separate operation." If an offender entered a room and assaulted three persons, three crimes were committed. If, on the other hand, the offender stole property from those three persons, only one crime occurred. Silverman presents some of the definitions used by Statistics Canada.

> Robbery ... If three persons in a store are held up and the store is robbed, score a single offence of robbery. If four persons rob one, or one person robs four at the same time and location, only one robbery is scored.

> Break and Entering ... When a building contains several independently occupied residences such as apartments ... each one entered should be scored. ... Score one offence for any number of box cars broken into when grouped in one location ... on the same spur or siding (Statistics Canada, 1986: 7-2, 7-3).

Silverman notes other potential inconsistencies; for example, if four box cars were on the same siding, it would be one offence; if two box cars were on one spur and two on an adjacent one, it would result in two offenses. However, these types of problems may not interfere with some types of research. If all police forces respond to these inconsistencies in a similar way, including *mis*classifying these events to the same degree, these would be random errors and the rates produced by each police jurisdiction would still permit comparison. Unfortunately, it is quite common for different agencies to apply the rules in a variety of ways.

The Centre for Justice Statistics has been working on these types of problems, and will be introducing "incident based reporting." Some of the pitfalls discussed in this chapter may be avoided in the future. The point that students of criminology should remember is that there are many potential problems in using crime statistics, but scholars can make use of them when they make reasonable assumptions and take appropriate precautions.

Crime Statistics in the U.S.: Two Systems

When discussing crime statistics in the U.S., one might be referring to the FBI's Uniform Crime Reporting System (UCR) or to the Bureau of Justice Statistics' National Crime Survey (NCS). There is a frustrating tendency for the two systems to produce very different numbers. The first measure reflects police recording while the second utilizes the response of victims. Attempts have been made to compare these two systems by adjusting them in a variety of ways. For example, victims do not report all of their experiences to the police. However, even after such adjustments are made, the NCS system routinely produces many more crimes than the UCR. More important for policy considerations is that NCS data based on victims point to a *decline* in crime at the same time *increases* in UCR rates dominate the headlines. These issues are discussed in detail by Albert Biderman and James Lynch (1991), where they discuss the factors that influence these two statistical systems. Naturally, the Canadian Centre for Justice Statistics learns about difficulties in data-gathering by noting the American research.

Canada also has gathered victimization data, and they will be utilized in Chapter 7. One might argue that victimization data are more appropriate, because they are less likely to be influenced by the activities of police. On the other hand, victimization surveys in Canada cover only small portions of certain populations, such as larger cities. For our purposes, it is worth noting that the NCS data in the U.S., which many scholars feel are the better measure of crime, indicate that the rates are going down, while the UCR data, which are more sensitive to the behaviour of the agencies, indicate that the rates are going up. Since the Canadian media focus almost exclusively on the official rates, more comparable to the UCR data, should we be surprised that the public mistakenly believes that crime is increasing?

The Misrepresentation of Crime Data

Agencies sometimes deliberately present crime data in a biased way to achieve a political goal. If the mayor tells the police chief that it would be nice if crime rates fell, there are ways to make the statistics coincide with that wish. New York City provides a classic illustration of this process. In the 1930s, New York City crime rates fell to ridiculously low levels. Efforts by the Federal Bureau of Investigation to secure greater compliance to the reporting methods were unsuccessful. Finally, New York City's crime rates were excluded from U.S. statistics because they were "incomplete, unreliable, and misleading" (New York Institute of Public Administration, 1952).

It was not until 1950 that data-gathering procedures were altered sufficiently so that the largest city in the United States was again included in U.S. crime statistics. Not surprisingly, official crime rates jumped dramatically. In April of 1950, only 214 burglaries were reported. In April of 1951, 4211 burglaries were recorded. It is safe to say that the twenty-fold increase in burglaries recorded was not a reflection of changes in actual crime. In Canada, we do not have such dramatic illustrations, but some of our older data can be used to illustrate problems better than more recent data.

Making Sense Out of Problem Statistics

P. J. Giffen (1965) provided some helpful illustrations of problem statistics by using data on fraud and assault from Canada's three largest cities, Montréal, Toronto, and Vancouver, in 1960.

Table 5.1 Fraud and Assault in Three Canadian Cities, 1960 — Number of Offenses

	Montréal	Toronto	Vancouver
Fraud	18	2536	60
Assault Causing Bodily Harm	99	1159	242

Source: P.J. Giffen, 1965: Table

Toronto had 2536 cases of fraud, compared to 18 in Montréal and 60 in Vancouver. Should we assume that Torontonians were more inclined to cheat others than those who lived in Montréal or Vancouver? Or did the police classify fraud in different ways in the three cities? Similarly, assaults causing bodily harm appeared to be more numerous in Toronto (1159) compared to Montréal (99) or Vancouver (242). Was it possible that the police in Montréal avoided the more serious category of assault causing bodily harm, and put some of these incidents in a less serious category? These distortions are so great that we are not misled.

Table 5.2 Selected Offenses - Reported, 1962 and 1971, Rates per 100,000

	Montréal		Toronto		Vancouver	
	62	71	62	71	62	71
Fraud	81	171	364	557	340	601
Theft Under $50	777	798	1134	1806	1430	2301
Break and Entry	754	1018	398	713	950	1832

Source: P.J. Giffen, 1976: Table II

A decade later Giffen (1976) revised his discussion, this time using rates per 100 000 people instead of raw numbers. Using 1962 data, the rates for fraud for the three largest Canadian cities were: Montréal, 81; Toronto, 364; and Vancouver, 340 (Giffen, 1976: 79). The 1960 pattern persisted somewhat into 1962. The differences still remained between Montréal and Toronto with Vancouver's rates increasing to those of Toronto. Adjusting the figures by using rates per 100 000 did not explain the changes. The police in each city were probably still recording fraud in different ways.

Do patterns persist over time? In 1971, the rates for fraud were: Montréal, 171; Toronto, 557; Vancouver, 601 (Giffen, 1976: 79). Have the con men moved to Vancouver? Instead of trying to interpret statistics without any background information, it might be wiser to supplement our knowledge about a specific system. My discussions with police in Montréal suggest that juvenile thefts are more likely to be handled informally than in other Canadian cities. If this strategy made sense for juveniles, was it used for adults as well?

In the rest of Canada, in contrast to parts of Québec, the police recorded about twice as many thefts as break and enters. This fits with common sense that people shoplift more frequently than they break into houses. However, Montréal produces official statistics that are frequently contrary to this pattern. This would make sense if the police frequently handled shoplifting informally. In 1971, the rate for break and entry in Montréal was 1018. For theft under $50, it was 798 (Table 5.3). In other words, the Montréal theft rate was unusually low compared to Toronto (1806) and Vancouver (2301). Instead of saying that the statistics are "wrong," it makes more sense to say they tell us something about the way police respond to certain types of events.

The illustrations provided by Giffen are so extreme that we know comparisons would be wrong. In recent decades, the figures begin to appear more plausible. This can lull readers into a false complacency and tempt them to make inappropriate comparisons. If we make direct comparisons across Canada, we can easily be misled. At this point, the reader may feel that crime statistics are fraught with so many errors as to be completely useless. If we naïvely assume that these figures are determined primarily by the behaviour of criminals, a view typically taken by the media, we will certainly be misled. But if we use statistics as just another piece of information, they help us understand crime as well as the agencies that respond to it.

COMPARING CANADA AND THE UNITED STATES

In an attempt to consider the merits of different policies towards violent crime, Laurel Gauld and I utilized a rather detailed study from Columbus, Ohio, and made comparisons with Edmonton, Alberta (Hackler and Gauld, 1982; Van Dine, Conrad, and Dinitz, 1979). The State of Ohio tended to have rates of murder, rape, and robbery that were similar to the U.S. average, with aggravated assault being slightly lower than average. Columbus itself had rates that were somewhat higher than the rest of the state. Edmonton and Columbus were similar in size, so we used the 1973 data that were used in Columbus and obtained comparable data for Edmonton.

Table 5.3 Violent Crime Profile, Columbus and Edmonton 1973

	Known	**Cleared by Charge**	**Adults**	**Juvenile**
Columbus	2892	792	342	126
Edmonton	5567	996	495	21

Source: Hackler and Gauld, 1982

Table 5.3 provides a Violent Crime Profile for the two cities. More violent crimes were known to the police in Edmonton, more offenses cleared by a charge, with 495 adult offenders compared with 342 adult offenders in Columbus. On the basis of this table, one might think that Edmonton was the more violent of the two cities. However, in Table 5.4, we see that, in Columbus, 15% of the 342 violent offenders were charged with homicide and attempted murder, while only 4% of the 495 Edmonton violent offenders were charged with homicide. It appears that the violent offenders in Edmonton were not as violent as the violent offenders in Columbus.

Table 5.4 Distribution of 1973, Violent Offence of Subjects Charged: Edmonton and Columbus

	Edmonton		**Columbus**	
	N	**%**	**N**	**%**
Homicide and Attempted Murder	18	4	53	15
Sexual Offenses	37	8	71	21
Assaults	268	54	57	17
Robbery	172	35	161	47
	495	100%	342	100%

Source: Hackler and Gauld, 1982

If we look at the number of assaults in Edmonton, we see that there were 268, and we note that this is much more than the 18 homicides and attempted murders. Columbus recorded only 57 assaults, similar in number to the 53 homicides and attempted murders. Are we to believe that Columbus had almost as many homicides as assaults? Or, is it more reasonable to believe that many assaults were simply not recorded? Clearly, the latter makes more sense.

We do not have the insights to interpret these data correctly, but it seems that the Edmonton system generates a larger base of violent offenders, by reporting and charging many assault cases compared to Columbus. Van Dine (1979) and his fellow researchers in Columbus, Ohio, lend support to this interpretation, since their study shows that many family assault cases do not result in charges leading to prosecution. When homicides are compared, Columbus is more violent than Edmonton. This is consistent with the general finding that the U.S. has more homicides than Canada. If we look at the number of assaults, Edmonton appears to be more violent, but it also appears fairly obvious that Columbus under-reports assaults.

This examination of crime statistics in Edmonton and Columbus should make us pause about other comparisons. A casual glance at the total violent-crime statistics would lead most journalists to conclude that Edmonton had more violent crime. A more careful look at the homicide data would lead to the opposite conclusion.

Paul Brantingham (1992) points out other potential faults in the above comparisons. Are the American aggravated assault categories the same as the Canadian categories of "woundings plus bodily harm"? Charges are different from reported incidents, and there are a number of filters between the police and the courts. These filters are probably different in Edmonton and in Columbus. Clearly, comparisons with other countries are risky.

Mapping the Distribution of Crime

Paul Brantingham has used crime data to look at the spatial distribution of reported crime. The graphic displays he presents provide a much clearer visual image of crime rates (1991: Chapter 14). He makes international as well as North American comparisons. However, this may be expecting more from the statistics than they can deliver, because some of the assumptions one must make may be untenable. For example, Brantingham would acknowledge that the way crime statistics are generated differ from place to place, but he could reasonably assume that much of this variance is random. Thus, some of the differences will cancel out. In addition, the number of jurisdictions that report crime in a similar way may be the clear majority, and therefore, general patterns may be valid even though there will be some areas that are represented incorrectly. My suspicion is that *uniqueness* in the way systems gather data is more common than uniformity. Thus, many of our attempts to make geographical comparisons may create unrealistic myths, as we have seen in some of the illustrations above. On the other hand, if everyone is clear that these comparisons refer to the *reporting* of crime instead of actual criminal behaviour, then the graphs that Patricia and Paul Brantingham (1981) have used so effectively in their past research provide a useful visual display.

Keeping the Edmonton - Columbus comparison in mind, let us look at Figure 5.1 (14.10 from Brantingham [1991]). It appears that Western Canada, as well as the Western U.S., has more theft than elsewhere. However, if the Western police forces cast a wider net and include more minor offenders among those who are charged, the higher theft rates in Western Canada could be a better measure of the *activity of agencies of social control* than of theft. In the following chapters, we will suggest that the justice systems of the Western Canadian provinces cast a wider net and process more cases. Could we argue that theft is actually similar across Canada, and that the differences in theft rates are caused by the way the police react? Dan Koenig (1991) might have sympathy towards such a view, but we simply do not know how much of the crime rate is determined by what the police do.

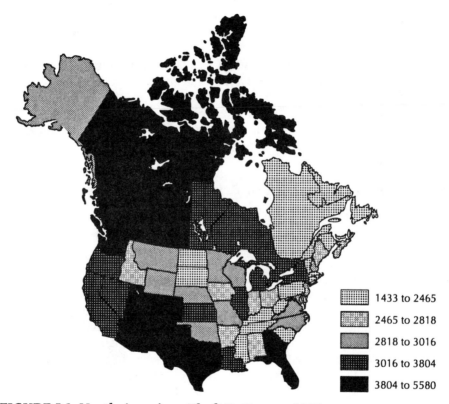

▦	1433 to 2465
░	2465 to 2818
▨	2818 to 3016
▓	3016 to 3804
■	3804 to 5580

FIGURE 5.1 North American Theft Patterns - 1989
Source: Paul Brantingham (1992).

Is Brantingham being courageous or reckless in providing these graphic depictions for us? Possibly a little of both. Unless people like Brantingham are willing to use statistical data, make the necessary assumptions, and try to interpret them, we will not engender the sort of debate that increases knowledge. On the other hand, I have reservations about Figure 5.1 (14.10 in Brantingham), and similar depictions of statistics. Most readers assume that these geographical representations can be used to test theories about *criminal* behaviour rather than the behaviour of agencies of social control. To say that Western Canada and the Western U.S. have more *reported* crime than the East is appropriate. To say that there is more crime in the West is less clear.

My caution about the use of this technique varies with the type of offense. For example, homicide is probably measured similarly across Canada and across the United States. Police behaviour may not influence the recording of murder to a great extent. Therefore, Figure 5.2, which was taken from Brantingham (14.7), shows the distribution of homicide in North America, and is probably based on data less influenced by reporting systems. Therefore, I would be willing to test theoretical ideas relating to homicide, even though I would be cautious about using measures of property crime. Clearly, the Brantinghams and I would both agree that criminologists who do not attempt to use empirical data forfeit valuable tools.

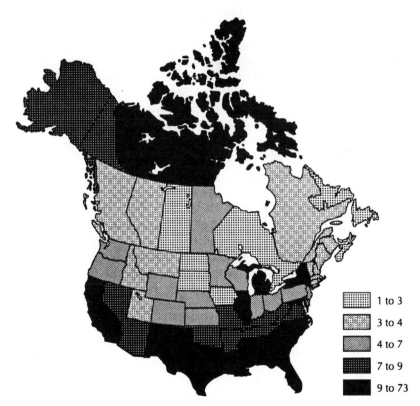

1 to 3
3 to 4
4 to 7
7 to 9
9 to 73

FIGURE 5.2 North American Homicide Patterns - 1989
Source: Paul Brantingham (1992).

Motor-vehicle theft is also a measure that might lend itself to geographical comparisons. The assumption is that most people report stolen cars regularly for a variety of common-sense reasons, such as insurance. Thus, motor-vehicle theft might be only minimally influenced by police practices. Notice, however, that auto-theft rates are standardized in the conventional way, thefts per 100 000 persons. While this makes sense for many types of crimes, would it not be more sensible to calculate the rate according to the number of automobiles instead of people? After all, the more automobiles, the more likely the risk. If computed as thefts per 100 000 autos instead of people, the comparative rates would drop in British Columbia and rise in Québec.

Using Data to Test Ideas

A major reason for gathering crime statistics is to test ideas relevant to social policy. Our confidence in our data fluctuates for a variety of reasons. Sometimes we feel reasonably secure in using crime statistics. At other times, our awareness of weaknesses in the data will make us very cautious about making an interpretation. Of course, we may *feel* rather confident but later discover that we have been misled.

P. J. Giffen (1976: 106) provides data that illustrate one of these dilemmas. Some scholars have argued that cultural conflict leads to crime. Thus, immigrants might get into trouble with the law more easily than others. In reality, most studies show just the opposite (Thomas, 1993). Immigrants tend to be more law-abiding than the native-born, despite claims that "the problem is with those foreigners." On the other hand, the cultural-conflict notion appears to have more validity for the second generation. Whereas first-generation immigrants try hard to obey the rules of the new country, their children are often caught between the wishes of their parents and the demands of a different teenage culture. Some theorists argue that delinquency is more likely for children caught between two cultures. Giffen presents data on delinquency according to the birthplace of the fathers.

Looking at the 1951 data, Giffen notes that the delinquency rates for the children of Canadian-born fathers and the children of immigrants does not differ dramatically. However, those who favour the culture-conflict notion might point to the relatively high delinquency rate of the children of Italian fathers. Children of Italian parents had a delinquency rate of 28, which was higher than children of native-born Canadians and others. Could it be that culture conflict is higher for second-generation Italian juveniles than for second-generation Scandinavians or Germans? The 1951 data appear reasonable, but let us turn to the 1961 data. One would expect some consistency. There isn't. The delinquency rate for children of Italian fathers drops from 28 to .9, the lowest of any of the categories. The rate for children of Scandinavian fathers goes from 10.7 to 19.3, the highest of the immigrants, exceeded only by the children of Canadian-born fathers, which has gone from 19.7 in 1951 to 37.6 in 1961.

Table 5.5 Birthplace of Fathers of Juvenile Delinquents, 1951 and 1961. Rates per 10,000 Males 25-64 Years of Age of Each Birthplace in the Canadian Population

	1951		1961	
	Number	**Rate**	**Number**	**Rate**
Canada	4,968	19.7	11,764	37.6
England and Wales	415	20.3	211	11.7
Scotland	192	24.8	71	9.9
Other British Commonwealth	11	13.4	13	7.9
United States	116	12.1	89	11.0
Germany	21	14.6	20	3.5
Italy	74	28.0	8	0.9
Poland	73	9.6	28	3.6
Russia	84	10.6	28	3.9
Scandinavia	32	10.7	54	19.3
Other European countries	230	19.6	59	2.8
Asiatic countries	25	13.4	11	5.8

Father's birthplace not stated: 1951—401, 1961—90

Source: Giffen, 1976: 106.

CONCLUSION: THE DANGERS OF "PLAUSIBLE" DATA

When data support widely held views, we tend to assume that the data are valid. The above illustration points to the danger of feeling comfortable with data because they appear plausible. The 1951 data "made sense." The 1961 data shattered that thinking. Should I question the data or the ideas? It is only after we have looked at crime statistics from many angles over a period of time that we can use them with any degree of confidence.

The purpose of this chapter has been to make the reader cautious. Being cautious regarding crime data does not mean that data cannot be used with a modest degree of success. Our comparison of Edmonton and Columbus, Ohio, contained weaknesses, but we learned something. The diagrams produced by the Brantinghams showing the distribution of official crime rates has inherent problems, but it also yields useful information if interpreted cautiously. The next chapter will attempt to make comparisons, using these imperfect data.

MAKING COMPARISONS WITH CRIME STATISTICS

I used to search for the truth; now I'll settle for an absorbing fantasy.

Anon

CHARACTERISTICS THAT COMPLICATE COMPARISONS

At this point, the reader may feel that making sense out of crime data is hopeless. The more we learn about these statistics, the warier we become, but in exchange, we gain insights about the settings in which crime statistics are produced. With these insights we are willing to make some comparisons, but hesitant to make others. Sometimes we would like to compare provinces. At other times we would like to compare cities. If all of the cities in Québec and Ontario do things the same way, then comparison between the two provinces is possible. However, if cities themselves do things differently or have different characteristics, comparisons among provinces or within provinces can be misleading. Therefore, it is important to look at some features of cities and the impact they might have on crime statistics. Let us first consider the "Central City Phenomenon."

The Central City Phenomenon

As every experienced policeman knows, crime is more likely in areas where there are goods to be stolen or victims to be robbed. Patricia and Paul Brantingham (1981) have spelled out conditions that influence the time and location of criminal acts. Some of these conditions are found in central cities (Gibbs and Ericson, 1976). Those cities that are surrounded by populated areas, such as suburbs, are more likely to act as "magnets" for people living nearby. Some cities, such as Calgary or Saskatoon, have relatively little population in the suburbs. There are no large surrounding populations that might use Calgary or Saskatoon for criminal exploitation. Central cities are not only attractive for work and culture, they also provide many well-known targets for crime (Boggs, 1965).

Victoria, British Columbia, offers one of the best illustrations of the "central city phenomenon" in Canada (Hackler and Don, 1989). According to official data, Victoria displays surprisingly high crime rates when compared to other metropolitan areas. The high crime rates in Victoria data do not get much attention in the media, because the city is not one of the larger metropolitan areas. In addition, in a city where you can purchase flowers in front of houses by putting money in an unattended box, the residents have difficulty thinking of their town as the crime capital of Canada. However, Victoria is a central hub for a half-dozen communities on the Victoria peninsula. Each community has its own police department. They are part of a general metropolitian area of approximately 200 000 people with Victoria as their central city, their downtown. If you are a drug dealer living in one of the suburbs and are looking for action, you would probably head for Victoria. Similarly, if you are a young woman living in the suburbs and decide to earn money by selling sex, you could try propositioning your neighbour while he is walking his dog, but you would probably do better in a bar in downtown Victoria. The central city phenomenon suggests that opportunities for crime in city centres attract the criminally inclined from the surrounding residential areas.

Table 6.1 shows crime rates for males charged with theft and break-and-enters. Vancouver is used as a comparison, since it frequently has the highest crime rates of any major city in the nation. Victoria is shown with its five major suburbs. Sidney, with a population of about 8000, is on the northern end of the Victoria peninsula. One can think of Sidney as using Victoria as its "central city," but it is useful to view Sidney as a small central city. Central Saanich is the semi-rural area adjacent to Sidney.

Our study looked at several other central cities in British Columbia but, for simplicity, we only include Langley City, about fifty kilometres from Vancouver. Past experience suggested that theft has a different pattern from break and entry, so data for these offenses are separated. In addition, data on adults and juveniles can be handled differently, so Table 6.1 separates them.

Theft and the Central City Phenomenon

As predicted, the five surrounding suburbs of Victoria have lower theft rates (52-254) than Victoria itself (627), possibly due to the fact that the criminally inclined go into the central city to do much of their stealing. The same phenomenon appears to operate elsewhere (Hackler and Don, 1989). Sidney, the shopping centre for a smaller area, has twice the theft rate of its nearby areas (206 compared to 73-90). Langley, a community of 16 000, fifty kilometres east of Vancouver, is surrounded by a large agricultural area with 47 000 residents. Where would people go to steal? We suggest that the higher theft rate in Langley City (428 to 148) is not because

Table 6.1 Males Charged With Theft and B & Es in 13 Communities* in British Columbia (Rates per 100,000 Population 1981 - 1985)

		Theft		B & Es	
	Population	5 Year Avg-Men	5 Year Avg-Boys	5 Year Avg-Men	5 Year Avg-Boys
Vancouver City Mun.	417 422	550	59	170	64
Victoria City Mun.	65 223	**627**	**215**	**239**	**72**
Saanich Mun.	79 025	150	82	74	90
Esquimalt	16,154	254	63	120	46**
Oak Bay Mun.	16 853	52	38	68	53
Colwood Prov.	33 152	126	105	164	181
Sooke Prov.	8619	78	107	176	170
Sidney Mun.	8448	**206**	**187**	**104**	**171**
Sidney Prov.	7104	84	42	167	135
Central Saanich Mun.	11 485	90	57	81	55
Ganges Prov.	6844	73	37	248	207**
Langley City Mun.	15 621	**428**	**132**	**268**	**101**
Langley Township Mun.	47 108	148	61	127	151

* The first police detachment in each set is the central city unit. Other units are the suburban police detachments.

** A rate of 0 was recorded for one of the years and was deleted from our analysis. Therefore, only a four year average was calculated.

Source: Hackler and Don, 1989:7

the criminals *live* there, but rather that it has more attractive targets; thieves come to town to steal.

Break and Enter and the Central City Phenomenon

Should we assume that these spatial patterns apply to burglary as well? This may differ according to age. For adult males, the central city phenomenon persists, but not as clearly as for theft. Juvenile boys, however, may be more familiar with their local community, and thus more likely to choose neighbouring homes to burglarize. In other words, adults may be more experienced and have a greater "awareness space" (Brantingham and Brantingham, 1984: 352). For them, going to other parts of their metropolitan area might be a good strategy.

Table 6.1 shows a high charge rate for B&Es in Ganges (248 for adult males, 207 for juveniles) where a half-dozen RCMP officers serve Salt Spring Island. These rates are higher even than Vancouver's, which often leads the nation. Should we notify the newspapers that the bucolic setting on Salt Spring Island is deceiving, and that they should give Ganges the title "B&E Capital of Canada"? Before raising the alarm, we should remember that the police usually do not have much information on most burglaries. When they do not have a suspect, it is difficult to make an arrest and lay a charge. Thus, it is difficult to clear "by charge" much more than 15% of the known B&Es. Salt Spring Island may be different, in that offenders are liable to be known. When Mabel notices that her TV set is missing, she may know the local policemen and they may even know her TV set. If they check the next ferry, they may check the autos waiting in line for Mabel's TV in the back seat. In other words, police in small communities may be more familiar with potential offenders and better able to lay charges. B&E is probably less common on Salt Spring Island than in Vancouver, but the *likelihood* of burglars being discovered and charged appears to be greater on an island with a limited road network.

Thus, some statistics may be augmented in small communities; others, such as public drunkenness, may be diminished. Marianne Nielsen (1979) argues that, in small communities, the police may know the offenders and let them dry out in a cell or take them home. In larger urban centres, such offenders may become part of the official statistics.

Are Vancouver, Montréal, or Toronto central cities? Vancouver contains about a half-million people policed by a separate department. Another half-million live in surrounding communities, which have separate police forces and generate separate statistics. Montréal and Toronto, by contrast, have larger police departments, which cover downtown cores but also secondary shopping areas and residential communities. Going downtown to steal in Montréal keeps the statistic in the same police district, but going from Burnaby to Vancouver is a move from one police jurisdiction to another. Thus, Vancouver could be influenced by the central city phenomenon more than Montréal or Toronto.

In Nova Scotia, does the bridge across the Narrows between Halifax and Dartmouth mean that it is easy to travel from Dartmouth into Halifax for certain illicit activities? Or is the distance a barrier? The central city phenomenon plays a different role in different parts of Canada. Victoria appears to be the best Canadian illustration. Therefore, we would anticipate official crime rates to provide a distorted image of that city. At present we do not have research that can do more than suggest the possibility of these impacts on crime rates.

COMPARING CITIES: EDMONTON AND CALGARY AS ILLUSTRATIONS

Each year, when crime statistics are released, journalists call local criminologists for explanations. The cautions about interpreting these figures usually have little impact on the media and are forgotten by the time statistics appear the following year. Edmonton is compared annually with Calgary, since Edmonton almost always displays much higher crime rates. The two cities are very similar in size and demographic characteristics, and thus the comparison is natural (Silverman, 1980). Edmonton typically joins Vancouver in the top three cities in the nation on a variety of offenses, but Calgary invariably reports a lower crime rate. When the Canadian Centre for Justice Statistics (1990) studied crime reporting procedures, part of the differences in reported crime rates was attributed to the operation of the information systems in the two police departments (Silverman, Teevan, and Sacco, 1991: 57). Crimes disappeared from the record-keeping after the first telephone call, but the disappearance rate was higher in Calgary — 9.9% versus 5.5% in Edmonton. At the next stage, but still before an offense report was written, 11% of the cases in Calgary were screened, compared to 1% in Edmonton. It is inappropriate to assume that one system is "correct" or that one system is deliberately trying to mislead. Rather, it calls our attention to the variability that probably exists across different systems.

Alberta has been fortunate in that the two cities are aware of these differences, and Edmonton has not tried to make its statistics look "better." The shared information between the police of these two cities provides insights into the dynamics of the crime-recording process, information that should help us in understanding crime data elsewhere in Canada in the future.

The central city phenomenon might also influence the crime rates of the two cities. Calgary's suburbs make up only 2.3% of the metropolitan area, while suburbanites make up 22% of Edmonton's population (Silverman, Teevan, and Sacco, 1991: 58). Crime rates are more similar between Edmonton and Calgary than the statistics suggest.

In general, inter-city and inter-regional comparisons are risky, even though this is constantly being done in the press (Hackler and Paranjape, 1983). If we wish to use crime statistics to compare cities, we should be aware that these indicators measure *the response of local justice systems to what they perceive to be crime.* This is a useful comparison, but it is misleading to think of such statistics as measuring the behaviour of criminals. On the other hand, if there is constancy in the way systems operate, statistics may be a reasonable indicator of *trends* for a country, province, or even a city. There are pitfalls, however, even when one attempts to examine trends. Let us turn now to some of these trends.

RECENT TRENDS IN HOMICIDE RATES

Since the 1960s there probably has been an increase in violent crime with a peak in the early 1970s (Figure 6.1). Debates on this issue are numerous, and criminologists do not agree, but similar increases have been reported in most of North America and Europe. Because of the consistency of this evidence, the best guess is that violent crime increased from the 1960s until the 1970s in North America and in Europe.

Some measures of violent crime are unsuitable for looking at long-term trends. Rape, for example, was clearly under-reported in the past. More cases are reported today. Similarly, more child abuse, wife abuse, and minor assaults are being reported. Homicide rates appear to be more reliable for assessing trends. One could also argue that homicide rates reflect violent situations; although most violent confrontations do not end in death, the more such confrontations, the higher the homicide rate. Figure 6.1 shows the homicide rates in Canada since 1926. The U.S. has a similar pattern. The peak in 1930 was not seen again until 1970 (Silverman and Kennedy, 1993:33-35). There was a steady decline following the stock market crash of 1929, through the economic depression and World War II, until 1944. From 1966 to 1975 there was a dramatic rise, followed by a gradual decline.

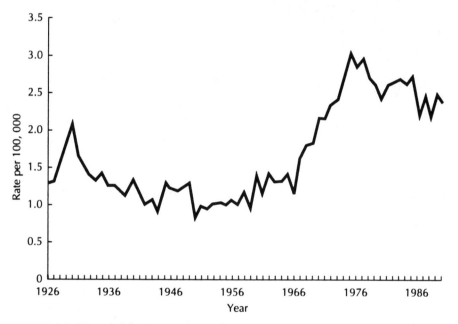

FIGURE 6.1 Homicide Rates Canada, 1926-1990

Source: Statistics Canada, 1983; Canadian Centre for Justice Statistics, 1988; Silverman and Kennedy (1993:33)

Homicide Rates for Canadian Native People

Figure 6.2 looks at the homicide rate since 1961, and calls attention to our Native Indian population. Silverman and Kennedy (1993:212) point out that definitions of who qualifies as a Canadian Indian have not been consistent over time. However, the rate rises dramatically between 1961 and 1975. The rate of 30 per 100 000 Canadian Indians in 1978 and 1979 is more than ten times that of the rest of the population.

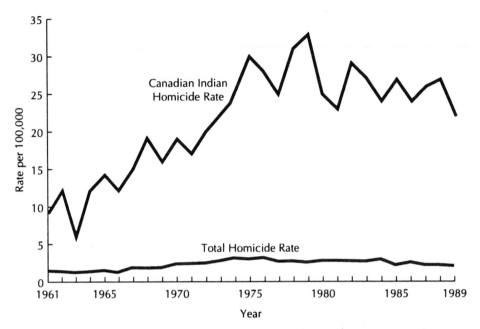

FIGURE 6.2 Homicide Rates for Canadian Indian Offenders Canada, 1961–1989*

*Population bases for calculation of rates are extrapolated from census data.

Later in this book, I will suggest that marginal groups in North America have suffered more than the dominant populations over the past couple of decades. The majority of Canadian Indian homicide is intraracial; i. e., they kill each other. Similarly, the majority of African-American homicide is intraracial. Those who are well off have apparently not endured the ravages of crime since the 1960s as much as those at the bottom of the social hierarchy.

Who Kills: Family, Friends, or Strangers?

Figure 6.3 shows that strangers tend to account for less than 10% of the murders. "Intimate murder, in the form of spousal and other family murder, accounts for about 40% of Canadian murder incidents during the 1980s, equalling the proportion of friend/acquaintance events" (Silverman and Kennedy, 1993:67).

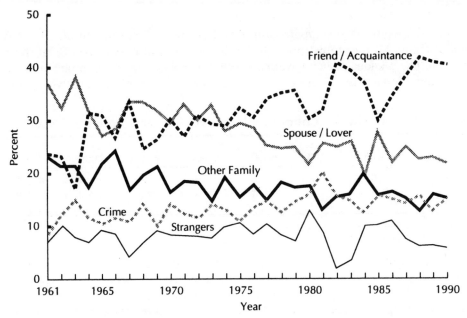

FIGURE 6.3 Social Relationship Between Victims and Offenders Homicides in Canada, 1961-1990*

*Proportion of all homicides.

In 1961 family murders accounted for 60% of Canadian murders. While murders among friends/acquaintances have increased and murders among intimates have declined, the family still accounts for the majority of homicides. The crimes feared most by the public, stranger- or crime-related murders, have not increased substantially since 1961, nor do they account for more than a quarter of Canadian murders. Since the 1970s, victimization studies in the U.S. show that violent crime has decreased. Canada displays the same pattern. Obviously, this is not the impression we get when we listen to politicians "wage war on crime."

Measuring Violent Crime: Nationally and Internationally

Although it is difficult to measure most crimes, many people assume that murders would be measured accurately. But how many hunting accidents were actually murders? How many suicides were actually murders? At some point, we must work with what we have. While not perfect, murder and car theft appear to be reasonable indicators that permit comparisons within Canada; but can we make international comparisons?

Comparing Homicide Internationally

Obviously, we need to compare countries if we are to test some of our theories about crime. Murder rates appear to be the best indicator available. Even there one must be cautious. Robert Silverman (1991) describes some of the problems making international comparisons even when the basic information is relatively good.

Table 6.2 Homicide by Countries, 1986 (Number and Rate per 100,000)

	U.S.A.	U.K.	F.R.G.	France	Canada	Japan	U.S.S.R.
Number	20 613	2160	2728	2413	569	1744	16 700
Rate	8.6	4.3	4.5	4.4	2.2	1.4	5.8

Source: Silverman, 1992.

It is tempting to draw conclusions from the selected comparative homicide rates summarized in Table 6.2. However, each country defines homicide slightly differently. The U.S. data include murder and manslaughter (but attempted murder and manslaughter *are not* included); the United Kingdom data include murder, attempted murder, threat or conspiracy to murder, manslaughter and infanticide; the Federal Republic of Germany includes murder, manslaughter, "murder on demand," and infanticide; France includes murder, manslaughter, parricide (parent killing), infanticide, and poisoning; Japan includes murder, manslaughter, attempted murder and robbery causing death; Canada includes first and second degree murder, manslaughter, and infanticide; homicide in the U.S.S.R. is undefined in the data source. No two countries define the data identically, and as a result, major differences can be noted (Silverman, 1992).

Somewhat different definitions of crime might not be a major problem if future scholars are able to provide us with estimates of the impact of certain practices. What adjustment should be made if attempted murders are included along with completed murders or manslaughters? A more detailed knowledge of recording factors might still permit valid comparisons. For example, Table 6.2 indicates that the Canadian homicide rate of 2.4 is higher than Japan's 1.4; but since Japan also includes attempted murders, we might assume that the difference between the two countries is *understated*. Thus, one can safely argue that Japan's homicide rate is less than half of Canada's. Testing hypotheses concerning murder in the two countries could safely assume that Japan's murder rate is less than Canada's.

Comparing Canada and the United States

The U.S. has different criminal laws for each state, but the similarities are still very strong. Canada has only one criminal code, and while this helps, the diversity in police practices may be as great across Canada as across the United States. Thus, comparing states, provinces, or states with provinces must be done cautiously. Edmonton has, at times, been "the murder capital of Canada," with approximately 30 murders a year in a city of 600 000 people. The Bronx, a borough of New York City with a population of about 700 000, has close to 400 murders per year (Silverman and Kennedy, 1993:3). Recording practices probably do not account for the higher murder rate in the Bronx.

At times, Vancouver and Seattle (and Toronto and Chicago) have been compared, in terms of homicide. The U.S. cities have higher murder rates, and some argue that Canada's more restrictive legislation regarding handgun possession may be a factor. While it is difficult to judge this argument on the basis of these data alone, comparing British Columbia with Washington, Oregon, and Idaho on a variety of crime statistics may be just as valid as comparing Canadian provinces.

Police Killings in Canada: An Illustration of Public Response to Crime Data

How do the media respond to crime statistics? In the latter part of 1984, seven policemen were killed in Ontario and two in Québec. Not surprisingly, the media spoke of increased attacks on the police and discussed the need to bring back the death penalty. Few people asked whether this unusually large number of police deaths was a *rare* event that might occur "by chance," or as part of a trend. Statistics since 1961 provided some insights (Hackler and Janssen, 1985). Most policemen killed on duty died in automobile accidents, like the rest of us, but homicides naturally got more attention. The largest number of police killings in Canada (12) was in 1962. The 23-year average was 3.6, but what was the long-term trend? Hackler and Janssen (1985) concluded that the trend was downward, and that the 1984 experience was statistically within the range of chance at the .05 level. In other words, it was the sort of thing that would normally happen occasionally, *even with* a downward trend.

What was the trend for the next five years, until 1990? Officially, six officers were killed in 1984 and five in 1985. The nine cases reported in the newspapers in 1984 were resolved and counted in these two years. In 1986, four police officers were killed, in 1987, three, and in 1988 and 1989, no officers were killed. Only in one other year (1963) since these data have been gathered have no police been murdered on the job (Statistic Canada, 1989, 1988, 1987). Naturally, we hope this downward trend will continue, but it is clear that the media are not interested in this type of information. No headlines announced that no police officers had been killed for two years. By contrast, in 1984, the media gave the public the impression that the killing of police officers was on the rise. Probably most Canadians, including those who make policy, have the same impression today. Being a police officer continues to be less dangerous than working in industry, and is much less dangerous than farming, fishing, forestry, and mining.

CONCLUSION

Some criminology texts introduce the section on crime statistics with national summaries of various crimes. That is not very useful. Instead, I review various pitfalls and biases that influence crime statistics, before presenting them. Crime data can be used for some purposes, but not others. It is difficult, but not impossible, to compare different geographical areas. Such comparisons are more useful when we are aware of the influence of the central city phenomenon and other factors that influence the production of crime rates.

Clearly, the statistics tell us more about agencies of social control, such as the police, than about criminals; but it is useful to understand these agencies. Eventually, we may be able to sort out the influences that come from the police, leading to better data on actual criminal behaviour. If we assume that the practices of the police remain constant in an area, then the changes in crime rates may, in fact, be due to changes in criminal behaviour. Thus, many Canadian criminologists would agree that homicide, and probably violent crime in general, increased moderately from the 1960s until the middle of the 1970s, but decreased in the 1990s.

In the next chapter we will look at the distribution of crime in Canada. and try to "correct" some of the data to see if they provide us with a better way of assessing crime in a particular city or province.

A STATISTICAL PICTURE OF CRIME IN CANADA

The less people know about how sausages and laws are made, the better they will sleep in their beds at night.

Otto von Bismarck

THE DISTRIBUTION OF CRIME ACROSS CANADA

Now that the reader has been warned about the problems with crime statistics, we can make some generalizations about the patterns of crime in Canada despite our many reservations.

The Distribution of Violence in Canada

Figure 7.1, showing homicides across Canada in 1991, could probably be used as an indicator of general violence across the country. The Northwest Territories and the Yukon are not included in most of these comparisons due to the large number of young, single males working in the North, which inevitably leads to higher rates of certain types of crime, particularly those related to violence. For convenience, we will focus on the ten provinces in our attempts to make comparisons. Generally, there has been an East-West differential in most crime rates. The Atlantic provinces tend to have lower crime rates, while the Prairie provinces and British Columbia tend to have higher crime rates.

For homicide, British Columbia often leads the nation, although recently Manitoba has contested that position. In 1990, the homicide rate for Canada was 2.4 per 100 000 inhabitants, which was the third-lowest rate since 1972. These data reinforce what seems to be a broad-based finding that homicide, and probably violent crime in general, peaked in the middle or late 1970s in North America. Whether this is simply because the baby boom of young males is getting older is still a subject of debate.

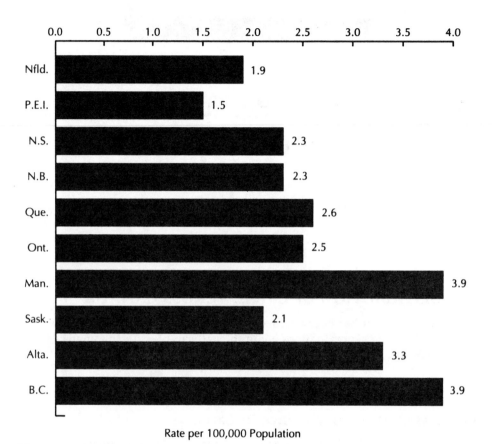

FIGURE 7.1 Rates for Homicide Offenses: Canada and the Provinces, 1991
Source: Wright, (1992), Figure 2.

There is some evidence that one type of crime is related to another. That is, we rarely find communities, or individuals, who are very criminal in one area while being very law-abiding in others. They exist, and are of interest to criminologists, but we are probably safe in saying that the higher homicide rate is probably a reasonable reflection of a higher-than-average assault rate and a higher rate of domestic violence. While most assaults do not end up as homicide, an important proportion of murders are the products of situations that began as assaults or some other type of violence.

Thus, we might argue that the East-West differential for homicide would also appear for other violent crimes, such as rape. The pattern also persists overtime. In 1977 British Columbia represented about 11% of the population, but contributeed about 18% of the rapes. The Prairie provinces also contributed more than their share. The Atlantic provinces contribute 10% of the population but only 5% of the rapes. We are assuming that the biases involved in reporting rape exist to an equal degree in different parts of Canada. Despite our cautions about most comparisons, the consistency of these East-to-West differences, using different types of data, leads us to conclude that there is more violence in the West, a pattern that has persisted for some time.

The United States shows a similar pattern. The West, as well as the South, consistently generates higher-than-average violent crime rates. New England tends to produce less violence. Some explanations of crime take these patterns into account, as we will see later in this book.

Although we tend to accept murder rates as valid, they are relatively small in number and become less useful for comparing smaller populations. If we expand our violent crime rate index to include more common offenses, such as assault, we increase the likelihood that local practices will influence these figures. Kim Don and I (1990) undertook a study to see if we could use the police response to minor violent crimes as a way of "adjusting" or "correcting" total violent crime rates.

"Correcting" Violent Crime Rates with a "Recording Index"

In Table 7.1, the total violent crime rates for five provinces are presented. Nova Scotia is fairly typical of the Atlantic provinces, and Alberta is somewhat representative of the prairies. In the first column, minor assault cases are the most numerous violent crime, and thus influence the total assault figure more than more serious offenses. They are also susceptible to discretionary screening by the police. Therefore, it is not advisable to make comparisons using the total violent crime rate.

Table 7.1 Violent Crime — 1985, Rates by Province (Per 100 000 Population)

			Robbery (Weapons)	
	Total	Homicide	Firearms	Other
Nova Scotia	591	3	6	9
Québec	514	3	68	36
Ontario	742	2	11	14
Alberta	882	3	11	18
B.C.	1136	4	22	29

Source: Statistics Canada, 1986. *Canadian Crime Statistics 1985*, Catalogue No. 85-205 Annual, Table 2

The second column utilizes homicide, but as we can see, the numbers are fairly small. While it might be reasonable to use homicide as a rate of comparison for Ontario and Québec, we would be hesitant to use them for the smaller provinces. Columns 3 and 4 show robbery rates where weapons are involved, which are probably recorded more accurately than minor assaults. Column 3 shows robbery with firearms, which might be viewed as a very serious violent crime. It is clear that Québec, with a rate of 68 robberies with firearms per 100 000 people, leads the country in this category. Montréal has been known as the bank robbery capital of North America for some time.

Screenable and Non-Screenable Crimes

The important question is what is the best measure of violence? Should we use *total* violent crimes, or focus on rarer but more serious offenses? Using one indicator, total violent crimes, Québec is one of the lowest provinces in the nation, but using robbery with firearms, it is the highest. One strategy is to create a *recording index* that measures the tendency of police to screen out less serious crimes. In Table 7.2, rates of assault and robbery are presented. Assaults include serious crimes, but the bulk of assaults are less serious and, to some extent, are "screenable" by the police at their discretion. Robbery, on the other hand, is comparatively "non-screenable." That is, we assume that police can use more discretion about recording minor assaults than they can about recording robberies. By dividing the assaults by the robberies, we create, in the last column, a *recording index*, a measure of the tendency of police to screen out potential offenses (Hackler and Don, 1990). The higher the index, the more minor assaults are recorded; i.e., the less they are screened, thus increasing the apparent crime rate.

Table 7.2 Assault and Robbery — 1985, Crime Rates by Province (Per 100 000 Population)

	Assault	Robbery	Assault/Robbery
			(Recording Index)
Nova Scotia	542	31	17.5
Québec	335	160	2.1
Ontario	666	58	11.5
Alberta	767	66	11.6
British Columbia	1003	109	9.2

Source: Statistics Canada, 1986. *Canadian Crime Statistics 1985*, Catalogue No. 85-205 Annual, Table 2

Once having worked out this *recording index* with 1985 data, we could apply it to 1986 data. In Table 7.3, we have taken the total violent crime rates for the same five provinces and "adjusted" them by dividing by the *recording index* obtained in the last column of Table 7.2 The new rate makes a dramatic difference in Québec, giving it a score of 262.7, almost twice the rate of British Columbia. With the exception of Québec, however, the traditional East-West differential persists for the other provinces.

Table 7.3 "Adjusted" Violent Crime Rates — 1986, (Using Assault/Robbery Recording Index 1985)

	1986	1986 Adjusted
Nova Scotia	621	35.5
Québec	549	262.7
Ontario	794	69.2
Alberta	908	78.1
British Columbia	1239	134.7

Source: Statistics Canada, Uniform Crime Reporting Statistics. Statistical Highlights 1986, pp. 21-32.

One should be cautious about using these "adjusted" rates. The assumptions may not be true, but it makes sense to see if we can separate out the characteristics of the social-control agencies from the behaviour of the potential criminals. If the recording index does reflect what the police do, and if we can adjust for that influence, the resulting measure of crime would be a better measure of what criminals do. If we are interested in crime in different parts of Canada, we need to somehow control for the responses of agencies in different parts of Canada.

We now face a dilemma of interpretation. Which province is the most violent in Canada? Using total violent-crime data, Québec appears low, but we suspect that this province also screens out more minor assaults. We also know that robbery rates are high in Québec. Is it likely that an area can be high on one violent crime but low on another? We cannot answer these questions at present, but it is probable that the level of violence in Québec is higher than suggested by the official statistics. Is it higher than B.C.? We simply do not know, but eventually, we may be able to apply "recording indices" or some other formula that will produce crime statistics that are more comparable.

The Distribution of Property Crime in Canada

Could we apply the same logic to property crimes? By arguing that theft offenses are " screenable" but break and entry cases are "non-screenable," we attempted to "correct" property crime statistics for 28 cities in Canada with populations over 1,000,000 (Hackler, Cossins, and Don, 1990). We ran into several problems. First, there is some indication that several police departments near Toronto (Peel, York, Halton, Waterloo, and Durham) had very low B&E rates, as did Toronto itself. It appears that B&Es can also be screened by certain reporting practices. This suspicion was supported by the fact that the Peel police had a clearance rate of 60% for B&E. Normally, the police do not know who commits burglaries. Without a suspect the chance of clearing them is low. Thus, a clearance rate or 10 of 15% is more reasonable. These data provide insights into police practices in the Toronto area, but they probably make it impossible to compare property crimes with other parts of Canada.

Using Victimization Rates to Create a Recording Index

So far we have been using data that indicates the activity of the police. However, victimization surveys measure crime as viewed by victims, and may be more useful for comparing parts of Canada. (Research and Statistics Group, 1986; Johnson and Sacco, 1990). Researchers with the Solicitor General of Canada surveyed victims in seven cities (Solicitor General of Canada, 1986). Usually, people underreport crime. Those interviewed only reported between 32 and 38% of the burglaries they experienced. There were no large regional differences.

Victimization data do not define all crime in precisely the same way as the official data, but break and enter (burglary) is defined similarly (O'Brien, 1985). Table 7.4 compares the official B&E rate with the rate reported by victims. The first column, official rates, shows Vancouver to be the highest of the four. Toronto has half the rate of Edmonton or Montréal and one third the rate of Vancouver. However, if we look at the victimization rate in Column 2, the picture changes. According to victimizations for burglary, Montréal shows the highest rate. It is reasonable to assume that the official rate is more likely to be influenced by police reporting practices, and therefore, the victimization report might be taken as the *best* estimate of actual burglary.

We can now estimate the degree to which the police recorded (or screened) the break and enters by dividing Column 1 by Column 2. This ratio appears in Column 3. In Vancouver it was .32, but in the two eastern cities of Toronto and Montréal, it appears that fewer burglaries were recorded (.15 and .19). In other words, the recording process used by the police in Toronto seems to screen out twice as many burglaries as in Vancouver. About 1 burglary in 6 is recorded in Toronto, while 1 in 3 is recorded in Vancouver. The *ratio* in the last column of Table 7.4 may provide a plausible measure of the level of screening.

We could go on and use this measure of screening to "adjust" other crime rates, but we will forego that exercise here. Suffice to say that the rates for B&E in Toronto and Montréal are probably reduced through police recording practices,

Table 7.4 Break and Enter Offenses Known and Break and Enter Victimizations (1986)

	Break and Enters Known to Police (Rate)	Break and Enter Victimization Rate	(Rate) Column 1/Column 2
Vancouver	3218	10 100	.32
Edmonton	2208	8600	.26
Toronto	1031	6900	.15
Montréal	2253	12 200	.19

Source: Solicitor General of Canada, 1986.

compared to Vancouver and Edmonton. At the present time I suspect that there is somewhat more crime in the West than in the East, but in addition, a higher rate of screening by the police in parts of Ontario and Québec exaggerates those differences.

We know that official statistics are influenced by recording strategies at the local level. In this exercise, we attempted to use some of the knowledge about these local systems, namely their tendency to screen certain types of cases, in order to produce a better estimate of crime rates that could be more useful. Whether or not this process actually is an improvement is not the point of this section. Rather, more sophisticated data-users in the future should be able to produce statistics that will allow us to compare regions, even though that is not possible at present for most offenses.

IS WESTERN CANADA MORE INCLINED TO USE AGENCIES OF CONTROL?

The bulk of discussion of crime statistics focuses on criminal behaviour. It is also important to use data to understand what criminal justice systems do. In fact, this is probably where crime data in their present form are most useful. Although criminal behaviour may vary across Canada, it probably doesn't vary as much as the behaviour of our criminal justice systems. From a policy standpoint, it makes sense to assess our agencies of social control and make deliberate decisions concerning their change. For example, are there any systematic patterns across Canada with regard to using the agencies of social control?

Western Canada appears more willing to record crime, use the courts, put people on probation, and use prisons. For example, in 1988 the percentage of young people appearing in Youth Court was highest in the four western provinces, with Alberta leading. Measures of incarceration, police reporting, and parole usually indicate higher rates for western provinces. Some might argue that these are more "punitive" responses, but that is less clear. Perhaps it would be wiser to simply say that some regions are more "reactive," the official system reacts more vigorously (Hackler and Paranjape, 1983; 1984).

Responses to Crime — The Use of Institutions Across Canada

Number of Inmates Detained in Custody

There are different ways of looking at prison population. Using the average number of prisoners in custody per 100 000 population does not tell you if you have 1) many people serving short sentences, or 2) fewer people serving longer sentences, but it is probably one of the easier measures to use for comparative purposes. In Figure 7.2 we see that the Prairie provinces rank high in terms of the number in custody per 100 000 population in 1990-91. Saskatchewan, with 184 per 100 000, has the highest ratio of offenders in custody, followed by Alberta and Manitoba with 130 and 123. Of those in custody in Saskatchewan, 68% were Natives, after remands were excluded. Manitoba follows with 49%, Alberta 36%, and British Columbia 18% (Canadian Centre for Justice Statistics, 1991). In Ontario, Natives make up 8% of the custodial population, while they comprise less than 5% of the custodial population in Québec and the Atlantic provinces.

The numbers *admitted to custody* (Figure 7.3) is different from the numbers in custody and can modify the pattern somewhat. Manitoba leads in terms of admissions, and this is influenced by the fact that 56% of their admissions are remands (held awaiting trial), compared with 41% in Saskatchewan (Canadian Centre for Justice Statistics, 1991). Thus, Saskatchewan has the highest percentage of people in custody, but Manitoba processes the most into prison. A similar difference exists between Québec and Ontario. In Québec 65% of the admissions are remands, but only 38% of admissions are remands in Ontario. Québec processes more but holds fewer.

Since the Yukon and NWT are somewhat unusual, we have eliminated them from most of these Figures, but a general pattern appears: the Prairie provinces hold more people in custody in provincial institutions. The data on P.E.I. should be interpreted with care. We are talking about a hundred or so inmates who are probably well known to staff. Custodial facilities may be a reasonable alternative in smaller communities to other shelters for people who are drunk, etc.. Thus, the custodial "rates" may provide meaningless comparisons for P.E.I.. The many very short sentences that are given in P.E.I. would be consistent with this argument. British Columbia has a custodial pattern more like the Atlantic provinces than the Prairies, and Québec and Nova Scotia seem to use prison less than the rest of Canada.

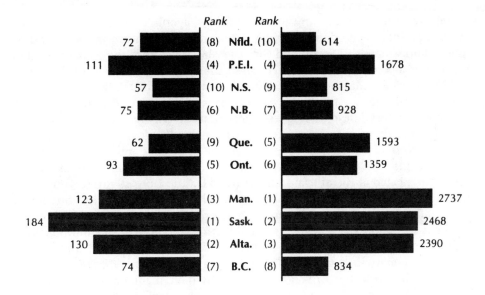

	Rank		Rank	
72	(8)	**Nfld.**	(10)	614
111	(4)	**P.E.I.**	(4)	1678
57	(10)	**N.S.**	(9)	815
75	(6)	**N.B.**	(7)	928
62	(9)	**Que.**	(5)	1593
93	(5)	**Ont.**	(6)	1359
123	(3)	**Man.**	(1)	2737
184	(1)	**Sask.**	(2)	2468
130	(2)	**Alta.**	(3)	2390
74	(7)	**B.C.**	(8)	834

FIGURE 7.2 Average Number of Offenders in Custody in Provincial Institutions per 100,000 Population (Includes Remands) 1990-91

FIGURE 7.3 Admissions to Custody in Provincial Institutions per 100,000 Population (Includes Remands) 1990-91

Source: Canadian Centre for Justice Statistics, 1991.

Interpreting Canadian Crime and Correctional Statistics

Speculation about the meaning of these data is very risky, but I will do it anyway. What explains the higher crime and incarceration rates in the Prairie provinces? Perhaps *official responses to crime are a measure of community willingness to reintegrate marginal people back into society.* Conceivably the Atlantic provinces and Québec are more willing to treat offenders as normal people who made a mistake. They may have done bad things, but they are still members of the community. We want them to be ashamed of what they have done, but then they should be reintegrated into the community. In the Maritimes, the police, as well as the courts, may share this thinking and thus may be hesitant to cast people out of society.

In the West, particularly on the Prairies, we may be more inclined to "cast the bastards out." Offenders are not just mistaken, they are bad. They are different from us. We do not wish them in our society. If the police and courts share this mentality and feel that one must use the formal agents of social control to cast out the deviants, then crime rates, conviction rates, and incarceration would be higher. Unfortunately, if Straus and Gelles (1986) are correct, these characteristics may be part of a *crime-producing society*. John Braithwaite (1989) would also argue that those societies that fail to reintegrate those who err create higher crime rates. In other words, has greater mobility and a lack of a sense of community in the West lead to a social order that is less tolerant, more willing to cast out offenders and stigmatize them, more eager to use prisons, and thus *create* more crime?

Let us continue this speculation with regard to Québec and British Columbia. We suspect that a large, heterogeneous city like Montréal actually has more crime than that reflected in the official statistics (Hackler and Don, 1990). However, the police appear to handle more minor cases in the community. This tendency to solve conflicts in the community may characterize Québec in general. Therefore, we might see fewer cases in the criminal justice system. British Columbia may not be as cohesive, may not emphasize the traditional family as much, and may reflect more mobility than Québec. The police may respond in a manner similar to the rest of the West, but British Columbia may have made conscious efforts to decrease the impact of the courts and correctional system. Thus, the high official crime rates in British Columbia, which we feel are somewhat exaggerated, may not translate into high custodial rates.

Statistics Canada warns us that comparing the cost of court services is very hazardous (Locke, 1993), but I shall continue with my reckless comparisons. By dividing court expenditures by population we learn that British Columbia spends $32.28 per capita on court costs and Alberta spends $29.25. Québec spends only $19.91. Such figures would support my thesis that the West resorts to the courts while Québec would be more likely to resolve things in the community. Unfortunately for my ideas, Nova Scotia spends $32.60 per capita on court costs, the highest in the nation. My above interpretation of Canadian data could be quite misleading, but persisting with such questions should eventually provide insights.

Another way of reading the above data is that the West simply has more Native people. It is possible that everywhere in Canada agencies of social control marginalize certain groups, Native people in the West and those from the Caribbean in the East. Thus, the Prairie provinces treat Natives the same as underdogs are treated everywhere; it simply has more of them. In other words, if the Prairies arrests, charges, convicts, and incarcerates more Native people, and has more of them, it is understandable that crime rates, court appearance rates, and custodial rates would be higher in these Western provinces.

At this point, we cannot make convincing arguments about the meaning of crime rates across Canada. The West appears to have higher crime rates, but there is the distinct possibility that the West uses its agencies of social control more than the rest of Canada. Or, stated differently, it has more marginal peoples; i.e., Natives, who are more likely to come to the attention of social control agencies.

SCIENTIFIC THEORY MAY HELP US

Data on crime do not explain themselves. They are products of dynamic systems and should not be treated as superior to other information. But they are relevant, even though difficult to interpret. Official statistics and other measures of crime are potentially useful for testing hypotheses and creating theories. If we use the scientific model discussed earlier, each of these measures is a potential operational definition for a concept. If there are too many factors influencing that operational definition, it may not be a good measure of a particular concept. For example, if we are interested in criminal behaviour, petty-theft rates are questionable, murder rates are better. On the other hand, if we are interested in societal response, theft rates might be very appropriate.

This process of matching concepts with measuring devices has many pitfalls, but it is still worthwhile. Some criminologists choose to not use these tools, but it is unwise to deny their utility. On the other hand, we should guard against the careless use of statistics that are influenced by many factors that are not well understood.

CONCLUSION

Despite the cautious approach taken in this book to crime statistics, a few generalizations are appropriate. Violent crime in North America appeared to be somewhat constant from World War II until the 1960s. Then there was a gradual increase, reaching a peak in the middle 1970s, followed by a gradual decrease for 15 years. The mass media and politicians exaggerated the increases and ignored the decreases. Compared to the East, Western Canada probably has more violent crime and responds more vigorously to crime, although Québec may not fit that general pattern. In the future, however, I predict an increase in violent crime in the U.S., and also in Canada. The gap between rich and poor has widened, social programmes have been eroded, and for over a decade government strategies favoured the production of material goods and creating wealth for those already well off. Official practices in the 1980s neglected the quality of life among marginal groups. The resulting damaged families are just now producing children who will soon enter the crime producing ages. But these arguments will be presented later.

PART II

EXPLANATIONS OF CRIME

These chapters follow a predictable sequence. The section moves through psychological (8), social psychological (9 and 10), and social structural discussions (11 and 12) of why individuals commit crimes. Chapter 13 deals with the ecology of crimes, spatial relations, and integrating theories. The policy recommendations arising out of many different criminological theories are often quite compatible even though there can be heated debates on the importance of various casual factors.

These discussions also reflect a historical sequence in that the themes about individual behaviour addressed in chapter 8 were more prominent in the early stages of criminology than the themes raised by the conflict theorists in chapter 12. The earlier arguments could be seen as more "conservative" and the later presentations as more "radical." The reader will also detect a bias with regard to the sort of social intervention which would be most appropriate for a Canada: structural changes would yield better returns at the present time than efforts to intervene at the individual level. The reasons for these recommendations will be clearer in Sections III and IV.

TRADITIONAL AND BIOLOGICAL EXPLANATIONS OF CRIME

Man is the only animal that blushes. Or needs to.

Mark Twain

THE CLASSICAL SCHOOL AND FREE WILL

Traditional explanations of crime focus on the question, "Why do they do it?" Less thought was given to the possibility that society itself could be a factor. The problem was to understand why some individuals did not conform to the rules of society. To many people that is still the issue, but today criminologists must also ask questions about the dynamics of different social settings and the nature of the larger society. For now, such questions will be laid aside, as we review these traditional arguments.

Cesare Beccaria and the Assumption of Rationality

Cesare Beccaria wrote an influential treatise in Italy in 1764, which was published in England with the title, *On Crimes and Punishment* (Beccaria, 1963). He placed great stress on man's rational faculties and ability to make reasonable choices. His thinking was in keeping with the growing concern over individual rights and prerogatives. There was an assumption that society evolved with contractual beginnings; that is, individuals surrendered a degree of sovereignty over their lives in exchange for protection from the hazards of total freedom. This social contract between individuals and the state required that laws be developed to make society viable. The resulting legislation was guided by the principle of creating the greatest happiness for the greatest number of people (Maestro, 1973).

Punishment should fit the crime. Prior to this period, punishments in many countries were capricious. Beccaria's logic assumed that people acted on the basis of free will. People have a choice between doing right and doing wrong. When they do wrong it is a deliberate choice. Since Beccaria argued that it was better to prevent crime than punish criminals, fear of the appropriate punishment would deter crime. The laws should be clearly written and not subject to the whims of judges. The roles of legislators and judges were to be distinct. Judges would be bound by the law, while legislators created it. While rigid, the laws should be impartial and apply to all, regardless of social status. His argument for the impartiality of the laws may be Beccaria's greatest contribution. Writing at the time when North America was just being Europeanized, these ideas were central to the thinking in these evolving societies. Impartiality has still not been successfully implemented in most societies, but the ideal is widely shared.

Jeremy Bentham: A Penal Pharmacy and the Hedonistic Calculus

Like Becarria, Bentham disliked the arbitrary, inconsistent, and cruel administration of justice in England during his lifetime (1748-1832). Similarly, he believed that punishment should prevent crime rather than be guided by retribution. He favoured *utilitarianism* or the "greatest-happiness principle." Human beings were assumed to be *hedonistic.* They chose those actions that would give the maximum pleasure and avoided those that would bring pain. There should be a proper quantum of punishment for each quantum of crime. In his *Introduction to the Principles of Morals and Legislation*, published in 1825, Bentham proposed a "penal pharmacy" prescribing certain punishments for specific crimes. Only enough punishment should be used to achieve the necessary deterrence for potential wrongdoers who use the *hedonistic calculus.* Thus, the potential rapist would calculate the pleasure gained from raping a woman, assess the pain that would be inflicted if he were convicted, and then make a rational decision. This logic assumed that people acted on the basis of free will. By manipulating the pain of punishment, the pleasure gained from the criminal behaviour would be outweighed.

Bentham concentrated on the laws and neglected human behaviour. He failed to consider criminals as complicated human beings with variegated personalities (Geis, 1972:53). Consequently, his arguments were based on overly simplistic assumptions about human nature.

The *positive school*, (sometimes "positivistic" is used) eclipsed the classical school about a century later, and made assumptions more compatible with the developing thinking in the social sciences.

THE POSITIVE SCHOOL, DETERMINISM, AND THE REJECTION OF FREE WILL

Cesare Lombroso and the Atavistic Criminal Type

The thinking of people like Lombroso paralleled that of Charles Darwin. While Darwin was to put together many different facts and observations about the natural world, to develop his theory of evolution in *On the Origin of Species* in 1859, Lombroso also concentrated on measurable facts, assuming this would lead to natural explanations. This approach is somewhat different from scientific theory as described in Chapter 4. Facts do not speak for themselves. Lombroso was part of a growing school of scientists who assumed that the amassing of data in and of itself would lead to explanations. In contrast, a preferable strategy is to spell out hypotheses, preferably linked together systematically, leading to a *selective* choice of empirical data that would confirm or reject the stated ideas. One needs to be selective in a world that is awash in empirical data.

However, when Lombroso was publishing his major ideas between 1864 and 1878 (1911), the straightforward accumulation of evidence made sense. One cannot propose hypotheses without this background work, but the danger of letting the data dictate explanations is similar to *ex post facto* reasoning. And that is what Lombroso did. His ideas were formulated after looking at the data, but that is typical of most scholarly work.

Lombroso concluded that criminals were different from law-abiding people. As a physician attached to the Italian army, he examined the physical attributes of many soldiers. These anatomical characteristics were examined in an intellectual atmosphere where scientists were finding it acceptable to view human beings as another animal, without the divine characteristics that had been imputed in the past. Since the breeding of animals to produce various characteristics was a familiar practice, it was reasonable to assume that genetics would influence human behaviour as well. Just as other species are "programmed" from birth to act in certain ways, why not humans? In other words, it made sense to ask if criminals were heavily influenced, if not actually determined, by biological antecedents which they could not control. Criminals were not rational beings with a free will, they were simply "born that way." Just as Beccaria and Bentham were products of their intellectual world, Lombroso was a product of this new intellectual stream a century later.

Enrico Ferri and Continuance of Positivism

Enrico Ferri (1856-1928) continued the positivist thinking of Lombroso. Although trained as a lawyer, he was particularly critical of classicism. For example, he argued that no one could develop a clear standard that would enable us to say a particular punishment would be equitable for a particular crime (Ferri, 1901; Brown, *et al.*, 1991:235). Ferri was also scathing in his attacks on the concept of free will, arguing that "every act of a human being is the result of an interaction between the personality and the environment of man" (1901: 54). Individuals live in different personal, physical, and moral conditions, which lead to a chain of cause and effect that disposes them towards crime. Ferri broadened the range of variables to be considered beyond those considered by Lombroso. He also noted that factors *interacted*, rather than causing behaviour directly. In many ways his thinking was very modern, but his primary argument was that crime was *determined*, not chosen.

Assessing the Early Positivists

Scholars differ on the contribution of the early positivists. A major contribution was to shift the focus of attention from the law and philosophy to the first-hand study of criminals. Empirical evidence began to play an important role. In this respect, they clearly broadened the discussion of crime causation. Marvin Wolfgang argues that Lombroso laid the foundations of modern criminology, by his emphasis on studying the differences among different groups and by his emphasis on the deterministic, or positivistic, approach to explaining behaviour, in contrast to the free-will perspective (1972).

Since born criminals couldn't help themselves, a policy for restraining criminals could not rely on a hedonistic calculus. Only through severe social intervention could these atavistic human beings be reformed. Like other animals, they had to be punished until they learned. This was not a matter of justice but "social defence." Society had to be protected. Raffaele Garafolo, a contemporary of Ferri's, argued that it was necessary to eliminate criminal offenders by death, imprisonment, or transportation. Following the thinking of Darwin on natural selection, he recommended that society eliminate those individuals who are too disruptive to social life (Brown, *et al.*, 1991). Since the problem was largely one of genetics, such individuals would then no longer produce problem offspring to plague the society in the future.

Both Garafalo and Ferri had considerable faith in science as a guide to social policy. They were less critical of the moral values held by scientists, politicians, and those in positions of power. The Italian Fascist party under Mussolini argued for measures that sacrificed individuals for the benefit of the larger society, and Garofalo, like Ferri, finished his life as a Fascist activist (Brown, *et al.* 1991:236). Adolf Hitler was also able to utilize the thinking of such scholars. Obviously, scholars do not necessarily clarify moral issues nor provide ideas for intelligent social policy.

Charles Thomas and John Hepburn are more critical of Lombroso and his followers, arguing that "the rise of the positive school, which quite probably marks the most significant event in criminological history, had the effect of blocking our progress for more than a quarter of a century" (1983:146). They acknowledge Lombroso's willingness to consider other variables influencing crime as his work progressed, such as climate, race, education, sex, population density, education, and economic factors; however, such factors were secondary to the notion of atavism and to the belief that criminals were inherently inferior. Poverty, for example, was seen as the fault of the individual rather than as a consequence of extreme inequality in the distribution of wealth and legitimate opportunities. "If thieves are generally penniless, it is because of their extreme idleness and astonishing extravagance, which makes them run through huge sums with the greatest ease, not because poverty has driven them to theft" (Lombroso, 1872; cited in Thomas and Hepburn, 1983:152).

In a book on *The Female Offender* Lombroso also reflected views that were acceptable at the time. Females are more primitive than males — naturally vengeful, jealous, insensitive to pain, and lacking any sense of morality. They have lower rates of crime than men because their natural deficiencies are neutralized by piety, maternity, a lack of passion, sexual coldness, weakness, and undeveloped intelligence. Indeed, women are so monotonous and uniform, when compared to men, that they not only fail to become artists, scientists, and political leaders, they also lack the zip to become criminal.

CONTRASTING CLASSICISM AND POSITIVISM

The classical school focused on legal terms. Crime was a legal entity. The positivists rejected this; they viewed crime as a psychological entity, that is, one tried to explain the individual and how he differed from others. The classical school assumed everyone responded in the same way. The classical school emphasized free will; the positivists focused on determinism. The classicists concentrated on the deterrent effect of punishment, while the positivists emphasized the treatment of criminals so as to protect society.

Both themes are still very much alive today. Our criminal justice system is largely a product of classical thinking. Punishments are supposed to be the same, regardless of the individual. However, judges are also influenced by the perceived impact of punishment on future behaviour; that is, they think in terms of the "social defence" logic offered by the positivists. Thus, the respectable person who has done wrong has already suffered by going through the criminal justice system, and only a modest penalty is required to bring about reform. Thomas and Hepburn would probably argue that this "social defence" logic favours the powerful and results in stiffer punishment for the lower classes. The application of classical thinking might justify harsher punishment for the powerful, since they had little excuse.

Neither of these schools serve us well in terms of reducing crime, but for now let us turn to some of the work that emphasized the biological determinism pioneered by Lombroso.

BIOLOGICAL DETERMINISM

In a 1950s genetics class, the professor displayed a chart showing the Adams family and their accomplishments throughout U.S. history. This family produced presidents, diplomats, and many distinguished individuals, providing evidence of the power of genetics. Others might argue that Bill Bennett became premier of British Columbia, that Preston Manning has achieved some renown, and that Stephen Lewis has had a successful political career at least partially because their fathers were important political figures. Some geneticists might claim that the success of these people was simply superior biology coming to the fore. Sociologists would argue that the offspring of Henry Ford had a distinct edge on other talented individuals, when it came to attaining the presidency of the Ford Motor Company. When my genetics professor turned his chart over, the Juke family was displayed. The catalogue of criminals and social degenerates went down through the generations. The original Juke possessed such a miraculous energy in his vicious genes that he transmitted degeneracy for five generations. Let us look at the research that produced this chart.

Richard Dugdale and the Creation of the Juke Myth

The Jukes: A Study in Crime, Pauperism, Disease, and Insanity, by Richard Dugdale, was seen as an authoritative book towards the end of the nineteenth century. A well known publisher, Putnam's, brought out three large editions, which were accepted as sociological gospel. Samuel Hopkins Adams (1955) reviewed his research and pointed out some flaws. Dugdale's qualifications are peculiar. After three years of schooling in New York, he left to become an assistant to a sculptor. He attended evening classes and won something of a reputation as a debater on social topics. The family then moved to the Middle-West to try farming, but failed. The Dugdales returned to New York and Richard turned to manufacturing. The business failed. Richard Dugdale was twenty-three and had a nervous breakdown. He writes that he could neither earn nor learn. So he became a criminologist.

In 1873, Dugdale was in police court where a youth was on trial. Five relatives were present as witnesses, but the family had a poor reputation. Dugdale invented the name "Juke" for the clan. The fact that the young man was acquitted did not discourage Dugdale. He found that the other relatives had done nasty things, although proof was often lacking. Two girls were listed as harlots. "Under the heading of harlots are included all women who have made lapses, however seldom."

Adams (1955) goes on to describe how Dugdale continued his precise definition of criminals and degenerates. "With comparatively little inquiry, it was found that of twenty-nine male adults, the immediate blood relations of the six, seventeen were criminals and fifteen others convicted of some degree of offense." Notice the impressive arithmetic. He got thirty-two out of a possible twenty-nine!

As Dugdale went sleuthing back through the generations, he discovered Old Max, an old Dutch reprobate who ran a hostelry in the middle of the eighteenth century. He had a reputation for drinking, gambling, and wenching. He gets the credit for starting the Jukes on their way to ill fame. Nothing criminal appears in his record, however. His two legitimate sons (presumably there were many illegitimate ones), married into six sisters. "One, if not all, of them were illegitimate." Delia is recorded as a "harlot before marriage," and Bell as a "harlot after marriage." Clara was reputed chaste, but she married a man who shot a neighbour. Notice that Old Max's genetic material seemed to leap over marriages and into his daughters-in-law and even on to their husbands.

One sister, Ada, *circa* 1760, gets credit for the distinctly criminal line of the family. Dugdale changes her name to "Margaret, Mother of Criminals," which does have a better ring to it. But she hardly lives up to her name. A daughter was a harlot, one son was a labourer, "somewhat industrious" and another was a farmer who had been "indolent" and "licentious in youth." Clearly, some eminent people have had similar backgrounds.

Dugdale developed his "facts" through the generations with a similar attention to accuracy. He created illegitimacy, negative characteristics, and crime when evidence was lacking. He fattened the record with entries like: petty thief, though never convicted; guilty of murder, but escapes punishment; supposed to have attempted rape; cruelty to animals; habitual criminal; impossible to get any reliable information, but it is evident that he was a leader in crime. There was also a "contriver of crime," and a hardened character who, in addition to frequenting a saloon, was accused of breaking a deaf man's ear trumpet. Like the Juke who started it all, he was acquitted.

By now the reader can appreciate that Dugdale's work was trash. However, it was not until after Dugdale's death that prison reformer Thomas Mott Osborne studied the work more carefully and noted that the data Dugdale used were practically non-existent. Tracing legitimate family lines is difficult; illegitimate ones were impossible beyond a generation or two. To put together so much detailed factual information over five generations in one year obviously required the use of "conjectural statistics." It takes a pretty skilled, or imaginative, investigator to learn that, in one branch of the Jukes, forty harlots contaminated 440 men.

Dugdale's nonsense, however, was viewed as appropriate sociology, and was still contaminating charts of genetics in college classrooms in the 1950s. The major lesson we might learn is to beware of fads in the intellectual community. One hopes that the intellectual debate that takes place in more mature scholarly circles would avoid the acceptance of such shoddy work.

THE CRITIQUE OF AND DEBATES OVER BIOLOGICAL DETERMINISM

Charles Goring has been given credit for refuting the atavism theme put forward by Lombroso. A psychiatrist, philosopher, and also a medical officer in various English prisons, Goring studied 3000 convicts, identifying some 96 traits (1913). These were compared with 1000 Oxford and Cambridge University students, hospital patients, and soldiers. The results refuted Lombroso's work. It is important to note that some of the traits identified by Lombroso characterized Sicilians. At the time, Sicilians were more likely to be in conflict with the rest of Italian society, and were perceived by other Italians to be more criminal. This is the type of error, a spurious correlation, that can lead reasonably careful research astray.

Another illustration of this type of error is the pencil-tapping test used in a study of English delinquents (West, 1969). When asked to tap as rapidly as they could, delinquents were much slower than non-delinquents. Was this evidence of motor coordination and other biological differences? Donald West and his colleague David Farrington were alert to the influence of the social setting. When well-mannered, non-delinquent boys were asked to tap pencils, they performed with enthusiasm. Delinquent boys responded skeptically. "Do *what?* What a stupid thing to do. OK, if you want, I'll tap. How's this?" And with sneers on their faces they leisurely tapped away for this weird interviewer who made strange requests.

Clearly, careful researchers can be misled as they lay out testable propositions that can be refuted in the future. Other work, such as that by Dugdale, has no merit to begin with. The work on biological determinism is mixed in terms of academic merit. One should not assume that research at universities automatically guarantees superior reasoning. For example, Earnest Hooton, a Harvard anthropologist, claimed in *Crime and the Man* (1939) that criminals were physically inferior. His massive work contained many errors (Martin, *et al.* 1990:128). Murderers should look different from rapists, and robbers from thieves. Murderers are tall, while burglars tend to be short, squatty men who are also associated with assault, rape, and other sexual crimes. The elimination of crime, then, required the elimination of these physically, mentally, and morally unfit individuals, or alternately, complete segregation from the rest of society. Interestingly, Hooton found that one of the characteristics was tattooing. Since one is not born with tattoos, it is difficult to see this as a genetic trait. Perhaps there is a biological tendency for getting tattoos. For such a book to be published in 1939 by a professor at a prestigious university is noteworthy; but it was also ominous that, in one of the most scientifically advanced countries, Hitler had already eliminated 50 000 non-Jewish mentally deficient Germans. The strategy spread to Jews, Eastern Europeans, and others considered to be subhuman (Hagan, 1986:409).

William Sheldon was influenced by Hooton. He developed the theory of three body types: ectomorph, endomorph, and mesomorph (1940). Stated more simply: skinny, fat, and athletic. The athletic types were more delinquent. One could argue that Sheldon had tunnel vision. While he measured biological characteristics with great precision, he pointedly ignored the other criminological thinking that was emerging around him (Martin, *et al.* 1990.) One might view Sheldon as an excellent illustration of the scholar who looks carefully, but has a limited range of vision.

Sheldon Glueck was a professor of law at Harvard, and his wife Eleanor was a professor of social work. They also found that mesomorphs were more likely to be delinquent (1950). Many faults have been found with the work done by the Gluecks, in addition to their arguments regarding the link between crime and body types. For example, studies comparing army recruits, bus drivers and truckers showed that they were more mesomorphic than delinquents (Kamin, 1986). Since the Gluecks were prolific writers, and their books were widely used in schools of social work, one might ask if these biologically deterministic ideas have been leading social workers astray for several decades. In a book focused directly on the many errors in delinquency research, Travis Hirschi and Hanan Selvin found that the work of the Gluecks alone provided them with more than half of their examples (1967).

I have deliberately chosen negative illustrations from scholars at Harvard to reinforce another theme in this book. We should be *more* suspicious of ideas that come from people who are more insulated from criticism, such as high-status scholars. What is fashionable in criminology is influenced by those who are custodians of intellectual activity. The authors of criminological theories, until the last few decades, have tended to be white, upper-class males. (Whether they were also more endomorphic and ectomorphic than mesomorphic I do not know.) It is not surprising that non-criminals were more inclined to resemble the authors, while criminals were somehow different.

RECENT WORK ON BIOLOGY AND CRIME

It is fashionable and "politically correct" to ridicule biological models of crime. In doing so, do I risk making errors similar to those described above? As a sociologically trained criminologist, I openly acknowledge my bias against genetic explanations; but there are arguments *for* some biological studies.

In the 1940s and '50s, social scientists began to appreciate that genes played a role in determining if an animal became a turtle or a human being, but once a human was produced, some sociologists began to ignore genetic differences. True, the quality of the work by people like Dugdale deserved ridicule, as did some of the theories of genetic superiority that argued that immigrants, blacks, and others were inherently inferior. But have we developed biases that blind us to considering the role of genetic factors? Some family studies (Robins, 1966) have long shown that one of the best predictors of antisocial behaviour was the father's criminality. There has always been a problem, however, in disentangling hereditary and environmental influences. Karl Christiansen and Sarnoff Mednick have attempted to separate these factors.

Karl Christiansen, Sarnoff Mednick, and the Studies of Twins

Karl O. Christiansen made use of data from the Danish national register of criminal behaviour to trace the fate of over 7000 twins born in Denmark. After his death, Sarnoff Mednick and other colleagues have continued this work (Mednick and Christiansen, 1977; Mednick and Volavaka, 1980). They attempt to separate the influence of environmental and genetic factors by comparing twins derived from one egg (identical twins) with those who come from two separate eggs (fraternal twins). If criminal traits are inherited, identical twins, whose genetic makeup is the same, would be more likely to have similar behavioural characteristics than fraternal twins, who have many genetic differences. Christiansen found that 35% of the identical twins were similar in terms of criminal activity, compared to 13% of the fraternal twins. Mednick notes that these findings point out the importance of *both* the environment and genes in the development of criminality (1985). The fact that 65% of the identical twins did not have similar records of criminality suggests that the environment is very important. However, identical twins were much more likely than the fraternal twins to be alike in criminal and non-criminal behaviour, suggesting that genetic similarity influences the likelihood of becoming criminal.

J. P. Rushton and His Theory of Racial Hierarchy[1]

J.P. Rushton (1988), a professor of psychology at the University of Western Ontario, argues that there are three fundamentally different races of humans (1988). This is in contrast to the more widely accepted view that human characteristics exist on a continuum, with some parts of the world giving rise to groups we crudely categorize as Blacks, Whites, and Orientals. Rushton claims that these racial groups evolved at different times: the African Blacks first, then the white Europeans, and finally the Orientals (Rushton, 1988). Those who evolved recently were more advanced. Life was easy in Africa with lots of fruit to be plucked from trees, thus allowing the Africans to be lazy. They didn't have to evolve to survive, but those who moved north into a cold Europe got a little smarter and showed greater sexual restraint. Things were even tougher for the Orientals as they evolved, and

---

[1]I would like to thank Doug Wahlsten for assistance with this section. For an extended discussion of genetic and environmental factors see (Wahlsten, 1990).

they developed still bigger brains and smaller genitals. The result, according to Rushton, is a clear hierarchy of the races with the Orientals on top, being more intelligent and less sexually active, and the Blacks on the bottom (Rushton and Bogaert, 1987). Thus, the superior Orientals committed fewer crimes, while the less evolved Blacks committed more.

Epling and Cameron (1991), in an article appropriately titled "Beyond Reason and Dignity," provide an humorous summary of Rushton's ideas. Biologically speaking, organisms differ in the way they take care of their offspring. Oysters, for example, produce many offspring but are negligent parents. Humans have few babies, and generally, do better at child care. Rushton argues that Blacks are more oyster-like than Orientals, who because of their smaller sex organs (and thus lesser sex-drive) produce fewer children but nurture them more effectively to become law-abiding adults. It is difficult to take Rushton seriously. He used sources carelessly (Wahlsten, 1992; Zuckerman and Brody, 1988; Weizmann, *et al.*, 1990). A detailed critique of Rushton's work is not needed here, but it is healthy to be reminded again that having a PhD, or teaching at a university provides no guarantee of clear thinking. For example, in Canada, our Aboriginal population is clearly of oriental origin, but they also are in trouble with the criminal justice system more often than white Canadians. This is inconsistent with Rushton's argument. Most criminologists would argue that those groups, racial or ethnic, that are towards the bottom of the social hierarchy tend to be viewed as the most criminal.

Genetic Influences Rather Than Determinants

Doug Wahlsten (1992) makes an argument that is compatible with the reasoning of Sarnoff Mednick (1985). Genes work at the level of molecules. They cannot move up the level of complexity to directly influence something like intelligence, much less a social variable such as crime. However, genes might have an influence on other factors that could eventually be related to anti-social behaviour. For example, people with certain genes have livers that cannot metabolize one amino acid, and this leads to a harmful buildup of the chemical in the blood. The high levels of this amino acid can retard brain development, which will influence intelligence. This, in turn, could influence success in school and a series of events leading to crime. The point to be emphasized, however, is that *there is no gene that codes directly for social behaviour, such as crime.*

Wilson and Herrnstein: A More Polished Version of Biological Determinism?

One of the most influential books of the 1980s has been *Crime and Human Nature* by James Q. Wilson and Richard J. Herrnstein (1986). They argue that to understand predatory street crime, we must move away from excessive attention to social and economic factors and look more closely at differences among individual people. They acknowledge the importance of interaction between family upbringing and genetic differences, and point out that bad families produce bad children. However, they discount societal characteristics, emphasizing instead the kinds of people and their individual personalities. These views are not new, as the sample of arguments presented in this chapter suggests, but during the 1980s they were endorsed by social critics of a somewhat conservative bent, such as Ronald Reagan.

The book was noted in popular newsmagazines and the press. While it was acclaimed by many, particularly conservative officials, it received very critical reviews by some noted scholars (Kamin, 1986). But why did this book receive so much praise from public officials? Some of the arguments use logic similar to Rushton's. One reason for the different reception may lie in the prestige of the authors. Wilson is a professor of government at Harvard and Herrnstein is a professor of psychology. They claim that their book is interdisciplinary and scientific, citing over 1000 research reports. Were these authors also shielded from criticism by their academic status?

Let us focus on some of their arguments. Delinquents are less willing to delay gratification. Unlike non-delinquents, who save money from their paper routes for future goals, delinquents snatch purses and spend their ill-gotten gains in wild abandon. One explanation is that during the 1960s more low-birth-weight babies survived, due to better medical care. The babies were smaller and sicker because of the smoking and drinking of their pregnant mothers. The resulting mental defects made them unable to defer gratification. No one questions the harmful effects of smoking and drinking during pregnancy, but the evidence that sickly children are less able to defer gratification, and hence are more criminal, is less clear. Wilson and Herrnstein discount the *social* conditions surrounding such families that might predict the same results.

Elsewhere in the book, Wilson and Herrnstein suggest that delinquents lie more than others. However, they neglect the studies that show that students studying for law and medicine tend to cheat more than other students. Since there is a tendency for sons of lawyers and doctors to follow their fathers' profession, we could use the biological theories suggested by the authors and conclude that the criminal tendencies of the fathers who became lawyers and doctors have been passed on to their offspring. This explains why prelaw and premedical students cheat more than others. Not surprisingly, my students do not take this proposition seriously.

Wilson and Herrnstein use evidence selectively to support their ideas. Kamin (1986) points to their explanation of the low crime rates in Japan. They say that cultural differences may grow out of biological differences. Personality has a biological basis, and the Japanese personality is less criminogenic. In one questionnaire study, the Japanese were classified as introverts. Since introversion tends to be related to lower crime rates, this explained the low Japanese crime rates. Americans tend to be extroverts, and thus more criminal. However, citizens of Uganda are even more introverted than the Japanese, but the authors ignore the high rates of violent crime in that country.

The authors conveniently ignore another aspect of this same study, which measured another criminological trait, psychoticism, which is associated with brutality and insensitivity to others. Which country was the most psychotic? Japan. Which countries were the least psychotic? Canada, the United Kingdom, and the U.S. Thus, these personality tests show the Japanese have low scores on one trait associated with criminality, introversion, but stunningly high scores on another criminal personality trait, psychoticism. However, the authors give us only part of the evidence.

In an earlier article Herrnstein wrote, "as technology advances, the tendency to be unemployed may run in the genes of a family as certainly as bad teeth do now (Kamin, 1986)." Unemployment, of course is a social phenomenon, however, like crime. Explaining it as "running in the genes" illustrates the confusion between correlation and causality. These comments also sound somewhat like Lombroso's comments regarding the poor, cited earlier in this chapter. Obviously skin colour is strongly influenced by genetics, but must we conclude that unemployment, doing poorly in school, and crime is *explained* by black skin? Is it not possible that a history of slavery, racial prejudice, and blocked employment has contributed to that correlation?

This book by Wilson and Herrnstein was, unfortunately, one of the most influential of its decade, but was its success related to the political thinking that was popular two years after Ronald Reagan was re-elected? The presentation is more polished than that of J. P. Rushton, but some of the flaws in thinking are similar.

Deborah Denno and Sex Differences in Crime

Deborah Denno (1984, 1985) is one of many who notes systematic differences between males and females. She also tries to control for the influence of other biological and environmental variables, such as social and economic factors. As a less well established scholar, perhaps she had to display logic superior to that of Wilson and Herrnstein in order to get her work published.

The Vulnerability of Males

Denno asks if males are more vulnerable to environmental damage and developmental problems. They are more likely to experience prenatal and infant mortality, childhood diseases, learning disorders, and retardation. These disorders are most common among the deprived and, to some extent, among criminals. Denno followed youths from birth to age seven, and then looked at school and arrest records from age 10 to 17. Not surprisingly, she found it difficult to distinguish biological and environmental factors. For example, intellect has a biological base, which can be socially altered. Thus, the greater incidence of delinquency in males may be attributed in part to Central Nervous System injuries, as well as to cultural pressures to be aggressive. Lorne Yeudall, in his research at the Alberta Hospital, argues that fathers play with their male children in a rougher manner than they do with the girls, and may inadvertently cause minor brain damage. In other words, brain damage can be linked to criminality, and boys may be more vulnerable than girls (Yeudall, 1987).

Denno (1984) noted faster physical maturation of black females, a disparity that is greater than among white samples, and suggested that this could influence the development of the brain. Thus, the earlier brain development of females may make them less vulnerable than males to environmental factors. In general, however, she found socioeconomic factors to be more crucial than biological variables. This study is significant in that *different variables influence males and females in different ways.* For example, school achievement was linked to delinquency for males but not females. Again, we have a problem of interpretation. Do males who fail in school turn to crime because social pressures are greater than those on females? Is this a biological or social variable?

In another study, which again utilized both biological and sociological variables, Denno (1985) worked with 800 black children in Philadelphia. After controlling for biological variables, economic and social stability of families predicted delinquency for males but not for females. Again, males seem to be more vulnerable, but the social factors still offer a better explanation than the biological ones. In addition, this study did *not* confirm earlier findings of direct relationships between delinquency and intelligence, retardation, left-handedness, or early central nervous system dysfunction. However, the incidence of some of these variables was low. Denno points to the possibility that past findings of biological links to variables such as intelligence or crime may be artifacts of environmental effects, such as socioeconomic factors. While this work does not lead to clear conclusions, it points to the possibility that boys and girls grow up differently, even though it is difficult to separate the causal factors.

CONCLUSION AND POLICY IMPLICATIONS

The better quality genetic studies being done today do not suggest a direct link between genes and crime: they point instead to the possibility of biological characteristics, such as biochemical abnormalities or neuropsychological defects, which lead to behavioural problems — impulsiveness, aggressiveness, and poor school performance. Children with such characteristics are disadvantaged and, if they fail in the traditional routes towards success, are more likely to engage in criminal activity.

Many criminologists share the view of Charles Thomas and John Hepburn. "We doubt that there is anything to be found inside the genetic, biological, or personality structure of the individual actor which will permit us to account for more than a very modest portion of ... antisocial behaviour. This notion will not please those of you who are wedded to the notion that the world can be divided into nice people like us and nasty people who come before our criminal courts. ... Criminal conduct ... is an entirely normal product of the manner in which our society is structured and the processes of social interaction that brings us into contact with one another"(1983: 158).

I also lean towards social variables, and am suspicious of the consequences of labelling potentially troublesome youngsters or adults. However, some supporters of genetic arguments advocate a range of volunteer, supportive programmes for a wide range of disadvantaged youngsters (Mednick, 1985). These could be something like the Head Start programmes, which seemed to help preschool children do better in school. Instead of guiding high-risk children into boring, repetitive, low-status positions, could they be directed towards challenging, varied, and demanding jobs that include some of the excitement that these individuals crave? If society were to devote considerable resources to creating a meaningful educational system, leading to meaningful work and a stake in society, then identifying children who are at risk might be seen as benevolent. On the other hand, there is little evidence that our governments are inclined to provide superior services to those faced with afflictions, genetic or social.

When those in the political arena are influenced by the biological explanations, they are less inclined to take the advice offered above by Sarnoff Mednick. Instead there tend to be predictable consequences:

1. Lower-status citizens are punished more;
2. There is a tendency to ignore the basic flaws in the structure of society;
3. There is less concern for social programmes that would help vulnerable portions of the population, which in the long run would reduce crime;
4. There will be more jobs for lawyers and prison guards in our booming, but inefficient, criminal justice system;
5. There will be more jobs for therapists to identify and correct the deficiencies in individuals.

Searching for the best explanations of crime is one aspect of criminology; understanding the impact of those explanations on public policy is another.

Let us close this chapter with a somewhat different thought. Is it possible that countries like Denmark have developed social programmes that have "evened the playing field" for disadvantaged parents and their youngsters, thereby making biological variables more visible and more influential? In the U.S., and probably in Canada, lack of such comprehensive social programmes means that economic and social factors weigh more heavily on poor families. Thus the *social environment* would explain more variance in crime in societies that have greater disparities in opportunities to achieve acceptance in the dominant society. By contrast, in those countries, such as the Scandinavian countries, that have reduced those disparities; that is, reduced the impact of social variables, biological variables might be more predictive of criminal behaviour.

One might even extend this thinking to sex differences, as demonstrated in Denno's study of 800 black children (1985). The sociological variables were more crucial to the boys. Is it possible that the disparities found in North American society weigh more heavily on boys than on girls? Poor school achievement appears to have more negative consequences for boys than for girls. Is it possible that the socioeconomic factors do not penalize girls as much as they do boys? If that is the case, biological variables might be more predictive of behaviour among girls than boys.

The same argument might be made for people from middle-class backgrounds. When socioeconomic factors become *less* relevant, genetic factors play a more important role. At present it is difficult to specify just how social and biological variables interact, but it is clear that biological variables cannot act on crime without going through some sort of social filter. In some societies, or for certain groups, the social filter might balance social factors, making individual variables more apparent.

While some people might interpret the twin studies and adoption studies from Denmark as a reason for *neglecting* social programmes, I would argue just the opposite. Creating greater opportunities for the underclass in North America to participate more fully in the riches of our society may be the necessary prerequisite to utilizing these genetic studies constructively. A logical public policy would focus on social disadvantages first; then it would be easier to diagnose physiological factors that persist in influencing behaviour.

PSYCHOLOGICAL PERSPECTIVES

Psychiatry is a way of correcting our own faults by confessing our parents' shortcomings.

L. J. Peter

THE PSYCHOANALYTIC EXPLANATION OF CRIME

Like the explanations offered in the last chapter, psychological views of crime focus on the individual. However, mental processes, personality, and early childhood socialization become the centre of attention. Psychoanalysis is relatively recent and, in a sense, began with Sigmund Freud. As a scholar and researcher, he fits nicely into the positivist tradition, expecting to identify "the causes" of human behaviour. An examination of his own life helps us to appreciate strengths and weaknesses in his theories. He was considered dogmatic and tyrannical by some, showing little tolerance for those who expressed differing opinions (Martin, et al., 1990). This led to ardent disciples and others who were rejected from his circle of followers.

According to Freud, humans are born with two basic instincts, the life or love instinct and the death or hate instinct. The complex interaction of these two instincts can lead to much variety in human behaviour. Aggression, for example, which is an innate part of the death instinct, is a *natural* part of human nature. It is not learned, nor is it just a response to frustration of certain needs. In other words, there is a constant struggle going on within the human psyche, and it is common for the bad components to prevail. In general, these instincts make the brain a "seething cauldron of conflict" (Freud, 1965).

The personality of the normal adult is composed of the *id, ego,* and *superego*. The id is present at birth and is not aware of outside forces, such as morality. It operates at the unconscious level and is intent on immediate gratification. It is governed by the *pleasure principle*, maximizing pleasure while avoiding pain. Although

121

some have portrayed the id as evil, it should really be seen as amoral. Morality is simply irrelevant.

As the baby becomes an infant, the ego develops when the child faces the real world. There are barriers to some of the wants demanded by the id. The ego represents the compromise between the unrestricted wants of the id and the rigid demands of the world. It operates on the *reality principle*, restricting the id when it is unreasonable. One matures with the development of the superego, which focuses on ethical concerns. Morality, remorse and feelings of guilt are produced when the well-socialized person does something wrong. Expectations and standards from parents and others have been internalized to produce a *conscience*.

Yablonsky (1990: 435) provides a simplified model to illustrate the operation of the Freudian id, ego, and superego: A child sees a cookie on the table. Her id demands immediate satisfaction and she grabs the cookie. Father takes the cookie away. Later, when she has developed an ego, she waits until father leaves before taking the cookie. She applied the reality principle and postponed, but did not give up, gratification. If father has made her promise not to take cookies out of the cookie jar, she may or may not obey, depending on the development of the superego. A developed superego would make her feel guilty if she broke her promise. If the superego had not developed, perhaps she could blame the stealing of cookies on her little brother.

The psychoanalytic position would view crime as having several causes:

1. Criminal behaviour springs from within. When the id is uncontrolled, as a result of faulty ego development, the individual has little capacity to repress instinctive impulses. Those dominated by the id are criminal.

2. When the ego fails to develop in the first few years of life, and the superego fails to develop later, the individual is antisocial.

3. An overdeveloped ego may make no provision for the satisfaction of the demands of the id. Crime can result from the compulsive need for punishment to alleviate guilt.

4. Crime can also represent displaced hostility.

Psychoanalytic explanations of crime are obviously more complex than this, but essentially crime is viewed as a symptom of underlying emotional problems. There are differences within this perspective, with some scholars including more family variables. However, psychoanalytic theory does not explain the "normal" crimes of those who learn to commit crime as part of their interaction with others. Peer pressures, the social environment, and social structure are basically ignored.

A major criticism of Freud is that his model of behaviour is not empirically testable(Redl and Toch, 1979). In a theory, concepts should be linked to operational definitions that can be measured. But how does one get a measure of the unconscious? Or the id, ego, or superego? Admittedly, theories can be tested when some of the concepts are unmeasured, but psychoanalysis offers few handles that would allow the empirically oriented researcher to get a grip on the theoretical ideas.

Freud's insights on women would also be questioned today. Clearly, women are inferior. This is obvious from observing their sex organs. Women have no penis. Boys and girls both recognize this difference instinctively and thus take male superiority for granted.

> Women are exhibitionistic, narcissistic, and attempt to compensate for their lack of a penis by being well dressed and physically beautiful. Women become mothers trying to replace the lost penis with a baby. Women are also masochistic ... because their role is one of receptor, and their sexual pleasure consists of pain (Klein, 1973:16).

Is it possible that Freud's view of women influenced a generation of psychiatrists, counsellors, and others so that they developed particular views about rape? Again we see the potential link between ideas and public policy. A "reality" created by a group of thinkers may find a receptive audience in practitioners and policymakers. One could speculate that Freudian ideas had an impact on the way some people viewed female victims.

THE PSYCHOLOGICAL TEST: A USEFUL TOOL FOR UNDERSTANDING CRIME?

Since World War II, social scientists have spent considerable effort developing a variety of questionnaires related to crime. Psychologists have created intelligence tests and measures of personality types, and a number of such devices have been used with the hope of identifying criminals and delinquents. In general, they have shown that there are correlations between different types of test scores and criminal behaviour. However, it is less clear that the tests measure what they claim to be measuring. For example, a well-known psychological test developed in California asks juveniles which president they prefer, Lincoln or Washington. Those who choose Lincoln are more delinquent. Since Lincoln did away with slavery, he has been more popular with Blacks in the U.S., while Washington has been favoured by Whites. It is not surprising that a test item that distinguishes Blacks from Whites in California is also correlated with crime.

While this type of error can trap researchers rather easily, those who are in the business of producing psychological tests are resistant to change. In the 1980s, I was told by a psychology student in Ontario that the question asking which U.S. president one preferred, Lincoln or Washington, was still being asked of *Canadian* young people on the same standardized test. Clearly, one must question the use of such an instrument for studying delinquency in Canada.

Circular Reasoning in Psychological Testing

A major weakness of some psychological tests is that they contain built in tautologies, or circular reasoning. The items in the test are basically the same as the thing they are trying to measure. For example, the *Minnesota Multiphasic Personality Inventory* (MMPI) is a widely used diagnostic tool with ten clinical scales. Some of the scales differentiate criminals from noncriminals. However, Gordon Waldo and Simon Dinitz (1967) pointed out the item, "I have never been in trouble with the law." This is an illustration of circular reasoning: a test item identifying people who have been in trouble with the law, not surprisingly is related to people who have been in trouble with the law.

This sort of faulty reasoning is illustrated in Canada by the psychopathic checklist popularized by Robert Hare (1980, 1985), presented as "reliable and valid" in a popular Canadian criminology text edited by Rick Linden (1987: 131). Among the 22 items on that checklist one finds, "juvenile delinquency" and "poor probation or parole risk." It is difficult to be on probation or parole without having committed a crime. Thus, when Wong (1984) finds that 22% of the inmates in eight federal penitentiaries were classified as psychopaths using this checklist, it is very difficult to see how one could avoid such a finding.

Hare has defended the scale in public discussions by claiming that the other items on the checklist also predict criminality, but let us look more closely at some of the other items: previous diagnosis as psychopath; pathological lying and deception; parasitic lifestyle; short-tempered/poor behavioural controls; promiscuous sexual relations; early behavioural problems; impulsivity; many types of offence. If one were asked to describe a criminal, is it possible that the adjectives used might be those used on the checklist? While some psychologists claim that their measuring devices "work" on the basis of a number of sophisticated statistical analyses, they seem to forget that they are not measuring concepts that are independent. Instead of measuring psychological constructs that *predict* crime, they may, in fact, simply be measures *of* crime. The ritualistic use of statistical techniques has obscured the *thinking* that must also be applied to the question of explaining crime. In all fairness, this type of problem is not rare in scientific work. Circular reasoning and undiscovered factors that lead to spurious relationships are often deeply embedded in the most careful research. Once these are recognized, however, scholars are obligated to take them into account.

Lee Robins (1992), famous for her psychological studies of crime, recognized the frequent tautologies in so much psychologically oriented criminology. She also pointed out factors that have trapped psychologists, and suggested how we might make better sense of the available data. For example, Whites who are arrested are more likely to have antisocial personalities than Blacks. In the general population, Blacks and Whites have similar rates of antisocial personality. Thus, other (social?) factors seem to lead to the arrest of Blacks. If social policies and societal change could reduce differences due to race, *then* personality differences might become more meaningful.

Since science tends to be self-correcting, why have some psychologists persisted in the use of faulty test instruments for such a long time? Is it because there is a "psychological test industry," which has perpetuated itself and which has a vested interest in the continuation of some of these measuring devices? This book cannot engage in a balanced debate on this issue, but the reader should again be aware that the creation of knowledge in criminology is influenced by the dynamics of the professional traditions of the involved researchers.

LEARNING AND CRIME

By deliberately beginning with some criticisms of certain research procedures, I hope to sensitize the reader to the fallibility of some of our thinking; but these cautions should not let us overlook the major contributions that have been made in this area, including the extensive and significant work by Robert Hare, whom I have criticized above (See, for example, Hare, 1970; Hare and McPherson, 1984). A major premise shared by psychologists and sociologists is that crime is learned. Different personalities may respond to situations in ways that lead to crime, but crime, or the failure to behave in a criminal manner, is learned.

Classical Conditioning and Instrumental Learning

Many people have heard of Ivan Pavlov's famous experiment with dogs who learned to salivate at the sound of a bell. Pavlov paired a neutral stimulus (in this case a bell) with a meaningful stimulus (food), which led the dogs to associate the bell with the food. In *classical conditioning*, animals or people have no control over the situation. The learning that takes place is not because of a reward but because of the association between the bell and the food. Gordon Trasler (1962) used these principles in arguing that learning experiences early in life influence the probability of crime at a later time. If parents punish a child for breaking rules, the child will experience anxiety. This will become a conditioned response, similar to the salivation of Pavlov's dogs. To avoid situations that cause anxiety, people will avoid certain types of behaviour. Essentially, conforming behaviour is escape or avoidance of that which is painful or stressful. The inhibition of criminality is learned through conditioning. It persists, or resists extinction, because it continues to reduce anxiety. As long as one conforms, one doesn't get punished.

Trasler notes that some people are more resistant to this conditioning. Those who are outgoing and crave excitement (extraverts) are more resistant to such conditioning, while quiet, self-controlled, introspective individuals (introverts) are susceptible to conditioning. Some individuals learn *not* to be criminals more than others; that is, they are more amenable to *passive avoidance conditioning*. Those who learned early in life that improper behaviour led to anxiety-producing punishment, physical or psychological, would be inhibited from improper behaviour later in life. They would still experience anxiety if they even considered committing a crime, even when the likelihood of punishment is negligible. In other words, learning has become coupled with a response from the involuntary nervous and glandular system, and these reactions create a barrier to criminal behaviour.

Instrumental learning or *operant conditioning* is different. The learner must *do* something in order to obtain a reward, or alternatively, avoid being punished. An important distinction between instrumental learning and classical conditioning is that when the former is operating the individual anticipates a reward (or punishment). Classical conditioning is the result of an association with a stimulus and takes place without a reward. In the book *A Clockwork Orange*, by Anthony Burgess, a psychopathic individual "learns" to decrease his aggressive behaviour by aversive conditioning. During his treatment something unpleasant happens to him each time he thinks antisocial thoughts. After a while, the aggressive behaviour automatically recalls the aversive stimuli (such as feeling sick or an electric shock). One learns that there are consequences for behaviour. The environments, of course, may differ. The two-year-old boy may learn that a temper tantrum can be used to manipulate Dad, but not Mom. Thus, he uses them when Dad is in charge, but abandons that strategy with Mom.

The best-known name in this area is the late B. F. Skinner, whose ideas influence the use of behaviour modification in correctional systems. Like other psychologists with a behaviourist orientation, Skinner believes that humans follow the same basic natural laws as other animals (Bartol and Bartol, 1986:78-83). He is also a *situationalist*. Individuals have no control or self-determination. Free will is a myth. Humans do not control their environments; they react to them. When a pigeon pecks in a certain way to get food, this is a reaction to a stimuli to receive a certain reward. It is not self-determination. The behaviour is molded by *reinforcement*, which can be positive or negative. Several criminologists, such as Ray Jeffrey (1965) and Ron Akers (1985), have made systematic use of operant conditioning theory.

According to behaviour modification, the reduction of crime requires the changing of the environment through behavioural engineering. Societal members must learn at an early age that they will be positively reinforced if they do good things, but will not be rewarded (or will be punished) if they do bad things. A major problem in this scheme is understanding how to provide adequate reinforcement. If a young man gains status among his peers, increased self-esteem, and feelings of competence for bringing off a daring theft, it is difficult for society to provide competing positive reinforcement for avoiding such behaviour.

Hans Eysenck and Criminal Personalities

For many psychologists, personalities make a considerable difference. Hans Eysenck (1977,1981) argues that criminal behaviour is the result of the interaction of environment and personality traits. Although he does not claim that people are born criminals, some have nervous-system characteristics that affect their ability to conform to the rules of society. Three major components of personality, *extraversion*, *neuroticism*, and *psychoticism*, are related to crime.

Extraversion

Using self-report questionnaires, Eysenck classified roughly 16% of the population as extraverts and another 16% as introverts. Extraverts are sociable, impulsive, and have high needs for excitement. They lose their tempers quickly, are aggressive, and are unreliable. (Eysenck say that the commonly used term *extrovert*, spelled with an *o*, differs somewhat from his classification of *extravert*, but many of us are unclear about this distinction). Behavioural differences are related to physiological differences in brain functioning. Extraverts handle stimulation to the cerebral cortex differently from introverts and others. They do not generate cortical arousal effectively, and thus need additional stimulation. The nature of the extraverts' nervous systems inhibits the internalization of the rules of society, and they are also drawn to risk-taking activities, such as joy-riding, drug-taking, and stealing. Eysenck would agree with Trasler that most criminals are extraverts.

Neuroticism

In contrast to those who are emotionally stable, neurotics react intensively to stress. They are moody, touchy, anxious, and complain about many physical ailments. They develop phobias and obsessions. These characteristics also have a physiological base (Bartol and Bartol, 1986), which will not be discussed here. Eysenck assumes that people high on neuroticism are more likely to be criminal, because it acts as a drive, pushing an individual to perform in a manner consistent with past habits. If those habits are of a risk-taking nature, such as those common to extraverts, the likelihood of crime is increased. Neurotic extraverts, then, are the most likely personality type to be criminal.

Psychoticism

While extraversion and neuroticism can be explained in neurological terms, such mechanisms have not been defined for psychoticism. It is characterized by insensitivity, disregard for danger, and hostility towards others. Eysenck suggests hardcore violent offenders are likely to be psychotic. We could get into circular reasoning, if one tries to define psychotics and then use this concept as an explanation. For example, a person who is high on psychoticism is "cold, impersonal, hostile, lacking in sympathy, unfriendly, untrustful, odd, unemotional, unhelpful, antisocial, lacking in human feelings, inhumane, generally bloodyminded, lacking in insight, strange, with paranoid ideas that people are against him" (Eysenck and Eysenck, 1976). Those with such characteristics tend to be serious and sometimes violent offenders. Is this an *explanation* or a *description*? Neuroticism and extraversion, on the other hand, are defined in neurological terms and, on the surface, may be defined more independently of the phenomena they try to explain.

While it might be more appropriate to place Eysenck's work with biological explanations, it also provides a convenient link with learning theories. If one accepts the role of conditioning discussed above, it suggests that neurotics, extraverts, and possibly psychotics, respond differently to the conditioning process. This orientation treats certain outcomes as inevitable, but human beings play an active, rather than passive, role in their environment.

Social Learning Theories

While Skinner and the behaviourists emphasize external factors as determining behaviour, learning theorists underscore thought processes, perceptions, and the way the environment is assessed. Social learning accentuates cognition, which we might simplify as thinking and remembering. In addition to conditioning, people learn by watching and listening to those around them. Reinforcement would be necessary to maintain behaviour, but criminal behaviour might be first acquired through association with others and through observation of others. The experience can be direct, or it can be based on modelling. For example, a boy watches his older peer (who acts as a model) steal something, so he tries it himself. If a store clerk spots the boy and grabs him as he leaves, the aversive experience may inhibit future theft. But if the theft is successful and if others applaud his skill and daring, the reinforcement could be positive.

Ron Akers (1985) has elaborated this argument as *differential reinforcement theory*. He and many other scholars have tested these ideas to explain delinquency and drug use, and find considerable support. People first learn behaviour, including criminal behaviour, through imitation or through observing what happened to others. Depending on the nature of the reinforcement, whether the behaviour is rewarded or punished, the pattern will be maintained or will be extinguished. The family, peers, and other significant others, such as teachers, are important as role models and as differential reinforcers.

Learning Aggression: Albert Bandura

One of the best-known scholars in learning theory, Albert Bandura, is noted for his work on aggression (1973). The late Robert Walters pursued this line of research in Canada, and James Check of York University continues this tradition (Malamuth and Check, 1981). Bandura's classic work with children notes that they can learn how to shoot a gun from watching TV; not in a skilled manner, perhaps, but enough to pull triggers, just as adults "know" how to use a pistol even if they have never done it before. Thus, when children watched a film showing adults beating an inflated rubber doll, they imitated the behaviour. When cartoons were used where a cat bashed Bobo the doll, children imitated the aggression. Not only did they hit Bobo more frequently than children who watched a peaceful film, they used dart guns, peg boards, and tether balls in a more aggressive manner than the control groups. Thus, we should not automatically view the Road Runner cartoons as harmless entertainment. Not many seconds pass before a violent message is delivered. The coyote, who is stalking the Road Runner, is crushed by rocks, blasted by dynamite, or flattened by a steamroller in a variety of ways. Despite the claim that all children know that these cartoons are fantasy, the potential for increasing aggression is there. Adults who observe aggressive acts also become more hostile. This should make us uneasy, since the amount of violence on television appears to be increasing. A recent study noted that there are five or six violent incidents per hour on prime-time American television, and 15 to 25 violent incidents for each hour of cartoons (Signorielli, et al. 1982).

Canadian scholars have raised similar concerns. An Ontario study noted that during popular viewing hours, 44% of the programmes portrayed crime and violence (Gautier, 1977). On weekend evenings, there were six violent incidents per hour. An interesting study of the impact of television in general was made in a small British Columbia logging town, which had no television until recently (Joy, et al., 1986). After the introduction of television, there was a greater display of physical aggressiveness.

Hartnagel, Teevan, and McIntyre (1975) used questionnaire data to ask if high school students who viewed more violent television programmes also admitted to more violent acts. They found a moderate relationship. The impact may have been less because previous laboratory studies, such as Bandura's, may focus the subjects' attention on the violent content of the simulated programmes and thereby intensify the impact. In addition, some studies measured the potential impact very soon after exposure to the film, in a setting that replicated the setting in the film. Another factor was that Hartnagel and his colleagues looked at junior and senior high school students, instead of very young children.

However, Hartnagel and his fellow researchers do not dismiss indirect influences of TV on violent behaviour through its impact on learned values and attitudes. It is possible that teenagers simply view violence on TV as normal. This may explain why some favourite TV programmes, which clearly contained violence, were perceived as having relatively little violence by many of the high school students. In addition, violent television content may produce attitudes that condone violence for resolving disputes. Thus, exposure to violent TV could have important indirect effects on actual violent behaviour. Students who actually were violent might understate such violence on a questionnaire, not because they were lying, but because they saw violence as less noteworthy.

Malamuth and Check (1981) extend this logic to violence against women. Male and female university students were shown two types of films; one with sexual violence and one without. This was done as part of a normal film series. Several days later, they were asked to respond to a series of attitude questions, unaware that there was a connection with the films they had seen. Malamuth and Check found that males who viewed the film portraying violent sex were more likely to express attitudes accepting violence against women. Admittedly, these studies of *attitudes* do not provide evidence of violent *behaviour*. However, the social learning theorists argue that the media are one source of modeling that contributes to the repertoire of patterns from which an individual can choose. In the film *Basic Instincts*, the first scene opens with a beautiful nude woman astride a man locked in sex. Just as the man reaches an orgasm, the woman murders him by plunging an ice pick into his chest many times. If potential murderers are short on imagination, such films could certainly make up that deficiency. Nor should policy-makers overlook the other side of the coin. There is evidence that constructive television programming, *Sesame Street* for example, can increase the likelihood of prosocial behaviour (Coates, Pusser, and Goodman, 1976; Forge and Phemister, 1987).

Cognitive and Moral Development

In their classic work, *Studies in Deceit*, the first of a three volume collection, Hartshorne and May (1928-30) generated a debate on some basic questions regarding the consistency of behaviour. Are honesty, and other moral characteristics, something we learn early in life and internalize so that they operate in all situations? Most of us tend to believe that people have "character," which makes them act consistently under different conditions. Another argument is that people respond to the *situation*. Thus, the individual's honesty and moral behaviour is determined by circumstances. This chapter focuses on studies that view moral behaviour as a characteristic of the individual. In the next chapter, we will note dynamic group situations that lead to behaviour that would not be anticipated from our knowledge of the individuals concerned.

Hartshorne and May surprised many people in the 1930s, when they found that children who were dishonest or ruthless in one situation were not likely to act the same way in different situations. However, Burton (1963, 1976) reanalyzed these data, omitting some that were unreliable, and found a general tendency for children to be somewhat consistent in terms of honesty or dishonesty. This general disposition was related to the social status of the child's family, with higher-status children displaying more honesty. Similarly, brighter children tended to be more honest and displayed more consistency in their honesty than those who were less bright. Of course, one might ask: do bright, higher-status children live in a less difficult world?

Consistency is what one would expect from the work done by Jean Piaget (1948), a Swiss psychologist who pioneered studies of how children organize social rules and make judgements. He argued that morality develops in a series of stages, depending on the intellectual or cognitive skills of individuals, as well as on their social experiences. Kohlberg (1976) continues this train of thought when he argues that the individual grows in an undeviating sequence through six stages of moral development. The individual must develop the skills and insights in sequence, building on each step before moving to the next. People progress through these stages at different speeds, and some do not progress as far as others.

There are three primary stages; *preconventional, conventional,* and *postconventional* morality, each of which is divided into early and late substages. At the *preconventional* stage, individuals act entirely out of self-interest. They have not developed notions of right or wrong. They defer to those in power, but the rules and expectations are external to the "self" of the individual. During the *late preconventional* stage, individuals become more practical. They learn to use others and understand that they must adapt in order to meet their own needs.

With the *conventional* stage, which characterizes the average adolescent, the individual strives for social approval and acceptance, particularly from peers. Their good behaviour is designed to receive social rewards and avoid negative experiences. Their image of what their peer group expects is somewhat stereotyped, but they have internalized the rules of society, particularly those with the power to reward or punish. At the *late conventional* stage the conscience develops; a sense of duty to the society emerges, but the individual does not question the morality of the authorities or the society at this stage.

At the *postconventional* stage, one begins to appreciate larger principles and rights of individuals. Customs are critically examined. A minority of adults after age 20 begin balancing rights of individuals with demands of society and the consideration that some laws may be unjust. The late *postconventional* individual is oriented to decisions of conscience and ethical principles that appeal to comprehensiveness and consistency. These principles can be abstract and reflect universal principles of justice (Jennings, Kilkenny, and Kohlberg, 1983).

Kohlberg argues that people pass through these stages at different rates, with many never going beyond a certain level. Criminals, like children, tend to remain at the *preconventional* stage. Although the stages represent a progression, Kohlberg acknowledges that individuals can display a wide range of moral judgements. However, they would cluster around a single stage. In addition, these judgements would be related to the individual's perspective. If the delinquent displays loyalty to his gang or the Mafia member adheres to the code of his society, he may be behaving in a manner consistent with higher levels of morality. One can see the problems of applying these arguments to criminals if someone has been socialized into criminal lifestyles. Can we assume that morality has a single dimension, or do different subgroups create different moralities?

A number of questions arise regarding the acquisition of moral character. Kohlberg suggests that it is something that is internalized and then remains fairly constant. Bandura's experiments and the work of Malamuth and Check, such as those mentioned above, suggest that *situations* lead to the imitation of others. Peers also exert a strong influence on criminal behaviour, particularly during adolescence. There are also situations where people *know* what is morally correct, but for other reasons do not do it. Our theories select certain factors as explanations for criminal behaviour when, in reality, many things are happening at once, or possibly coming into play at different times or under different circumstances.

CONCLUSION

The explanations reviewed in this chapter focused on the individual, but clearly individuals do not operate in a vacuum. While many psychologists tend to concentrate on characteristics of individuals and the immediate environments in which they are socialized, it is difficult to explain criminal behaviour without looking at other forces in the community and in the larger society. Theories of offenders' attributes, personalities, or social background and conditions, do not explain why others with the same traits, same personality type, or similar upbringing do not persist in criminal careers. Criminological theories that stress individual traits or offender pathology also fail miserably at explaining spatial patterns of crime, regional variations, intercity and intracity differences, or changes in crime over time.

A murderer, after savagely killing a woman and robbing her house, took the utmost care to feed the victim's dog and cat (Fattah, 1971). He even left them enough food, for fear that nobody would come to the scene of the crime for some time. Violent offenders who exhibit extreme cruelty and callousness towards victims sometimes show tender love and compassion for others, and even for animals. In other words, concentrating on attributes of the individual alone cannot yield an adequate explanation of crime. The following chapters will review perspectives that bring in group dynamics and situations that increase the likelihood of criminal behaviour.

GROUP DYNAMICS, COLLECTIVE BEHAVIOUR, AND CRIMINOGENIC CIRCUMSTANCES

The school teacher was trying to explain why obedience was necessary in the classroom. She told the story of a lamb that had strayed from the flock and had been eaten by a wolf. "You see, had the lamb been obedient and stayed with the flock, it would not have been eaten by the wolf."
"No, ma'am," answered one small boy. "It would have been eaten by people."

Anon

SITUATIONAL DYNAMICS

The automobile was left on the streets in an eastern U.S. city across from the campus of a large university; the licence plates were removed and the hood was raised. Then the researchers unobtrusively observed the car for 64 hours. Within ten minutes the first visitor arrived. The observer noted, "family of three drive by, stop. All leave car. Well dressed. ... Mother ... stands by car on sidewalk keeping watch. Boy, about eight years old, stays by father throughout, observing and helping. Father (neatly) dressed ... opens trunk, rummages through, opens car trunk which is full of tools, removes hacksaw, cuts for one minute. Lifts battery out and puts in his trunk."

Another thief was a distinguished looking, middle-aged man pushing a baby carriage. He stole something from the trunk and put it in the baby carriage. After twenty-six hours the car was stripped of the battery, radiator, air cleaner, radio antenna, windshield wipers, chrome strip, hub caps, a set of jumper cables, a gas can, a can of car wax, and its only good tire. Nine hours later random destruction began when teenagers tore off the rear-view mirror.

While this experiment was being conducted in an eastern U.S. city, a similar procedure was followed in California near the Stanford University campus. After sixty-four hours the car in Palo Alto was untouched. In fact, when it began to rain, one passerby lowered the hood so the motor would not get wet.

This experiment by Philip Zimbardo and Scott Fraser (Zimbardo, 1970) might suggest that eastern urban dwellers are more criminally inclined than Californians. Attempts to explain such behaviour, however, in terms of characteristics of individuals, ignore many dynamic factors. For example, several adults observed the family of three stealing the battery but did nothing. Furthermore, most of the vandalism was done in broad daylight by well-dressed, apparently middle-class people. One can focus on the setting, but clearly there seems to be considerable *interaction* among a number of factors. The setting is dynamic rather than static, and outcomes are somewhat different from what would be predicted by looking at isolated factors.

The Setting and Deindividuation

Some settings and circumstances appear to encourage *deindividuation*, where people lose their identity and become part of a group. Zimbardo predicted that the large concentration of population in the eastern U.S. would mean that people would be more likely to lose their identity and feel less responsible for their actions. In addition, the anonymity in the larger city, in combination with situational clues, suggested that no one else cared what the "thieves" were doing. In the setting near Stanford University, people could be more easily identified. Somehow, this explanation seems incomplete to me. What is it that makes someone take the first step towards a criminal act?

Robertson Davies, in his book *The Manticore* (1972: 150), provides a description of how the central character in the book, while a teenager, joined other boys in breaking into a cabin owned by elderly people. The leader began damaging things and goaded the others into following his lead. Their appetite for destruction grew with feeding. The leader piled photographs on a table, jumped up on the table, stripped down his trousers, squatted over the photographs, and defecated on them. At that point, the central character in the book comes to his senses and tries to understand what is happening. The scene dramatically captures the transition from normal boys to destructive criminals. In this case, it is difficult to view the boys as being inherently criminal or the setting as criminogenic; instead the *dynamics* of the group play a more important role.

Mutual Excitation and Circular Reactions

Andrew Wade (1967) provides an explanatory argument for vandalism that is quite compatible with these ideas. In describing the damages done by a group of boys in a feed mill warehouse, the boys explained how they originally gained entry to play tag among the stacks of feed bags. Soon the motorized fork-lift trucks were discovered, and the boys began having fun driving them. They didn't *deliberately* drive them into the feed bags, but they were unskilled pilots of the fork-lift trucks. The first time the grain sacks were damaged, the boys may have hesitated, perhaps a bit anxious about what they had done; but they may have also wondered how deeply you could drive the forks on the trucks into a bag of grain if you really took a run at it. The challenge, the dare, the competition, and the perverse pleasure in the destruction stimulated others to go further than they had earlier planned. This is *mutual excitation*. In earlier studies of collective behaviour, Blumer suggested the term *circular reaction* (1951). This is the type of interstimulation where the actions of one individual stimulate another, which in turn is reflected back to the first person, providing reinforcement. Soon there is group contagion. Wade documents five stages in this process:

Stage I: Waiting for Something to Turn Up
The actors are poised for some action-provoking suggestion. Sometimes "games" are being played, such as trying to shoot bottles with a BB gun. It doesn't take much of a shift, however, to find that street lights and windows can be exciting targets.

Stage II: Removal of Uncertainty (the Exploratory Gesture)
The unstructured situation changes when an action-provoking suggestion is offered. The exploratory gesture is sometimes made cautiously, sometimes boldly, but it provokes interest in contrast to what might have been prevailing boredom. Of course, the exploratory gesture could be rejected. In the above description of the boys vandalizing the cottage, the process might have failed to develop if the exploratory gestures were rejected, if the circular reaction was stifled initially. But let us postpone such thoughts until later, when we consider antidotes to this type of crime. Assuming, however, that the exploratory gesture is not rejected, how does the uncertainty change into direct action?

Stage III: Mutual Conversion
A number of pressures may be operating to cause the individual to go along with the actions implied in the exploratory gesture; challenges to one's self-image related to courage, manliness, or daring. One does not want to be viewed as "chicken." There can be a struggle between the internalized norms of the larger social system, norms that favour prosocial behaviour, and the demands of loyalty to the peer group, which may favour deviant behaviour. When the peer group wins in this struggle, mutual conversion has taken place. Obviously, the likelihood of conversion depends on background factors. Highly delinquent boys will not need much encouragement to engage in vandalism. On the other hand, those who perceive that others in the group would think badly of them if they responded favorably to an exploratory gesture to do something wrong would resist such conversion.

Stage IV: Joint Elaboration of the Act
In this stage there can be large-scale property destruction. The *circular reaction* and *mutual excitation* accelerate the potential for reckless behaviour, so that a veritable orgy of vandalism can take place. Any impact of favourable family socialization

must be submerged and replaced, at least temporarily, by pressure from peers to conform to new norms. The individual must respond to challenges and call the bluff of the others. The *deindividuation* described by Zimbardo appears to fit these other situations. The temporary loss of identity and sense of security in the peer group reduces feelings of individual responsibility. Cautious individuals, who would normally be very reluctant to engage is criminal behaviour, now feel they can hide behind the perceived anonymity. An *impression of universality* is created, giving the appearance of group solidarity.

Stage V: Aftermath and Retrospect
In a *retrospective view of the act*, the participants may redefine the criminal behaviour as "getting even" with someone who did them wrong: this is not a meaningful "explanation" but instead an *ex post facto* rationalization. Most of the boys thought the vandalism was simply "fun" at the time and were carried away by events, rather than seeing any reasoned attempt to get revenge against some real or imagined enemy. Feelings of shame and guilt will depend on the importance of other reference groups. If the primary source of self-definition comes from prosocial elements, such as parents, guilt will be strong, but even so, Wade found that some boys still expressed some malicious delight at having been participants in these wild acts. Adult males, holding respectable positions, often delight in retelling stories of past misdeeds. The passage of time makes the description of their previous daring more status-enhancing than the shame they should exhibit for such thoughtless behaviour.

Breaking the Chain of Events

The sequence of events is not inevitable. In the scene above, where the boys were trashing the cottage, what event would have interrupted the process? Jack Katz (1988) used the behaviour of soldiers as an illustration of mutual excitation and other group dynamics, which led from routine interrogation of Vietnamese peasants to brutality. A soldier was beating a woman when she had a spontaneous bowel movement. "The soldier stopped. I'm beating up this girl, for what? What the fuck am I doing? I just felt like a shit" (1988: 7). Crime prevention involves making potential deviants "feel like a shit," preferably before the behaviour takes place.

Neutralization Theory

Some explanations of crime emphasize that underdogs are striking back against injustice in society or juveniles are rebelling against the boredom of the schools (Sykes and Matza, 1957). Injustices in society *are* criminogenic, as we will see in later chapters, but when Sykes and Matza (1957) describe juveniles as neutralizing guilt feelings about certain types of behaviour, we should be careful to look at the time sequence of these events. Since the rationalization usually takes place after the acts, it should not be seen as a *cause* of the behaviour. The Sykes and Matza argument is an explanation about neutralizing guilt, rather than about crime.

In a demonstration concerning funding for the university, a student at the University of Alberta crushed an egg on the head of the Alberta Minister of Higher Education. One student spokesman said that the act illustrated the frustration students felt, but is this an "explanation" or a rationalization? Was the act done on a dare? Was this student more frustrated than others? Or did the group encourage him? Such *ex post facto* explanations of deviant acts should be treated with suspicion. On the other hand, *ex post facto* rationalizations are part of the sequence. People naturally search for "explanations," but the process should not be confused with predicting the behaviour.

Neutralization "theory" is almost always covered in criminology and delinquency textbooks in those sections that deal with explanations of *causes* of crime, but the work by Wade (1967) is largely unknown. In terms of explaining the dynamics of certain types of crime, however, I find the single article written by a relatively unknown probation officer (Wade) far superior to the frequently cited article written by two scholars at prestigious universities (Sykes and Matza, 1957) and published in the top sociology journal, *The American Sociological Review*. Matza's later book *Delinquency and Drift* (1964) was also well received, even though I found it obtuse and less successful than Wade's work in providing clear insights into criminal involvement, particularly because Wade dealt with the time sequence more effectively. These comments are not intended to denigrate the work of Sykes and Matza, but rather to remind the reader again that the popularization of theories of crime and their selection for criminology textbooks is, like criminal deeds, subject to dynamic factors. Students should not assume that the ideas about criminology forced on them in school will automatically be those that are superior. The political climate, prevailing cultural fads, and authors being part of established universities are some of the variables that will influence our preferred explanations.

The Definition of the Situation

In addition to the group processes operating as Wade described above, people perceive situations differently. In the abandoned-car experiment referred to earlier, the reader will recall that the automobile near the Stanford campus was not vandalized. Zimbardo argued that it was not clearly identified as abandoned (1970). The experimenters decided to damage it somewhat to see if others would follow suit.

> There is considerable reluctance to take that first blow, to smash through the windshield ... but it feels so good after the first smack that the next one comes more easily, with more force and feels even better. Even though the sequence was being filmed, the students got carried away. (Zimbardo, 1970:290)

Everyone was eager to use the sledge-hammer. One student jumped on the roof and began stomping it in, two were pulling off the door, another broke all the glass he could find. They later reported that the experience was stimulating and pleasurable. Observers, who were shouting to hit it harder, finally joined in and turned the car completely over on its back. This was another illustration of mutual excitation. The experimenters realized that they had gone too far and that there was little likelihood that such a badly wrecked car would be vandalised further. However, that night three men with pipes and bars were pounding away at the carcass. The situation had been redefined. The car was clearly "abandoned." Sometimes it is not clear when a car has been abandoned, as the following anecdote suggests.

> A motorist pulled his car off the highway in Queens, New York, to fix a flat tire. He jacked up his car and, while removing the tire, was startled to see his hood being opened and a stranger starting to pull out the battery. The stranger tried to mollify his assumed car stripping colleague by telling him, "Take it easy buddy, you can have the tires; all I want is the battery". (Zimbardo, 1970: 292)

It appears that circular reactions and mutual excitation can make people go further than they had originally intended, but there is often the need to have the situation defined as "okay" before people begin to commit questionable acts. Having a person in authority define things as "okay" has considerable impact on this process.

The Role of Authority in Producing Wrongful Behaviour

Group members do not all have the same influence. People defer to others even when they encourage actions contrary to what they feel is right. Soldiers kill when ordered to do so. People at the bottom of hierarchies sometimes do things because they assume that the people above them have superior knowledge that enables them to see consequences not visible to those who must do the dirty work. This makes the questionable acts acceptable. At times, the underling feels she has no choice. At other times conscience wins out.

The Milgram Experiment on Obedience to Authority

Stanley Milgram (1963) did a controversial study where the subjects gave electric shocks to others to "teach" them. The subjects were told they were studying the effects of punishment on memory. They would be the "teachers" who would administer the punishment, but they did not know the "learners," who pretended to feel the electric shocks, were part of the experiment. When the subjects met the learners, a coin was flipped to see who would be the teacher and who would be the learner. In fact, the naïve subject always "won" the toss and became the teacher. The learner was then taken into an adjacent room and strapped into an "electric chair" in front of the naïve teacher. The teacher would then go into the next room, containing the "shock generator," which had labels indicating different levels of shock from 15 to 450 volts. The labels also provided descriptions, such as "slight shock" and "danger: severe shock" and further on the scale "XXX." Each time the learner gave a wrong answer, the researcher told the teacher to administer a stronger shock. The confederate learner, of course, gave wrong answers, displayed increasing discomfort, finally screamed in agony, banged on the wall, and pleaded with the teacher to stop.

How far would people go in administering painful shocks when told to do so by the authority figure (the researcher)? Milgram was surprised that two-thirds of the subjects went past the danger level, all the way to extreme level. While obeying the instructions, many of them displayed considerable discomfort, sweating profusely, biting their lips, etc., especially when the victim began pounding the wall (Milgram, 1963; 1974).

Milgram varied the physical distance between the teacher and learner, and by varying how much the teacher could hear, varied the "psychological" distance. For example, in the closest physical and psychological distance, the teacher sat next to the learner. In general, the subject resisted the instructions of the experimenter more when close to the victim.

However, the nearer the *experimenter*, who remained calm, got to the teacher, the higher the rate of compliance. While compliance was similar for male and female subjects, female teachers displayed greater discomfort. These distance factors may be relevant to violent crime. The more *impersonal* the weapon, the greater the likelihood of damaging behaviour. Is someone more likely to shoot another at twenty feet than stab someone at two feet? Is stabbing easier than strangling someone with bare hands? Can a manufacturer run a factory, using poisonous substances that hurt workers, if she does not know the workers in the plant? This may seem a digression from the theme of this chapter, but there are implications for social policy in these experiments.

The subjects rationalized *after* having administered the severe shocks. They were sure the experimenter would not permit the victim to be harmed: "He must know what he is doing." Still others had faith, perhaps unwarranted, in the merit of social science research: the knowledge gained justified the method. However, as cautioned above, these rationalizations may reduce guilt after the fact, rather than "explain" the behaviour.

This work by Milgram and others who have investigated the pressures of group dynamics raises questions about the nature of society, including those countries that take pride in producing individuals who love democracy and are, therefore, capable of resisting the wishes of malevolent authorities. One thing is abundantly clear: personality factors or levels of moral development are simply not enough to explain many types of antisocial or criminal behaviour. Let us turn even more to group processes, not only for more complete explanations, but for insights into intelligent social policy.

Criminogenic Settings

A number of factors described above come together in the well-known Stanford prison experiment initiated by Zimbardo (1973). Student volunteers were screened and paid $15 a day. The experiment required two roles, guard and prisoner, assigned by the flip of a coin. The next day, "prisoners" were unexpectedly "arrested" and brought in a police car to a simulated prison at Stanford University, where they were handcuffed, searched, fingerprinted, deloused, issued a prison uniform, and placed in a 6' by 9' cell with two other "inmates." The guards wore uniforms and mirrored sunglasses and carried night sticks, whistles, and handcuffs. They drew up formal rules for maintaining order in the "prison."

Both guards and prisoners took on their roles completely by the end of six days. Previous socialization and values seemed to count for little, as the guards treated the prisoners as if they were animals, taking pleasure in cruelty. The prisoners became servile, thinking only of their own survival, with mounting hatred towards the guards. Three prisoners had to be released during the first four days when they became hysterical and depressed. Others begged to be "paroled," willing to forfeit the money they had earned from the experiment. None of the prisoners simply said, "I'm quitting the job, and if anyone tries to stop me I'll have you charged with kidnapping." Instead, they continued to play their role as inmates, trying to escape or get better treatment by following the artificially created rules. Even Zimbardo, as prison director, got caught up in his role. Suspecting a "prison riot," he had taken some counter-precautions. When another professor dropped by to see how the experiment was going and began asking questions about psychology, Zimbardo was annoyed. Here he was with a potential prison riot on his hands, and this ivory-tower type was asking questions about dependent variables. Zimbardo had *become* a prison director instead of a psychologist.

A third of the guards abused their power, but even those who were seen as fair but tough never supported the prisoners against guards who were treating the inmates badly. The exercise of power was self-aggrandizing and self-perpetuating. The most hostile guards moved spontaneously into leadership roles and became role models for others. The situation became such that Zimbardo terminated the experiment in six days instead of proceeding through the planned two weeks.

There have been criticisms of this study, but in less than one week normal young males learned to behave in a pathological and antisocial manner. It has been said that prison guards tend to be recruited from those with a lust for power and other antisocial characteristics. An alternative argument is that when a situation is created where some have power and others are powerless, everyone learns to despise lack of power. Prisoners and guards learn to admire power for its own sake. Real prisoners learn how to gain power through informing, sexual control of other prisoners, or forming powerful cliques. Despite the articles in the press that describe some prisons as country clubs, there are many criminologists who argue that it is very difficult to create prisons that are humane and that can create positive experiences for an inmate.

Although the Stanford prison experiment calls into question some of the assumptions about incarceration, it also fits into the larger issue of pathological behaviour being raised in this chapter. The *characteristics of individuals* are often insufficient to explain antisocial behaviour. Criminogenic situations exist that will increase the likelihood of violence and physical abuse. By the same token, different situations could be created that make people more caring, more altruistic, and more inclined to come to the aid of someone in need. Criminologists tend to ignore this constructive side of the coin. On this note, let us turn to studies that involve the role of bystanders.

BYSTANDER BEHAVIOUR AND COMING TO THE AID OF OTHERS

In February 1981, a young University of Alberta student was stabbed and clubbed to death by six men, as his horrified girlfriend looked on. Bystanders watched curiously, but made no effort to help (*Edmonton Journal*, February 23, 1981). In July of the same year, several people waited unconcernedly for a bus while an elderly man lay at their feet, dying of a heart attack. "The guy was lying in front of the bus stop and his face was turning blue, but nobody even glanced at him" (*Edmonton Journal*, July 29, 1981). The man was pronounced dead on arrival at the hospital.

Upon hearing of such events, it is tempting to offer explanations in terms of moral depravity or lack of humanity on the part of the non-intervening onlookers. It is unlikely that Edmonton, where the above events took place, is much different from other cities in Canada. These sorts of situations, unfortunately, occur regularly in many different types of communities. If one attempts to explain these phenomena in terms of the characteristics of the bystanders, our reasoning is often deficient in the way that it fails to explain criminal acts. Characteristics of communities, the dynamics of the situation, and other factors also influence the likelihood of crime or antisocial behaviour and, in addition, influence the bystanders or observers of crime. It is reasonable to argue that bystanders can make a difference. Therefore, it is worthwhile to review studies of bystander behaviour, and expand on the principles reviewed in the earlier part of the chapter to those people who have a potential for intervention. We could ask, "In what type of setting do antisocial acts take place?" For now, however, we will ask, "What type of stimuli do people need to act in a prosocial or antisocial way?"

The Willingness to Help and the Diffusion of Responsibility

The Smoke-Filled Room

This experiment placed undergraduate males in a room, completing a questionnaire. The experimenter began to introduce "smoke" into the room. When a subject was alone in the room, he would glance up from his questionnaire. Most subjects would get up from their chairs and investigate. No subject showed any sign of panic, but three-quarters of the men reported the smoke. However, when a naïve subject was in the room with two "stooges" who were instructed to ignore the smoke, the behaviour of the subject was quite different. Only one in ten reported the smoke, "the other nine stayed in the waiting room as it filled up with smoke, doggedly working on their questionnaire and waving the fumes away from their faces. They coughed, rubbed their eyes, and opened the window — but they did not report the smoke" (Latané and Darley, 1968: 218).

In a third test situation, three naïve subjects were placed in the room. To a large extent, the three naïve subjects acted like the single naïve subject placed with the two stooges. In general, *the presence of others led to a delay in noticing the smoke, and inhibited prosocial action.* This leads us to question the assumption that the presence of many people at an emergency will increase the likelihood that aid will be provided.

The Lady in Distress

Perhaps there was no real danger in the smoke-filled-room study. Individuals might respond differently if someone was actually in pain. In a related study, naïve subjects were ushered into a room by a young woman, to fill out a questionnaire. A few minutes later, they heard the young woman fall in the next room and cry out for help. "Oh, my ankle. I can't get this thing off me" (Latané and Rodin, 1969). Of those who heard the fall while *alone* in the waiting room, 70% offered to help the victim. When an inactive stooge was present, only 7% of the subjects intervened. Similarly, a second naïve subject, instead of the stooge, tended to inhibit the action of the subjects. However, one of the test situations included two persons who were *friends*, rather than strangers. They were more inclined to offer help than when the subjects were strangers. The researchers suggest that friends are less likely to worry about looking foolish in front of each other than in front of strangers.

Asking the Wrong Questions

Criminologists may not have been asking the best questions, when it comes to explaining crime. "Why do some *individuals* commit crimes? Why do some *individuals* object to antisocial behaviour in others? Why do some *individuals* come to the help of others in distress?" They sound like reasonable questions, but the characteristics of individuals, their moral development, their socialization, and their personalities may play a smaller role than had previously been thought. The situational factors, particularly those factors that influence the dynamics of the immediate social environment, may be more crucial in determining whether a person will take part in criminal behaviour or interfere with others when they observe acts of deviance.

Helping Models

It would be inappropriate to leave the reader with the impression that the interesting experiments by Bibb Latané, John Darley, and their colleagues provide the definitive answer to certain types of behaviour. In the "flat-tire" study by James H. Bryan and Maryanne Test (1967), a woman was standing by an automobile with a flat tire. An inflated tire was leaning on the car. The young woman, flat tire, and inflated tire were conspicuous to passing traffic. A quarter of a mile towards the traffic another car had a flat tire. This time a young man had pulled his car off the road and appeared to be changing the flat tire for the woman. Of two thousand vehicles that passed the automobile where the young lady was being helped, fifty-eight stopped at the second car where the second young lady was alone.

In a second experiment, there was no "helping model" to be seen shortly before coming upon the lady with the flat tire. If one uses the "diffusion of responsibility" model, one could argue that the evidence of someone helping would *decrease* the obligation on a passer-by to help. If others are willing to help, there is less need to do so. But the flat-tire study indicated the opposite. Only thirty-five cars stopped when there was no helping model to remind drivers of the social-responsibility norm. It seems, then, that we are encouraged to act in a prosocial way when we have seen others acting in a prosocial manner.

Attribution Theory

Social psychologists have explored many different avenues in their attempts to explain why people do something, or why they are willing to intervene when someone needs help. My purpose has not been to come up with some "best" explanation, but to alert the reader to questions that get less attention when we attempt to explain crime. The purpose of this chapter is to illustrate the type of thinking that might be profitably used to provide more adequate explanations of crime.

Attribution theory has been of considerable interest to social psychologists. To simplify, people attribute certain "causes" to situations, and such attributions lead to their taking a certain course of action. One can see how this might help to explain the beginnings of some of the dynamics described above. For example, a person with some potential for criminal behaviour is observing a potential victim. Let us assume that a few youths are observing someone who is sleeping on the sidewalk. The youths may believe the man is drunk. If they attribute the drunkenness to the faults in the man, they may identify him as responsible for his problem. They may feel disgust and fail to help him. Or they may see him as worthless and undeserving, and therefore an appropriate victim of theft.

They may view a well-dressed business man, who is walking towards them, as someone who lives by exploiting others, a person not worthy of respect. He may also be seen as partially to blame for the type of system they live in that makes it hard for them to find jobs. Thus, robbing him becomes acceptable. In a similar manner, they may attribute certain characteristics to the owner of a store. He cheats his customers, it is easy to dislike him, and once having shared this dislike with peers, robbing his store becomes a more likely response.

Of course, the reasoning of the youths could proceed along different lines. The man lying on the street may remind the young men of someone they know; they may believe that he is having a heart attack. At any rate, they may attribute the situation to circumstances beyond the victim's control. It is not his fault that he is laying there; therefore he is deserving of sympathy. Providing help might be the final response.

Similarly, the well-dressed business man may be someone to admire. The boys might attribute his successful manner to the fact that he worked hard, displayed intelligence, was honourable in his business relations, earned the trust and respect of others, and as result now has an important position. If he were to slip on the ice, the young men might go to his aid.

The owner of the store might have been someone who came to North America from the old country with the grandfather of a friend of one of the boys. He worked hard, got ahead, treated customers well, granted credit to deserving people facing tough times, and gave jobs to kids in the neighbourhood. He and his store have been welcome in the area, so if the youths pass the store at night and see someone trying to break in, they might frighten the burglar off and call the police.

The illustrations just provided, as well as the others offered in this chapter, do not provide a sophisticated explanation of crime, but they call attention to some of the group dynamics that make a difference. The way people perceive and interpret the world around them influences their actions, but the factors that influence those perceptions and interpretations are not always of their own making. It is appropriate to end this chapter with a study that links some of these ideas to other elements in the society.

Social Ties and Their Impact on Norms and Expectations

In order to control children, or adults for that matter, and see that they are following the norms of society, we have to know what they are doing. We audit books of a company to be sure they are behaving properly, we reveal certain aspects of our lives to assure others that we are not doing something wrong, and if parents are to socialize their children properly, they need to know where they are and what they are doing. Based on this last assumption, Barth, Watson, and Blanchard (1966) did a survey where they asked the following hypothetical question:

> Suppose that a young girl, about fourteen, was seen by some neighbours climbing out of her first floor bedroom late at night, after her parents were in bed, to keep a date with a boy who picked her up in a car.

The respondents were then asked:

> In this situation, what do you think the neighbours *should* do? What do you think most of the people actually *would* do? What would you, yourself, do in this situation?

The first question represented the preferred norms, what *should* people do. This is the *right* thing to do. Of course, people do not always do what they should. We expect them to fall short of the mark some of the time. The second question represents the *expectations*, the sort of thing people would do in reality. Finally, what would you do? Would you do the *right* thing? Or would you hold back somewhat?

The respondents were also asked to answer these questions depending on their relationship to the girl's parents: 1) friends, 2) acquaintances, or 3) strangers. The results are summarized in Table 10.1

The data show that, under conditions of close friendship, there was a very high consensus on the proper course of action. If the neighbours were friends, 95% of the subjects thought they should tell the parents that their daughter was climbing out of windows at night. This was the *right* thing to do. Telling the neighbours was clearly wrong; that would be gossiping. Only 5% thought you should say nothing to anyone. As the social ties or degree of intimacy with the neighbours decreased, so did the obligation to tell the parents, dropping to 74% for acquaintances and 48% for strangers. However, it was clear that one should *not* gossip with neighbours, even though, in the case of strangers, telling no one came close to the norm of telling the parents (44% compared to 48%).

Having established the norm, the *right* thing to do, one might ask what is likely to happen in reality. Would your neighbours do the right thing? The expectations fell short of the norms. If they were friends of the girl's parents, the respondents thought people would follow the norms fairly well, reporting the behaviour 85% of the time, but the respondents expected acquaintances and strangers to fall below the norm. In fact, they would do what one should not do, that is,

Table 10.1 Norms, Expectations, and Predicted Behaviour in Reporting a Deviant Act

	Tell Parents	Tell Neighbours	Tell No One
Norms: What *should* the neighbours do if they were:			
Friends of the parents	95%	0%	5%
Acquaintances	74%	3%	23%
Strangers	48%	8%	44%
Expectations: What *would* the neighbours do if they were:			
Friends of the parents	85%	7%	8%
Acquaintances	40%	38%	22%
Strangers	11%	47%	42%
Prediction of *Own Behaviour* if parents were:			
Friends	94%	0%	6%
Acquaintances	68%	4%	28%
Strangers	34%	13%	53%

Source: Barth, Watson, and Blanchard, 1966.

gossip, or tell the neighbours. In the case of acquaintances, it was 38% and strangers, 47%. In other words, with the decline of intimacy the respondents felt that others would violate the norms.

When asked to predict their own behaviour, the respondents reported a pattern similar to the norm. Of course *they* would follow the proper course of action. If the parents were friends, the respondents said they would tell the parents in 94% of the cases. Absolutely none of them said they would tell the neighbours. Even if the parents of the 14-year-old girl were strangers they would tell the parents 34% of the time, much higher than the 11% they would predict for others. They confessed they might gossip in 13% of the cases, but certainly they were much better than other neighbours, who would gossip 47% of the time.

How much faith should we put in the respondents' assessment of their own behaviour? I can't speak for you, readers out there, but of course *I* would certainly do the right thing. If Morris Milgram asked me to move a lever, sending a shock to the person in the next room who began groaning in pain, *I* would quickly tell Dr. Milgram to take his shock generator and stuff it. If I were with those teenagers who broke into the cottage as described in Robertson Davies' book, *I* would have strenuously opposed their vandalism. You wouldn't catch *me* driving fork-lift trucks into grain sacks the way those nasty boys did. *I* would certainly not become a nasty guard in the Stanford Prison Experiment. A young lady in distress, yelling to get a table off her, would assuredly find *me* quickly at her side. On my honour as a Canadian criminologist, *I* would have done what was right.. ... Or would I? ... Or would you? And would the respondents of the survey above have really acted according to the norms they expressed in the first portion of the survey? It is probably more realistic to assume that people would act according to the *expectations* expressed in the second portion of the survey, rather than according to the *norms* expressed in the first part. In fact, some of the studies reviewed above suggest even poorer performance on the part of most people. Surely, we were surprised at how many people were willing to give severe shocks on the instruction of the experimenter. It is surprising that, under certain conditions, people did nasty things or failed to do the "right" things. However, the Barth, Watson, and Blanchard study suggests that when people are friends, they are more likely to follow the norms.

It appears that friends communicate more accurately with each other. Assuming that most of us respect the norms of society, is it important to have conditions where people form more genuine friendships? To what extent are groups of boys *really* friends? When they are unsure of themselves and less confident in the quality of their relationships, are they more inclined to respond to dares, to do something outrageous? One might argue that, when people are comfortable and secure in their relations with others, they may be freer to disagree, to express values that are consistent with their convictions. They may be under less pressure to portray themselves according to expectations they assume other people have. Is "pluralistic ignorance" reduced; that is, do we make fewer false assumptions among friends about other's expectations for us? At times those expectations, especially among male groups, could lead to conditions and situations that are criminogenic.

CONCLUSION

Normal people do strange things, including criminal acts, under a variety of different situations. Criminologists, of course, focus on the dynamics that produce crime, but may neglect those that produce prosocial behaviour. My argument is that similar dynamics are operating, and therefore, students of criminology should be asking what makes people do the *right* thing as well as the wrong thing. Characteristics of the individual, including socialization, will not provide adequate explanations of criminal behaviour. At the same time, what the individual brings into a group situation can make a difference.

Some of the difficulties of sorting out these factors are illustrated by attempts to explain why some people helped Jews escape from the Nazis during World War II (Fogelman and Wiener, 1985). While some made deliberate decisions to rescue Jews, others got involved accidentally. One person reluctantly agreed to let his secretary's husband hide from the Nazis in his office. As he was drawn into the situation, he became more compassionate, eventually rescuing about two hundred people. Some were very religious, others were atheists, and surprisingly, a few were even anti-Semitic.

In their attempt to explain why these people helped Jews, Fogelman and Wiener (1985) searched for differences in their backgrounds, but this can lead to another type of error. When rescuers are asked to look back on the factors that led them to take action, they also have potential explanations in their minds. Do they reconstruct motives and socialization practices in such a way as to "explain" their actions? It is possible, of course, that these reconstructions will become perceptions of their world, rather than accurate descriptions of the factors that influenced their behaviour *before* they played the role of rescuer.

Fortunately, we do not need "final" explanations before applying knowledge to policy decisions regarding crime. Although the arguments about television raised in the last chapter have not been resolved, there is enough evidence to suggest that some of our current media practices are potentially dangerous. When it comes to group dynamics, even our imperfect knowledge suggests that there are ways to structure some of our activities, settings, and communities to increase the likelihood of prosocial behaviour.

CHAPTER 11

SOCIAL INTERACTION: FAMILIES, FRIENDS, AND SCHOOLS

I have on my table a violin string. It is free. . . . But it is not free to do what a violin string is supposed to do – produce music. So I take it, fix it in my violin and tighten it until it is taut. Only then is it free to be a violin string.

Sir Rabindranath Tagore

INTERACTION IN THE FAMILY

Criminology books organize ideas into compartments, even though the border-lines between explanatory arguments are fuzzy. This chapter focuses on theories that emphasize families, friends, and schools. The family plays a central role in control theory and several Canadian scholars have made important contributions related to these ideas.

Ties to Conventional Society: Control Theory

The notion of "social control" arising out of social bonds that link young people to families and significant others has been part of the thinking of many criminologists. Two American authors are summarized, to provide background. Then a Montréal study is presented, to indicate that policy implications are inherent in this research.

Walter Reckless — Containment Theory

Walter Reckless was an early contributor to "control theory" (Reckless, Dinitz, and Murray, 1956). His version was called "containment theory" and contributed insights into crime committed by relatively normal people. Reckless asks: What makes people conform? He suggests that there is an inner control or containment system, as well as outer containment.

Inner containment focuses on components of the self: self-control, good self-concept, high frustration tolerance, sense of responsibility, goal-orientation, ability to find substitute satisfactions, tension-reducing rationalizations, and other characteristics that have become internalized.

Outer containment represents characteristics of the surrounding world that provide restraints: a consistent moral front presented by family and others, institutional reinforcement of norms and goals, a reasonable set of social expectations, effective supervision and discipline, opportunities for acceptance and identity, as well as safety-valves for dealing with crises.

These containments act to restrain the tendency of juveniles to get into trouble because of *internal pushes,* such as restlessness, hostility, anxiety, and the need for immediate gratification (Reckless, 1967:469-483). There are also *external pressures* arising out of poverty, unemployment, being a racial minority, and limited opportunity. *External pulls* would include delinquent companions, membership in deviant groups, and the mass media. To a large extent, Reckless attempted to synthesize current knowledge in a comprehensible manner, but his attempts to test these ideas have been criticized for a variety of reasons (Schrag, 1971:84; Schwartz and Tangri, 1965).

Travis Hirschi — The Social Bond

Like other control theorists, Travis Hirschi does not ask: Why do they do it? Instead, he assumes that most people would commit crime if they dared, particularly children. Thus Hirschi focuses on why people do *not* commit crime, what prevents them from becoming lifelong criminals. An individual's *bond* to society, largely through the family, ties individuals to social groups. We are moral beings to the extent that we have internalized the norms of society, and have become sensitive to the needs of others. What they think is important to us. On the other hand, if an individual does not care about the opinions of others, is insensitive to them, he is free to deviate.

Hirschi also makes certain assumptions about society; i. e., the members of society are tied together by a common value system. Morality is self-evident. Having conflicting value systems within a society is contrary to Hirschi's assumptions. Being loyal to groups that have different values would mean that a person could be tied into a group that is deviant, but Hirschi rejects this view for the bulk of crime. In a stable society, *almost everyone* agrees on what is improper behaviour, and those who are bound by the *social bond* to society will be constrained from deviant behaviour.

The social bond consists of four major elements. *Attachment* refers to the ties of affection and respect to people like parents, teachers, and friends. A strong bond with all three will be a major deterrent to crime. Parents are the most important. If families are broken by divorce or separation, the attachment can still remain strong and help children internalize the norms of society. They also have more respect for people in authority, such as teachers. Alienation from parents increases the likelihood that they will be alienated from others.

The second element of the social bond is *commitment*. To the extent that children are committed to the ideal requirements of childhood, they will be less likely to engage in delinquency. Spending time and energy on education, saving money, and other conventional activities increases one's stake in the conventional world. One avoids risk-taking behaviour and postpones drinking and other adult activities, to avoid risking that stake.

Involvement in school, family, and recreational activities doesn't leave much time for delinquency. Idleness and boredom make one consider disapproved activities. Finally, *belief* in a shared moral world-view includes sensitivity to the rights of others and respect for the laws of the land.

Biron and LeBlanc - Implications of Control Theory

At the Université de Montréal, several researchers have done empirical work on social control theory. Since this book empasizes policy implications that arise from criminological research, the work by Louise Biron and Marc LeBlanc (1977) offers an excellent illustration. The conceptual model in Figure 11.1 begins with *structural aspects* of the family, which influence the *supervision of children* and childrens' *identification with parents*. Identifying with parents leads to better *communication with children* which, in turn, makes supervision more effective. Finally, supervision and communication have an impact on *home-based delinquency*, the final variable in the model.

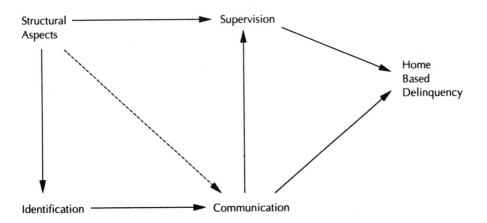

FIGURE 11.1

Source: Biron and LeBlanc, 1977.

Structural aspects of the family are measured by asking: 1) Is the mother employed outside the home? 2) Are there fewer than three children? 3) Are the parents living together? In other words, are there family characteristics that make it difficult to create the social bonds that link the adolescent to the family and the society? Using questionnaires, of course, limited the type of information that could be gathered. Admittedly, the measure of structural characteristics of the family, as stated in the three questions above, is imperfect. However, one could argue that, if the mother is working outside the home, or if there is a large number of children, supervision is more difficult. One could debate the impact of working mothers and whether Québec might differ from the rest of Canada, but for now let us simply recall the earlier discussion in the theory chapter: social scientists typically work with measures that are far from perfect.

To measure *supervision*, parents were asked if they knew where their children were and who they were with. *Identification* was measured by asking questions such as: 1) Do parents make unfair rules? 2) Do you want to be the kind of person your parents are? *Communication* was assessed by estimating the hours spent discussing things with parents and siblings. *Home based delinquency* in Figure 11.1 was measured by running away. At first, running away may not seem like a serious crime, but in reality it is highly correlated with other acts of delinquency.

Figure 11.1 also uses arrows to indicate the direction of causality. Normally, questionnaire studies at one point in time do not permit tests of causation, but statistical techniques can be used that permit causal inferences (Blalock, 1964). When Biron and LeBlanc applied the techniques for testing causality, the model was moderately supported. However, the link shown by the arrow going from structural aspects to communication did not appear to be direct. Instead, the causal link was indirect, it occurred *because of* the linkage through identification. Thus, one might argue that if the mother works (a structural aspect) it may not have a *direct* impact on communication with children. It depends on identification: whether parents make unfair rules and whether the children want to be like their parents. Thus, the link between structural aspects and communication is indirect, with a broken line. The main linkage between structural aspects and communication is through identification, as indicated by the solid arrows.

Why have I presented this tedious discussion? Testing the subtle aspects of our theories can make a difference for policy decisions. Biron and LeBlanc concluded that the structural aspects of the family were less important than anticipated. If one can improve *supervision* and *communication* in a family, even if there are structural problems, there should be a decrease in delinquency. What public policies are suggested by this research? Adequate day-care centres might assist a working mother in providing supervision. *Even if* there are divorces, if women must work, and if there are many children in a family, improving the supervision of children is one place where public policy might make a difference.

A general theme in this book is that governments can have an impact on crime. Unfortunately, the "get-tough" policies so popular with politicians do not prevent crime. The research in Montréal is compatible with a general argument supported by considerable research: strengthening families and helping with supervision lessens some of the stresses that increase the likelihood of crime in the future. Naturally, this is easier said than done, but some countries have done better than others. Sweden, for example, has made systematic efforts to provide family support. Research has assessed the impact of these programmes.

> The striking finding ... was that mothers in the different categories [of social and economic class], report similar family relations, hold similar attitudes toward child-rearing, report similar rules of child-rearing, express similar aspirations for the child, involve themselves equally actively in the child's schooling, etc. (Martens, 1981: 159).

Sweden has accomplished, at least in part, what many of our theories and research advocate: creating the kind of family environment for less privileged children that exists for those more fortunate. The Montréal study by Biron and LeBlanc points to areas where society could intervene. Sweden provides an example.

As we go through other explanations of crime, one could make similar observations about how governments could intervene. Those who claim, "theories are fine for professors, but we are talking about the real world," display ignorance of what theories are about. The work by Biron and LeBlanc is one illustration of the *direct* link between theory, empirical research, and implications for practical policy decisions.

Ties to Unconventional Society: Sutherland — Differential Association

One of the most influential explanations of crime was offered by Edwin Sutherland in 1939. In some respects it fits with learning theory in an earlier chapter, but it also provides a link between psychological and sociological thinking, which characterizes control theory. Sutherland revised his ideas in various editions of a popular criminology text, with a final version appearing in the 1947 edition. It has appeared in each revised edition since (Sutherland and Cressey, 1978). Most of the nine points in the theory can be summarized as follows:

> Criminal behaviour is learned in interaction with others in intimate personal groups. A person becomes criminal because of an excess of pro-criminal definitions. Associations with different types of others will vary in: 1) how often exposure takes place (frequency), 2) how long each exposure lasts (duration), 3) whether it takes place during the early, impressionable stage of life (priority), and 4) how close the personal bond is with the message sender (intensity). Learning crime is like other learning. While crime is an expression of general needs and

values, it is not explained by them since non-criminal behaviour is an expression of the same needs and values.

This argument cannot simply be summarized as having bad companions. Rather, it leads us to study the ratio of messages for and against criminal behaviour being sent from associates. These messages do not necessarily have to come from individuals who are criminals, nor do all criminals always present criminal definitions to children and friends. For example, some gangsters have been known to present very pro-social messages to their children, even though different messages are sent to their criminal colleagues. Similarly, a non-criminal mother may say that it is all right to steal bread if one is starving. This theory also differs from some of our previous arguments with regard to the impact of the mass media. Sutherland emphasized interaction in *intimate* personal groups. The mass media may make a person receptive, but the message doesn't have the same weight. When the TV hero corrects problems around him by leaving a trail of blood and gore, it is not the same as having a loving father send a similar message.

When differential association was first proposed, it broadened explanations beyond the personal pathology arguments that dominated criminology in the 1930s. It explained why normal, sociable, gregarious, active males in slum areas could easily become criminals, while similar boys taking part in Boy Scout activities in middle-class neighbourhoods did not. Isolated individuals would also respond differently. These ideas helped to explain why certain minority groups, lower-class individuals, and males, in contrast to females, were more likely to become criminal. Sutherland also applied his ideas to white-collar crime. Those in positions of power, who interacted regularly, reinforcing messages about the appropriateness of certain activities that were, in reality, illegal would be systematically engaged in corporate criminal behaviour (Sutherland, 1949).

There are problems with the theory, including the difficulty of measuring certain elements. For example, how does one *know* when there has been an excess of pro-criminal definitions? If one uses the commission of a crime as the indicator of such an excess, one commits the same tautological mistake we accused psychologists of making in an earlier chapter. Despite these problems, differential association has been one of the most influential attempts to explain crime.

Combining Differential Association with Control Theory — Eric Linden

One of the criticisms of control theory is that it assumes that everyone would be criminal if they were not restrained. It does not account for separate *motivations* to commit crime. This doesn't square with our knowledge of human interaction. Crime is not necessarily that attractive to everyone. In addition, some people "go along with others," even though they have reservations. Rick Linden combines differential association with control theory to provide a more complete explanation (Linden, 1987; Linden and Hackler, 1973; Linden and Filmore, 1981). For differential association, the *presence of* ties with others is crucial to provide definitions and messages that encourage crime. For control theorists, the emphasis is on the *lack of* ties with others, which would restrain antisocial behaviour. Originally, Hirschi felt those who had ties with peers, even deviant ones, would be less delinquent than those with no ties at all. Linden argues that the *direction* of the tie, conventional or unconventional, is also important. Lack of ties with the conventional order not only frees the individual to deviate, it also increases the likelihood of association with deviant peers and a source of definitions favouring crime. This extension of control theory explains more of the variation in delinquency than can either of the parent theories alone (Linden and Filmore, 1981; Linden and Hackler, 1973). The relationship among the interacting variables is shown in Figure 11.2.

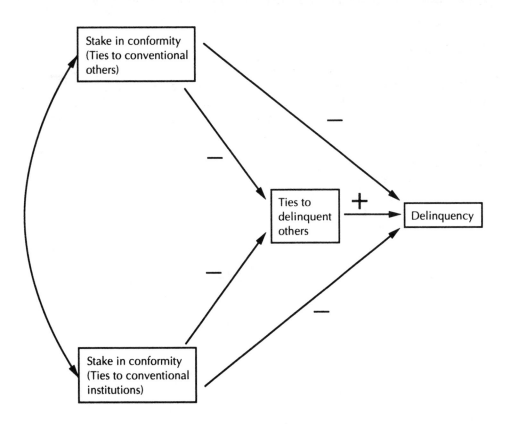

FIGURE 11.2 The Relationship Between Control and Differential Association Variables

Source: Linden and Fillmore, 1981.

Research by David Brownfield and Kevin Thompson of Erindale College, University of Toronto also supports the idea that taking peer relationships into account is important to extending the implications of control theory (1991), and personality characteristics and social status were incorporated into control theory models by scholars at the University of Montréal (Caplan and LeBlanc, 1985; Fréchette and LeBlanc, 1985; LeBlanc and Tremblay, 1985).

Gillis and Hagan (1990) note that the nature of the social bond may differ for delinquents. On self-reported questionnaires, delinquents do not express the same willingness to be Good Samaritans as conventional juveniles. However, in crisis situations involving direct and instant intervention on behalf of family or friends, the delinquents expressed a greater willingness to intervene. It appears that the notion of delinquency as simply being produced by a lack of social ties does not adequately take into account the nature of the networks that link delinquents to others.

Extending Control Theory and Differential Association to Economic and Political Elites — John Hagan And Rick Linden

Social control theory is typically applied to lower-class adolescents, but John Hagan (1991: 100-103; 1985: 170-174) notes that economic and political elites often find themselves relatively free of the ties that restrain most of us from criminal behaviour. Some powerful individuals feel that they are above the law. They operate in areas where the general public has difficulty assessing their "badness." Robbing a bank is clearly wrong, but when corporate leaders appoint each other to serve as directors on the company boards, and then vote themselves many privileges, it is harder to evaluate their wrongdoing. They have fewer ties to ordinary people. The powerful rationalize their behaviour. Without being constrained by the disapproval of intimates who would be shocked at their actions, such individuals are psychologically free to pursue their interests without moral or legal constraint. Hagan uses the Watergate affair in the United States as an illustration. After an unsuccessful break-in of the Democratic National Headquarters in Washington's Watergate complex, it became clear that powerful people were regularly committing crimes during the early 1970s. These events finally lead to the resignation of President Richard Nixon and the imprisonment of some of his aides.

Hagan asks a basic social control theory question: Why aren't all upperworld citizens criminal? One might answer that inner and outer restraints operate to keep most of them, to a reasonable degree, in line. However, the inner restraints, such as morality, seemed to be lacking in the Watergate affair. The principal actors were not ashamed of their criminal behaviour. Thus, only outer restraints, the risks imposed by other institutions and their representatives, needed to be assessed. Since these external control mechanisms also seemed to be weak, violating public trust became more likely as the main actors saw some clear rewards and the risk appeared to be low.

In his reading of the transcripts of the case, Hagan notes that there were few references to societal values, to those internal constraints that arise from an uneasy conscience. Instead, there were discussions of the rights and obligations of the executive branch and the limits of executive privilege. In addition, the criminals in this case were also the people who controlled the institutions of social control. It is ironic, however, that the criminals of Watergate had a high stake in conformity. Control theory argues that people calculate the costs of breaking the rules, but it appears that Richard Nixon *mis*calculated those costs over and over again. The price paid by the criminals in the Watergate affair was clearly much greater than they had anticipated.

One could argue that the way Linden combines differential association with control theory offers an even better explanation of the Watergate affair and upperworld crime than the use of control theory alone, as suggested by Hagan. Powerful members of the economic and political elite *learn their behaviour in interaction with others and provide consistent definitions which favour "bending" certain rules.* When Hagan reviews white-collar and corporate crime in Canada (1987), he does not explicitly use the social control model he has offered elsewhere, nor does he consider the combined model suggested by Linden and Fillmore; but the conditions Hagan describes in his chapter on white-collar and corporate crime appear to fit the combined theory suggested by Linden and Fillmore, summarized above. If Edwin Sutherland were alive today, he would approve of this use of differential association, since he clearly saw adequate explanations of crime as part of broader theories of behaviour. Linden and Hagan have carried on this tradition.

Contrasting Control and Learning Theories

Theories call attention to different factors and sometimes suggest social action. This point is illustrated by contrasting social control and learning theories, which underscore modelling. While learning theories emphasize what the role models *do*, control theory emphasizes the *nature and quality* of the social bond. Let us consider tobacco use — the most dangerous drug, as far as health is concerned, currently being used in North America. Our discussion of drugs will be postponed until later, but we can all agree that it would be desirable if young people could grow up as non-smokers. The question is: which is more important, the closeness of the bonds that parents establish with their children or the role model they present?

According to control theory, parents who smoke, but also have close ties with their children, should be able to inhibit drug use on the part of their offspring. Many of us are aware of children who nag their parents extensively about their smoking, sometimes because of the close ties of affection. The parents agree that their behaviour is unwise, convey the message that the children are correct to oppose it, but plead human frailty. The message and the social bond can be more important than the role model.

Learning theory would make a different argument. Close ties with drug-using parents might *not* inhibit juvenile drug use. Modelling may be more important. The desire to imitate parents may make juveniles decide that smoking is the proper thing to do. In fact, close ties with the parent may increase the likelihood of imitation.

Clearly, a combination of a good role model and close parental ties would be preferred, but in a complex social world it may be important to ask which variable is more important — the social bond or modelling behaviour. In addition, we may also wish to condition young people to respond to drug users, such as smokers, in a tolerant way. An argument will be made for such a strategy later, when we discuss *reintegrative shaming*, where pressures are placed on people to change while still considering them members of our community. Ideally, we might wish to have young people, as well as adults, disapprove of crime, be surrounded by those who behave properly, be bonded to intimate others who behave well and preach the correct messages, but simultaneously be ready to encourage others who are in error to change their ways rather than cast them out of normal society.

Family Factors and the Low Rate of Female Criminality

Questioning the Traditional Female Stereotypes — Ngaire Naffine

In his well-known work on control theory, Hirschi (1969) excluded females from his analysis, even though he had collected data from them. Since women have higher levels of conformity than men, they are seen as having stronger attachments to the conventional world. In addition, they experience higher levels of parental supervision than boys. Ngaire Naffine offers a different view on female criminality (1987). She is critical of the view that females are passive, compliant, and dependent, and thereby bonded to the conventional order. Nor does she share the view that "liberated" females become more criminal. Law-abiding women are not helpless and insipid, clinging to conventional society. Rather, they are responsible, hardworking, and immersed in conventional activities. They are rational in their decision not to place the gains achieved by the feminist movement in jeopardy by committing crimes. Being involved in both work and child-rearing, modern women already have more powerful attachments to conventional society. Thus, Naffine would argue that increases in female crime, if there are any, should be seen as a response to the increased economic marginalization of women, rather than as a result of liberation from traditional female roles.

So far, theories have been reviewed that link individuals to society. However, peer groups can create subcultures of their own which may develop norms contrary to the dominant society. These subcultures may then influence behaviour and also the ties with others. But how do subcultures evolve?

INTERACTION AMONG PEERS

Albert K. Cohen — The Subculture of the Gang

When Albert K. Cohen presented some very influential ideas about the "subculture of the gang" (1955), few efforts had been made to link group dynamics and social ties. Cohen argued that the middle class establishes certain standards for behaviour in school, a "middle-class measuring rod." This includes an emphasis on good appearances, selling oneself, restraining aggression, being sophisticated, displaying respect for authority, and deferring gratification. The theories during this period ignored female delinquency to a large degree, on the assumption that juvenile crime was primarily a male problem and that girls did not face the same type of problems. The proper middle-class boy works hard at his paper route, saves money to go to college, and so on. Adherence to these standards makes one popular with teachers and leads to success in school.

Lower-class children may not be socialized in the same way. They are told to stick up for their rights, not to let others push them around. Adult role models from the lower classes also provide a different set of norms. Winning a few hundred dollars at Bingo may lead to buying drinks for all your friends at the pub, displaying generosity rather than putting money away for a rainy day. These lower-class standards of behaviour may serve to integrate one into male peer groups, which probably have chauvinistic attitudes towards females and a somewhat devil-may-care outlook towards life, but such a world-view rarely makes boys popular with the more straitlaced expectations of his middle-class teachers. These boys do not do well against the middle-class measuring rod, and achieve relatively little status in the classroom.

Reaction Formation and Mutual Conversion

What can the young male do when things are going poorly in school? One possibility is to change — adopt behaviour consistent with the middle-class measuring rod. This is not easy. The teacher may not even recognize such efforts. There may be little support from home, in terms of facilities, such as encyclopedias, quiet rooms for study, or in attitudinal support from parents. A second possibility is to withdraw and become something of an isolate. A third option is to alter your immediate social world. This might be achieved through *reaction formation*, a psychological mechanism for redefining standards, from those that cannot be achieved to standards that are achievable. The middle-class norm is to defer to authority. This can be changed to: don't let people push you around. The middle-class student is polite to the teacher. This can be changed to: don't suck up to the teacher. The middle-class student dresses in a presentable way: the gang wears jeans at half-mast, unique hairdos and leather jackets ripe with many months of sweaty wear in hot weather. And so it goes. The middle-class rules have been reversed, turned up-side-down. These new norms are now achievable for those who failed in the past.

However, *reaction formation* does not come into existence spontaneously. It evolves through collective action brought about by *mutual conversion*. It is a gradual process. Imagine that a boy, who has done poorly in school, is on his way home to the wrong side of the tracks. He is walking with another boy who also finds school unattractive. "How did you like school today?" asks the first. The second responds cautiously, "How did you like it?" "Not much," says the first. "Neither did I."

Each boy tests the waters carefully. How did you like the teacher? ... Not much ... She isn't always fair ... I think she stinks ... Each boy sticks his neck out a little further. They respond as most of us do, cautiously sending out signals when we are not sure of the feelings of others. Gradually, however, the boys find that they have similar ideas. Or they mutually convert each other towards norms that are contrary to the middle-class measuring rod. It is also possible that the final convergence is more extreme than the views held by the individual boys.

Certain individuals can also be defined in new ways. "What do you think about the little girl who sits up front and wears pink ribbons?" "You mean the one that brings an apple for the teacher?" "Yeah, the one whose father is a professor." (The first boy asks himself: could the other boy like this little girl? I'd better be careful.) "She always does her assignments." "I think she's the teacher's pet." (OK, he does-n't like her either.) "I think she's a kiss-ass." "She's really stuck on herself." Notice that the boys do not offer firm opinions at first, but lead up to it. Again, the final con-clusion may be more extreme than the original opinions held by either. When this process goes on among a number of boys who are losing out in the conventional school system, Cohen argues that they can create a delinquent subculture and a gang with values contrary to those of the dominant society.

Once the subculture is established, the new norms make the action of the gang very visible. Their toughness is advertised. Fighting is a way of gaining status. Having a "rep" and "heart" provides prestige within the gang. As the gang mem-bers increase their solidarity and loyalty to one another, they become more isolated from the conforming society. In control theory terms, the bonds with conven-tional institutions, such as school, and possibly family, become weakened. In dif-ferential association terms, their interaction with deviant peers provides many definitions favourable to violating the law. Even pluralistic ignorance, as discussed earlier, adds to the criminal norms. Each youth may *assume* that others hold more criminal norms than he. Thus, more extreme members of the gang may be perceived as expressing universal standards.

Some Implications of Criminal Subcultures

As losers in the dominant system turn to the deviant subculture for support, sta-tus can only come from the gang. Cohen warns us that these phenomena can occur when societies go through certain crises. Hitler rose to power with the Nazi Party, which gave young males who were unemployed and unsuccessful a chance to define themselves as superior. Today, similar pressures appear to be operating, particularly in the former East Germany. Young men who have not done very well under communism now find themselves part of a larger Germany, which also defines them as second class. Being "losers" in several respects, it is understandable that they, in turn, would blame others for their situation. Immigrants, particularly those with different-coloured skin, make ideal targets. The racist young males in eastern Germany today may be responding to factors similar to those facing German youth more than half a century earlier. As they become more dependent on their fellow gang members, the negative opinions of conventional members of society become less important to them.

As long as societies can provide opportunities for the vast majority of their young people to succeed in conventional society, these gangs may recruit relatively few members; but in pre-World War II Germany, the high unemployment rate provided potential members for Nazi organizations. Cohen's ideas should be reconsidered for the current period. The link between failing in school and/or the workplace, criminal subcultures, and extreme political parties should not be forgotten.

SCHOOL ATTACHMENTS — WHO NEEDS THEM THE MOST?

Allen Liska and Mark Reed (1985) offer insights into control theory that are relevant to Canada. The relationships among the variables in control theory should be seen as being *reciprocal*. That is, one factor influences a variable which, in turn, has a counter-influence, either directly or indirectly. For example, attachment to school affects delinquency but delinquency, in turn, influences school attachment. Furthermore, some of these dynamics may differ by race. An attempt to explain the sophisticated statistical techniques used by the authors will not be attempted here, but the reader can appreciate that dealing with causal and reciprocal relationships can be complex. However, a simplified argument is still useful.

Figure 11.3 suggests that parental attachment affects delinquency, which affects school attachment which, in turn, affects parental attachment. In other words, the bonds with parents reduced delinquency, but influenced school attachment less. In fact, being delinquent was more inclined to reduce attachment to school than the reverse. Being delinquent could threaten relations with parents as well, but Liska and Reed suggest that attachment between parents and their children is less conditional on behaviour. Even when juveniles act badly, parents still support them. By contrast, the link that ties teachers to their students is more dependent on behaviour. The social bond in the other direction, from student to teacher, may be

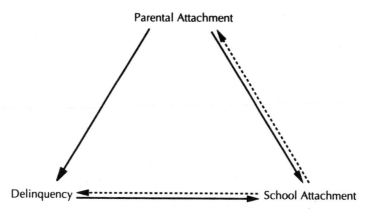

FIGURE 11.3 Ties to School and Delinquency: Possible Reciprocal Effects

A pattern which may be appropriate for white boys but not for black boys. The arrow from School Attachment to Delinquency appears to be stronger for black boys.

Source: Liska and Reed, 1985.

overrated, at least for white boys. The notion that students control their delinquency in order to curry the good opinion of teachers is questioned. Perhaps bonding with their teachers is more relevant for younger students, but for adolescents, the good opinion of teachers is less important than that of their parents.

For black students, however, Liska and Reed found a strong effect of school attachment on delinquency. Is it possible that school is the only link to conventional institutions that is available to many black youths? Thus, black youths who aspire to college and decent jobs may place more importance on relationships with teachers; avoiding crime might also be part of their thinking.

Would these ideas have merit in Canada? Do minorities see the school system as being more meaningful than the majority population? One might suspect that an immigrant family from Hong Kong would view success in the schools as an important step towards success in the larger society. It is less clear how the Native peoples of Canada view our school system, although one might argue that there are some parallels between the school success rates and crime rates of Native youth in Canada and black youth in the United States.

The causal structure of psychosociological forces is much more complex than the simple models that have been offered by most social control and related theories, but policy implications are evident. Just as the work of Biron and LeBlanc indicates that providing support to struggling families might reduce delinquency, the Liska and Reed work suggests that making schools attractive to marginal youth may also deter delinquency. These ideas are not original, but they are frequently put aside while more politically expedient ideas prevail. For example, punishing parents of delinquent children is a popular theme expressed by many indignant citizens from time to time. However, there is little evidence that parents who are struggling with problems of their own benefit from further harassment. While most of the theories offered here are crude, they offer superior guidelines to the sort of comments frequently offered by politicians in the press.

A Developmental Theory of Delinquency

Many of the recent theories on crime are explicitly stated in causal sequences. While this makes it more difficult to test some of these theories, there are clear advantages for clarifying time sequences. If one is hoping to launch a delinquency prevention programme, it helps to know if one's efforts are directed towards conditions that *precede* potential delinquency. The Opportunities for Youth Project in Seattle produced a body of data that was utilized by several Canadian scholars (Hackler, 1966; Hackler and Lautt, 1969; Hackler and Linden, 1970). The theory was created to guide the strategy of a delinquency prevention programme and has occasionally been reprinted in collections of readings (Hackler, 1988). Figure 11.4 spells out the sequence.

The developmental sequence systematically links specific variables in a causal chain, as follows: (1) Having low esteem leads to (2) the anticipation on the part of others that ego will act badly or at least not be able to act properly; this leads to (3) ego's *perception* that others anticipate improper behaviour if (a) opportunities to play conforming roles are perceived as blocked by those in dominant positions, such as teachers, and if (b) ego views the self-relevant responses from primary and non-primary significant others as valid; this would lead to (4) the development of a delinquent self-concept, which leads to (5) the search for roles compatible with a delinquent self-concept; this leads to (6) delinquent behaviour; and finally leads to (7) the selective endorsement of delinquent norms through dissonance-reducing mechanisms.

While these ideas are similar to many other sociological arguments, they treat the role of norms differently. Traditionally, we assume that people have certain norms and attitudes which guide behaviour. The above formulation argues that such norms and attitudes are the *product* rather than the *cause* of behaviour. That is, people get involved in activities and then justify that behaviour by rationalization and adopting new norms. Admittedly, the relationship between norms and behaviour is more likely to be of a reciprocal nature, as described by Liska and Reed above. However, if the dominant causal direction is for deviant norms to develop *after* actual deviance, it would have certain implications for intervention. With the above model, one would not attempt to change delinquency by changing the attitudes or norms of youth. To be effective, one should start at the *beginning* of the causal chain. It is difficult, however, to change the esteem of a boy or his family (Step 1 in Figure 11.4). We assume that certain groups will be held in low esteem

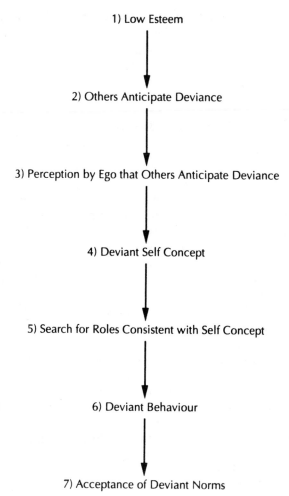

1) Low Esteem

2) Others Anticipate Deviance

3) Perception by Ego that Others Anticipate Deviance

4) Deviant Self Concept

5) Search for Roles Consistent with Self Concept

6) Deviant Behaviour

7) Acceptance of Deviant Norms

FIGURE 11.4 The Sequence in a Developmental Theory of Delinquency

in certain communities, and changing that status would be far beyond most delinquency prevention programmes. Step 2 is also difficult to alter. Teachers and others who are in contact with children frequently anticipate that children from "the wrong side of the tracks" will be more delinquent than those from higher-status families. Ideally, we would like to change teachers, police, and other representatives of societal institutions, so that they do not anticipate deviance from low-status groups, but in the Opportunities For Youth Project, we felt it was more realistic to focus on Step 3. Could we change the *perception* of the boys that other people actually thought they were *not* delinquency-prone? The experimental programme focused on this particular variable. The main experimental techniques utilized (1) boys testing teaching machines in a structured setting, guaranteed to make them successful, and (2) a supervised work programme that made success very likely.

The portion of the programme using teaching machines asked the boys to evaluate the machines. Teachers sent a message that *assumed* the boys were capable. We wanted them to perceive that we anticipated competent behaviour. Similarly, the work experience conveyed the idea that the boys were good workers and that we naturally anticipated that they would succeed. In general, the programme aspect of Opportunities for Youth was carried out successfully, but did it have a measurable impact on delinquency? Four thousand computer tables, using forty-nine different criteria for success, suggested that, as far as delinquency was concerned, we were irrelevant (Hackler, 1966).

Nor could we determine accurately whether the various activities lead to changes, as predicted by the theory. Despite the fact that the programme activities appeared to be successful, the actual impact of the experiment on the boys was so negligible that it was not possible to test any of the theoretical possibilities (Hackler, 1978; Ch. 3). What does one make of such a result? One possibility is that most of our programmes have little impact on the lives of young people. Opportunities for jobs with real futures may have permitted a test of these ideas, but one day a week for a year did not make a great deal of difference.

However, the data gathered in the study were used for less direct tests of causal sequences (Hackler, 1970). The data analysis supported the causal theory somewhat, but was not particularly convincing. In addition, Hagan (1973) points out that the patterns of relationships displayed were compatible with the proposed causal sequence, but they were equally compatible if the anticipations of others, such as teachers, were *accurate* in their predictions of deviance. The causal model argues that various adults in the community, such as school teachers, *anticipate* deviance on the part of juveniles who come from low-status families. The assumption made in the OFY project was that boys from low-status families were really just like everyone else, and it was the *anticipation* of their deviance by their teachers, correctly perceived by other boys, who then developed deviant self-concepts, etc., which finally led them to delinquent behaviour. But as Hagan points out, if boys from the wrong side of the tracks *in fact* were more delinquent, and if teachers correctly predicted that delinquency, the data would appear the same as those predicted by the causal model. In other words, simply using a causal format for a theory of delinquency does not necessarily lead to clear tests that support or reject a theory. Of course, if a theorist simply states that certain variables are related, without stating a causal sequence, the tests become even weaker. An even wider variety of plausible explanations will be consistent with the same set of findings. The OFY project illustrates that even well-conceived research projects do not always yield clear results.

Implications for Policy

This proposed causal theory of delinquency, like the other theoretical ideas discussed here, is not offered as a particularly adequate explanation of deviance. They may suffer from a variety of weaknesses, but causal theories provide more opportunities for rigorous testing, modification, and rejection. If they are supported, they give clearer indications to policy-makers. They indicate what might happen if certain changes were made. For example, if the causal theory of delinquency had received more support, teaching machines and supervised work might be promising delinquency-prevention tools. Actually, the project produced mixed findings (Hackler and Hagan, 1975).

Another policy implication implicit in the causal model is expressed by the sequence of Steps 6 and 7 in Figure 11.4. The claim is that deviant attitudes and norms will *follow* deviant behaviour. In other words, boys become deviant not because of the attitudes they hold, but because they are striving to play a coveted role. *After* engaging in deviant acts, boys will justify their behaviour by endorsing deviant norms, thereby reducing dissonance which would result from discrepancies between behaviour and the attitudes they hold (Festinger, 1957). For example, when a well-socialized Mormon is offered a drink, he usually refuses because this behaviour would be incompatible with deeply held norms. However, if the Mormon finds himself in a situation where the social pressures lead to drinking, he faces a dilemma: his behaviour and his norms are at odds. If the pressure to continue drinking persists, it is quite possible that the Mormon would begin to rationalize, and finally come to believe that drinking is not so bad after all.

What does this discussion have to do with crime and delinquency-prevention programmes? Many programmes assume that if they can just change boys' attitudes, the behaviour will change. If, in fact, the sequence goes from behaviour to attitudes, instead of from attitudes to behaviour, then such programmes would be similar to shutting the door after the horse has left the barn.

CONCLUSION: A GENERAL LESSON REGARDING THE APPLICATION OF THEORIES OF SOCIAL INTERACTION

The average citizen may wonder why criminologists have not produced scientific theories that lead to effective prevention or rehabilitation programmes. There are many pitfalls in transferring research findings into social action. The social interaction models reviewed here concentrate on individuals, families, and small groups, but when these insights are applied to actual programmes and social policy, other things must be considered. These ideas neglect factors external to individuals, their families, and groups. Thus, it should come as no surprise that our growing knowledge of human behaviour does not automatically lead to effective anti-crime policies.

Although psychologists will frequently disagree, those of us with a sociological orientation might argue that the theories discussed so far will *never* be very adequate as a basis for social policy. The developmental theory suggested in Figure 12.4 may be somewhat correct in claiming that a juvenile's perception of what others think of her is important; but if families are worried about having enough money to pay the rent and buy food, the impact of other factors may be hard to detect. Elliott Currie (1985:248-252) identifies a number of family-support programmes that do make a difference to delinquency, but they offer a range of services which have a small impact in different ways. The weakness of the Opportunities for Youth Project, and other crime-prevention programmes that follow the logic based on theories presented here is that they focus on a *few* critical variables. In reality, there are *many* variables, which contribute in small ways and interact with each other to have a meaningful impact. Until factors that influence the structure of society can be modified, efforts at this small-group level may not be effective. Thus, the next chapter moves from small groups to characteristics of the larger society.

FOCUSING ON THE STRUCTURE OF SOCIETY — THE CONSENSUS TRADITION

We hang little thieves and take off our hats to great ones.

German Proverb

SOCIAL STRUCTURE AND CRIME[1]

Previous chapters focused on individuals in a variety of small-group settings. It is not possible to develop a complete explanation of crime by looking at a single level of abstraction; that is, by focusing on individuals or on small groups. Nor is it possible to explain crime by looking only at the characteristics of societies. However, for those interested in social policy, theories that deal with the structure of society provide particularly useful suggestions for reducing crime.

Theories that integrate psychological and sociological levels of thinking into an integrated theory will eventually be needed. At present, such attempts are still in their beginning stages, and therefore it is useful and more understandable to simplify things by reviewing explanations at a single level. When we concentrate on the "structure" of society, we are not being very precise. However, there are some important sociological traditions that take a broad view of the way societies function. Before these characteristics of society can be translated into crime at the individual level, several links are needed. Thus, theories of crime that focus on the structure of society are inevitably somewhat crude. On the other hand, policymakers may find this level appropriate for introducing change. When attempting to reduce crime, it is unrealistic to talk about cures. Rather, we should be asking if we can achieve a modest reduction in crime. Changes at the societal level, then, may be practical even though they are difficult to predict.

---

[1]Portions of Chapter 9, "Strain Theories" (Hackler, 1992) have been incorporated into this chapter.

THE CONFLICT-CONSENSUS DEBATE

It is convenient to think of two major orientations towards explaining crime. The older tradition can be viewed as the *consensus* perspective. This approach assumes that the vast majority of the population holds similar views regarding right and wrong. Morality is universal, with values being shared by all members of the society. Customs persist, and the laws represent a codification of societal values. This perspective assumes that people who go through the criminal-justice process and are convicted would be the criminals. Thus, adjudicated offenders represent the closest possible approximation to those who have, in fact, violated the law. They are the people whose behaviour needs explaining. Although most citizens acknowledge that powerful, upper-class law-breakers are less likely to be arrested, tried, and convicted than lower-class offenders, a traditional perspective would agree that those who have been convicted of crimes are more criminal than those who have not been convicted.

The *conflict* perspective on what is crime and who is the criminal questions such assumptions, and argues that criminal law may be regarded as part of a body of rules that prohibit specific forms of conduct and indicate punishment for violations. The character of these rules, the kind of conduct they prohibit, the nature of the sanctions, etc. depend on the character and interests of those powerful groups in the population that influence legislation. In other words, the set of rules that represents criminal law does not necessarily represent the moral values of the majority, but will vary depending on which groups are in a position to create and enforce those laws. The social values that receive the protection of the criminal law are ultimately those that are treasured by the dominant interest groups. It is not the *majority*, but rather the most *powerful*, whose values and concerns will be represented in the justice system. Ronald Hinch of the University of Guelph has organized these *conflict* theories into categories (1992), and we expand on these ideas in the next chapter. This chapter reviews some historical traditions that reflect the *consensus* perspective.

THE CONSENSUS PERSPECTIVE — STRAIN THEORIES

Consensus theories assume a reasonable degree of agreement on things that matter in society. One assumes that large portions of the population share these views. Crime occurs when people are subjected to unusual influences. Those special, crime-producing influences come from strains, frustrations, or stresses generated by the way society is organized or evolved. The term *strain theories* has been used in describing these ideas since the 1970s, even though the ideas are much older. They emphasize adaptive processes that arise from barriers to success or the failure to achieve widely held expectations.

While it is convenient to separate our discussion into the consensus and conflict perspectives, the reader should be aware that this arbitrary classification oversimplifies reality. It may be more appropriate to think of particular crimes as being of the consensus or the conflict type. In most societies, there is a high level of agreement that robbing someone and doing them bodily harm is a crime. Other activities, such as smoking marijuana and committing adultery, will lead to less agreement regarding the need for criminalization. Laws regarding homosexuality illustrate not only varying attitudes, but changes in attitudes and laws over time. Thus, elements of consensus and conflict are always present in modern societies.

Durkheim: The Functions of Crime and Anomie

In his book *Division of Labour in Society*, first published in France in 1893, Émile Durkheim argued that social solidarity, that is, social groups working together towards agreed-upon goals, was an essential characteristic of human societies (1933). In pre-literate societies social groups were isolated and self-sufficient. There was little division of labour outside of the family. All men had similar skills and all women did similar work. Such societies had *mechanical solidarity*.

Modern industrialized societies, by contrast, have a highly developed division of labour, with individuals specializing in unique tasks. Since individuals are dependent on others, group solidarity evolves because of this diversity. We need each other to satisfy our needs. This type of interdependence Durkheim called *organic solidarity*.

Crime was normal, even necessary, to define the boundaries of that which was acceptable and for the creation of laws that would identify certain behaviour as criminal (1933). The process varied in different types of societies. In societies with mechanical solidarity, crime served several functions. Since everyone was so uniform, deviance was easy to spot and reaction against the offender strengthened social bonds. Crime is also functional in that it reminds members of a community about the interests and the values they share. Community bonds are strengthened. The deviant act inspires indignation. And, even more important, deviance reassures the "good" members of a community that their morality is the acceptable one. Since crime is functional, society encourages, or at least permits, a certain amount of deviance.

In addition, crime tested the social limits, making groups evaluate social norms. In complex societies, pushing the legal limits led to change. When Judge Emily Murphy pushed for legal rights for women, she was not content with laws as they were. The same could be said when Louis Riel led a revolution in Manitoba. Mahatma Gandhi and Martin Luther King clearly opposed the established authorities, and Jesus Christ was a deviant in his day.

There must be a balance between the functional and dysfunctional aspects of deviance. Excessive crime and deviance would destroy a society, but if there were none at all, society would be compelled to create some. Even in a society of saints, someone must push the limits of proper behaviour. For Durkheim, every society needs its quota of deviants.

The Dilemma of Diversity

If a society is made up of many different elements, social cohesion is more difficult to achieve. There will be less consensus on what is good, and a higher rate of crime. This simple explanation has been generally supported in many different situations. It also presents us with a dilemma. If we believe in a heterogeneous and diversified society where people with different cultures, languages, and tastes can mix, there will be more problems of social cohesion and crime. Some of us are not happy with the implications of such explanations. We feel that diversity makes for interesting societies, leads to expanded ideas, and helps us to be tolerant. For example, the Canadian prejudices against the Chinese and the Japanese during the first fifty years of the twentieth century have gradually given way to tolerance, acceptance, and finally the appreciation of valuable cultural traits which enrich Canada. Similarly, adapting to both English and French cultures leads to stress, but it also generates mechanisms for dealing with diversity. There is a price, however. Diverse populations have more crime.

Anomie and Normlessness

Durkheim popularized the concept of anomie to explain crime in more advanced and differentiated urban societies. Heterogeneity and increased division of labour weakened traditional societal norms. The resultant changes loosened the social controls upon people, allowing greater materialism and individualism. When social cohesion breaks down and social isolation is great, society loses its traditional social control mechanisms and crime increases.

In his classic work on suicide, Durkheim argues that similarity of attitudes leads to social cohesiveness (1951). Suicide, crime, and general deviance are inhibited in cohesive communities. By looking at religious similarity in various districts in France, Durkheim noted that some communities were homogeneous with regard to religion; that is, 100% Catholic or 100% Protestant. Other communities were heterogeneous, perhaps 50% Catholic and 50% Protestant. Those communities with great similarity in religion tended to have low suicide rates, while heterogeneous ones tended to have higher suicide rates. Although one could certainly measure homogeneity and heterogeneity using other variables besides religion, (for example race, language spoken, etc.), it is interesting to see that similarity on *religion alone* had a powerful explanatory value. One can also extend this argument from the specific act of suicide to crimes in general. That is, lack of similarity leads to less social cohesion and, finally, to more crime. In other words, suicide and crime are both products of societies that are less cohesive. Of course, cohesive societies may be less able to change and adapt.

Durkheim's theory may have merit, but I am not content with a theory that tells me that we have to be more homogeneous to reduce crime. Instead, I want a theory that tells me how to attain a diverse, multi-racial, multilingual society which still has a reasonable degree of social cohesion and a reasonably low rate of crime. In other words, I want theories that provide policy guidance in directions that fit my values.

Merton: The Gap Between Aspirations and Means

In the 1950s and '60s the most cited article in criminology was by Robert K. Merton (1938), where he discussed social structure and anomie. Crime was viewed as a symptom of the *dissociation*, or gap, between *culturally prescribed aspirations* and the *socially structured avenues* for realizing those aspirations. The culturally prescribed aspirations are the *goals* held up for all members of society. Merton argues that in America the accumulation of money, and the status that results from material wealth, is a universal goal. Socially structured avenues, such as schooling, are the accepted institutionalized *means* of reaching these goals. Socially structured avenues to achieve these universal goals are no problem for well-off members of the society. If father is a medical doctor, it is more realistic for the son to aspire to the same occupation and social status. One attends schools that condition students towards thinking about a college education, and the home environment encourages reading and getting good grades. Although certain individual characteristics, such as minimal intelligence, may be required, the means to achieve culturally prescribed aspirations is available to many middle-class youths.

By contrast, the son of an immigrant family, or a member of a racial minority, could find things more difficult. If the father has abandoned the family, if an older brother has been in trouble with the law, and if mother has been on welfare, the means to achieve success is not readily available. A youth coming from such an environment may not respect the school system, his grades may be poor, and his likelihood of entering college could be minimal. However, he might also like to be a doctor and have both the material and social rewards that accrue to that occupation.

The gap between goals and means is small for certain portions of the society but large for others. The strain resulting from the gap between goals and the means to achieve those goals could result in "innovation," often criminal in nature. In simpler terms, when society encourages people to want things, but makes it difficult for certain groups to get them, they are more likely to steal, sell drugs, cheat on their taxes, or go into prostitution.

Merton's argument seems to fit many forms of lower-class crime. It may also fit certain upper-class crimes where people aspire to great wealth. The legitimate avenues to success may not be sufficient because of severe competition; other business people may be "cutting corners" in a variety of ways. Thus, if there is a gap between the desired goals and the means, innovation or illegitimate tactics are more likely.

Opportunity Structures and Their Influence on Crime

Durkheim argued that human aspirations had to be regulated and channelled. Since human aspirations are boundless, and people cannot always have what they want, they must be persuaded to accept what they receive. When people are not persuaded, society becomes anomic, and moral guidelines are unclear. Social control breaks down and some people violate the norms of those in power.

While Durkheim emphasized the restraints that control crime, Merton focuses on opportunity structures. He begins his argument similarly to Durkheim's and suggests that American society has an overriding dominant goal, material success, but the guidelines for achieving that success are not always clear. If this type of anomie is so widespread, however, why isn't crime distributed evenly throughout society? Merton accepts the argument that crime is distributed unevenly, that it is higher in the urban slums, for instance. To explain this social-class-specific crime by anomie, he redefines anomie as the disjuncture between the cultural goal of success and the opportunity structures by which this goal might be achieved (Box, 1971: 103-106). This is another way of explaining the gap between culturally prescribed aspirations and socially structured avenues, as described above. Anomie was shifted from normlessness, according to Durkheim, to *relative deprivation*. Instead of viewing an entire community as anomic, specific individuals felt deprived if committed to the goal of wealth, while barred from the means that would lead to the realization of this goal.

Interpreting Merton

A frequent application of Merton's work has been to explain delinquency. Many scholars have worked to translate these ideas into measures that could be tested empirically. Debates arose over what Merton meant. Were his ideas intended to explain the behaviour of individuals or, as Thomas Bernard would argue, the behaviour of aggregates or groups (1987a)? Bernard argues that it is not correct to interpret *strain* or *anomie* in psychological or social psychological terms; instead these are properties of social structures. Merton uses the word *anomia* as the sociological counterpart of the psychological concept *anomie*. According to Bernard, Merton's theory suggests that societies whose cultures overemphasize monetary success and underemphasize adherence to legitimate means will have high rates of instrumental (in contrast to irrational, impulsive) crime. If legitimate opportunities to achieve those monetary goals are unevenly distributed, then instrumental crime will be unevenly distributed.

One must note the distinction between *cultural* factors and *structural* factors in a society. In societies where structural features create an uneven distribution of legitimate opportunities — that is, where there are many blocked opportunities — there will be pockets of instrumental crime, regardless of cultural values. *Individuals* facing blocked opportunities would be those who were more criminal. If, by contrast, the culture emphasizes the ruthless pursuit of wealth and everyone has equal opportunities, then crime will be widespread, and such a *society* will have a high rate of crime. Both elements could be operating, and one might argue that the United States is the best illustration of such a society today.

Perhaps Bernard is correct in his warning that Merton's ideas should only be applied at the societal level, but many of us find it useful to apply Merton's ideas to individuals (Agnew, 1987). For example, Merton describes one type of adaptation to strain as *innovation*, where there is an acceptance of cultural goals but rejection of institutionalized means. It is easier to visualize *persons* who are frustrated in their striving for monetary gains than aggregates. Whether or not Merton meant to confine his arguments to groups is an appropriate debate for scholars, but one can also ask if the hypothesis applies to individuals. We are less concerned with fairness to Merton than with the validity of various interpretations and extensions of these influential ideas.

Some Criticisms of the Concepts Used by Merton

Gwynne Nettler is critical of the clarity of Merton's concepts (1984). Is what people *say* they want out of life an adequate measure of their *aspirations*? When asked what we'd like, it is easy for us to answer — money and status. But Nettler questions the uniformity of wants or values in society, at least in terms of acting on those wants. The serious offender may have a philosophy that is different from the majority, in terms of being cynical, hedonistic, hostile, and distrustful. Citing Hy and Julia Schwendinger regarding the philosophy of serious offenders, you should "do unto others as they would do unto you ... only do it first"; and, "If I don't cop it ... somebody else will." (1967, p. 98)

Nettler also feels that the concept of "opportunity" is vague. Is there a difference between *perceived* opportunities and *real* ones? "*Opportunities are by their nature much easier to see after they have passed than before they are grasped.*" (1984, p. 209) If people do not end up equally happy and rich, is this due to differences in opportunity? We must avoid the tautology, or circular argument, of explaining the cause by using the outcome. Problems over the meaning of these concepts have led to considerable debate, as scholars have tried to develop operational definitions to test these ideas.

Merton's strain theory is also unhelpful in the explanation of lower crime rates for women. Merton takes into account differences in opportunity that arise out of social class, but does not apply the same reasoning to blocked opportunities based on gender (Comack, 1992). Women, like disadvantaged lower-class males, might be expected to be more criminal as a means to achieve universal goals. While many conventional theorists have assumed that women experience less strain than men in the struggle to achieve through institutionalized means, many feminist scholars reject these statements as assumptions and biases rather than fact (Morris, 1987; Naffine, 1987). While the strains women are subject to may differ from those experienced by men, they may be just as severe. Unless one assumes women have more modest goals, strain theory does not explain why women are less criminal.

Despite these arguments, or perhaps because of them, no theory of crime has engendered as much work by criminologists. For decades, sociologists found support for these ideas. Critics joined the debate during a later period. Recently there has been renewed interest in strain theory, but the debate gets rather involved. Instead, let us summarize some original ideas by Sol Kobrin, who noted that communities differ in the availability of opportunities (1951).

Kobrin: Opportunity Structure in Different Communities

Although there may be strains that create a pressure towards criminal behaviour, there are also different opportunity structures that facilitate breaking the law. Some communities, or some situations, may not provide opportunities for crime even though individuals are discontented. In one of the most seminal articles in criminology, Sol Kobrin (1951) argues that opportunities differ in various communities, which could be organized in the following typology suggested originally by Clarence Schrag.

Kobrin points out that we live in communities that sometimes offer a variety of opportunities, both legitimate and illegitimate. The means available to attain aspirations within these communities are, in actuality, not just present or absent; rather, they offer a range of possibilities. Figure 12.1 simplifies those possibilities to make the theoretical point, and treats opportunities as simply available or not. If communities have legitimate opportunities and/or illegitimate opportunities, four types of communities are possible. No community actually fits the pure examples illustrated in the figure, but there are approximations.

In Type I communities, there are illegitimate opportunities as well as legitimate ones. One might call this type of community a "stable slum," where prostitution, gambling, and a variety of other illegal activities are well organized. The organized criminal element may concentrate on certain activities and avoid, or even discourage, violence and other types of crime that would upset the community and the forces of control. In such stable, lower-class neighbourhoods, one

Type of Community	Type I "Stable Slum"	Type II "Transitory Slum"	Type III "Suburbia"	Type IV "Unlikely"
Legitimate Opportunities	Present	Absent	Present	Absent
Illegitimate Opportunities	Present	Absent	Absent	Present

FIGURE 12.1 Typology of Community Opportunity Structures Implicit in Kobrin (1951)

would expect a number of legitimate opportunities that reflect the normal, ongoing activities of a city. This would include restaurants, stores, repair shops, and the like, and the normal economic activities that would arise to meet the needs of any urban society. In fact, well-organized illegitimate activities might provide the capital for legitimate economic enterprises. This typology oversimplifies reality. In actuality, there will be gradations in terms of opportunities, but it is useful to think in terms of ideal types.

The Type II community might be called a "transitory slum," as typified by a decaying housing project. In such a disorganized community, there is extensive unemployment. No business dares to establish a store in the neighbourhood, because of the fear of robbery. Paperboys do not deliver in the area, because customers would lose their papers, the paperboys might be attacked, and newspaper publishers would find it unprofitable. Restaurants are not established; thus, there are few opportunities for waitresses, dishwashers, or cooks. In other words, it is an area with very few legitimate opportunities for earning money. Even the illegitimate opportunities are unprofitable, because the neighbourhood is poorly organized. Prostitutes find it dangerous to work there, those who wish to gamble go to the more stable slum areas, and although the residents may frequently attack each other, the pickings are slim. In these disorganized areas, crimes are more likely to be predatory and vicious. There is little community life and families are poorly integrated. Minimal opportunities exist in either the legitimate or illegitimate world.

The Type III community, "suburbia," has legitimate opportunities but no illegitimate opportunities. Teenagers can find work mowing lawns, especially if the neighbour knows that the teenager comes from a reliable family. Paper routes are available, and because of various contacts in the community, juveniles may learn of opportunities for summer work and other part-time jobs. The adult and adolescent worlds are involved in economic activities, which create opportunities for work and the anticipation for future work. On the other hand, illegitimate opportunities are rare. If some of the young ladies reading this book decided to sell their bodies to earn a little money, they might have difficulties wandering about their suburban communities, approaching men walking their dogs. Even if they went downtown to the appropriate streets, their middle-class background leaves them unskilled in this business, and the competition might make them unwelcome. Similarly, college students from middle-class homes may be unsuccessful selling an armful of stolen hubcaps door-to-door in suburbia. In other words, suburbia may be lacking in illegitimate opportunities.

What about the Type IV community? Although such a combination is theoretically possible, it is unlikely that any neighbourhood could develop a wide range of profitable illegitimate opportunities without also spawning some legitimate ones. If the illegitimate opportunities were well organized, we would expect restaurants, stores, laundries, and other facilities to develop, to provide those stable lower-class communities with normal services. If either organized crime or the citizenry had things fairly well under control, the community could become viable. Control mechanisms may differ in such neighbourhoods, but a community with well-organized illegitimate opportunities alone is very unlikely.

Kobrin (1951) emphasizes the *dual* characteristics of lower-class communities. Both legitimate and illegitimate opportunities exist together in greater or less degree. How these two structures interact and what draws people to one versus another has generated considerable debate among sociologically oriented criminologists. Policy-makers must take community characteristics into account and be aware that a uniform strategy is unlikely to work, because of the different nature of communities.

Richard Cloward: Illegitimate Opportunity Structures

Just as there are differences between legitimate and illegitimate opportunities, there are different *kinds* of illegitimate opportunities. Francis Cullen points out the importance of "structuring variables" (1984: Ch. 3). Richard Cloward asserts that simply being subjected to socially generated strain does not enable a person to deviate in any way she chooses. People can only participate in a given adaptation if they have access to the means to do so (Cullen 1984:40). Even though lower-class persons may be under a great deal of strain, they are less likely to engage in violations of financial trust, political corruption, and other white-collar crimes in order to achieve their goals. Such opportunities are simply not available.

In an article (1959), and then in a book with Lloyd Ohlin entitled *Delinquency and Opportunity* (1960), Richard Cloward extended the ideas of Merton by combining them with themes found in Sutherland's "differential association." Sutherland argued that criminal behaviour is learned through associations with others who define criminal activity favourably. While Merton emphasized *legitimate* means, Sutherland called attention to the concept of *illegitimate* means (Cullen, 1988). People under strain cannot become any kind of criminal they choose; they are limited by the opportunities available to them. Dealing in drugs is not automatically available to a "square" college professor as a means of supplementing his income; he probably lacks the skills and contacts. In other words, illegitimate means are not readily available to anyone simply because they lack legitimate means. While Durkheim and Merton developed plausible theories of structurally induced pressures, they did not explain the resulting adaptive behaviour as Cloward tries to do.

Merton appreciated Cloward's insights and extension of his ideas. The editor of the *American Sociological Review* persuaded Merton to write a commentary on Cloward's 1959 manuscript, which appeared immediately after that article. Merton noted that earlier research indicated five times as many criminals convicted of fraud in Texas as in Massachusetts. Perhaps it was more difficult to sell someone a dry oil well in Massachusetts than in Texas. Illegal opportunities for certain types of fraud are clearly more available in some areas than others.

Opportunity theory fits many different types of deviance, but Cloward and Ohlin are best known for the application of these ideas to juvenile delinquency. Although undergoing "strain," juveniles face different barriers to resolving that strain. The way they respond to social barriers for achieving goals could lead to three different types of gangs or subcultures, namely, *criminal, conflict*, or *retreatist* gangs. Herbert Costner, in lectures at the University of Washington, used the diagram illustrated in Figure 12.2 to explain how these gangs were formed.

There are barriers to conventional goals and middle-class values, such as respectability and conventional success. If one overcomes those barriers, as most middle-class juveniles do, there is little crime. However, the lower-class male may actually have different goals. Instead of respectability, he may be more interested in money, a car, and, assuming he shares the chauvinistic views of many of his peers, having a "good-looking chick" on his arm. Under certain economic conditions, this might be achieved by working in areas where his skills are scarce, working in a hazardous occupation, or possibly being fortunate as an athlete. In other words, it is possible to be successful in a working-class style of life. These ideas differ somewhat from Merton's in that aspirations are not *universal* as Merton had argued. Striving for success can mean different things to different people.

Cloward, however, emphasizes the barriers to lower-class goals as well as to middle-class goals. Even if certain working-class people aspire to different things,

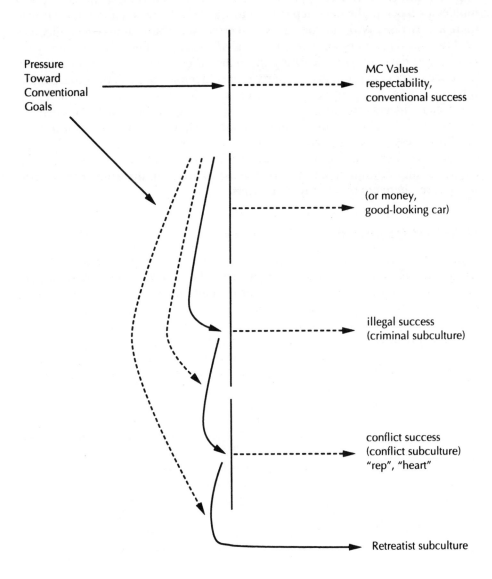

FIGURE 12.2 Barriers to Legal and Illegal Opportunities Implicit in the Work of Cloward and Ohlin (1960)

the means to achieve them, even working at unskilled jobs, are not necessarily available. But crime has an opportunity structure of its own. If legitimate opportunities are blocked, the next step may be to search for illegal success, but even here there are barriers. Without contacts with certain subgroups, it may be difficult to get into illegal gambling or learn the skills of a successful safecracker. Many juveniles will have difficulty learning the skills necessary to succeed. However, if there are barriers to profitable property crime, juveniles can still turn to a conflict subculture as a means of attaining status, at least among their peers. Juveniles unskilled as thieves can show their bravery by fighting for their "turf." This demonstrates "heart," and their courageous behaviour will give them a "rep." But even conflict success has barriers. Not every juvenile is keen on wielding a bicycle chain in a gang war. One may lack strength or courage or both. These juveniles may employ a third delinquent alternative: the use of drugs. In the drug or "retreatist" subculture, there are practically no barriers.

Marginal Opportunity Structures

Francis Cullen (1988) feels that many scholars have not fully appreciated the extensions made by Cloward, because they focused on the gap between aspirations and perceived opportunity. In fact, other deviant adaptations become apparent when one looks beyond traditional types of crime and at different settings. Fred Desroches describes the way some men adapt to pressures related to homosexual activity in public restrooms in Ontario (1991). The "tearooms," those public toilets where homosexual activity takes place, provide an opportunity structure for those under certain types of strain. Desroches does not attempt to explain why these men engage in the activity, but he adds Canadian content to ideas put forward by Laud Humphreys (1970). Whatever it is that drives men to the public restroom for homosexual activities, alternatives do not seem to fill the need; thus, this marginal opportunity structure is used, with the risk that police action will create additional problems in their lives.

Another marginal opportunity structure is illustrated by the oil company spy. In Alberta, many oil companies drill wells in wilderness settings and try to keep their findings secret. Spies from rival companies sometimes pose as hunters or fisherman to observe drilling operations without being detected. This activity can be hazardous, but it highlights the presence of particular opportunities and particular barriers to potentially profitable tasks. Kobrin and Cloward have applied these ideas to conventional crime, but there may be a much wider range of marginal behaviours that might fit these models.

Figure 12.2 indicates a number of barriers or "structuring variables" that influence the choice of activities. If all opportunities are blocked, skid row may be the alternative. P.J. Giffen describes the "revolving door" in Toronto, where skid row alcoholics go in and out of jail on a regular basis (1966). If the retreatist subculture is the end of the line for certain types of delinquents, we might argue that skid row represents a similar situation for those who find other barriers insurmountable.

Which Is Better: Marginal Opportunities or None at All?

The question of opportunity structures, including illegitimate ones, poses an interesting policy question for society. Which is more desirable: having skid-row alcoholics with no opportunities, or having people engaged in marginal criminal activities? Prostitutes and gamblers engage in activities that are seen as deviant by society. Is this better than a skid-row lifestyle? While legitimate opportunities are clearly preferable to illegitimate ones, is it possible that the integration of some borderline, or even obvious, deviance would be better than the total breakdown represented by some of society's rejects? In a society that must sometimes choose between levels of evils, would policy-makers be wise to consider the nature of different opportunity structures and assess the impact of selected illegitimate opportunities on society?

Empirical Evidence for the Theory of Illegitimate Opportunity Structures

Cloward's theory of illegitimate opportunity structures suggested that specific types of subcultures would develop. According to Figure 12.2, he predicted three distinct types of gangs, corresponding to the criminal, conflict, and retreatist subcultures. However, there has been little empirical evidence for three distinct types of gangs corresponding to these adaptations (Short and Strodtbeck, 1965). It seems that stealing, fighting, and drug use were more likely to be found in combination rather than in distinct subcultural forms. Even though specialized subcultures are not readily apparent, the idea of barriers to illegitimate success has been a major contribution. Other characteristics, such as race, may be related to some of these barriers. Thus, Asian youth in Vancouver may have opportunities to work with Asian gangs who extort money from restaurant owners, while Black youth in Toronto and Montréal may be more represented in drug subcultures, finding it more difficult to overcome barriers to both legitimate and certain illegitimate success. Violence and drugs may be the only things left. In Canada, Natives' abuse of alcohol may also be influenced by barriers to both legitimate and illegitimate opportunities.

Do certain groups assess opportunities correctly? Young Black males in Chicago seemed quite aware that they would face financial problems if they got married and raised children (Short and Strodtbeck, 1965: Ch. 2). In periods of depression, Native people in Canada, Blacks who have lived in Nova Scotia since the American

Revolution, Jamaican immigrants in Toronto, Haitian immigrants in Montréal, and others, probably have a realistic view of the barriers to material success, both in the short and the long term.

Educational versus Financial Goals

Some critics, such as Hirschi (1969), argue that the gap between aspirations and expectations is not as meaningful as the aspirations themselves. He believes strain is redundant as an explanation of delinquency; goal commitment is enough (Kornhauser, 1978). Margaret Farnworth and Michael Leiber (1989) provide evidence of the potency of educational aspirations but, in addition, find that the *dysjunction* between economic goals and educational means is an even better predictor of delinquency. That is, those who want lots of money but don't anticipate college are more likely to be delinquent. As opportunities for education decrease in Canada, along with less employment, the criminogenic conditions described by Farnworth and Leiber seem to be increasing.

THE POSSIBILITY OF MULTIPLE GOALS: CRIME IN THE FACTORY

So far we have been viewing crime as something disruptive. Is it possible that complex societies have multiple goals that are often in conflict? Is crime necessary as a way of achieving a balance among these goals? Bensman and Gerver (1963) describe a factory where one task was to assemble plates of metal that utilized recessed nuts and bolts. At times the plates got out of line, and it was not possible to get the bolt to turn into the recessed nut. Under these conditions, a tap was sometimes used. A tap is a cutting tool of extremely hard steel, which can be used to rethread the recessed nut. When this is done the holding power of the bolt is weakened, and the improper work cannot be seen by an inspector. In this factory, the use of such a tap was "illegal" and provided grounds for immediate firing. However, the tap was used from time to time.

New workers were socialized into the way the tap was used. It was not to be used carelessly or unnecessarily; but despite the dangers of getting caught, there were times when the tap expedited the flow on the assembly line. The new worker was constantly reminded of the dangers: "If it snaps, your ass is in a sling." New workers who displayed the appropriate caution and followed the informal rules regarding the use of the tap eventually bought their own and occasionally loaned them to others in need. When a foreman asked him to perform a tapping, the worker had established his identity.

The agencies of "law enforcement" in the factory had several levels. The purchaser of the product had the ultimate control, but there were only two inspectors from the purchaser in the plant. The second level of control came from the 150 plant quality-control inspectors. They fraternized with the workers and hoped they would not "louse him up." The inspector could not maintain quality simply by his efforts alone. Thus, he counted on the willingness of the workers to do good work. Since the penalties for the use of the tap were so severe, an inspector was hesitant to report a violation. There were subterfuges: don't use the tap in the presence of an inspector; an inspector may move a tap to the bottom of a tool box, expressing his good will and his awareness of what goes on; at times the inspector may catch a worker and issue a stern reprimand.

The third level of enforcement lay with the foreman. Like the inspectors, the foreman gave a tongue-lashing to the occasional new man caught using the tap. The foreman usually made it clear that it was only his intervention that kept the man on the job. One learned not to use the tap unless it was absolutely necessary. The worker was obliged to accept the reprimand. If he took it lightly, then the foreman genuinely got mad. The worst crime was to take the rituals surrounding the use of the tap lightly.

Note the contradictions in behaviour. On the one hand, the foreman taught the use of the tap and assisted in evading rules; on the other hand, he performed rituals of punishment. A certain "double-think" was necessary. The foreman was primarily concerned with production, not quality. Despite the emphasis on the illegality of the tap, and the fact that its use was grounds for immediate firing, no workers were ever fired when they were caught.

The taps were also brittle and could break, leaving the tell-tale piece in the recessed nut. Naturally, the company tool room did not supply taps, but it did supply tap extractors to remove the piece of a tap that had been left behind.

As we attempt to explain the persistence of tapping in this factory, deviance, in the sense of rejecting the norms of the social system, does not fit here. Tapping is intrinsic to the system. The "crime" is as central to the system as the norm it allegedly violates. It is difficult to say what is functional and what is dysfunctional. If one attempts to use the Mertonian scheme, what are the goals of the *system*? It may be possible to locate the goals for *individuals* in a system, but the goals of the system are much more difficult to specify.

There seems to be a multitude of goals, which have different meanings for different people in the system:
the company wants to earn profits;

the purchaser wants a high rate of production, good quality, and low cost;

the foreman wants production and promotion. Maintaining his production quota is the means for his private goals;

The inspectors want to get along, to avoid "buying" jobs that might be rejected later. The tap represents a compromise;

The worker needs to get the work done and stay out of trouble.

The semi-secret use of the tap represents a way of bringing these diverse goals together.

What may be a means for one group may be a goal for someone else. Production is the goal for the worker and for the foremen, but it may be the means to achieve profitability for the company. "It is the plurality of ends (goals) that accounts for 'deviant behaviour' rather than the conflict between means and ends (goals)." (p. 596) Different goals become more salient for different persons in the system. If you accept the dominance of the ultimate goal and view crime as a conflict between means and goals, you overlook the possibility that this conflict is really conflict between the means to one goal and the means to another. Crime is not a form of anomie here. The use of the tap is not innovation, but rather a permanent part of the organization. The major result of this conflict of goals is a form of double-think, where the major crime is to show lack of respect for the ceremonials surrounding the use of the tap. The major crime is the violation of the rules of criminal behaviour. It is important to note that the use of the tap is rigidly controlled. A careless worker is ridiculed and sent elsewhere, but is never fired. This would expose the practice.

Another Definition of Crime

This leads Bensman and Gerver to a new definition of crime:

> A 'crime' is not a crime so long as its commission is controlled and directed by those in authority towards goals which they define as socially constructive. A violation of law is treated as a crime when it is not directed and controlled by those in authority or when it is used for exclusively personal ends (p. 598).

This study calls our attention to the fact that, in a complex society, the goals and means to achieve goals differ for various groups and various individuals. At times, the system will not fit together very smoothly. Bensman and Gerver have tried to give us a new definition of crime; but when we look at the above statement more carefully, four situations are possible, as described in Figure 12.3.

In Figure 12.3 we have the use of the tap falling in Cell 1, directed by those in authority towards goals defined as socially constructive. The opposite diagonal, Cell 4, is clearly a crime according to Bensman and Gerver. But what about the other two cells? If the activity is directed by people in authority but the goals are defined as unconstructive (Cell 3), is it a crime? Who is going to define the activity as unconstructive? If the manager of a furniture factory is having a crew make furniture privately for him on the side, that would probably be defined as criminal. If an auto manufacturer decides not to shift the position of a gas tank, even though aware that many deaths and injuries will result, should this be defined as a crime? (In the case of the Ford Motor Company a court decided it was not.) If the province of Alberta refuses to pass seat-belt legislation that would protect children, should this be seen as criminal? While one might agree with Bensman and Gerver that

		Directed by People in Authority	
		Yes	**No**
Goals Defined as Socially Constructive	Yes	No Crime	?
	No	Probably Crime	Crime

FIGURE 12.3 A Classification of Questionable Behaviour

breaking rules in society under the conditions existing in Cell 1 might not consti-tute crime, other combinations are less clear.

The other diagonal (Cell 2) provides different problems. When environmen-talists or peace advocates protest in ways that are illegal, such activity is not directed by people in authority; yet some would argue that the goals are socially con-structive. To what extent can people who lack authority break the law without being considered criminal? It may depend on how many people they can con-vince that their goals are those shared by the larger society.

Misbehaviour by Those in Authority

When the RCMP broke the law many times in Québec, breaking into buildings and stealing property belonging to certain political parties (Canada, 1981), how did the public respond? The activity was directed by people in authority; and the goals, at least as defined by those in power and by much of the general population, were probably defined as socially constructive. Thus, were the RCMP activities crimes?

The ideas offered by Bensman and Gerver would be very traditional according to the more radical criminologists, but they call attention to the *structure of society* and to the multiplicity of goals in the various segments of society. They point out difficulties in using the structural-functional approach to explain crime as a re-sponse to striving towards a common universal goal.

ASSESSING CONSENSUS, FUNCTIONALIST AND OPPORTUNITY THEORIES

Despite renewed idebate over strain theory, there is considerable agreement that the contributions emerging from Merton, Kobrin, and Cloward are still useful (Bernard, 1987a; Bernard, 1987b; Agnew, 1987; Cullen, 1988; Farnworth and Leiber, 1989). Nor do traditional theoretical perspectives have to be seen as distinct and competing explanations. There has been a convergence of ideas that permits strain theory, differential association, and control theory to complement one another. In addition, the policy implications of the different theories can be similar. For example, enabling the disenfranchised to participate more fully in what society has to offer is probably related to greater social bonding with others, and a stronger belief in the rules that guide the larger society. However, if social bonds are primarily with people who condone or rationalize criminal behaviour, and with those who face similar blocked opportunities, criminal behaviour is likely. In such situations, control theory, differential association, and strain theory complement each other.

When Durkheim introduced his ideas, the scholars of the day were explaining crime primarily by genetics and inner psychological forces. Durkheim turned the attention towards social forces, a radical idea at that time, but it is now the dominant view for explaining crime. His attempts to explain the link between crime and modernization may not be completely accurate, but the basic ideas have had broad applicability. They make considerable sense for patterns of crime that have evolved in Western Europe, and also in Eastern European socialist countries and the emerging nations of Asia, Africa, and Latin America as they move towards modernization (Shelley, 1981).

Durkheim was less correct in his description of premodern nations as stable, crime-free societies. In fact, many had, and still have, high levels of violence. Furthermore, there seems to be a long-term decline in crime over the last few hundred years in Western countries (Gurr, 1981). Despite the continual complaints we hear today, during the seventeenth century the average citizen in most cities in Western Europe would rarely leave the security of a locked home after dark.

Merton's distinction between means and ends also presents some difficulties. Why did Olympia and York, the company owned by the Reichmann family, borrow twenty billion dollars and invest so heavily in real estate, buy Gulf Canada, and build futuristic office buildings at Canary Wharf in London? Did they want more money? Or is it more realistic to see a blurring of means and ends? The process of achieving may be as important as the achievement itself. It would be difficult to explain the behaviour of the Reichmann family or the Bronfmann family in terms of striving for wealth. Doing the job well becomes both the means and the end. Thus, an explanation of crime that concentrates on a *gap* between goals and means may be inadequate if goals and means become blurred.

Kornhauser (1978) argues that delinquents have *both* low aspirations and low expectations. Such youths are not strained because they don't expect to get much, but they don't want much either. Elliot Liebow's work among street-corner men illustrates these ideas. Among these Black, lower-class men, values were not passed from father to son as part of a valued cultural heritage, but both father and son experienced the same failures and maintained certain fictions to protect themselves against these failures. ("I got divorced because I was too much of a man for any one woman.") These fictions have been interpreted as "lower-class culture," but Liebow concludes that, "what appears as a dynamic, self-sustaining cultural process is, in part at least, a relatively simple piece of social machinery which turns out, in a rather mechanical fashion, independently produced look-alikes (1967: 223)." It is the *structure of society* that guarantees blocked economic opportunities, not *culturally induced values* that create unrealistic aspirations. Liebow feels that these men are driven to do things they would rather not do, not by cultural values, but by socially structured situations that guide behaviour. Liebow's strain theory does not reject Merton, Kobrin, and Cloward and Ohlin. However, it argues that the behaviour of these lower-class males is "independently produced" by similar social forces.

Neglecting the Question of Gender

A long-standing deficiency of most strain theories is their neglect of the gender issue. Differential rates of crime for men and women have frequently been discussed by criminologists, and some strain theorists might argue that women are less concerned about educational and economic opportunities, or that the female role is not as subject to stress as the male role. Such assumptions have clearly been questioned. Traditional thinking in this area illustrates male biases and ignores the stresses and frustrations that women face in the work place and in the family. Opportunities appear to be more limited for women; stresses may actually be greater than those faced by men. Why aren't they more criminal? It remains to be seen whether strain theories can be recast to explain the continuing lower crime rate for females.

Other evidence that questions strain theory comes from a study showing that blocked opportunities were more associated with delinquency among Whites than among Blacks (Cernkovich and Giordano, 1979). Blacks may develop an attitude of resignation towards future occupational goals. It is also possible that strain and delinquency are the result of degradation and loss of status that occur when juveniles fail in school. They may not be viewing school as a means to an end, but failure in itself is demeaning and frustrating. In a broader sense the whole notion of opportunity structures may not take into account the fact that people can find satisfying roles in life that do not emphasize material success. The skilled craftsman may take pride in his work, the academic may be comfortable in his role, but material success could be modest. Merton's contribution overlooks the broader notion of simply having a niche, even a modest one, as part of being a conforming member of society. Thus, strain theory calls attention to some characteristics of society that create situations that increase the likelihood of deviance, but it might be wiser to view these ideas as heuristic rather than as complete explanations. They call our attention to *settings* that might be potentially criminogenic.

POLICY IMPLICATIONS

The Application of Strain Theory: Employment for Ex-Felons

Strain and other theories suggest that having a job would help individuals to avoid crime. Thus, helping ex-felons find and hold jobs should also reduce crime. While such an idea seems obvious, only recently has the evidence become convincing. The Transitional Aid Research Project (TARP) provided unemployment benefits to released prisoners in Georgia and Texas. The findings suggest that unemployment benefits can be helpful, but one should be careful not to reward ex-inmates for not working (Berk, Lenihan, and Rossi, 1980). Successful work experiences also help to break a vicious cycle of self-defeating behaviours and attitudes that interfere with future employment (Liker, 1982). Research of this type, unfortunately, is rare in Canada.

While these social structural consensus models have their limitations, they provide suggestions for modest but meaningful contributions for improving society. Rossi believes "fine-tuning" social programmes is an appropriate role for social scientists (1980) and strain theories offer some appropriate tools.

Opportunity Structure, the War on Poverty, and Crime

In the 1960s the Mobilization for Youth Project was launched in New York City, following the principles outlined by Cloward and Ohlin (1960). This project attempted to improve education, create work opportunities, organize lower-class communities, and provide a variety of social services. There is little evidence to suggest that the project was successful in an overall sense (Maris and Rein, 1973; Short, 1975; Helfgot, 1981). However, the programme was probably unable to alter the social structural arrangements that create barriers to opportunity. Later, the programmes were taken over by traditional social-service bureaucracies, which normally act to protect and enhance their own interests. Thus, actual implementation involved attempts to change individuals instead of making basic changes in the structure of society. In his book *Betrayal of the Poor*, Rose (1972) argues that the War on Poverty in the U.S. failed because it was transformed to serve the interests of poverty-serving agencies. In Canada, little research examines this type of problem. Do we tend to reward agencies and professionals who work *with* the disadvantaged, without necessarily changing structural opportunities *for* such clients? If so, there is little reason to expect our expanding bureaucracies to reduce crime.

Opportunities for Youth (OFY) in Seattle was another attempt to use work opportunities to reduce delinquency that met with little success (Hackler, 1966). One might argue that temporary job programmes do not make a meaningful impact on the larger community. However, this same project had an impact on the attitudes of the adults living in the four communities where the project was conducted (Hackler and Linden, 1970). Furthermore, parents of Black children seemed particularly responsive and positive towards the idea of job opportunities for their children. Like so many programmes launched during the 1960s, OFY attempted to utilize strain theories. Lower-class populations did respond and became involved. Although evidence of crime reduction in the short term is lacking, the opportunity structure may have been altered for some lower-class families.

CONCLUSION: IGNORING THE WARNINGS

Scholars do not have to be in complete agreement regarding strain theory before applying many of these principles to public policy: decreasing the gap between rich and poor makes sense. Nor should we ignore the warning Merton voiced in his 1938 article: *the ruthless pursuit of profit creates a criminogenic society.* That is the basic philosophy that has guided government thinking in North America: encourage everyone to make money. Increasing opportunities for the less privileged members of society makes more sense, if the goal is to reduce crime, than some pious hope that rewarding the wealthy will encourage them to invest (for a profit, of course), so that some of the wealth will trickle down to the poor. The self-serving policies advocated by powerful people in North America during this past decade, should, according to any version of strain theory, lead to more crime.

Unfortunately, blocked opportunities for the lower classes have increased in North America in the past fifteen years. There has been a dramatic increase in the wealth available to the upper classes, but the frequent visual display of a luxuriant lifestyle, especially on television, creates all the more strain for those who aspire to a share of that material wealth.

This chapter began with a review of the structural-functionalist perspective and applied it to several situations. Durkheim argued that crime was more frequent when social cohesion was less, when there was anomie or normlessness. Merton modified the idea of anomie to that of relative deprivation caused by the gap between goals and means. The focus on opportunity structures grew out of these ideas. Kobrin showed that communities offer different types of opportunities, and Cloward suggested that juvenile gangs performed similar functions. Opportunity structures make sense for other types of crime, as well. Governments can influence these opportunity structures. Despite the criticisms, strain theory has been applied with some utility to a number of policy-relevant issues. These traditional ideas are still very useful and, at times, compatible with more radical perspectives, which are offered in the next chapter.

FOCUSING ON SOCIETAL REACTIONS, MARXIST THEORIES, AND CONFLICT

Laws are like spider's webs which, if anything small falls into them, they ensnare it, but large things break through and escape.

Solon

ASSUMING CONFLICT RATHER THAN CONSENSUS

The traditional emphasis on structural-functionalism was fairly accepting of societies as they were. Cultures and societies evolved into something that was imperfect but reasonably workable. Conflict theorists do not assume that the societies that result are necessarily desirable. In this chapter we use the term *conflict theorists* to include a variety of critical thinkers who differ from liberal-humanitarian thinkers who hope to "do good" within the framework of the current society. The liberal-humanitarians want changes, but they worry that revolutions are often disappointing. Conflict theorists are less satisfied with capitalist societies and more willing to see dramatic changes. Instead of viewing societies as stable entities, conflict theorists view modern, complex societies as collections of competing elements, each struggling to make gains, usually at the expense of others. They see evidence of economic disparity and inequalities in the distribution of power. Conflict theorists bring criminology back to some of the broader themes that are part of other sociological thinking. They are critical of the assumptions made by business and political leaders during the period of unrestrained capitalist expansion in the nineteenth century, and still accepted by many people today.

In actuality, the distinction between consensus and conflict thinking is quite arbitrary. John Lowman (1992) points out that most critical criminology concerns itself with the social construction of consensus as much as with conflict. The oversimplifications and categories used in this chapter distort many of the elaborate arguments made by those whom I lump together as "conflict" criminologists.

These ideas had only a modest impact on criminology until after World War II, even though they were raised by previous social thinkers. Robert Ratner (1984) points out that the impact was even slower in coming to Canada. A number of developments in mainstream criminology, however, led to conceptualizing crime and criminality differently, and cast doubt on ideas that had been taken for granted. For example, what did criminal statistics mean? For years many criminologists assumed that crime and delinquency statistics were good measures of criminal behaviour, but now we know that the dynamics of the agencies, as well as a variety of other factors, influence those numbers tremendously. To avoid this type of bias, Nye and Short (1957) led a minor methodological revolution by asking people (usually school children) to report on their own crimes and delinquent acts. These studies found that the relationship between crime and lower-class status was much weaker than anticipated (Nye, Short, and Olsen, 1958). Middle-class juveniles also committed many crimes, although admittedly, few of them were serious. Other studies found that the relationship between race and crime, which existed when official statistics were used, diminished considerably with self-reports.

LABELLING CRIMINAL BEHAVIOUR — A SOCIETAL REACTION APPROACH

Some criminologists began to argue that the over-representation of the poor and others at the bottom of the social hierarchy was the result of discriminatory practices of agencies of social control (Tannenbaum, 1938). It was not that they stole more; but when they did, the system reacted more strongly, hence generating biased statistics. This type of thinking led to research focusing on the agencies themselves. The labelling theorists concluded that attempts to punish or even treat individual offenders were likely to increase subsequent illegal conduct, by stigmatizing them as criminals and by modifying their self-concepts. This *labelling approach*, and its attention to the role *societal reactions* to deviance, has raised additional questions, which have provided fuel for conflict thinking.

Several scholars have summarized the labelling approach, but Clarence Schrag (1971) shows how it breaks with traditional thinking and develops links with conflict theories.

1. No act is intrinsically criminal. It is the law that makes an act a crime. Crimes are defined by groups that have the power to influence laws.

2. Criminal definitions are enforced in the interest of power groups through their official representatives.

3. A person is designated a criminal by the reactions of authorities, who confer upon him the status of outcast.

4. Dividing people into criminals and non-criminals makes little sense. Most of

the time criminals conform with the law, while some of the behaviour of supposed conformists violates the law.

5. Although many people violate the law, few are caught and singled out for special handling. This processing in the criminal justice system subjects the individual to unique experiences, which "tarnish" his image in his own eyes as well as in the eyes of others. If convicted, he is condemned not only for what he has done but also for the evils attributed to other criminals. He becomes a scapegoat.

6. Penalties vary according to characteristics of the offender. Recidivists are usually treated more harshly than first offenders, reflecting the view, "Once a criminal, always a criminal."

7. Sanctions also vary according to non-criminal characteristics of the offender. Males, the unemployed, the poorly educated, members of minority groups, transients, and residents of deteriorated urban areas are treated more severely. These categories are precisely those who continue to have high offense rates.

8. Criminals are assumed to be pariahs — wilful wrongdoers who are morally bad and deserving of the community's condemnation. This is achieved by status-degradation ceremonies. Attempts on the part of the offender to change this status by changing behaviour and attitude are likely to be unsuccessful. The public will probably not recognize such changes because the justice system dramatizes evil people rather than acts. If the former offender mends his ways, his efforts may be viewed as a devious device for concealing criminal inclinations. If he continues his criminal activities, it confirms the community's previous verdict.

9. Being labelled evil makes it difficult to maintain a favourable image. Initially, she may blame her low status on discrimination or other things beyond her control, thus resisting the negative opinion others hold. However, she will also be inclined to reject her rejectors and develop antagonism towards the community, especially its officials, increasing the probability of further offenses. Eventually she acquires the traits first imputed to her and becomes the evil person she was labelled.

Empirical Evidence for the Labelling Approach

Obviously, it is important to know which of the claims made by labelling theorists are correct, or at least to what degree. The empirical evidence is mixed, because people in different situations differ in their resistance to deviant labels. In addition, it is difficult to tell if a teacher, for example, has been giving a child a negative label or has simply been perceptive in identifying characteristics that would later lead to delinquency. Clearly, higher status people can resist negative labels even when their behaviour is reprehensible.

The term "teflon man" has recently entered our vocabulary, referring to important people to whom "the mud doesn't stick." The former Premier of British Columbia, William Vander Zalm, was charged with illegal acts in connection with the sale of his Fantasy Gardens. Although Vander Zalm was acquitted, the judge felt that the former premier exercised poor judgement. Will the acquittal change the label of *criminal* created by the charge? Powerful people can resist negative labels more effectively than those who are weak. Will the criminal conviction of Don Cormie in the Principal Affair in Alberta lead to an ongoing criminal label, or will his wealth (most of which is still shielded from claimants outside of Canada) enable him to resist stigmatization?

One reason the labels do not stick is because laws have been formulated to benefit powerful groups (Williams, 1980). Laureen Snider's study of corporate crime in Canada would fit in this category (1978, 1993). While Snider does not claim that her study offers overwhelming proof for this general argument, she concludes that those who control the major economic resources have been able to use their power to prevent the introduction of laws that threaten their positions. At the least, they have resisted being classified as criminal, despite the clear criminality of some of their behaviour.

Lower status people may face discrimination and differential processing in the criminal justice system, but it is more difficult to document, possibly because it is hard to separate out so many causal factors. Williams (1980) concluded that over 80 percent of both racial and socioeconomic studies failed to support differential processing. Similarly Wilbanks (1987) concluded that there was insufficient evidence to support the charge that the system is racist today. Coramae Mann (1993) and others argue that Wilbanks is simply wrong (Reiman, 1990). Mann argues that racial discrimination is endemic in the U.S. and permeates social institutions, including the criminal justice system. Native people in Canada probably face similar experiences.

The criminal justice system may be less biased against the poor and the minorities than it was in the past, but it still functions to *weed out the wealthy* (Reiman, 1990: 84). Agents of social control may not deliberately discriminate, but in Canada, as in the U.S., it comes down more heavily on the weak (Ericson, 1982; Ericson and Baranek, 1982). In addition, Canadians should not be smug about contrasts with the United States. While Canadian police have better reputations than their U.S. counterparts, increasing Canadian research on agencies of social control demonstrates more similarity than differences.

It is not clear if our systems simply *reflect* societal biases or *contribute* to the criminalization of those at the bottom. If courts, for example, make decisions on the basis of a prognosis for the future, middle-class defendants are clearly a better risk. If the playing field is uneven before people enter the system, it may be unrealistic to expect the system to even the odds. If a child from a stable family appears in Youth Court, it is unlikely that she will spend time in an institution. However, if

the child comes from a badly disorganized home, the likelihood of institutional-ization is much greater, even if the offense is the same. Statistically, this will appear to be a bias, but the judge may have fewer options for some juveniles. Any serious attempts at crime reduction must influence situations and lives *before* people come into contact with agents of social control.

Improving Labelling Theory

Early labelling theories were somewhat oversimplified, but recent formulations take into account some of the subtle ways in which the reactions of agencies am-plify or stabilize patterns of deviance. It is not just the public labelling, but also self-labelling that may amplify deviance. Bruce Link and his colleagues (1987; Link et al. 1989) note that when individuals are socialized, they learn that people in general see the "mentally ill" in a certain way. If an individual becomes a patient, these beliefs become very relevant and begin to apply in very personal ways. The more patients believe that they will be devalued and discriminated against, the more they feel threatened as they interact with others. They may try to keep their treatment a secret, and withdraw from social contacts that they perceive as re-jecting. This can lead to the loss of social support networks, problems with em-ployment, and loss of self esteem.

Bruce Link has focused on mental illness, but one can see possible parallels with criminal justice. If someone is convicted of a crime, that person can feel de-valued and may hesitate to interact with others whom she believes will reject her. Unlike the mentally ill person, a person labelled as a criminal may be able to find others who will reward her for her criminal label. In other words, this reformulation of labelling theory might be even more potent for crime than for mental illness.

The Link Between Labelling and Conflict Theories

One aspect of labelling theory that is particularly suspect is the claim that labelling *causes* criminal behaviour. Obviously Don Cormie, Richard Nixon, and Spiro Agnew did not commit their crimes *because* they had been labelled criminals. For conflict theorists, the labelling approach is primarily important because it emphasizes the other side of the coin — instead of focusing on criminals, it looks at the function-ing of bureaucracies that come into direct contact with potential criminals, such as police units, courts, and probation offices. Conflict theorists are inclined to view these bureaucracies as merely pawns acting on the wishes of powerful members of so-ciety, but one can study these units without this assumption and gain insights that are relevant to criminology. Studies of agents of social control suggest that they are often not particularly benign, and the dynamics involved in these bu-reaucracies can lead to agendas that differ from publicly stated goals. However, it is not clear to what extent they are simply extensions of those in power.

Labelling theorists looked at the dynamics of specific agencies, but most conflict theorists concentrate on power relationships among different elements of society. This is probably where conflict theory makes its most important contribution, even though these issues are not new. Social scientists, philosophers, journalists, and others have made similar points in the past. Edwin Sutherland called attention to white-collar or corporate criminality (1949), and Frank Tannenbaum (1938) saw crime as related to the activities of an entire community, not just selected members from a certain social strata. In the 1930s, Thorsten Sellin (1938) presented arguments very similar to those made by later conflict theorists, but the major expansion of this thinking in criminology began in the 1960s and 1970s.

One of the influential documents of this period was produced by the American Friends Service Committee (1971). In a very coherent report, they argued that actions that bring the greatest harm to the greatest number of people should be labelled criminal. This would apply most frequently to official actions of government agencies. The most murders of this century have been committed by governments in wartime. The greatest theft of property in the U.S. was the theft of lands belonging to Indian tribes. The evacuation and internment of Japanese-Americans during World War II was carried out by the government with the approval of the courts. (Canada's record in this area may even be worse.) Civil rights demonstrators, exercising constitutional rights, have been beaten by police.

By the 1970s, the conflict perspective was a major force in criminology. Robert Ratner describes the growth of radical criminology in Canada as in competition with "entrenched foes" (1984: 159), and the ongoing debates were at times acrimonious, but there is little doubt that the "mainstream" of criminology was taking these arguments into account. I find it difficult to present a systematic overview of this thinking, but I will begin by going back to Karl Marx and Friedrich Engels, who made major contributions by calling attention to economic factors. While "conflict" theory, as used in this book, covers a number of somewhat different perspectives, the Marxist views provide a convenient starting point. Ron Hinch (1992) argues that Marxist theories should not be grouped with other conflict theories, but this chapter joins with others who do so.

MARXIST THEORIES

By the middle of the nineteenth century, the Industrial Revolution had led to mechanized factories, coal was used to drive steam engines, and a variety of economic activities became integrated. Cottage industries were replaced by large factories. Wealthy owners had great power over workers and were rarely concerned about the terrible working conditions. Trade unions began challenging that hegemony, but were ruthlessly suppressed.

Marx and Engels concentrated on the means of economic production and its influence on social life. Capitalism led to unequal distribution of property and power which, in turn, led to the inevitable class conflict that characterized most complex societies. Ron Hinch (1987) warns us that there are several Marxian theories of crime and criminality and that debates over *economic determinism* continue among Marxist scholars. However, many claim that class conflict is a major factor influencing the definition of crime and who gets criminalized. These arguments can be grouped into *instrumental* and *structural* perspectives.

An Instrumentalist Perspective on Marxism

From a historical perspective, instrumentalists argue that Canada evolved as a colony providing resources for England and France (Panitch, 1977). The leaders of society felt that what was good for those on top was also good for those on the bottom. When Canadian Pacific built the railroad across Canada, it received extensive amounts of public lands and money on the assumption that this would eventually benefit everyone. Similarly, providing tax concessions to the West Edmonton Mall, giving public support to companies refining oil in the Tar Sands of Alberta, or drilling in the Hibernia oil field off Newfoundland were viewed by those in power as appropriate government investments. Charles Reasons (1984) contends the government apparatus served the interests of the capitalists. From the perspective of conservative governments at least, what was good for Imperial Oil was good for everyone.

Brickey and Comack (1986:17-21) summarize these ideas succinctly. The instrumental position is that the state acts at the behest of the capitalist class, those with the power. The institutions within the state, including the police, the courts, and the prison system, are the tools of the capitalists. One view of the creation of the Northwest Mounted Police was that it was designed to control workers and Native peoples; that is, serve the interests of those in power (Brown and Brown, 1973). Concepts such as "the rule of law" and "equality before the law" are means of obscuring the reality of *lack of equality* in most situations. Taken to its extreme, the instrumentalists would view capitalists as immune from legal sanctions (Quinney, 1975; Chambliss, 1975). They not only make the law, but control those who enforce it.

Such a view offers a "conspiracy theory" involving all powerful people, which ignores structural restraints on the influence of the capitalists. It also fails to recognize that laws are often passed that restrict the interests of the capitalist class, such as anti-combines legislation and right-to-strike legislation. Powerful individuals clearly have advantages, but they are not immune, as evidenced by the conviction of Donald Cormie with regard to the Principal Group fraud, Colin Thatcher, Saskatchewan cabinet minister and son of a former premier, in connection with murder, Charles Keating as an outcome of the Savings and Loan scandal in the U.S., Michael Miliken with his criminal involvement in finances, and Leona Hemsley, the New York hotel queen, as a result of her income tax evasion. In addition, the law does not serve the powerful alone — at times it serves the weak as well.

A Structuralist Perspective on Marxism

Nicos Poulantzas (1973) sees many of the descriptions of the state as an instrument of the capitalists as oversimplifications. The state is neither completely free of control by the dominant classes nor simply dominated by them. Instead, it is relatively autonomous, allowing it to serve as a "factor of cohesion" and help regulate the overall equilibrium of society. Brickey and Comack note that, in contrast to instrumentalism, the structuralist position argues that the state acts on *behalf* of capital rather than at the *behest* of capitalists. The state acts as an "organizer"; it mediates between capital and labour, usually to the advantage of the former. It creates the conditions that will aid in the process of capital accumulation. It also tries to maintain and create conditions of social harmony by convincing the economically oppressed classes that this is for the good of all. Clearly, during the 1980s in Canada and the United States, many of the "lower" classes bought into this argument and elected governments that generally accepted this view. At the beginning of the 1990s, there was fairly wide acceptance of the view that if those at the top prosper, so will those at the bottom.

To achieve these goals, the state requires a certain degree of autonomy from direct manipulation by many elements of the dominant class. They must be able to resist the specific demands and *immediate* interests of certain dominant individuals or groups, in order to ensure the *long-term* interests of capital. The state evolves out of the constraints and contradictions inherent in the capital-labour relationship. Thus, laws that favour workers, such as the length of the working day and health and safety regulations, also protect the long-term interest of capitalistic enterprise. Smandych (1985) notes, for example, that Canadian anticombines legislation arose in the late nineteenth century to mediate the conflicts among large capitalistic forces, which were attempting to eliminate competition, and small businesses, which were trying to maintain competition.

Similarly, the police, courts, and other systems of the state need to maintain the appearance of neutrality in order to win the acceptance of the dominated classes. Despite the formal equality that is maintained in law, the economic inequality of reality frequently compromises the ideal. One might argue that the instrumentalists exaggerate discrimination in the operation of the law, while other critics claim that structuralists err in the opposite direction by minimizing it.

Testing Marxist Hypotheses

Tony Platt's book, *The Child Savers* (1969), might be said to reflect the instrumentalist view. He claimed that the juvenile justice system was created to serve capitalist interests. New categories of youthful deviance were "invented." Child-savers (mainly middle-class women who·had the psychological need to do good) and other representatives of the powerful recommended increased imprisonment or other control systems, in order to rehabilitate juveniles. The entire "juvenile court system was part of a general movement directed towards developing a specialized labour market and industrial discipline under corporate capitalism by creating new programs of adjudication and control" (1974:377).

Hagan and Leon (1977) used data from Toronto to test this argument, and found that juvenile justice in Canada evolved without the apparent concern of the industrial elite. The key proponents of the *Juvenile Delinquents Act* of 1908 seemed to be a news reporter and a philanthropist. Opposition came primarily from the police. The developing role of probation seemed to be crucial to the new legislation and, as a result, imprisonment rates went down as informal methods of dealing with delinquents and the family became more popular. Hagan and Leon suggest that capitalism may not be particularly relevant to some aspects of criminal justice, such as the evolution of responses to juveniles.

Platt's work assumes that corporate capitalism *directly* influenced the juvenile court. The work by Hagan and Leon illustrates the type of micro-level work that reveals a number of processes operating within these agencies of social control. *The link with dominant powers in society remains a hypothesis to be tested.* The workings of agencies of social control will be influenced by external and internal factors, but Hagan and others would argue that it is an oversimplification to assume that the wishes of the power elite are transmitted directly to and through elements of the criminal justice system.

A more benign view of the agencies of social control is that a lot of the people involved mean well but, for a variety of structural reasons, they serve their clients poorly (Hackler, 1991). To summarize, many criminologists probably accept that portion of conflict theory that argues that the powerful have undue influence in the creation of legislation and that they successfully resist laws that interfere with their perceived well-being, but there is less agreement on the levers of power that guide the agencies of social control in their dealings with troubled and troublesome people.

The Future of Marxist Theory on Crime Policy

With the break-up of the Soviet Union and the failure of communism in Eastern Europe, some people assume that Marxist theorists have lost all credibility. It is a mistake to believe that radical thinkers in the West were unaware of the deficiencies of communist dictatorships. Like the rest of us, conflict theorists knew that crime was common in Russia and that these states lied about their social problems. In addition, changes recommended in the *Communist Manifesto* in the nineteenth century have, to a large degree, become the reality in most western nations,

thanks to the efforts of progressive thinkers and others who saw the need for change. Nor are Marxist theorists unaware of some of the benefits of reasonably free enterprise, and their good fortune in living in a society where they can criticize the powerful. Their contributions to an understanding of crime, and hopefully its eventual reduction, will continue to be important simply because economic factors and power relations have a crucial impact on human behaviour. While some criminologists will not appreciate all of the arguments coming from the far left, by calling attention to deficiencies in capitalist societies, the Marxian conflict theorists turn the spotlight on criminogenic conditions that cannot be ignored in modern complex societies.

Of much greater concern to me is that the so-called "victory of capitalism" will lead North American governments in particular to ignore some of the dangerous consequences of the shift to the right since the early 1970s. Galbraith (1992) talks about a "culture of contentment," where reasonably well-off Americans represent such a powerful voting block that they prevent governments from taking important steps which directly influence the quality of life. For example, the "contented majority" may not be interested in universal medical care (Hackler 1993). The infant mortality rate for the U.S., acknowledged as the best measure of a country's medical care, is now worse than in 28 other countries, tied with Barbados and Martinique and behind Spain and Italy.

The deterioration of inner cities in the U.S. and the concomitant increase in crime, suggests that the brand of capitalism espoused by many leaders in the U.S. offers an *unattractive* option. Galbraith's message seems particularly appropriate for Canada. Our "contented majority" is more concerned with protecting individual wealth than creating a society with less crime. Eastern Europe and developing nations unfortunately look only at the material successes, particularly in the United States. They ignore the failures in the social area. The emphasis on a single yardstick of goodness, material wealth, coupled with uneven access to such wealth and the perpetuation of myths about social equality, leads to conditions conducive to crime. The break-up of the Soviet Union might be viewed as an illustration of the deficiencies of corrupt dictatorships, but there is no evidence that unrestrained free enterprise, particularly the American model, reduces crime and other social problems.

When the majority of the people are told that everyone should be treated equally, but those in the working classes are convinced that certain elites are favoured by the law and by the agencies of government, *criminogenic* conditions exist. Obviously, this is an oversimplification; but when people believe that many others are cheating, they see less reason for being honest themselves. The basic assumption of capitalism and free enterprise, that greed for individual profits leads to the greatest social good, simply tears at the fabric of society. Traditional criminologists also agree with conflict theorists that this leads to crime.

Previous chapters dwelled on traditional views, which did not challenge the appropriateness of the rules. Not only do Marxists and other conflict theorists question the rule-making process, they examine *conditions* that increase the likelihood of crime. Marxists do not deny that psychological factors and small-group dynamics contribute to an understanding of crime, but they see them as *shaped by larger social structures.* The Marxist conflict theorists call attention to economic factors and power. When these benefits are not widely distributed, even when societal members believe they should be, crime is more likely. Marx believed capitalism was an inherently self-contradictory economic system. Its very success in profit-making tends to "unglue the social structure (McDaniel and Agger, 1982: 57)." In addition to creating the circumstances of its own destruction, during the time the social structure is coming unglued, there would be more crime.

The Crimes of the Powerful

One of the major contributions of the Marxist theorists and others with a radical perspective is to call attention to the crimes of the powerful. A rich literature has been produced (Barak, 1991; Chambliss, 1988; Goff and Reasons, 1978; Reasons, Ross, and Paterson, 1981; Snider, 1993), but this discussion will be postponed to those chapters dealing with specific forms of criminal behaviour. It is appropriate, however, to end a discussion of Marxist criminology with a comment on who and what criminologists should be studying. Friedrich Engels (1958), writing in 1844, summarizes the point rather well.

> If one individual inflicts a bodily injury upon another which leads to death ... we call it manslaughter; ... if the attacker knows beforehand that the blow will be fatal we call it murder. Murder has also been committed if society places hundreds of workers in such a position that they inevitably come to premature and unnatural ends. Their death is as violent as if they had been stabbed or shot. ... Murder has been committed if society knows perfectly well that thousands of workers cannot avoid being sacrificed so long as these conditions are allowed to continue. Murder of this sort is just as culpable as the murder committed by an individual.

CONFLICT THEORIES, MACRO-LEVEL ARGUMENTS, AND CRIMINOGENIC CONDITIONS

Organizing conflict theories into meaningful categories depends on how one wishes to use them. It is a convenient simplification to say that some focus on macro-level arguments, that is, the larger structure of society, while others concentrate on micro-level arguments, that is, on the agencies that define crime and handle those identified as criminals. By the 1950s, a number of scholars were finding consensus theories limiting. Dahrendorf (1959), Sellin (1938), and Vold (1958) offered suggestions to supplement and extend some of the traditional theories.

Vold and Group Conflict Theory

Various groups in society interact; that interaction is not always peaceful. In fact, modern societies are characterized by a constant state of conflict. Groups ally themselves with others in defence or for advancement within society. Such interaction includes groups involved in making or enforcing the law, as well as groups that are required to obey the law. Legislation represents the triumph of a particular group, or an alliance of groups, over other groups. Naturally, those who succeed in having a law passed are likely to conform to it, while those who oppose it, or whose actions were the target of the new law, are least likely to obey the law and most likely to get in trouble with the enforcers of the law, usually the police.

Vold calls attention to the political nature of law creation and law enforcement and specifies the types of situations that would most likely lead to criminalization. Some conflicts do not escalate. When students march on legislatures, usually the disagreements do not result in the police arresting the participants. On the other end of the continuum, the actions of the "minority" *and* the actions of the dominant group may lead to the criminalization of the minority group. In 1970 a Québec-based protest group, the FLQ (Front de Liberation du Québec), kidnapped Pierre LaPorte, the Labour Minister of the Québec government, and James Cross, a British trade official. The goal of this group was the independence of Québec, but its actions included terrorist tactics and violence. There were bombings and police casualties. The federal government under Pierre Trudeau responded to the kidnapping by invoking the *War Measures Act*, which suspended certain liberties. When LaPorte was found murdered, the FLQ lost any claim to legitimacy in the eyes of the majority of Canadians.

Austin Turk and the Conflict Between Authorities and Subjects

Many of today's conflict theorists were influenced by Vold, including Richard Quinney and Austin Turk. In his book *Criminality and the Legal Order* (1969), Turk offers a useful illustration of this branch of conflict theory. I use Turk's work for two reasons: Turk taught in Canada at the University of Toronto for many years, and his conflict theory of crime is stated in such a way as to be testable. A major criticism of many conflict theories is that they are statements of faith and are not formulated as testable propositions that could be refuted or supported with evidence. Turk notes that *criminalization* is distinct from the *behaviour* of deviants. For him, criminality is a *status* and is determined by what authorities do. Social order is viewed as conflict among those seeking to protect and improve their life chances. Political power determines legality. Criminality is the study of the relations between authorities, those with power, and subjects, those without power. His typology utilizes three variables, in an attempt to predict conditions that lead to high or low rates of criminalization.

The most important variable in this typology is *congruence*. When there is congruence between social norms — what people actually *do* — and their cultural or "announced" norms — what people *say* is important — the likelihood of criminalization is high. For example, let us assume that the police, the most visible symbol of the authorities, accept the cultural norm against the use of marijuana. That is the law. But the "social" norm is more relaxed. The police may not be enthusiastic in enforcing the stated norm. Thus, there may be low congruence on the part of the authorities. Stated differently, high congruence exists when people really feel strongly, and act in accordance with those beliefs. With low congruence, people accept the norm but are not inclined to sacrifice a great deal for it.

Congruence varies among authorities and, similarly, among subjects. Some young people (subjects or norm-resisters) may feel they have a right to smoke marijuana, just as adults have their tobacco, but they are not dedicated to this behaviour. Therefore, congruence would be low. With low congruence on the part of the subjects *and* the authorities, the probability of conflict and criminalization is minimal. However, if there is high congruence between the beliefs held by those young people and their actions, if they flaunt their marijuana and blow smoke in the faces of the police, the likelihood of conflict increases. Figure 13.1 illustrates the typology at this stage.

The four cells in Figure 13.1 indicate different situations, which vary in the probability of conflict and criminalization. Focusing on the upper left-hand cell, imagine a group of young males showing how tough they are by defying the police. They are committed to this activity and the police are just as determined not to take any crap from these "hoodlums." Both subjects and authorities display high congruence. The possibility of a clash and someone being charged with a crime is high.

Moving to the next cell to the right, we might find that individual prostitutes feel strongly that they should be able to sell their wares any way they like; the police may believe this is unlikely to change and, since prostitution is not a crime (although soliciting customers is), they may not enforce the anti-soliciting laws enthusiastically. The probability of conflict is moderate.

The lower left-hand cell might represent casual marijuana smokers who are not particularly committed to the behaviour, but they live in an area where the police are really eager to enforce the law to the letter. Their risk of arrest might be moderate.

The lower right-hand cell might illustrate jaywalkers in Edmonton. In most cities, such laws are rarely enforced. The police in Edmonton do not consider this

AUTHORITIES

		Authorities	
		High Congruence	Low Congruence
SUBJECTS	High Congruence	High Probably of Conflict	Moderate Probability of Conflict
	Low Congruence	Moderate Probability of Conflict	Low Probability of Conflict

FIGURE 13.1 The Probabilities of Conflict and Criminalization (Austin T. Turk, 1969)

Source: Austin T. Turk, 1969

top priority either, but are sometimes pressured to give tickets. From the subject's point of view, there may be low congruence between the importance of the norm and their commitment to jaywalking as a practice. They just don't want to walk down to the corner to cross. For most situations, criminalization is unlikely.

Congruence is the most important variable; the second is *organization*. One assumes that all authorities are organized; but when subjects (or norm-resisters) are organized, conflict and criminalization is more likely. A single norm-resister can be overwhelmed rather easily by the authorities, but an organized mob or gang can lead to serious confrontations. A single marijuana smoker can be ignored, but a mob of them blowing smoke in the faces of a group of policemen increases the likelihood of a response, and thus, criminalization.

The third variable is *sophistication*. When either the authorities or the subjects are sophisticated, they know the behaviour patterns of the others and are better able to manipulate them. Sophisticated norm-resisters or subjects can assess the strengths and weaknesses of their position relative to authorities, and thus avoid open warfare. For example, skilled safe-crackers adapt to police practices. Some develop reputations for "quality" work that the police have learned to admire, albeit grudgingly. "Joe can peel back the door of a safe with nitro and not even shake up the tea-cups." Similarly, Joe does not carry a gun and is therefore less dangerous. Besides, he specializes in supermarkets, which have insurance. Since Joe doesn't leave evidence laying about, and if he doesn't get greedy and blow too many safes, he may not get charged for some time. Many white-collar criminals are sophisticated, can assess the enforcement activities of officials, and avoid confrontation. Leona Helmsley, the New York hotel queen, may have considered herself a sophisticated income-tax evader, but evidently she misread the situation and overestimated her own invulnerability.

On the other side, authorities who are less sophisticated rely more on power and are less able to utilize avoidance, persuasion and compromise. Skilled police avoid riots while handling crowds; clumsy ones might create one.

For the time being, let us ignore the congruence variable and combine *organization* and *sophistication*, to see which situations are more likely to produce conflict. In Figure 13.2, the eight cells illustrate the different combinations.

The cell in the upper left-hand corner (number 1) combines organized but unsophisticated subjects with an unsophisticated authority. Let us imagine that we have a gang of unsophisticated young males confronting unskilled police. The likelihood of conflict and criminalization is high. In the cell in the lower right-hand corner (number 8) imagine a single experienced shoplifter dealing with a highly skilled police force. The police realize it is hard to catch this skilled thief, and simply warn merchants to arrange their goods differently.

The ranking of these cells from 1 to 8 is somewhat arbitrary. Turk has assumed that modifying one variable at a time would change the likelihood of conflict systematically. In reality, these combinations are not that neat. There are degrees of organization and different levels of sophistication, but the contribution that Turk makes is to specify outcomes in the real world.

Figure 13.3 adds the *congruence* variable. This combines Figures 13.1 and 13.2. Since congruence is such a powerful variable, cells ranked 1 to 8 are in the upper left-hand quadrant. That is, when the police feel strongly about what they are doing, and when the subjects feel strongly about their resistance, clashes and criminalization are high, regardless of the other variables. Again, the ranking in Figure

			AUTHORITIES	
			Unsophisticated	Sophisticated
SUBJECTS	Organized	Unsophisticated	1 (very high probability of conflict)	5
		Sophisticated	3	7
	Unorganized	Unsophisticated	2	6
		Sophisticated	4	8 (very low probability of conflict)

FIGURE 13.2 The Probabilities of Conflict Using Sophistication and Organization (Austin T. Turk, 1969)

Source: Austin T. Turk, 1969

13.3 is based on the assumption of a systematic change each time a variable is altered, and the various combinations provide a rank order of situations that are most or least likely to result in conflict and criminalization. The precision of this ranking is unlikely to match reality, but what is important about Turk's model is that it makes propositions that can be tested. His model is *refutable*, as any scientific theory must be (Gibbs, 1985; 1989). Many conflict theories are presented in a manner that makes them impossible to refute or test scientifically. In the final chapters of his book, Turk uses crime statistics to test his model. The empirical evidence is less than convincing, but this model is somewhat unusual among conflict theories in that it spells out ideas *explicitly* and suggests evidence that would support or reject the theory.

The explicitness of Turk's model makes it easier to criticize; a desirable characteristic of a theory. In Figures 13.1, 13.2 and 13.3 it is not easy to describe situations and crimes that fit the various boxes. Many traditional crimes do not fit very well. For example, murdering someone would result in a high congruence response from the police, but from the side of the subject, murderers usually do not have high congruence nor are they usually organized. And yet, the likelihood of criminalization for murder is high. In his book Turk does not link many traditional crimes with his theory, so it is not clear whether he had them in mind. When Turk talks about subjects as relatively powerless "social groups," he proba-

			AUTHORITIES			
			High Congruence		Low Congruence	
			Sophistication		Sophistication	
			Low	High	Low	High
SUBJECTS — High Congruence	Organized	Unsophisticated	1	5	17	21
		Sophisticated	3	7	19	23
	Unorganized	Unsophisticated	2	6	18	22
		Sophisticated	4	8	20	24
Low Congruence	Organized	Unsophisticated	9	13	25	28
		Sophisticated	11	15	27	31
	Unorganized	Unsophisticated	10	14	26	30
		Sophisticated	12	16	28	32

FIGURE 13.3 The Probabilities of Conflict When Congruence, Sophistication and Organization are Used (Austin T.Turk, 1969)

Source: Austin T. Turk, 1969

bly does not mean this to be safecrackers, marijuana smokers, and murderers. These may not qualify as "social groups," which are important to conflict thinking. However, he attempts to test his ideas with conventional crimes later in his book.

Interestingly enough, criticisms of Turk come less from empirical tests of his work than from his theoretical positions. Brickey and Comack (1986) criticize Turk for not clarifying the sources of power that differentiate authorities and subjects.

> How authorities come to be authorities is irrelevant; it is sufficient that a social structure built out of authority relations exists which is to say that authority and subject status categories are implicit in actual behaviour patterns ... (Turk, 1969: 51).

Other conflict theorists have criticized Turk's work as an "elitist conclusion" (Taylor, Walton, and Young, 1973: 246). He "accepts the retrenchment of existing orders of domination and repression" (266).

> Turk's work is permeated by an acceptance of the fact that authority-subject relationships ... must necessarily be relationships of domination and subjection. Were it to be otherwise, the demoralized and unhygienic ... could fail to learn ... their roles as subjects dominated by a legitimate authority. (Taylor, Walton, and Young, 1973: 246).

However, I view Turk as *describing* society, rather than *condoning* such situations. Taylor and his colleagues continue:

> Turk's formal conflict theory stands indicted ... as a form of theory which informally attempts to stabilize the ongoing dynamics of social conflict. ... So far from being a theory which appreciates the merits of deviant action not only in itself but also for its contribution to the defense of freedom in divided social organizations, Turk's conflict theory is an exercise in retrenchment.

Are all conflict theories *required* to appreciate the merits of deviant action? Must we appreciate Roger Caron's desire to pull off the big armed robbery? These criticisms by Taylor and his colleagues illustrate some of the problems with certain conflict arguments. Instead of making testable propositions about the real world, which might lead to the accumulation of data that would enable some arguments to be set aside, much of the debate is based on ideology and some presumed motives of the author. Recently, some of the conflict theorists have criticized the lack of realism in some of the work by their colleagues. Jock Young (1986), one of the co-authors with Taylor and Walton, appears to be more objective in works he has authored alone. He is among those conflict theorists who are concerned about the unwillingness of the "left idealists" to test many of the assumptions that permeate their thinking. In a later section on "left realism" we can see that some of the thinking from the left is compatible with that of the "liberal humanists" who argue that ideas require testing.

The theorists discussed above illustrate macro-level thinking that has influenced most criminologists, including those of a more conventional persuasion. Micro-level work calls attention to the specific dynamics of agencies of social control and how those dynamics influence the definition of crime and those who are labelled as criminals. These scholars do not ignore macro-level issues; but their focus on agencies of social control has had more impact on those of us inclined toward tinkering with agencies. In addition, this type of research may have more direct relevance for social policy in the near future.

MICRO-LEVEL ARGUMENTS AND THE POSSIBILITY OF CRIMINAL JUSTICE REFORM

During the 1970s, many radical thinkers rejected the possibility of participating in criminal justice, arguing that crime problems could not be solved within the capitalist system. Mucking about with band-aid solutions would not change a corrupt system. Other well-known radical thinkers, such as Nicole Hahn Rafter (1986), disagree. It is silly to claim that laws prohibiting serious kinds of rule-breaking, like homicide, rape, and robbery, are expressions of class conflict and instruments of class oppression. Radical criminologists must also address the mundane problems of crime causation, look at empirical evidence objectively, and not be concerned if they occasionally find their thinking compatible with mainstream researchers. Rafter states, "dirty hands are preferable to having no hand at all in the formulation of criminal justice policy" (1986:18).

One of the bridges between conflict theorists such as Nicole Rafter and middle-of-the-road liberals is the hope that research will lead to reforms in the criminal justice system. Thus, those conflict criminologists who focus on specific agencies of social control offer insights into changes that might produce improvements. For example, Richard Ericson and Pat Baranek (1982) bring a critical perspective to the processing of defendants through the criminal justice system. In my own work on juvenile justice, I am critical of Canadian practices (Hackler, 1991) and argue that our failure to be aware of juvenile justice systems in other countries limits our vision and imagination (Hackler, 1988). Conflict theorists might focus on what keeps authorities in a position to continue these abuses; those of us with a liberal perspective criticize the workings of the system *without* assuming it is necessarily entrenched in relationships of dominance, which the authorities are striving to maintain. Liberals also assume those in authority are concerned with their own self-interest, but this is not limited to capitalism. Rather, self-interest characterizes groups and individuals in all societies, including those with benign and humanitarian orientations.

Although it is clearly an oversimplification, the liberal non-conflict theorists are more optimistic about making changes *within* the present system. Some of us, perhaps naïvely, assume that many people in positions of power mean well and, given the right set of conditions, would help to modify the system and make it "better" for the more disadvantaged members of the society. We liberals do not expect heroism or great self-sacrifice from those in dominant positions, but as we criticize the system we cling to the notion that many people are somewhat noble and that virtue brings about its own psychological rewards. This faith sometimes persists even when continually confronted with evidence to the contrary.

Conflict theorists are less charitable, less sanguine, more cynical, less optimistic, and perhaps less naïve. They see the need for more *basic and sweeping* changes in the structure of society. For example, in assessing the reality of reform in the criminal justice system in Canada, Richard Ericson (1987) argues that supposed reforms may be initiated by those in authority as a smoke-screen to conceal other agendas which, in fact, serve the status quo.

A Conflict Perspective on Reform

Maeve McMahon and Richard Ericson (1987) illustrate this perspective with the development of the Citizens' Independent Review of Police Activities (CIRPA), an organization established to reform the police in Toronto. They argue that the reform group was co-opted by the authorities. This allowed the issues to be redirected by the police. In reality, the reform effort may have solidified the power of the authorities by providing the appearance of change. As one CIRPA board member stated, the police "have to be a bit more careful about what they say. It doesn't mean they have to be more careful about what they do, but at least they have to keep a facade" (65). Thus, the intended reformers assist in maintaining the status quo, and the police give the impression that they are willing to be accountable and take heed of civilians who criticize. Reformers working from within the systems always attempt to co-opt, neutralize, or use the "true" outside reformers to achieve their own goals.

Here again, ideology and explanation become somewhat confused. Traditional supporters of the system are puzzled by the criticisms levelled by Ericson and McMahon, because from their traditional standpoint the main goal of criminal justice is to protect society. Co-opting recommendations from outsiders is reasonable *because* it may improve the system, for the average citizen as well as those who are disadvantaged.

A Liberal Perspective on Reform

Ezzat Fattah, of Simon Fraser University, has written on reform from liberal and critical perspectives. His arguments against capital punishment were among the most influential in Canada. He also points out that reform efforts should not be judged from a radical or critical perspective alone (1987). Reforms that perpetuate authoritarian social control, as described above, may yield an unanticipated negative result, but that does not mean this was a carefully thought-out strategy of the power elite. At other times, something quite different happens: relatively minor attempts at reform lead to positive changes that are even greater than what was anticipated.

Fattah (1987) also criticizes an approach that often characterizes radical criminology: the elite are eager to criminalize the weak and the poor, while the lower classes are assumed to be benevolent. In fact, it is not the elite who consistently demand harsher penalties, more severe police powers, and so on, but the members of the middle and lower classes. They, rather than the elite, persistently complain about the molly-coddling of offenders, the country-club-like conditions in penal institutions, and the bleeding hearts who wish to help wrong-doers. They are the ones who are the strongest advocates of stigmatization and exclusion of offenders. It is the middle and lower classes, not the elite, who call for an extension of the powers of social control authorities.

In addition, Fattah (1987) points out that the distinction between inside and outside reformers is not appropriate, because those who are genuinely interested in reform do not care if it comes from within or without, or whether it is achieved by confrontation or co-operation. Fattah's thinking would be compatible with the left realists, those critical criminologists who point out that radicals should broaden the scope of their thinking and consider a wider range of reform efforts. Such an orientation leads to considerable overlap with the reform efforts of liberal criminologists, and the border between conflict and liberal reform becomes blurred. For many criminologists with reform inclinations, less concern with ideological purity is preferred.

One should not exaggerate the differences between conflict theorists and other criminologists. Most criminologists agree that crime reflects the way society is organized, and even conflict theorists admit that there are "bad" individuals. Many of these points of agreement appear in what Jock Young (1986) refers to as "left realism."

Left Realism and the Potential for Reform

Some radical criminologists have a tendency to romanticize crime, or assume that the only serious crimes are those committed by the powerful. While income-tax evasion certainly involves more stolen money than bank robbery, the majority of direct victims of crime are poor people victimized by other poor people. Crimes of violence usually involve one poor person hitting another, and half of the time it is a man hitting his wife. Conflict theorists like Nicole Hahn Rafter (1986), David Greenberg (1981), and Jock Young (1986) criticize some of the conflict theorists for ignoring the fact that crime really is a problem, particularly for poor people. Brown and Hogg (1992) review left realism in England and Australia and note some promising new directions. For example, some left realists devote considerable attention to police-community relations (p. 200). Heavy-handed proactive policing often alienates communities plagued with crime problems. In fact, these concerned communities can be the most important resource in helping to reduce crime. Instead of just seeing police as oppressors, the left realists recommend that the police be responsible to, and responsive to, the communities being policed.

Left realism does not ignore the impact of crimes of the powerful, but notes that people who are more vulnerable economically and socially will be caught in compounding problems, which create criminals and victims. While left realism argues that crime illustrates the antisocial fruits of capitalism, it also takes seriously the specific risks to vulnerable people; the dangers of a woman being in a public place at night, the widespread occurrence of domestic violence, and the fears of working-class people in crime-prone areas. Official statistics, despite their flaws, provide insights that help us understand the risk of crime in working-class areas. In general, left realists share with liberal humanists a practical concern for the day-to-day damage crime does to the most unprotected part of the population.

Following the Fads

To understand current theoretical thinking, one must take into account the fads that come and go in criminology. Those who work with statistical techniques are aware of the rise and fall in popularity of certain analytical tools. In the 1960s, for example, it was a rare data set that escaped being "factor analyzed." Some psychologists ask if every correlation is "significant at the .05 level of probability." Often, these tools reflect the latest fad and may be irrelevant for the intellectual question at hand. Theorists go through similar fads. The tendency to emphasize single causes of crime weakened the contributions from some theorists. These included: capitalism is practically the only cause of crime; unemployment automatically leads to crime; poverty leads directly to riots; and increases in crime are simply the consequence of greater criminalization on the part of the police (Young, 1986; Greenberg, 1981). Simplification and generalization are necessary, but we must be ready to modify, specify, and reject. Rigidity based on ideology, rather than caution based on evidence, characterized the work of some conflict theorists, just as the ritual and unthinking use of statistical techniques characterized other criminological work.

In summary, left realism recognizes and criticizes faddishness and extremism, and attempts to develop a balance between two themes. First, we should not underestimate the problem of conventional crime, but we must resist the hysteria that exaggerates certain types of crime. The second theme is illustrated by the systematic distortion of images of crime, victimization, and policing by the media (Ericson, Baranek, and Chan, 1987 and 1989; Voumvakis and Ericson, 1984; Cohen and Young, 1981). Despite overwhelming evidence that most violence takes place among acquaintances, the media exaggerate the role of the dangerous stranger. This provides ammunition for repressive and ineffective social-control tactics. For example, the headlines about sexual abuse in daycare centres shocked the public but probably misled policy-makers. Such abuse is rare in daycare centres; it is much more common by parents. Our concern should still be with families. Hysterical reactions to distorted images of crime lead to political and popular support for law-and-order campaigns that do little to protect victims in the future.

Left realism resists the hysteria, but does not deny the severity of crime as a problem. It is sceptical of official statistics and agencies of control, without rejecting figures and data out of hand. Nor does it automatically reject the possibility of reform. For a period, radical criminology concentrated only on the crimes of the powerful, the state, and its agencies, noting the impact on those at the bottom of the hierarchy (Chambliss, 1989; Chambliss, 1988). These themes are still important, but the left realists, in contrast to the "left idealists," argue that one cannot ignore the structural determinants of everyday crime. Nor can one accept uncritically that every action of the police and other agencies, such as school teachers, social workers, etc., is a deliberate act pursued and directed by the agents of capitalism.

It is appropriate to turn now to areas of overlap between conflict and traditional thinkers, especially among those who see the economic and political structures of society as crucial elements in explaining, and eventually reducing, crime.

BRINGING CONFLICT AND OTHER THEORIES TOGETHER

The Age Structure of Society: David Greenberg

David Greenberg (1977) sees many areas of compatibility between conflict and other theories. He builds on Merton and points to the structural sources of adolescent crime, which can be summarized in several points.

1. Juveniles are excluded from the world of adult work. This exclusion exaggerates teenagers' dependence on peers for approval, and eliminates the possibility of obtaining funds to support their social activities. Juveniles fear, with good reason, that this lack of employment will persist into adulthood. Males become anxious over achieving traditional male role expectations. This anxiety can lead to violence.

2. Freed from ties to conventional institutions, teenagers *have* become more irresponsible. This is characteristic of modern capitalistic societies, where children of *all* classes are not allowed to produce. The responses differ by class — lower-class youth use more violence, middle-class youth may be vandals, but their reactions are similar in that they are blocked from productive roles.

3. The explosion of a teenage labour supply from the baby boom came just as women began entering the labour force in large numbers. Teenagers lost out. The prolongation of education was associated with a diminished labour market. The way education is organized contributes to delinquency. The notion that complex technology requires more education applies to only a small minority of students and rests on the dubious assumption that schooling is superior to apprenticeships. School is designed to keep juveniles out of the labour market.

4. Delinquency in the former Soviet Union was associated with youths who were academic failures, not working, or had unrewarding jobs. Like capitalist countries, the Soviet Union was trying to create a docile, disciplined, and stratified labour force. A meaningful decrease in delinquency would require a thorough integration of teenagers into the labour force. This would require a major restructuring of work and education, which is unlikely in the foreseeable future. In other words, there are barriers not only because of social class, but because of age as well.

These ideas are compatible with work done by Bill Stephens of Dalhousie University (1979). In studying delinquency in different types of communities in Nova Scotia, he found that in those families where the work done by the children was *genuinely important* to the success of the family, delinquency was low. Farm families illustrate this situation. The child who gathers eggs at an early age, drives a tractor in adolescence, etc. knows that she is contributing to the welfare of the family. By contrast, the jobs held by most teenagers, in either affluent or impoverished families, permit them to purchase items relevant to adolescent lifestyles, but often these jobs do not make a significant contribution to the overall well-being of the family.

Adolescent Subcultures and "Stradom Formations": Herman and Julia Schwendinger

Herman and Julia Schwendinger (1979; 1985) use a Marxist perspective to explain delinquency and adolescent subcultures, and therefore may be surprised when I use their work as an illustration of bringing theories together. However, their analyses fit many of the positions shared by traditional criminologists, and are compatible with mainstream thought about delinquency. Like Greenberg, they argue that the structure of capitalist societies excludes juveniles from their previous important role as apprentices in meaningful occupations. As society becomes more industrialized, unskilled jobs are less common. This process prolongs the dependency of youth on parents and on school.

In school, delinquency is concentrated in peer groups, which they call *stradom formations*, (*stra*tified *dom*ains). The Schwendingers argue that these stratified adolescent formations are relatively independent of social class, and help to explain why self-report studies show high rates of delinquency across social classes. The different *stradoms* are a product of the adolescent period, which marks the transition from childhood to a more regulated and responsible adulthood. Along with expectations for adult-like behaviour, the juveniles find themselves dependent on parents for the material goods that provide status, at a time when they are trying to be independent.

Three types of groups emerge. The *socialites* come from middle-class parents who often imitate affluent lifestyles. Also known as elites, preppies, ivy leaguers, swingers, frats, and soshes, their delinquency may be more frequent than lower-class groups but is less serious in nature. Other *stradoms* are the *street corner* types: greasers, hoods, homeboys, hodads, dudes, and honchos. Usually they come from lower-class families, and their delinquencies, while not more numerous than those of the socialites, are more serious. Between these two socioeconomic levels are more independent peer formations, organized around special interests, such as cars, athletics, or surfing. These may be the hot-rodders, jocks, surfers, or gremmies.

The Schwendingers argue, along with many others, that if adolescents were afforded a more central and meaningful role in the society, and if they were integrated more effectively into the economic structure, delinquency and adult crime would be reduced. Some adolescents see themselves becoming prepared for such adult roles, and anticipate becoming integrated into the adult world. The *intellectuals*, those referred to as egg-heads, bookworms, brains, pencil-necks, edges, and encyclopedias, may not be in stradoms but in organized, adult-controlled activities, such as science clubs, the Scouts, the 4-H club, and church groups. Those who do well in school may face other adolescent pressures, but delinquency is less, since they are not part of the stradom culture which encourages delinquency. They view themselves as moving more or less in a direction compatible with the demands of society. Others, the nerds, clods, and turkeys, suffer the disdain of their peers, but they are less delinquent than those attached to street-corner and socialite stradoms. They may also find a place in adult-controlled activities.

Delinquent Modalities

With age changes, these stradom formations go through different delinquent modalities. The first phase is a *generalized modality*, organized around consumption, peer styles, and cynicism. During these preteen years, they are indifferent to the needs of others, and boys and girls engage in petty delinquencies. The *ethnocentric modality* begins by late junior high school. Group rivalry is intense, and graffiti proclaim the superiority of one stradom group over another.

During the middle adolescent period, delinquency becomes instrumental. The *illegal market modality,* or informal economic stage is characterized by robbery, burglary, prostitution, and drug sales; they shift their illegal pursuits from stealing things to use, to stealing things to sell. Economically deprived stradoms are more likely to engage in economic delinquency than middle-class stradom members.

The Schwendingers' work disputes the view that delinquency is a function of normlessness or feelings of inferiority. Juveniles develop their own norms. Delinquent groups form early in adolescence, before most youths are aware of their limited social standing. Their work also disputes the notion of blocked opportunities, but this puzzles me since the difference between the *socialite* and *street corner* stradoms and the *illegal market modality* stage appears to be a reflection of differential opportunity. The Schwendingers' work also does not share the social control theory perspective of viewing the delinquent as having weakened bonds with parents and schools. Instead, the delinquent is well tied in to a close peer-group pattern.

CONCLUSION

Perhaps the main contribution of the conflict theorists has been to bring criminology back to some of the broader societal themes, which must be considered to understand why those countries that advocate free enterprise the most are also the ones that seem to have more crime. It is difficult to test many of these ideas, to know which ones are true as compared to those that are statements of faith, but there are growing empirical data that fit many of the claims made by conflict theorists.

CHAPTER 14

THE ECOLOGY OF CRIME: SPATIAL RELATIONS AND INTEGRATING THEORIES

We have got to organize ourselves against Communism. We must keep the worker from red literature and red ruses. We must see that his mind remains healthy.

Al Capone

INTRODUCTION TO DANGEROUS PLACES: RODNEY STARK

Some areas have more crime than others. Is it because of the "kinds of people" who live there? Or is it possible that certain "kinds of places" produce a disproportionate amount of crime? A school of thought evolved at the University of Chicago prior to World War II that saw neighbourhoods as disorganized. Using this framework, Norman Hayner (1942) described a high-crime-rate area in Seattle. He recounted the social and cultural shortcomings of the residents, largely Italians of Sicilian origin. The businesses of the area were run down, and vacant and dilapidated buildings were common. Fifty years later the district remains a high-delinquency area, but very few Italians live there. Instead, it is the heart of the black community.

Rodney Stark (1988) asks how neighbourhoods remain high-crime areas *despite a complete turnover in their populations*. Those who grow up in those neighbourhoods and leave do not necessarily commit excessive amounts of crime elsewhere. Stark concludes that there must be something about *places* that sustains crime. Criminologists have focused on why individuals commit crime, but Stark reviews the findings from studies of human ecology. He notes that there are five characteristics, or essential factors, that distinguish high-crime-rate areas:

1. high population density,

2. poverty,

3. mixed use of buildings for residential and commercial purposes,

4. transience, and

5. dilapidation.

In addition, these factors influence the way people respond. These responses can be grouped into four categories:

1. moral cynicism among residents,

2. increased opportunities for crime,

3. increased motivation to deviate, and

4. diminished social control.

These responses further *amplify* deviance, through the following consequences:

1. by attracting crime-prone people and criminal activities to the neighbourhood,

2. by driving out the least deviant, and

3. by further reductions in social control.

Stark spells out thirty propositions, to form a theory of dangerous places. In selecting only some of those propositions, the argument is not complete, but the reader gets a flavour of this attempt to explain the ecology of crime.

1. *The greater the density, the more association between those most and least disposed to crime.* In low-density neighbourhoods, it may require an effort for one twelve-year-old to see another. Thus, kids and parents can limit contact with bullies and those in disrepute. In dense urban neighbourhoods, the "bad" kids are close by, dominate the playground, and are difficult to avoid. All young people living there will be under peer pressure to deviate.

2. *The greater the density, the higher the level of moral cynicism.* In low-density suburban neighbourhoods people keep up good appearances in public. In dense urban neighbourhoods, this is harder — discreditable information is more likely to leak. Teenage peers will know more embarrassing things about one another's parents. This colours their perceptions about what is normal, reducing respect for conventional moral standards. People in dense neighbourhoods become inferior role models — these same people would *appear* to be more respectable in less dense neighbourhoods.

3. Where homes are more crowded, there will be a greater tendency to congregate outside the home in places where there are opportunities to deviate. Crowded homes cause family members, especially teenagers, to stay away (Gove, Huges, and Galle, 1979).

4. *Where homes are crowded, there will be less supervision of children.* Parents may be relieved if children are out of the house, but then supervision is less.

5. *A reduced level of supervision results in poor school achievement, with a consequent reduction in stakes in conformity.*

6. *Where homes are crowded, there will be higher levels of conflict within families, weakening attachments and thereby stakes in conformity.*

7. *Poor, dense neighbourhoods tend to be mixed-use neighbourhoods.* The encroachment of commercial use leads to neglect of residential buildings and dilapidated conditions.

8. *Mixed-use offers increased opportunity for congregating outside the home in places conducive to deviance.* In dense, poor, mixed-use neighbourhoods, when people leave the house they go to street corners, pool halls, etc.

9. *Poor, dense, mixed-use neighbourhoods have high transience rates.*

10. *Transience weakens extra-familial attachments.*

11. *Transience weakens voluntary organizations, thereby reducing informal and formal sources of social control.* If neighbourhoods are transient, there is less of a commitment to the area, which leads to dilapidation. As areas get stigmatized, there is a reduction in an individual's stake in conformity.

12. *The more successful and potentially best role models will flee stigmatized neighbourhoods whenever possible.*

13 *Stigmatized neighbourhoods will tend to be overpopulated by the most demoralized kinds of people.* (We now skip the intervening propositions to Stark's final proposition.)

14. *The higher the visibility of crime and deviance, the more it appears to others that these activities are safe and rewarding.*

Policy Implications of Ecological Theories

Rodney Stark's ecological theory of crime has some interesting policy implications. A single social variable doesn't provide an explanation. Take poverty, for example. The ecological theory predicts less crime in poor families where their neighbourhood is less dense, where homes are not crowded and dilapidated, where there is less transience, where the police are not permissive of vice, and where the unemployed and demoralized are not concentrated. Effective action would probably require *many changes at once*, but it is important to note that each change would increase the effectiveness of other changes.

In France, I observed housing projects that illustrated both ends of the continuum. One housing project west of Paris had "matured," with people living there who no longer qualified according to income. However, the authorities did not require these people to move. Schools and other facilities were good, because they shared facilities used by wealthier neighbourhoods. With more successful and better role models remaining in the neighbourhood, there was admittedly less opportunity for demoralized residents to move in. With less transience, there were more voluntary organizations. One could argue that fewer poor and demoralized residents were being provided with low-cost housing, but from society's standpoint would it not be wiser to offer a larger number of housing projects containing smaller percentages of poor and demoralized residents, rather than concentrating them in one area? A few formerly poor people get subsidized housing, but are they not adding something to the community that would be expensive to replace?

Not far from Marseilles, I observed the type of disorganized slum that characterizes some urban areas in the United States. Although the high-rise apartment building was impressive architecturally, the residents were almost entirely Arab-speaking and on welfare. Successful Arab-speaking migrants moved out, and other dynamics illustrated the propositions developed. Other welfare families refused to move in, and the police avoided the place. Not only did it contribute to crime, but this type of residence also increased the friction between the French and Arab populations.

Ecological Arguments as an Antidote to Racist Thinking

I chose an illustration from France because it represents something that could happen in Canada. Some French arch-conservatives believe their crime problem is caused by the presence of immigrants. Right-wing politicians in France are willing to state the nature of the crime problem in a way that is rarely expressed, in public anyway, in North America. At least, not yet. For the right-wingers in France, crime is a "kind-of-people" problem. There are many Canadians who feel the same way.

In the U.S., when American social scientists talk about poor central-city neighbourhoods, they mean Black neighbourhoods. In Canada, when we talk about central-city neighbourhoods, we sometimes mean areas where there are large numbers of Native people. Social scientists are not comfortable trying to explain crime rates of Blacks or Natives. While poverty plays a role, it is only part of the explanation. Stark argues that, to a large degree, high Black crime rates are the result of *where* they live. Can we extend this argument to Native populations in Canada? To Haitians in Montréal? To Jamaicans in Toronto? To the many generations of Blacks living near Halifax? Although the reserves for Native people may not be densely populated, many of the other characteristics described by Stark would apply.

In the U.S., "kinds-of-people" theories have been well received during the past decade of conservative thinking (Wilson and Herrnstein, 1985). In Canada, some unsophisticated "kinds-of-people" theories have fared badly (Rushton, 1988; Rushton and Bogaert, 1987), but a portion of the population find such ideas attractive. The U.S. offers striking contrasts for both types of arguments. A friend attended a conference of Black mayors in the U.S. in the 1960s. There were only a handful. Twenty years later, she attended again. There were hundreds. In the 1990s, there are Black mayors of large American cities with large White majorities. It is rather remarkable for people with supposedly inferior genetic characteristics to make such progress. These talented individuals may have been able to escape dangerous places.

Stark also calls our attention to the strange fact that racial patterns in arrest and imprisonment are *more* equitable in the South than in the North and West. In South Carolina, the ratio is 3.2 Blacks for every White inmate. In Minnesota, it is 22 Blacks to each White inmate. Minnesota is not more racist than the Southern states, but the ecological distribution of Blacks is more *normal* in the South. Only 9% of Blacks in South Carolina live in the central core of large cities, compared with 80% in Minnesota. Outside of the South, Blacks live in areas where the probabilities of *anyone* committing a crime are high.

To summarize, community settings have a powerful influence on behaviour, which cannot be explained by individual characteristics. For example, we know that sex is an individual characteristic that influences behaviour, including crime, but males behave differently in all-male groups, compared to being the *only* male in a group of females. Similarly men or women, Blacks or Whites, Natives or non-Natives will be more or less criminal, depending on the social settings in which they live.

DEFENSIBLE SPACE AND ROUTINE ACTIVITIES

Crime Prevention Through Environmental Design: Oscar Newman

Another type of ecological study has concentrated on "crime prevention through environmental design." Oscar Newman (1973) is an architect who believes that citizens could be involved in crime prevention, if one constructed residential complexes that deterred crime by creating *defensible space*. Housing can be designed that allows residents to notice and identify strangers, and encourages them to have an interest in the protection of their territory. For example, the area enclosed by the wings of a building often becomes the focus of surveillance and informal control by residents of the facing apartments, particularly if the building is not very tall. Children playing in such areas are often under the watchful eyes of neighbours. Having play equipment and benches in such areas attracts people and keeps children closer to home. Residents feel safer if they can see and be seen, hear and be heard. When people are less anxious they spend more time in "shared" space, thereby increasing surveillance and informal control. Such settings increase the willingness of residents to intervene when deviance is observed, as suggested by some of the studies of bystanders discussed earlier.

It is unlikely that defensible space design can dramatically reduce crime, but studies in Great Britain suggest that there has been an impact in English public-housing areas (Baldwin, 1979). It is possible, of course, that crime is merely displaced from well-designed areas to nearby targets that are more vulnerable. In addition, the emphasis on the design of space may ignore social and demographic characteristics. For example, a project with many teenagers may have a higher crime rate, whereas one with many older people who observe enclosed areas may have higher surveillance and reduced crime. Areas with residential mobility may fail to develop a community spirit, whereas stable neighbourhoods may become more cohesive and reduce crime. High-population-density areas may attract more police officers, leading to an increase in formal control of crime (Gillis and Hagan, 1982). In general, the physical environment interacts with other factors associated with formal and informal social control. The concept of defensible space has been broadened by some scholars, and combined with other factors. The routine-activities approach could be viewed as an expansion of this logic.

Routine Activities: Lawrence Cohen and Marcus Felson

It is difficult to steal something if there is little to steal. The availability of increasing numbers of consumer goods in stores and in homes has provided new opportunities for crime. There was a fundamental shift in lifestyle after World War II. Personal affluence and the accumulation of household property rose, and provided opportunities for theft. This pattern appears in Europe as well. The availability of consumer goods in Sweden was related to theft (Stack, 1982). The importance of the availability of criminal opportunities has been observed before, with regard to money in banks (Gould, 1969) and the availability of cars in Canada (McDonald, 1969; Giffen, 1976). The routine-activities perspective builds on these findings, but combines them with other factors to provide a more complete explanation.

The routine-activities approach treats the motivation to commit crime as a constant. Thus, Cohen and Felson (1979) explain the volume and distribution of predatory crime as related to the routine activities of people's everyday lives. These elements can be grouped into: 1) the availability of suitable targets (such as homes containing goods which could easily be resold) 2) the absence of capable guardians (homeowners, watchful neighbours, friends, and relatives), and 3) the presence of motivated offenders (such as unemployed teenagers). Thus, when motivated offenders are around suitable targets that are not protected, there is a greater likelihood of predatory crime. This approach has been used to examine trends in crime and make suggestions for criminal justice services and programmes (Cohen and Cantor, 1981; Felson and Cohen, 1980; Cohen 1981; Cohen, Kluegel, and Land, 1981).

With increased affluence, people spend less time in home-based "routine" activities. Outside of the home, especially if people are in bars or other places that generate "excitement," people are more at risk. Similarly, their unguarded residences are more likely to be targets of crime. In addition to going outside the home for recreational purposes, since 1960 more women have been working outside the home. With children in daycare, homes are left unguarded and therefore become more suitable targets for crime. Similarly, suburbia usually does not have as many neighbours who are relatives or close friends and who are effective guardians of nearby homes.

The growth of easily transportable wealth, such as colour television, VCRs, etc. tends to be a factor, in that the more wealth a home contains, the more likely it will be victimized (Massey, Krohn, and Bonati, 1989). Other research suggests that a large supply of youths, competing for a smaller number of jobs and educational opportunities, provides a surplus of "motivated offenders" (O'Brien, 1989).

In Canada, this orientation has been used by Leslie Kennedy and David Forde to look at different *lifestyles* (1990), using data from the Canadian Urban Victimization Study (1984), which covered seven Canadian cities. Young, lower-class males who go out late at night to bars, work, classes, or for a walk or a drive are the most likely to become crime victims. Sacco and Johnson (1990) also used Canadian data to support a lifestyle/exposure theory. Those who averaged thirty or more evening activities outside the home per month were more than twice as likely to be robbed. One might conclude that it is safer to stay at home. However, these arguments apply to victimization from strangers; those who stay at home are more likely to be killed by family or friends (Messner and Tardiff, 1985).

While the routine-activities perspective helps to identify high-risk situations, a number of factors are interacting. Kennedy and Forde note that one must take into account the setting, and other parties who interact with the victims. They also point out the need for conflict-resolution tactics to resolve problems beyond simply avoiding high-risk conditions (1990: 150).

Extending and Testing Ecological Theories of Crime

Developing appropriate measuring devices to test hypotheses can be challenging. We mention only a few problems that inevitably face most theory-testing activities. For example, routine activities treats "motivated offenders" as a constant, but this runs contrary to much of our theoretical thinking. We assume that people respond differently to opportunities for crime. Not every unemployed teenager is inclined to rob someone who leaves a bar or break into an unguarded house. Massey, Krohn, and Bonati (1989) suggest that the notion of "motivated offenders" should be replaced with a more straightforward concern about the presence of "potential offenders." This should be treated as a variable to be measured as part of the test of the theory. It may be difficult, however, to find data sets that combine measures of all of the concepts one wishes to assess.

Miethe, Stafford, and Long (1987) faced the typical problem of not having the most desirable measures available when they used the U.S. National Crime Survey. They examined lifestyles based on day and nighttime activities, both in and away from the home. The patterns for property crime seemed to fit ideas suggested above, but violent crime did not. The authors suggest that violent crime involves interpersonal conflict and is often spontaneous, and therefore is not explained by the rational assumptions and calculated decisions underlying routine-activities theory. While high-risk situations are necessary, they are not enough to explain violent crime. The study by Kennedy and Forde (1990), however, suggests that even though Miethe and his colleagues have a logical point, the situational factors are powerful enough to shed some light on the incidence of violent crime in the larger cities in Canada. In summary, more complete theory-testing, for routine activities or other perspectives, involves being able to work with and control for a fairly wide range of variables.

Designing Out Crime: Hong Kong Mass Transit Railway

Although ecological models of crime are still relatively selective, the knowledge that is available can be of use. Mark Gaylord and John Galliher (1991) describe how the Mass Transit Railway (MTR) in Hong Kong utilized an awareness of "defensible space" to "design out crime." Unlike governments in many North American cities, the Hong Kong government took seriously the knowledge that automobiles stifle cities. They were also aware that subways are potentially dangerous places in some cities. Therefore, the achievements of the MTR in Hong Kong are somewhat remarkable. It was completed ahead of schedule, within budget, and is the world's busiest subway in terms of passenger density per mile. It is also the world's cleanest and enjoys the lowest accident and crime rate. Passengers are safer *within* the MTR than when they are at street level. In Paris, some residents avoid the Metro late at night, because of concerns for their safety.

Mark Gaylord, a sociologist who does research and teaches in Hong Kong, spent many months studying the way the police and MTR authorities monitor the system. He and his co-author also describe the interaction between the police and those planning the system. Stations were designed to minimize alcoves, dog-leg passageways, and columns, thus denying would-be criminals hiding places (Gaylord and Galliher, 1991: 19). Where this was not possible, mirrors and closed circuit television were installed. There are no chairs, public toilets, fast-food facilities, or left-luggage lockers where bombs or drugs can be planted. Loitering is discouraged.

Every police constable is in constant contact with headquarters, due to the installation of a Leaky Coaxial cable during construction. Each station is equipped with a closed-circuit television camera. These help train operators gauge when they can close the doors of the train, but the same image goes back to the central control room. The MTR police claim that, for spotting criminals, the TV is better than foot patrols.

Each car has a Passenger Alarm Plunger, which permits passengers to talk directly to the train operator, who will then request that police meet the train at the next stop. The operator will keep all doors closed until the police are ready to enter the train. Over the years, both passengers and criminals have learned that a police officer will be at the scene within ninety seconds of notification. Trains are built with a "straight-through" format, allowing passengers and police to walk freely between cars. One can often view the entire length of a train from either end. At the coupling that connects the cars, there is a slight rise which permits police to gain a good view over the heads of standing passengers. Stations offer a limited number of entrances and can be sealed off quickly, but since this can interfere with traffic flow, risks must be balanced. Since most stations are nearly a hundred feet below surface level, the chance of a suspect reaching the street without being captured is very low.

Hong Kong provides some other important insights to some of the principles discussed earlier. Some of our notions of population density must be considered within the context of a specific culture. Hong Kong has the highest population density in the world: 13 600 per square mile. It also has a low crime rate, even when we recognize the problem of international comparisons. In 1986, New York City had 1,582 murders, London registered 210, and Hong Kong, with 5.7 million people, recorded 67. Obviously, the low rate of crime in the MTR is related to the relative safety of residents on the streets of Hong Kong.

Designing in Crime: The Destruction of Public Transportation in the U.S.

Most people would agree that public transportation and other aspects of urban design have an impact on pollution and other environmental problems. Fewer people would extend that thinking to crime. Governments can improve this aspect of city life. Public transportation is particularly important to that portion of the population most likely to be affected by crime. Some transportation specialists argue that urban sprawl and auto dependency generate alienation and encourage problem neighbourhoods like those described by Stark. These ecological factors, which seem to plague U.S. cities more than European ones, reflect the effectiveness of city planners and government officials. Admittedly, some economic interests find urban sprawl to be profitable, even though it damages the environment and probably contributes to the weakening of the social fabric that helps to control crime.

The U.S. love affair with the automobile was obviously encouraged by auto makers. Beginning in the 1930s, General Motors, in league with Standard Oil of California, Firestone Tires, and some cement companies, secretly purchased over a hundred public transportation systems in the U.S., and systematically destroyed them (Fischer, 1979). When they took over the Los Angeles system, the GM cartel destroyed the largest electrified transportation system in the world. The electric streetcars were replaced by GM buses, using Standard Oil diesel fuel and Firestone tires, and the expansion of freeways was profitable for the cement companies in the cartel. Auto sales increased, bus companies (owned by the cartel) lost money and petitioned for subsidies as public transportation declined and more people purchased cars. Los Angeles has become an ecological disaster, many more lives are lost on freeways as compared to public transportation but, in addition, has urban sprawl created criminogenic communities?

The San Francisco-Oakland Bay area also suffered from the activities of the General Motors cartel. A light rail system could have been accommodated under the Bay bridge, but it was many years before it was discovered that the GM cartel controlled the bridge and sabotaged public transportation plans. The tunnel under the San Francisco Bay was a much more expensive option. By the time a congressional investigator discovered the activities of the GM cartel in the 1970s, public transportation in much of the U.S. was in a shambles.

The point to be made here is that in Hong Kong public transportation is not only *profitable*, it reduces crime *directly* and provides service to working-class residents that *indirectly* influences criminogenic conditions. Most Canadian governments neglect public transportation, despite the inevitable concentration of population in large urban centres. The application of ecological theories can create safer ways to move people about, contribute to community cohesiveness, and reduce crime.

Let us turn now to the perspective of the potential offender. A number of studies have focused on "crime prevention through environmental design" (CPTED). The work by Patricia and Paul Brantingham of Simon Fraser University is a good illustration of this type of research.

The Criminal's Viewpoint

Peter Letkeman, from the University of Lethbridge, used a study of safecrackers in Vancouver to make some generalizations widely shared among scholars who have studied professional criminals. "The criminal, like the tourist, the farmer, or potential resident makes evaluations on the basis of factors relevant to his interests" (1973:9). One gap in ecological studies is that little research has been done on the actual decision-making criteria of criminals in choosing particular targets.

The Geometry of Crime: Patricia and Paul Brantingham

One study used twenty-three ex-burglars, who examined a series of slides and visited the sites of some burglarized apartments (Phelan, 1977). For the ex-burglars, familiarity with an area was critical, and techniques used to promote territoriality, as suggested by Newman and others, did not seem to be as important. Instead, Phelan found that the burglars emphasized surveillance as the major deterrent. Would they be seen and reported by residents, passers-by, and patrol personnel?

Sarah Boggs (1964) noted that crimes committed by Blacks were committed most often in neighbourhoods where the offenders lived, but crimes committed by Whites were more dispersed. Carter and Hill (1979) studied the way offenders viewed Oklahoma City, and found that Black and White offenders saw the city differently. Black offenders avoided areas that had good crime targets, because they were not familiar with them. White offenders, on the other hand, moved about the city more freely, and were aware of a greater range of targets.

Carter and Hill are cautious about the ability of policy-makers to use this knowledge to control crime effectively. They came to conclusions similar to those of Jane Jacobs, a perceptive observer of neighbourhoods, who has become well-known in Toronto. Her influential book, *The Death and Life of Great American Cities* (1961), argues that neighbourhoods are not protected primarily by the police, necessary though they may be. Rather, it is the intricate, almost unconscious, network of voluntary controls and standards among the people themselves that keeps the peace. No level of police enforcement can prevent crime, if this informal mechanism is working badly (33).

Patricia and Paul Brantingham are aware of these dynamics, but they start from the perspective of the potential offender (1981). They argue that the actual commission of an offense is the end result of a multi-staged decision process, which identifies targets positioned in time and space. The potential offender uses cues to locate targets. She begins close to home because of familiarity, but she is also more likely to be known and therefore discovered. For simplicity, they focus on the "routine activities" of the potential offender. The figures that follow simplify the stages of exploration that might lead to crime. Figure 14.1 shows the *search area* of a cluster of potential offenders. Although conscious of surveillance in the immediate neighbourhood, offenders may look for potential targets fairly close to home, and also explore areas adjacent to their neighbourhoods.

Like others, offenders move about the city and acquire knowledge about other parts of an urban area through working (even sporadically), school, shopping, or recreation. Criminals develop an *awareness space* about parts of the city. In general, offenses occur within the criminal's awareness space (See Figure 14.2).

Depending on how a city is arranged, the awareness space of criminals will be larger or smaller. If shopping, recreation, and work locations are dispersed, awareness spaces should be larger. The way one moves about the city will also influence awareness. While travelling on the subway in Toronto, it is very hard to examine nearby targets in apartment buildings. By car or on foot, it would be easier. At the subway station, while waiting for a connecting bus, opportunities to observe shops and other targets would be greater. Figure 14.3 suggests a more complex search area for a cluster of offenders, perhaps a gang.

Although the search area may be large, the subarea that contains good targets is smaller. For an individual offender, Figure 14.4 illustrates adding areas with good targets. Some targets are outside the individual's awareness space, so only the cross-hatched areas are places of likely crime.

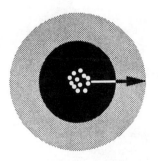 

 Offenders

Search Area

FIGURE 14.1 Search Area for Clustered Offenders
Source: Brantingham and Brantingham (1981)

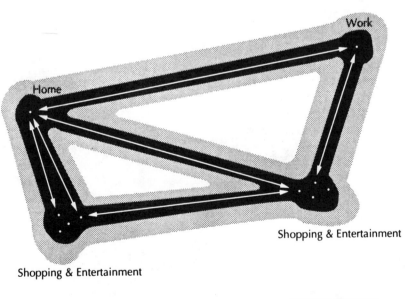

Movement paths   Search Area

FIGURE 14.2 Complex Search Area for Individual Offender
Source: Brantingham and Brantingham (1981)

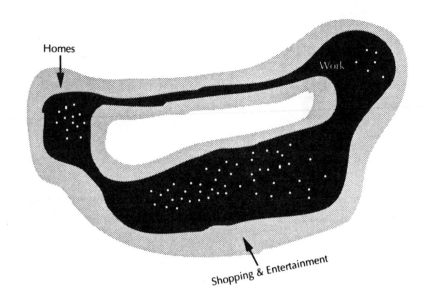

FIGURE 14.3 Complex Search Area for Cluster of Offenders

Source: Brantingham and Brantingham (1981)

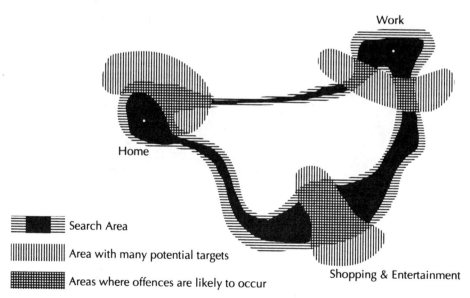

FIGURE 14.4 Selective Complex Search Area for Individual Offender

Source: Brantingham and Brantingham (1981)

However, perceived risk is another factor; therefore, things like escape routes are considered. Dufala (1976) found that convenience-store robberies in Tallahassee, Florida, were more common near major roads that had no surrounding evening business activity. On the other hand, if the store were in the middle of the West Edmonton Mall, an escape route might be rather confusing. The Brantinghams also note that awareness space is dynamic and can change over time. The novice looks for targets within her limited awareness space, and may search fringe areas. Over time, she expands her awareness space to include adjacent areas. If she has many social contacts among like-minded individuals, she may expand her area of high crime activity (Figure 14.5).

Like other routine-activities approaches, the above ideas only deal with a limited aspect of crime; but they may help to explain changes in crime patterns in cities. For example, newer cities with a mosaic of shopping centres, work areas, and entertainment locations will have dispersed crime patterns. Potential offenders travel more and have broader target search areas. This has obviously been influenced by the widespread use of automobiles. In Canada, cities in the West are newer than cities in the East and probably have poorer public transportation systems. Is this a partial explanation of the differences in crime rates from East to West?

LINKING ECOLOGICAL STUDIES WITH OTHER SOCIOLOGICAL STUDIES

Large cities are often seen as having more crime, but people distinguish between the entire city and their own neighbourhood. Quite often, people perceive their own neighbourhoods as relatively safe, even though they see the city in which they live as fairly dangerous (Hindelang, Gottfredson, and Garafolo, 1978). Vince Sacco (1985) also found this to be true of Canadian cities. He notes, however, that American cities may experience greater perceptions of danger because there are large and visible inner-city populations, and people link urban crime problems with these populations. This exacerbates ethnic hostilities, which influence crime in the U.S. Canadian cities are smaller than their American counterparts, and ethnic neighbourhoods in Canadian cities may be less concentrated and are frequently viewed as interesting and exotic. However, the potential for developing neighbourhoods that are perceived as dangerous is there.

Neighbourhood Integration and the Willingness to Intervene

Wesley Skogan and Michael Maxfield studied neighbourhood integration and crime in Chicago, Philadelphia, and San Francisco (1981). One of their findings is that neighbourhoods that displayed social cohesion and integration were less likely

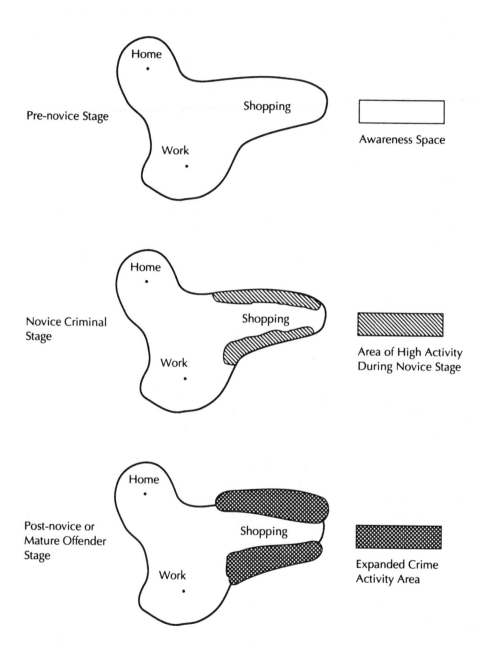

FIGURE 14.5 Maturation of Crime Search Area
Source: Brantingham and Brantingham (1981)

to perceive that they had a serious crime problem and, in fact, had lower crime rates. Although the three cities did not appear to differ remarkably overall, neighbour-hoods *within* the cities did vary considerably.

Skogan pursues this theme in his book *Disorder and Decline* (1992), where he concludes community disorder appears to interfere with the ability of communi-ties to exercise social control, and thus is related to crime and the fear of crime. While this confirms what most people suspect, Skogan also examines community policing programmes that attempt to address these problems. It seems that com-munity policing does increase police-citizen contact, but the citizens most in need of help are the least likely to be affected. Thus, the quality of urban community life is crucial to crime control, but programmes that deal effectively with disordered com-munities are difficult to enact.

Part of this chapter emphasizes physical characteristics of communities, but there is considerable interaction among a number of factors. In an earlier chapter, I discussed the "collective behaviour" that takes place in small groups. Under some conditions, people were more willing to intervene when deviance was observed. When people in those small-group experiments *knew* each other, it increased the likelihood of intervention. One might assume that in *integrated, cohesive* neigh-bourhoods people would know each other. In an early study of these phenom-ena, Maccoby, Johnson, and Church (1958) studied two neighbourhoods that were similar in educational levels and occupational status, but had different delin-quency rates. The residents in the low-delinquency-rate neighbourhood liked the area, knew their neighbours, and were willing to take action if they saw a child com-mitting a delinquent act. Skogan and Maxfield (1981) would probably consider this community *integrated, a* neighbourhood with greater *social cohesion.* These stud-ies suggest that social isolation may decrease the level of social control.

Macobby and her colleagues assumed that the two communities would dif-fer in their *attitudes* towards delinquency, with the high-delinquency area consid-ering delinquent acts less serious than the low-delinquency area. In fact, they found that the attitudes were very similar. I wish to emphasize this point, because many criminologists and policy-makers argue that criminal behaviour cannot be changed without modifying internalized values. In fact, there are many things that can be done *without* concentrating on changing attitudes. Some people argue that attitudes must change *before* behaviour will change. As was discussed earlier when we summarized cognitive dissonance, situations can be changed quickly and dramatically. Sometimes behaviour changes because of circumstances; then at-titudes change last, or perhaps they never change. Therefore, it behooves us to look at situations in different cities and neighbourhoods that might increase inte-gration, regardless of attitudes.

Shared Communication Networks

Vienna, Austria, seems to provide evidence for and against some of the ecological arguments. I lived in an area that was densely populated, but during my year of residence the crime on my street that generated the most discussion was dogs defecating on the sidewalk. Dogs who did not wear muzzles, another offense in the city of Vienna, did not generate the same outrage. Property- and violent-crime rates were perceived to be low. Like the Swiss, Austrians carried reasonable amounts of cash, merchants displayed goods on sidewalks without exercising excessive guardianship, and bicycles were often seen without locks. On the other hand, Jane Jacobs would have quickly noticed the informal networks in the neighbourhoods, which provided social cohesion, the societal glue. Windows at the street level were often open during the summer. A walk to the store usually meant several conversations with neighbours along the way.

A century ago in Vienna, when each apartment did not have its own water supply, people would meet and talk at the common water faucet. The term *Bassenagespräch* arose, which referred to the gossip that developed while standing around the water fountain. Although the term has negative connotations of gossiping about neighbours, it also illustrates how a physical characteristic of a building brought people together to share information. With modern plumbing in each apartment, it is now easier to isolate oneself from the communication network that existed at the water fountain. While Rodney Stark suggests that this lack of privacy may have made it more difficult to present a better moral front, it also created pressures to conform. Minding everyone else's business may be viewed as an advantage or disadvantage to North Americans who live in Vienna, but a communication system that spreads information probably reduces crime.

In Glasgow, one term for neighbourhood gossip was "havin' a hangin'". That is, you hung out the window and talked to your neighbour across the narrow street. Naturally, with modern apartment buildings this is harder to manage if you are on the thirtieth floor and the neighbouring apartment is a hundred metres away. The conditions I am describing in Glasgow and Vienna obviously mean that there are more people watching what goes on in the street.

Eyes on the Street

A bridge crossing the North Saskatchewan River in Edmonton was occasionally the scene of an accident that blocked traffic. No residences are close to the bridge, but years ago someone watched the traffic, and when an accident occurred, immediately called the police. No one ever learned who the caller was, but when those involved in the accident, or someone trying to help, finally walked to a telephone they were often surprised that the police had been notified. In fact, the police often arrived before anyone got to a phone.

To what extent do eyes on the street deter crime? In some areas of Québec, front porches are common: residents often sit on them, and sometimes chat with people as they go by. However, I know of no study that attempts to assess this type of architecture in Québec in terms of its impact on social cohesiveness and crime deterrence. As we saw in the chapter on collective behaviour, observing events does not necessarily mean that someone will act. Not only do we need conditions that encourage people to watch, we also need the type of community integration that increases the likelihood of action. In planning apartment complexes, architects thought that they could create inner courtyards and grassy areas where people would congregate. But these somewhat private inner courtyards are not where the action is. In some apartment complexes, mothers take their small children out next to the parking lots in playpens, and sit in their chairs knitting or whatever, because the comings and goings of people in the cars provide topics of conversation (who was driving a new car, who bought a new dress, etc.). The asphalt and auto exhaust fumes win out over the shade and green grass of the courtyard because the parking lot provides more interesting subject matter.

Jane Jacobs describes a setting where a man was standing by a bus stop. After a few minutes a lady opened a window and called to the man, asking where he was going. When he explained, the lady said that the bus he wanted didn't stop there anymore. He needed to go around the corner. How would this sort of activity be related to crime prevention? If a stranger were doing something suspicious in the neighbourhood, would she be noticed? With the advent of television, it is possible that many "eyes on the street" have been lost. The violence and crime on television are more intriguing than observing the rare real thing out the window.

Imagine a little girl playing on a sidewalk. A car drives up. The man in the car tries to get the little girl to get into the car. She shakes her head and refuses. The proprietor of the small hardware store behind the girl has been watching. He now steps onto the sidewalk holding a hammer in his hand. The butcher in the shop next door has also been observing the scene. He comes to the doorway with the meat cleaver still in his hand. Let us ruin the suspense by mentioning that the man in the car is the little girl's father, but the point should be clear. Jane Jacobs and others argue that busy sidewalks with many interested observers looking on make for safer environments. We would add that the social psychological studies described in an earlier chapter suggest that when people know each other in the community it also makes them more willing to intervene.

Jane Jacobs Areas

In a study of the community cohesiveness in a dozen census tracts in Edmonton, we found ourselves referring to one section of town as the "Jane Jacobs Area" (Hackler, Ho, and Urquhart-Ross, 1974). It was low in socioeconomic status, but it had characteristics that suggested social cohesion. From one street-corner we could see six small churches on one street. This suggested the possibility of smaller organizations where people could communicate more easily.

Fences can be barriers to communication, or they can expedite it. In this area, the lots were small, perhaps twenty-five feet wide, with small houses. Many fences were three to four feet tall, topped by a two-by-four with heavy wire used as the fencing material itself. One could lean on such fences and chat with a neighbour, perhaps about the vegetables in the front yard. In the home where I grew up, the fence separating the two back yards made communication among neighbours fairly easy. It was a wire fence with large openings. Many years ago, when my sister was about four years old, she was given a bone to take to the dog next door. When she did not return, we looked out the window. My sister was putting the bone through the fence so the dog could take a bite; then she would take the bone back and chew for a bit while the dog waited patiently for his turn. Surely, such a fence was no barrier to neighbourliness.

COMBINING DIFFERENT PERSPECTIVES AND INTEGRATING THEORIES

Criminologists have traditionally developed their theories on a psychological or sociological level, or have utilized a single perspective. For research purposes, that has a certain amount of merit. In addition, some criminologists argue that many theories are incompatible because they make different assumptions about human behaviour. The real world, however, does not function that way. Many factors are constantly interacting. Theoretical models might describe criminal behaviour more accurately if they could reflect the interaction among variables at the sociological and psychological levels, and included ecological factors, biological variables, and so on. Theories offered so far focus on limited aspects of social behaviour. Integrating several perspectives together would probably offer a better overall explanation of crime. A number of scholars have attempted this, but we select only a few for illustration.

Terence Thornberry's Interactional Theory

This approach challenges the one-directional causal order that is inherent in many theories of crime (Thornberry, 1987). That is, factors are viewed as exerting a causal influence on delinquency, without taking into account that delinquency may, in fact, influence these very same factors. Arguing that human behaviour develops dynamically over time as people interact with one another and as the consequences of prior behaviour are felt, interactional theory posits that delinquent behaviour may also have reciprocal causal influences on such variables as attachment to parents and commitment to school (Thornberry, et al., 1991). As a result, there is a potential for spiralling a person along an increasingly delinquent behavioural trajectory. Thus, delinquency is viewed as part of a larger causal network, affected by social factors but also affecting the development of those social factors over time.

Some scholars in Canada have combined variables from control theory and differential association that might be seen as moving towards integration (Linden and Fillmore, 1981; Linden and Hackler, 1973), but what makes the work of Thornberry and his colleagues different is that it specifically calls attention to developmental issues and the reciprocal, or looping, effect of these interactions. Such interactions are complex, and one must ask if this complexity is worthwhile. Since this book is interested in the policy implications of criminological theories, how might interactional theory provide some guidelines? Delinquency contributes, in a very real sense, to its own causation. That is, it causes a deterioration in the attachment and commitment to family and school, which further erodes the restraints on delinquency. Thus, comprehensive, holistic treatment strategies are required, rather than looking for a single key variable (Thornberry, et al. 1991). Rodney Stark uses a similar logic when he discusses "dangerous places." This means that effective interventions will be expensive and difficult to manage. On the other hand, successful intervention in one part of the system will have a ripple effect throughout the system, helping intervention efforts targeted at another factor. Family interventions that improve attachments to parents should also indirectly improve commitment to school, thereby making the efforts of teachers a little easier.

Another implication is that family interventions should start early, because the impact of parents on the behaviour of their children weakens as they become adolescents. In addition, schools must attempt to break the cycle of alienation from education early. Enjoying the classroom during the early years has an impact on the other factors that are related to delinquency. By late adolescence, the focus should shift and aid in a smooth transition from school to meaningful work. If the early problems are left unattended a behavioural trajectory is established, which increases the likelihood of adult crime. By the same token, if early problems are dealt with successfully, the same reciprocal quality of the system works to *decrease* crime.

Delbert Elliott's Integrated Theory

Delbert Elliott (1985) argues that scholars often make empirical tests to determine which of two hypotheses is better, but overlook the fact that "both hypotheses might be correct and might account for independent portions of the variance in the crime" (p. 126). When Elliott, David Huizinga, and Suzanne Ageton (1985) combined various aspects of learning, control, and strain theories, using data from a nationwide survey of adolescents, they tested an integrated theory. Structural models account for strains that lead to delinquent acts, but do not explain why some youths continue into careers of crime while others drop out. Control theories portray the delinquent as a loner, lacking close ties to important others in society. Thus, control theory suggests that delinquents are those freer to deviate but lacking the group support for prolonged criminal involvement. Learning theories often portray delinquents as somewhat passive, simply responding to delinquency-producing reinforcements.

By integrating the stronger features of these perspectives into a single theoretical model, Elliott and his colleagues argue that the perceptions of strain, inadequate socialization, and living in socially disorganized areas lead to weaker bonding with conventional others. When bonds to conventional people are weak, the attractions of delinquent peers are stronger. Such peers provide role models for crime and give psychological support and reinforcement for delinquent behaviour. These scholars concluded that variables from social learning explained the greatest amount of delinquency; social-control predictors came next, with strain and social-disorganization variables accounting for relatively little variation in delinquency.

Colvin And Pauly: An Integrated Structural-Marxist Approach

Both Elliott and Thornberry have concentrated on social-psychological, or microsociological factors. Ecological and macrosociological-level variables may be more amenable to social action if we recognize the erosion of certain structural supports in society. Mark Colvin and John Pauly (1983) developed an integrated structural-Marxist theory, which incorporates social-psychological factors into a macrosociological framework. They argue that lower-social-class employees who work in environments where there is coercive control are more likely to become hostile and alienated.

The capitalist system creates social relations in the workplace that do not inspire loyalty and respect for authority. This hostility and alienation comes home with the disgruntled worker, and is reproduced in the family. Children of alienated workers, particularly boys, are socialized differently than boys who live in families where the parents are more satisfied with their work and with the system. The attitudes in the workplace influence the attitudes in the home, and shape the initial bond or ties to authority. Lower-class parents who face coerciveness at work transfer this to their children. This influences the way children relate to other adults, the school, and peer groups.

Legitimate opportunities are more available to those from the proper social class with the appropriate socialization, but those who see barriers will be attracted to illegitimate opportunity structures. The resulting association with delinquent peers, and the interaction that follows, would fit the models described above. In terms of policy, this structural-Marxist model suggests changes are needed in the workplace. Since North America has many illustrations of companies "down-sizing" and laying off workers who are already vulnerable, this theoretical model predicts more discontent among lower-class families, more criminogenic conditions, and more crime in the future.

John Braithwaite: Reintegrative Shaming

John Braithwaite (1989) offers an integrated and general theory of crime, particularly those predatory acts that are seen by the community as reprehensible. Central to his own thinking is the concept of *reintegrative shaming*, in which both negative and positive responses of community members must be considered. The key to crime control is to shame offenders in ways that are "reintegrative." He builds on control theory, labelling, opportunity, subcultural and learning perspectives.

Crime is committed more frequently by young, unmarried males who live in large cities and who experience high residential mobility. They differ in their *interdependency* from married people and females. The employed are also more interdependent than those who are unemployed. Interdependent people are less likely to commit crime because they are more susceptible to shaming. Societies where people are interdependent are more likely to be *communitarian*, and shaming is more widespread and potent. Urbanization and high residential mobility undermine communitarianism. Japan is communitarian, even though modern and highly industrialized. The U.S. provides a stark contrast.

Shaming can become stigmatization, or can be followed by reintegration. Community disapproval ranges from mild rebuke to severe degradation ceremonies, which may or may not be followed by gestures of reacceptance and ceremonies that bring the offender back into the fold with other law-abiding citizens. Reintegrative shaming is more likely to bring the wrongdoer back into line. In communitarian societies shaming is likely to be reintegrative and crime rates low, because disapproval is dispensed without the deviant rejecting those who disapprove. Thus, the potential for, and the power of, future disapproval remains intact.

Stigmatization, by contrast, is a form of disapproval that often drives offenders to further acts of criminality. Stigmatizing shaming casts the deviant out of the circle of supporters and makes other groups, such as criminal subcultures, more attractive. When shaming becomes stigmatization, for want of reintegrative gestures and ceremonies that decertify deviance, the deviant is attracted to criminal subcultures and cut off from non-deviant interdependencies. To the extent that shaming is stigmatizing rather than reintegrative, and that criminal subcultures are accessible, higher crime rates will result. High levels of stigmatization encourage subculture formation, by creating outcasts with no stake in conformity.

In societies where individualism is the prevailing ideology, citizens are more inclined to shun and isolate offenders and endeavour to control crime through stigmatizing punishments, which pushes them into interdependencies with other violators. Systematic blockage of legitimate opportunities, exacerbated by the stigmatization, fosters criminal subcultures. Such blockages are most evident for those trying to climb out of poverty, but Braithwaite points out that these principles apply to white-collar offenders as well. When affluent corporations see barriers to even greater wealth accumulation, they look to each other and develop corporate criminal subcultures as a means of achieving certain goals. To counter such corporate crimes, Braithwaite argues that punitive measures against white-collar crime should emphasize direct adverse publicity, so that the offenses and the people who commit them are known to the rest of the community.

CONCLUSION

Clearly, the physical environment can influence social relations. Spatial factors are related to characteristics of the neighbourhood and create circumstances that influence crime. Even if the impact of these factors is small, it behooves policy-makers to take them into account. Modest gains can sometimes be achieved with relatively little cost. The Hong Kong Mass Transit Railway offers an excellent illustration of intelligent public planning that can reduce the level of crime.

Relatively few theories integrate spatial, sociological, and psychological elements. In addition, few theories note the reciprocal effect of variables, particularly crime itself which, in turn, has a strong impact on other causal factors. Rodney Stark and Terence Thornberry emphasize the reciprocal effect of variables, which suggests that public policy should direct efforts at many different points. The modest impact of each change could reinforce other changes. Colvin and Pauly incorporate structural variables that are identified by Marxist thinking, and suggest policy measures at the macrosociological level. Braithwaite feels that wrongdoers should be shamed, at all levels of the social hierarchy, but after they have repented, they should be brought back and reintegrated into the mainstream of society.

We have often heard that theorizing has nothing to do with the real world. This is simply wrong. The ecological perspectives and integrated theories summarized here emphasize different strategies, but they clearly offer something that policy makers could use.

PART **III**

THE SHAPE AND FORM
OF MODERN CRIME
PATTERNS

Instead of using the conventional categories which reflect different types of crimes, these chapters focus on patterns that generate a variety of social responses. Chapter 15 deals with women's issues, Chapter 16 with drugs, and Chapter 17 with violence. However, chapter 17 spends less time on murderers and more time on murderous situations. Chapter 18 reviews conventional and unconventional views on crimes for profit. In Chapter 19, prostitution and homosexual activities in public places are reviewed. As in the discussion on drugs, the focus is on the way agents of social control might respond. My assumption is that certain activities will continue and intelligent policies will work toward minimizing harm rather than eradication. Traditional questions are not always appropriate, and therefore, criminologists should reorient some of their thinking.

WOMEN'S ISSUES AND CRIMINOLOGY

Being a woman is a terribly difficult task, since it consists principally in dealing with men.

Joseph Conrad

THE NEED FOR A FEMINIST PERSPECTIVE ON CRIME

Marie Andrée Bertrand (1969, 1979, 1983), at the Université de Montréal, is one of the better-known Canadian criminologists to emphasize the male bias in criminology. First, there has been an intellectual sexism in theories of female crime. This typically took the form of emphasizing biological factors, which "naturally" had certain consequences. Men were innately more aggressive and females were naturally more care-giving. Social inequality was often denied and economic forces were ignored. Secondly, the criminal justice systems institutionalized sexism in their responses to females in trouble. A double standard was frequently applied. Sexual deviance and "immorality" were included with criminality. Traditional theories ignore the way agencies of social control reinforce womens' place in a male-dominated society (Chesney-Lind, 1989).

Historically, most criminologists have been men. Thus, it is not surprising that traditional theories of crime pay little attention to gender or the impact of patriarchal power relationships. Until recently, criminology has been a male bastion. When women became producers of knowledge, the new ideas were not always well received by those who have had a monopoly on the creation of wisdom. New issues were raised that have largely been ignored by traditional scholars. Such transitions take place in all disciplines, but it is appropriate to describe how a male-dominated discipline has responded to feminist views in criminology over the past three decades.

The Transition: Male Adaptations to Female-Created Knowledge

The fact that this book has a separate chapter on feminist thought illustrates a phase in criminological thinking. Traditionally, criminology texts reviewed crimes *by* women and how women are victimized, but the issues raised have been limited. As male textbook writers have become aware of their traditional thinking, and the need to incorporate feminist thinking into modern criminology, they have responded in predictable ways. One strategy is to ask a feminist criminologist to write a chapter on the topic, and add it to your book. Thus, when Rick Linden's *Criminology: A Canadian Perspective* was revised (1992) an additional chapter on Women and Crime, by Elizabeth Comack, was added.

Another strategy for male textbook authors is to learn more about feminist thinking. As a result, chapters on feminist thought will appear in new criminology texts. But this may be a transitional phase. As these views broaden our perspective, modify our theories, and lead to gathering facts in areas that had been neglected, feminist thinking may permeate other parts of criminology texts, and the practice of simply adding a separate chapter may be seen as a quaint, intermediate adaptation to an area that required fundamental changes.

Admitting Females to the Bastions of Male Criminological Knowledge Production

As a discipline, criminology has probably resisted feminist thinking more than other academic areas. Similarly, women have been slower to move into positions of influence in criminological academic organizations. In academic associations in anthropology, psychology, sociology, even medicine, women have been members of boards of directors, served as president, etc. for several decades. The process was slower in the American Society of Criminology (ASC), the most influential organization for Canadian criminologists. Few women served in leadership roles, and a woman did not become president until Joan McCord was elected in 1988[1]. By contrast, Canadian male criminologists have been able to participate in the American "old boy network" for some time, even though they represent a much smaller proportion of the ASC membership than do women.

While one should not use election to office as the only measure of intellectual acceptance, it is reasonable to argue that, compared to other areas of academic endeavour, criminology has been slow to utilize female talent to expand certain areas of knowledge. The Society for the Study of Social Problems (SSSP), recruited females for leadership positions in the 1960s, and by the late 1970s competent fe-

---

[1]The Canadian Association for Criminological Research and the Canadian Criminal Justice Association had women serving as presidents at a much earlier time.

male scholars were easily winning elections and leading the society. The old boy network broke down more quickly in the SSSP than in the ASC. Feminist thinking broadened sociological perspectives on social problems. In criminology, feminist thinking has been more isolated from other areas of interest.

The abilities of women in the American Society of Criminology were not readily appreciated, nor were their intellectual contributions incorporated into programmes to the extent they were in the Society for the Study of Social Problems. In response, women in the ASC organized a section on Women and Crime. In other organizations, such as the SSSP, there appeared to be greater intellectual interaction among male and female scholars. Admittedly, some members of the Women and Crime Section may have felt a need for a "sisterhood" as an understandable response to the situation in the American Society of Criminology, but the major thrust of the Section has been to expand intellectual horizons. These scholars "take into account a woman's perspective or interests" (Boyd and Sheehy, 1989: 255; Boyle, 1986). It is my impression that male criminologists, compared to other social scientists, have found it more difficult to interact with female colleagues who are bright, young, strong-minded, and who challenge traditional ideas. As a result, the fertilization of ideas that comes with the infusion of feminist thinking has lagged behind in criminology compared to other disciplines.

Male-Generated Myths on Feminism

When you are "one of the boys," it is easy to develop a certain perspective on feminist views of criminology. Part of that masculine bias might be summarized with three myths:

1. feminist analyses of crime are not objective;

2. feminist analyses focus narrowly on women; and

3. there is only one feminist perspective.

Kathleen Daly and Meda Chesney-Lind (1988) address these myths. Their ideas are paraphrased here.

Myth No. 1: The Lack of Objectivity

Until recently, depictions of the differences between men and women have been made almost exclusively by white, privileged men. Men have no monopoly on objectivity and, as a consequence, biased interpretations of human evolution and behaviour, are offered as authoritative. For example, theories of the evolution of "mankind" emphasize how bipedalism and expanded brain size resulted from *men's* tool-making and tool-use in the hunting of large game. Some feminist anthropologists asked, "Have only men evolved?" (Hubbard, 1982) Other new ideas have arisen in the past that offer alternative accounts of social life, but feminist ideas are assumed to be biased while the dominant and traditional modes of inquiry are *a priori* accorded greater legitimacy.

Myth No. 2: The Narrow Focus on Women

Feminists do not ignore men, although they give more attention to women. Obviously, traditional criminology focuses more on men, but *whose* social reality is worthy of explanation and *who* can be trusted to get it right? Much feminist work has focused on the way men think, theorize, collect, and marshal evidence. This contributes to a broadened awareness about how knowledge is created. Eleanor Miller's *Street Woman*, for example, provides a vision of the world from the perspective of the subjects. It not only provides insights about women, it makes us aware of other marginal people who struggle to survive in a society that claims to care about the weak, but has allowed practices that fall short of that goal. Traditional non-feminist criminology is more likely to be narrow, focusing on the lives of men with minimal attention to gender relations. Feminists will also make mistakes, but the movement has broadened, not narrowed, the discipline.

Myth No. 3: The Single Feminist Perspective

This is simply nonsense. There is a variety of views. It would be more accurate to say there is a *set of perspectives*, based on certain common assumptions about gender inequality. The dominant voice of American feminism is admittedly white, middle-class, and heterosexual, but other voices are beginning to reflect different social concerns. In addition, men are also engaged in feminist investigations, although criminology may lag behind other social sciences in this respect.

FEMINISM AND LAW IN CANADA

This brief summary of feminist legal scholarship since 1970 is provided by Susan Boyd and Elizabeth Sheehy (1989). Law and criminology are not identical, but organizing these feminist orientations into liberal, result equality, Marxist and socialist, radical, and integrative also makes sense in criminology.

Liberal Feminism and Result Equality Feminism

The 1970 report of the Royal Commission on the Status of Women argued for sex equality by eliminating laws that differentiated people by gender. The thrust of these liberal feminist scholars was equality before the law, with some authors arguing that discriminatory assumptions in statutes perpetuated stereotypes of female roles. The *Constitution Act* of 1982 and the accompanying *Charter of Rights and Freedoms* met the basic demands of liberal feminists, but gender neutrality in legislation does not necessarily eliminate inequality between the sexes. *Result equality feminism* looks at actual effects. For example, a provision that entitles a husband or wife to support from the deserting spouse gives no recognition to the reasons for the desertion or the tenuous financial position of the typical deserting wife (Shrofel, 1985). A man who leaves his wife is probably in better financial shape than a woman who leaves an assaultive husband.

Marxist and Socialist Feminism and Radical Feminism

Feminist views utilizing Marxist thinking noted inequalities arising out of the structure of society. Women's unpaid labour in the home was undervalued; rape was seen as more serious when the woman "belonged" to a man or had not been "married off" by parents. Traditional Marxism ignores the fact that women give birth and are the primary care-givers of children. Jane Ursel (1986) shows that, historically, family, labour, and welfare laws let men control women. Shelley Gavigan (1986) contends that the law provides the medical profession with authority over women's reproduction. *Radical feminism* rejects liberal and socialist perspectives in favour of a more direct attack on patriarchy — the systematic male domination of women that permeates society. Laws governing reproduction and sexual assault are seen as extensions of patriarchal control over women.

Integrative Feminism and the Application of Feminist Legal Theories

Integrative feminism is similar to and differs from these other perspectives, but it looks carefully at male control over women through the law, and asks how women might be empowered. Integrative feminists, however, are somewhat cynical about the potential for legislation to change the position of women in Canada, since judges, who are mostly male and traditional, must evaluate the constitutionality of legislation designed to reverse sexism.

How can these feminist legal theories be applied to crime? Rape legislation offers an illustration. Lorenne Clark and Debra Lewis (1977) took a Marxist perspective when they argued that rape was viewed as a crime against male property, rather than an offence against a female person. Traditionally, husbands could not be guilty of raping their wives. The requirement of proof of penetration further supported the argument. Physical integrity *per se* was not the primary factor. Feminists using a gender-neutral principle might argue that men as well as women could be victimized by rape, but radical feminists note that degenderization of rape masks reality. A *result equality* approach to sexual assault would ask if women are actually more protected. Gavigan (1986) warns against assuming that legislation and strategies of intervention will resolve such issues. We should focus instead on gender relations and politics. This is pursued in my later discussion of family violence.

Feminist views are broadening, rather than narrowing, criminological inquiry. They may shed light on certain puzzles, such as the fact that those who are repressed and disadvantaged are more criminal, or at least become officially labelled as criminal. Women are disadvantaged in our patriarchal society. Why aren't they more criminal? True, disadvantaged women are more criminal than those who are not, but it is still difficult to explain the low rate of female crime. Feminist questioning goes beyond women and crime, to include basic questions about the structure and function of the larger society and the dynamics of institutions that influence our lives.

TRADITIONAL EXPLANATIONS OF FEMALE CRIME

A short review of some of the thinking about female crime is useful to set the stage for both criticism and change. The traditional approach to female crime tends to focus on sex, and is almost oblivious to the fact that it takes two to tango. Clearly, males who have sex are not deviant but unmarried women are. This double standard permeates the traditional earlier "studies" in criminology.

The Sexualization of Female Crime

In *The Unadjusted Girl* (1923), William I. Thomas used case studies and equated female criminality with sexual delinquency. Thomas was influenced by biological models of crime. The reader will recall from earlier chapters that Lombroso and Ferrero (1895) viewed women as less intelligent, more passive, and morally deficient, when compared to men. Unless carefully supervised, their sexual instincts would get them into trouble. Thomas also emphasized instincts and assumed that the need for love was more intense for women than for men. Prostitutes did not receive enough love in a socially approved manner. The double standard is blatant, in that unmarried men seeking sex are "normal," but unmarried women doing so are "unadjusted." Women are "objects" to be adored and desired and to learn to play the appropriate social role through interaction with others. The differences between good and bad girls are often due to their social-class position and upbringing. Middle-class females are socialized to treasure their chastity. Lower-class girls lack this socialization. Good women sell their bodies for marriage, bad ones trade their bodies for excitement.

While these ideas are clearly sexist, they reflected a common view of female crime and had a great deal of impact on academia, the police, and other agents of social control. This basic theme persisted in criminology so that Otto Pollak, almost forty years later, in *The Criminality of Women* (1961), still saw women as basically inferior. He argued that official crime data under-reported the criminality of women. He emphasized the "chivalry hypothesis." The male-dominated justice system is lenient with women. But women are also deceitful. The deceitfulness of women is biologically based and socially induced. Men are less deceitful, because they must have an erection in order to have sex and cannot hide their failure. Men cannot pretend. A woman's body, however, permits pretence, and lack of orgasm does not prevent her from having sex. With the assurance gained by deceiving men, women can commit crimes that go undetected. It is hard for me to imagine how having sex without having an orgasm provides training for crime, but Pollak was considered an expert in the 1960s.

Women's social roles as homemakers also provide cover for other crimes: sexually abusing young children and poisoning the sick. In addition, women mastermind the crimes and men carry them out. These ideas from Pollak suggest that, compared to other areas of intellectual endeavour, criminology lagged behind. Such thinking persisted, even among women. Edith de Rham writes that females have an "inordinate talent for concealment and deception which characterizes the feminine style and makes the female lawbreaker harder to catch" (1969: 5). We are assured that most husbands are aware of this.

The reader can recognize the drift of the argument, so there is no need to summarize the many other scholars who wrote in this vein. However, it important to note the consequences of this thinking. The agents of social control were imbued with this logic and applied the double standard; thus, there was an institutional reinforcement of these "explanations."

By the 1960s many criminologists were suspicious of biological models and favoured socialization to explain female crime, as well as the tendency to commit less crime than males. Essentially, boys and girls learn different roles. Boys learn to become breadwinners and girls learn to be homemakers and caregivers. Boys are taught that they must take risks and be assertive, while girls are instructed that they should be passive, cautious and dependent (Bertrand, 1969; Naffine, 1987: 43-47). Thus, we tolerate boisterous and aggressive behaviour among boys but not among girls. The attributes compatible with crime are those that characterize masculinity. When women commit crime, then, they are seen as poorly socialized or having taken on masculine traits.

An earlier chapter, reviewed Lawrence Kohlberg's ideas on moral development (Kohlberg, 1976; Jennings, Kilkenny, and Kohlberg. 1983). According to Kohlberg, females do not move up the levels of moral maturity as much as males. They develop concern and sensitivity to others, but they are less inclined to develop insights into the abstract and universal rights that are part of the final stage of moral development. Carol Gilligan (1982, 1987) questions this conclusion. If women operate at a lower level of moral development, why do they commit less crime than men? She goes on to point out the masculine bias in Kohlberg's work, and in psychology in general.

Institutional Support for the Sexualization of Female Crime

Meda Chesney-Lind (1989) and Holly Johnson (1987) draw on considerable empirical research, which shows that the justice system not only has been a means for controlling females who do not conform to certain expectations, but has been part of the pattern of patriarchal power that put females at a disadvantage in society in general. Psychiatric institutions also play a role in controlling women. Women are placed in the "sick" role when they do not perform in traditional ways. Diane Hudson (1987) contends that women are more likely to be lobotomized than men, to solve behavioural problems. A bias on the part of psychiatrists is illustrated by the following case history.

> C was diagnosed as 'reluctant to accept authority' when she found it difficult to relate to a male psychiatrist after disclosing ... a long-term stable lesbian relationship. Her lesbianism was interpreted as a personality disorder for which she received drugs. She was diagnosed as 'hostile and aggressive' towards the stepfather who had sexually assaulted her when she was thirteen, ... She confided, just before she died, that a 'brain operation' to help her had been discussed. She perceived this as a threat rather than as a mode of treatment and the fear instilled by this threat probably contributed greatly to her suicide. (Hudson, 1987: 117)

It is also obvious that a woman who kills her children is "sick." Psychiatrists could not view her as "normal," but overwhelmed by circumstance. If she were to attempt suicide, that would confirm the diagnosis that the dysfunction was with her, not with her situation. Dorothy Chunn and Shelley Gavigan summarize this point rather well.

> Criminalization is the control mechanism reserved for the few women not constrained by fear and medicalization, that is, those who directly attack male power. Historically, men have frequently used criminal law against women who attempt to assert control over their own reproduction and sexuality. (1991: 291)

Menzies, Chunn, and Webster (1992) summarize much of the research that has been done on the processing of women vis-à-vis men by clinicians. When accused of crime, females are more likely than males to get a clinical evaluation. Those males who are remanded for clinical assessment are more likely to have criminal records than the women, who are more likely to have a psychiatric history. Men who commit serious crimes of violence are more likely to be seen by psychiatrists as legally and morally guilty and deserving of lengthy prison terms (Allen, 1987a, 1987b). Female offenders are transformed into pitiful victims who lack moral culpability.

When Menzies and his colleagues analyzed data from the Metropolitan Toronto Forensic Service, gender did not play as important a role in predicting outcomes as one might anticipate from previous research. Instead, the dominant characteristic of both the females and their male counterparts in this study was their marginality. They tended to be homeless, unemployed, and isolated, and were repeatedly involved in criminal justice, welfare, and mental health agencies. As research looks at the impact of gender more closely, we may find that the interaction of a number of factors must be taken into account.

In the past, however, privileged women supported a general pattern of patriarchy during periods of reform, such as those that led to the creation of Children's and Family Courts, which came into existence in South Australia in 1895, Illinois in 1899, and Canada in 1908. These middle-class women typically supported the stereotypes of the model female, and were active in the creation of monitoring systems designed to keep young girls from engaging in inappropriate behaviour (Feinman, 1980; Messerschmidt 1986).

Although most reformers probably had a genuine desire to help young females (others would be less generous here; see Platt, 1969), the institutional response by police and other agencies usually victimized women. For example, physical examinations for venereal disease and pregnancy were typically given to women, regardless of the charges against them. The results could then be used as evidence that these women were promiscuous (Chesney-Lind, 1973, 1989). Sanctions were also severe. Traditional views of women placed them in one of two categories: madonna or whore. (The word *madonna* has been redefined in recent years.) While chivalry may have been extended to the madonnas, it was not available to the whores (Feinman, 1980).

In Chicago, where the family court was introduced to North America shortly after it had been founded in South Australia, girls were more likely to be sent to reformatories than boys. A similar pattern has existed in Canada. In the 1960s, Barbara Nease (1971) found that even though girls in Hamilton, Ontario, seemed to be screened out of the system somewhat by the police, once they appeared in court, they were more likely to be incarcerated than boys. Caution is appropriate here, however, since other Canadian studies indicate more favourable treatment for girls and women than boys (Chunn and Gavigan, 1991).

Sexual behaviour, however, is still more likely to be noted for females, when sentencing or charging is being considered. Dorothy Chunn studied the Toronto Juvenile and Family Court before World War II, and found that status offenses were twice as likely to lead to court hearings for girls as for boys (Chunn, 1992). In Australia, Linda Hancock (1981) found that 40% of the referrals of girls to court specifically mentioned sexual and moral conduct, while such comments were made in only 5% of the referrals of boys. Christy Visher (1983) examined 785 police-suspect encounters in three American communities, and found that younger females received harsher treatment than their older counterparts. The police adopted a more paternalistic and harsh attitude to deter future inappropriate sexual behaviour. Furthermore, female suspects who violated typical middle-class standards of traditional behaviour did *not* receive chivalrous treatment.

Chesney-Lind's work in Hawaii provides a useful illustration of how the morality of one culture was imposed on another, creating particular hardships for the females. In Honolulu, during 1929-30, over half of the girls were charged with "immorality." Another 30% were charged with "waywardness." Girls were twice as likely to be detained as their male counterparts. Even in the 1950s, girls were half of those committed to training schools in Honolulu (Chesney-Lind, 1989).

Similar practices existed in England. Lorraine Gelsthorpe (1986) noted that English police were concerned about the sexual behaviour of girls. In the case of a 14-year-old girl, the police pursued a truancy application over objections from parents and Social Services, and despite a written medical report that the girl was premenstrual. The reason was, in one officer's words, "I know her sort ... I'm still suspicious that she might be pregnant. Anyway, if the doctor can't provide evidence we'll do her for being beyond the care and control of her parents, no one can dispute that. Running away is proof" (p. 136).

A word of caution is appropriate here. While perceived sexual behaviour influences the treatment of women in the criminal justice system, in Canada they appear to receive more lenient treatment for crimes of violence and property offenses (Church and Gavigan, 1991). This may be due to the double standard, where one assumes that a woman who is "acting that way" must be sick and irrational. In addition, women may be viewed as the unwilling accomplices of men. Clearly, the double standard and the "chivalry hypothesis" influence the way laws are administered, but the result is a mixed bag. Men and women are treated differently, but the debate over who gets treated worse by the system may obscure a more important point — what type of criminal justice system marginalizes *both* men and women, and decreases the likelihood that they can participate more adequately in normal society?

Women in Prison

This sexualization of female crime continues through the justice system into prison. Margaret Shaw and her colleagues (1991, 1992) have examined the situation of female inmates in the Canadian federal prison system. Sentences under two years are served in provincial facilities, but sentences over two years are served in the federal system. In 1992, of the 12,000 federal prisoners in Canada, about 250 were women. Because of the relatively small number of women in Canada receiving long sentences, a single federal penitentiary for women was built in Kingston, Ontario, in 1934.

Although Aboriginal Indian women make up only 2% of the population, they represent 23% of the federally sentenced population. Both Aboriginal men and women are over-represented in prison in Canada, but it is greater for Aboriginal women than for men (LaPrairie, 1987, 1990). The majority come from the Prairie provinces. Thus, when they are sent to prison in Kingston, they are effectively cut off from family visits. Women are also now serving longer sentences. With the abolition of the death penalty in Canada in 1976, women (and men) sentenced for first-degree murder must serve twenty-five years before they can be considered for parole. For second-degree murder it is ten years.

This has created more hardship for women than for men, because of their removal from homes and families. Recent programmes have allowed some federally sentenced women to serve time in provincial institutions closer to their families. Unfortunately, serving time in separate wings of provincial institutions may mean that programmes and facilities are unavailable to federally sentenced women. When provincial institutions are coeducational, it may be an improvement for both men and women; but there are risks. Usually, security concerns about the men take priority over coeducational programming. The use of minimum-security institutions for women is often not considered because of the long sentences. However, the risk to the public may not be as high as the length of the sentence suggests.

Some of the problems faced by female offenders in Canada may be exacerbated by geography, but others are similar to problems in other countries (Rafter, 1990). Although females make up a small proportion of prisoners in Western countries, there has been a dramatic increase in the use of imprisonment for women in the United States. By contrast, Australia and England and Wales show less dramatic increases. Scotland seems to have very few women in prison (Carlen, 1983). Canada tends to be between the U.S. and other English-speaking countries, in that we imprison women at a higher rate than England (Shaw, et al. 1992) but less than the United States.

From the standpoint of understanding women and crime, what can we learn by studying this small group of long-term female offenders in Canada? How different are they from the 8,800 women sentenced for less than two years in provincial prisons? Of the 338 women admitted to the Vanier Centre in Ontario during 1970-71, 37% had no previous convictions (Lambert and Madden, 1975). Three quarters of the federal offenders studied by Shaw neither had been convicted of a criminal offence before, nor had been convicted for minor offenses. What purpose is being served by these long sentences in prison? Shaw argues that most of these women come from backgrounds where a caring and protective environment is unknown. Over half of these women said they had injured themselves or attempted suicide at some stage in their lives. Can they be expected to respond without anger in a prison environment? Should, for example, a woman with a history of depression, found crouched under a wash basin, crying, be punished for hiding? Is rehabilitation possible under the present prison circumstances? While acknowledging that these women have committed crimes, they are often victims of abuse, violence, or poverty. Ongoing research by Elizabeth Comack (1993) on 727 women imprisoned between 1988 and 1993 in a provincial prison in Manitoba presents a picture of female offenders as victims (Comack, 1993). Seventy-eight percent had been sexually and/or physically abused. For Native women, it was 81%. Interviews reinforced the image of women who had gotten a poor deal in life, but Comack found these heart-wrenching stories were really about survivors rather than simply victims. She saw incredible strength in these women, reinforcing her doubts about concepts like "learned helplessness" being applied to women in abusive relationships.

Margaret Shaw recommends a shift in strategy, which is more compatible with the reintegration argument made previously by John Braithwaite. It involves changing the basis of sentencing to one that focuses on the effects upon the victim and the community, and how these might be redressed, rather than on the breach of the law itself. A number of mediation schemes have demonstrated the scope for using such an approach even for offenses involving violence. Canada has been slow to use mediation programmes (Nylund, 1991), but there is reason to believe that more emphasis on dispute resolution, mediation, and group processes, along with treatment and support, rather than on punishment and control, would yield a better return for the society as well as for female offenders. In her book, *Partial Justice*, Nicole Hann Rafter (1990) presents a similar perspective for the United States. She examines prisons for women in the U.S. from 1800 to 1935, and notes that in one New York prison for women at least half of the inmates were convicted of sexual misbehaviour, including such "crimes" as premarital pregnancy. Rafter argues that, although prisons have changed, women still suffer from sexual stereotyping.

Reorienting Thinking About Females and Crime

Feminist theories of crime focus on the consequences of the roles women are expected to play, including problems caused by racism and poverty. This includes the impact of the agencies of social control, which respond differently to males and females. For example, parents use these agencies to resolve conflicts with daughters. In 1929 and 1930 in Honolulu, 44% of the girls who appeared in court were referred by parents (Chesney-Lind, 1989). Other research shows that juvenile courts have traditionally received referrals for females more often than males for "deviant" activities that differ from regular crime. In other words, parents, the agents of social control, and the society in general "control" the behaviour of girls differently than they do the behaviour of boys, and *these differences in the control process must be incorporated in explanations of deviance*. "Anyone seriously interested in examining women's crime ... must carefully consider the role of the contemporary criminal justice system in the maintenance of modern patriarchy" (Chesney-Lind, 1986).

Radical theorists have long called attention to such differences in power relationships. Sometimes referring to themselves as "critical" criminologists, they now include women in their categories of disadvantaged. Similarly, feminists who look at agencies of control make arguments similar to the arguments of those who have examined these agencies critically for years. The gap between feminist thinking and much other work done in criminology is not as great as some people imagine. Perhaps feminist authors have not made the link with the larger issues concerning marginal people in general as often as they should, but many of them certainly do (Daly, 1990; Daly and Chesney-Lind, 1988).

Systems That Respond More Sensibly: Juvenile Justice in France

The biases in our agents of social control have been documented, but we have few illustrations of systems that respond more intelligently to females in trouble. French juvenile justice offers some alternative strategies (Hackler, 1988). I have often heard North American judges say that they felt compelled to lock female juveniles up in order to help them. French juvenile court judges have rarely locked up female juveniles since the 1970s. France has numerous and varied residential facilities for girls, but practically no place for keeping them in closed custody. In one jurisdiction of 1,500,000 people in southern France, about thirty boys were incarcerated, and one girl. She had strangled her mother. The girl was held in a portion of the women's prison. There simply was no prison or closed-custody facility for juvenile females, because the incarceration of a girl was seen as a very rare event.

On the other hand, the *juge des enfants* is viewed as a clear source of help for juveniles. One girl, working as a prostitute, was trying to leave her pimp and give up the business. She went to "her" judge for help. (Locking up girls for sexual deviance is seen as pointless by French juvenile court judges.) The judge ordered social services to buy her an airplane ticket to relatives in another country. After her pimp left the area, she returned to her family in France and started a new life. The essential point is that family court judges can, and do, assist juveniles, even though they also have the capacity to punish.

The French judges and social workers I interviewed argued that one cannot help and incarcerate at the same time. Since sexual deviance no longer provides grounds for custody, and since very few crimes by girls constitute a threat to society, specialized closed-custody facilities for girls are not needed. The fact that the majority of juvenile court judges and prosecutors in France are now female may have had some impact on the system.

The Desexualization of Female Crime

Traditional images of female roles and female crime obviously influence the response of the agencies of social control. However, the behaviour of the agencies persists, even when evidence indicates that those traditional images and explanations are faulty. Even before feminist scholars introduced innovative thinking in this area, empirical research was pointing out that the *similarities* in criminal patterns between men and women were greater than the differences, except that the frequency and seriousness of female crime is less (Cernkovich and Giordano, 1979;

Canter, 1982). Michael Hindelang (1971) found that female delinquency was not particularly specialized, but tended to parallel that of the male delinquents. The sexualization of female crime may be understandable, in that many marginal women are struggling for survival. Selling and using sex may be one of the few areas where they have an advantage over males. Female crime is closely connected to the fact that females are more vulnerable as victims. Girls are more likely than boys to be abused in the family, and their abuse begins earlier and lasts longer (Finkelhor and Baron, 1986). Females from disadvantaged settings, particularly juveniles, require more protection, and admittedly, it is difficult to know how to provide effective protection. However, the crimes they commit tend to be similar to those of males, but of a lesser volume. Instead of sexualizing female crime, feminist thinking calls our attention to the needs of marginal people and less powerful groups in a patriarchal and hierarchical society.

Power-Control Theory: Hagan, Gillis, and Simpson

At the University of Toronto, Hagan, Gillis and Simpson have developed power control theory to explain different rates of female crime (1985; 1987). The focus is on the relative positions of power held by husbands and wives. Power in the workplace is translated into power relations in the household. These relations influence the way boys are controlled, as distinct from girls. In a *patriarchal family*, the husband is employed outside the family with a wife not working outside the family. In such families, husbands tend to be dominant and daughters are expected to be like their mothers, that is, they should prepare to enter the "cult of domesticity." The sons are expected to prepare for participation in the external labour force.

In the *egalitarian family*, both parents work in positions of influence outside the home. Therefore, consumption and production activities are shared by males and females. In egalitarian families, parents produce sons *and* daughters for entry into the production sphere of the labour force.

In the patriarchal family, females are more controlled. Both father and mother exert more control over daughters than sons, but daughters are even more controlled by their mothers. In egalitarian families, parents treat sons and daughters more equally. In general, mothers gain power relative to husbands, and daughters gain freedom relative to sons. The result is that, in patriarchal families, girls are less inclined to take part in risk-taking activities, although this is acceptable for boys. In egalitarian families, risk-taking is more acceptable for girls. Thus, *differences in delinquency by gender are greater in patriarchal than egalitarian families.*

As females become more "empowered," their risk-taking and offending should increase. Chesney-Lind (1989) feels that power control theory offers a limited definition of patriarchal control, which focuses on parental supervision and variations in power, primarily economic, *only within the family*. When mothers participate in the work force, particularly in high-status occupations, they provide "egalitarian" models for their daughters, which leads to increased risk-taking and hence delinquency. This is a variation on the earlier liberal feminist approach, only it is the mother's "liberation" that causes daughter's crime. Chesny-Lind argues that there is no evidence that, as women's labour-force participation and female-headed households have increased, girls' delinquency has increased. Instead, it appears to have declined or remained stable (Ageton, 1983). Merry Morash and Meda Chesney-Lind (1991) partially tested power control theory, and found that identification with a nurturing mother was a more important variable than control. Power-control theory is generally compatible with liberal feminist thinking. Freda Adler's book, *Sisters in Crime*, argues that by striving for social and economic independence, women have begun to alter social institutions that protected males in positions of power (Adler, 1975). As women successfully compete with men, they will also be exposed to similar forces. Thus, the women's liberation movement will produce increased amounts of female crime, because it creates an environment where the roles of males and females converge. Similarly, Rita Simon, in *The Contemporary Woman and Crime* (1975), analyzed changes in arrest rates for females, and concluded that these increases are a function of the changing role of women. However, it appears that the increases in female crime are modest, compared to the increasing female participation in roles previously limited to males.

TRENDS IN FEMALE CRIME

With more empirical research focusing on women, different theories arose to explain female crime. One aspect of this work was that it sharpened the use of official criminological data and the assessment of trends. Central to this debate was the question, "are women committing more crime?"

The Liberation Hypothesis

Feminist criminologists disagree over the "liberation or convergence hypothesis," which suggests that as women become more liberated and have greater job opportunities, they will also engage in more crime. Male and female behaviour will converge (Adler, 1975; Simon, 1975; Smart, 1976). Women now have increased opportunities to commit larceny, fraud, and embezzlement. Fox and Hartnagel (1979) examine Canadian trends in female conviction rates for theft from 1931 to 1968. Conviction rates increased, along with female labour-force participation and post-secondary education rates. Although there were changes in female work patterns during this period, it preceded the strong feminist movement that developed in the 1970s in Canada. Rita Simon and Jean Landis (1991) revised Simon's 1975 theme, adding more recent data. They again argue that the data supports an "opportunity thesis," which asserts that, as women assume positions of greater authority and prestige, they will use the new opportunities to commit white-collar crime.

Criticisms of the Liberation Hypothesis

Correlation is not the same as causation, and others have criticized the interpretations of data offered to support the liberation perspective. Shelley Gavigan (1983; 1987) notes that the increase in female crime does not support the hypothesis. Paul Maxim and Carl Keane (1992) found little support when they looked at violent deaths in Canada between 1950 and 1986. Meda Chesney-Lind (1986) points out that, since the 1800s, criminologists, as illustrated by Otto Pollak (1961), have issued warnings that the emancipation of women would result in dramatic increases in female crime. In reality, female offenders are not liberated professional women, but are still minority women from backgrounds of poverty.

Peggy Giordano and her colleagues (1981) agree that, recently, women are more likely to enter the labour force, but they occupy disadvantaged positions with poor security and pay. Thus, the increase in female property-crime rates are the result of the economic marginalization of women, rather than an expansion of opportunities. Steffensmeier (1980, 1981) note that the increase in female crime was so small, it doesn't take much to show an increase. For example, there was an increase of 600% in Canada in the number of women charged with first-degree murder between 1976 and 1984. This shocking figure is less menacing when we realize that the increase was from two to fourteen offenders (Johnson, 1986: 8). Police decisions to use first-degree charges instead of second-degree could have played a role. In a study of female homicides in Canada from 1961 to 1983, Silverman and Kennedy (1987) report that, of all homicides in Canada, the proportion committed by females has been stable.

Another view is that the chivalry response is fading, in terms of the sanctioning of women. Instead of seeing actual increases in female crime, the greater equalization of gender roles leads to women being treated less leniently (Steffensmeier, 1980). Others argue that the chivalry hypothesis is still operating, particularly for juveniles (Chunn and Gavigan, 1991). Johnson and Scheuble (1990) found that girls were more likely to be dismissed than boys, particularly for less serious offenses. With most of these studies, data are analyzed at one point in the criminal justice process, and thus, it is very difficult to detect the effect of small but incremental influences that operate at many levels (Bishop and Frazier, 1988; Bortner and Reed, 1985).

Patterns of Female Homicide in Canada

Silverman and Kennedy (1987) found that Canadian females kill males more often than other females. Part of this is accounted for by the fact that they kill their husbands, but an examination of victims who are neither spouses nor children shows that 68% of the other victims are also male. This finding is interesting, in that Holly Johnson (1986) reports that most of the victims of women who committed *non-lethal violent acts* were females. At the same time, U.S. data show that females are almost twice as likely to be homicide victims as offenders (Wilbanks, 1982). Non-White women have the highest homicide victimization rate. Murders involving women of all races, whether the women are victims or offenders, are likely to be intraracial events. Wilbanks also found that U.S. women are unlikely to kill other women. They tend to kill men rather than members of their own sex, and are more likely to be killed by men.

Silverman and Kennedy also look at women who kill children. This is complicated by the distinction in the law made between *infanticide* and women who kill children, some of whom are under the age of one year. In one case, a 16-year-old hid her pregnancy, gave birth to the child alone, was afraid of the consequences, and suffocated the infant. She was too psychologically confused to remember what she did. Her charge was reduced from first-degree murder, which carried a mandatory life sentence with no parole for 25 years, to infanticide, for which she received two years probation. Infanticide may involve the assumption of post-partum depression, which may explain the maximum sentence of five years. In other words, the small number of infanticides (45) in Canada from 1961 to 1983, compared with the mothers who killed their children (230), probably has something to do with mitigating circumstances, which led to the lesser charge of infanticide being used.

Canadian women are treated more leniently than men in the courts, when they kill their children (Greenland, 1988). Comparing 37 women with 32 men prosecuted for child-abuse deaths, the women faced less serious charges, were more likely to receive a nonpenal disposition, and received shorter prison terms when convicted. The "battered-wife syndrome" has also been used as grounds for self-defence, for women who have killed husbands (Chunn and Gavigan, 1991).

In general, homicides by women are largely within the family. Husbands and common-law husbands are the most likely victims, but 24% of the homicides were directed against their children.

It is interesting to note that Canadian Native Indian mothers are rarely charged with killing their children, even though they are involved in spousal homicide. Killing children is more likely among Caucasian mothers in Canada. Caucasian women appear to transfer their anger from the actual source of frustration, and use the child as an available target. Why is it then, that Native women respond to domestic turmoil with violence against husbands, but rarely against their children? Since Native women are frequently incarcerated for violent crime (Johnson, 1986), it would be helpful to understand if there are factors that *inhibit* infanticide. If Native women rarely kill their children, do they abuse them less than non-Native women?

When mothers kill their children, they are declared mentally ill 67% of the time. However, this diagnosis is made by the police. William Willbanks (1982) points out that killing children is inconsistent with the gender stereotype of motherhood. Thus, "if they killed their kids they must be crazy." However, infanticides may be unique. These women are usually very young, unmarried, and very distressed about their pregnancy. This fits into a general pattern: *female crime is often related to their marginality in the society and their limited means to influence their own destiny.*

Long-Term Trends in Informal and Formal Social Control — Boritch and Hagan

Boritch and Hagan (1990) reconceptualize the problem differently. As we have noted in earlier chapters, official crime rates reflect criminal behaviour rather poorly, but they are accurate measures of police responses to crime. They are measures of *criminalization.* Official statistics become measures of formal *social control.* While men have historically been formally controlled by the police, women have been informally controlled within the family (Hagan, Simpson, and Gillis, 1987). The impact of formal versus informal control mechanisms for men versus women can change gradually over time. Thus, arrest rates in Toronto for men and women from 1859 to 1955 provide insights into changing societal responses (Boritch and Hagan, 1990).

The century-long Toronto data show a steady decrease in arrests for violent crime *for both men and women* from the end of the nineteenth century until the 1920s, followed by a gradual increase.[2] Arrest rates for property and public-order crimes were not as even in their changes, but displayed a similar pattern. Female arrests for public-order crimes, as a percentage of other crimes, were particularly high at the end of the nineteenth century, raising questions about the chivalry hypothesis. Early in the twentieth century, reformist groups began offering more help to elderly female vagrants and young female runaways, which diverted deviants from formal social control procedures into informal control mechanisms.

Although much has been made of recent increases in arrests for both men and women, these rates were much higher in the nineteenth century than in the 1990s. Modest increases in female arrests in the twentieth century predate women's liberation. Finally, the steepest part of the decline in female arrests occurred during a period of increasing, though often exploitive, female employment opportunities. The liberation argument would suggest increases in female criminalization, but the opposite occurred at the turn of the century, when women increasingly entered the labour force.

---

[2]Some studies indicate a different pattern. Paul Brantingham (1991) uses data from Statistics Canada (1983) showing that *convictions* showed a gradual increase in Canada between 1885 and the early 1970s. However, convictions represent the final step in how society has responded to crime, rather than initial stages of criminalization.

Criminal Justice and Women in the Urban Reform Era — Helen Boritch

Another historical study looked at how the criminal justice system responded to women in Middlesex County, Ontario, between 1871 and 1920 (Boritch, 1992). The decades spanning the late nineteenth and early twentieth centuries represent an epoch of significant changes in gender roles, social control policies that affected women, and levels of official criminality. This period, generally called the Urban Reform Era in Canada and the Progressive Era in the U.S., saw a steady movement of population towards the cities, accompanied by the growth of many social problems. During the Urban Reform Era, moral reform was at the centre of the progressive tradition in Canada and reflected the class bias of its advocates. As long as women performed their expected roles, courts were lenient, but working-class women who violated those expectations were treated severely. For vagrancy and drunkenness, for example, men were treated more leniently than women. In addition, prostitutes who worked in brothels (those serving wealthier men) were treated better than those women who worked the streets and served the poor. This was consistent with the hypocrisy of the times. Crimes that occurred in public represented the most flagrant affront to feminine values and, hence, were punished the most. Judges reserved their harshest responses for socially and economically marginal women, as illustrated by the harsh treatment of older women, who were more likely than younger women or older men to incur prison dispositions.

> Lacking ... employment opportunities ... frequently widowed or abandoned by their husbands, having lost their capacity to reproduce and, consequently, much of their social value, and viewed as too old or entrenched in their criminal tendencies to be reformed, these older women were victimized by society and the criminal justice system alike (Boritch, 1992: 318).

These Canadian findings contradict the myth of chivalry towards female offenders, at least for women who deviate from accepted standards of feminine behaviour. Daly (1987) argues that the state can compensate more easily for men's economic role than for women's parental role, therefore, judges are more reluctant to incarcerate married women than married men. This may be true in modern times, but economic factors differed during the Urban Reform Era, when there were few state supports to compensate families for the loss of a male wage-earner. Men's economic role in maintaining the family unit was more crucial seven decades ago. Thus, women's responsibility as primary care-givers did not confer the same special advantage during the earlier period.

WOMEN AS VICTIMS

It is not possible to understand female involvement in crime, or their interaction with the criminal justice system, without examining the ways in which they are victimized.

Institutional Response to Victims of Sexual Abuse

So far, I have concentrated on the way agents of social control respond to females who are viewed as deviant. Another side of the same coin is the response to females who have been victims of sexual assault. Since many violent crimes take place between people who know each other, and since such crimes are viewed as less serious in comparison to crime between strangers, victimized women are not always taken seriously (Stanko, 1985; Stanko, 1982). In their Canadian study, Loreen Clark and Debra Lewis (1977) found that police procedures led to the "unfounding" of the majority of rapes that were reported, that is, the allegations were false, that a crime actually didn't take place. When Clark and Lewis looked into these cases further, they found that only ten percent were seen as false allegations; rather, they were eliminated because of difficulties of predicting outcomes in court. Evidence of the victim's drinking, drug use, or sexual activity outside of marriage leads jurors to doubt the defendant's guilt. LaFree, Reskin, and Visher (1985) also found that jurors were less likely to judge a male defendant guilty when the complainant was a black woman. A juror arguing for an acquittal said a girl from "that kind of neighbourhood" probably wasn't a virgin anyway (p. 402).

Changes in Canadian rape legislation limited lawyers defending men accused of sexual assault in the questions they could ask about the sexual history of the victim. This "rape-shield" provision (Section 246.6 of the *Criminal Code*) was struck down by the Supreme Court of Canada in a seven-to-two ruling, in August 1991 (Comack, 1992). This issue continues to be debated in legal and criminological circles (Boyle, 1991; Currie, 1990; Hinch, 1985; Hinch, 1988). In addition to the laws, Comack claims that male biases regarding sexual assault persist. During a 1984 case, a Manitoba judge told a Crown attorney he "would have to have to have grown up in a vacuum not to know women often at first resist sexual advances only to give in to their instincts eventually" (p. 138). In 1989, a Québec judge commented, "Rules are like women, they are made to be violated." A lawyer involved in the case responded: "Exactly." Comack also described a 1988 Vancouver case where a man who admitted a sexual incident with a three-year-old girl was given a suspended sentence, because the judge found the victim was "sexually aggressive."

An incident in 1989 at Queen's University, in Kingston, Ontario, illustrates the persistence of male-chauvinist thinking, which influences police and court responses to attacks on women. The student council had launched an anti-rape campaign with the slogan, "no means no." Students in one male residence responded with signs bearing slogans of their own: "No means more beer" and "No means harder."

When Marc Lépine entered the École Polytéchnique at the Université de Montréal on December 6, 1989, he yelled, "You're all a bunch of feminists," and then killed fourteen women and wounded thirteen others. Explaining the Montréal Massacre is not easy, but the response by some men reflects continuing biases. In call-in radio shows, some men felt that the problem lies with women who make men feel insecure. Women are still to be blamed, to be seen as "legitimate," or at least "understandable," targets by a portion of the population.

During the U.S. Supreme Court nomination hearings of Clarence Thomas, Anita Hill, a young lawyer who had worked for Thomas, testified that he had made comments that could be interpreted as sexual harassment. In a survey asking people to rate the credibility of both Clarence Thomas and Anita Hill, a large number of women, as well as men, doubted Hill's testimony, even though I thought she was the much more credible witness.

One may criticize the all-male committee of U.S. senators who cross-examined Anita Hill, for insensitivity to women's concerns, but we can also point to the Canadian House of Commons as an illustration of a predominantly male body displaying insensitivity to female fears of violence. When research was introduced in the House of Commons in May 1982, estimating that one in ten Canadian women living with a man is battered (MacLeod, 1980), many of them laughed. In some respects, this crude response by our elected leaders raised the level of awareness on this issue.

Female Crime as a Product of Victimization

Holly Johnson (1987) argues that prostitution thrives in a society that values women for sex more than for their labour. Entry into prostitution often follows running away from home, frequently to escape abuse. The street, unfortunately, puts women at greater risk of violence. They tend to become psychologically and economically dependent, often on males who abuse them. This increases the likelihood of arrest. Comack (1992) points out that women are concentrated in jobs where the wages are the lowest. Canada has a "feminization of poverty." Single mothers are especially at risk. "As many as 85 percent of single-parent families are headed by women. In 1987, 57 percent of these families were living below the poverty line" (p. 142).

Jill Rosenbaum (1989) studied the records of women who had been sentenced as girls to the California Youth Authority in the 1960s. Approximately twenty years later, it was clear that these programmes did not help much in avoiding crime.

All but 6 of 159 cases (96%) were arrested as adults, even though two thirds of these women had earlier been sentenced to the Youth Authority *only* for status offenses, mostly running away. The girls (now women) uniformly came from extremely troubled homes and received little help after contact with authorities, even though the majority were not initially convicted of delinquent acts.

The mothers of these girls also had very troubled lives. By the time thy were sixteen, their mothers had been married an average of four times, experienced abuse, at the hands of other and, in turn, abused their children: 37% of them had been charged with child abuse and/or neglect. These mothers of CYA wards tended to marry young. The girls in this study, who became wards of the state of California in the 1960s, were running from miserable family situations and, as Rosenbaum states, they were double victims: victims of their families and of the criminal justice system. However, she also makes it clear that to say the system was primarily at fault is simplistic. It is impossible to disentangle system effects and family effects on the adult criminality of these girls, and the options for dealing with runaways was limited.

Domestic Networks Among Disadvantaged Women

Eleanor Miller's *Street Woman* (1986) goes beyond individual case histories of prostitutes, and describes the social networks that support street hustling. It provides a strong argument that the bulk of women's crime, and prostitution is only one expression, usually evolves out of the severe social and economic problems confronted by teenage girls. Women of colour are particularly vulnerable. Recruited by older males with criminal records, these women organize into "domestic networks." These networks secure a semblance of financial and emotional security among impoverished and alienated segments of a highly stratified society. Carol Stack first used the term "domestic networks" in her book, *All Our Kin* (1974). Female kin who share in the care of children, sometimes including the father's female kin, as well as friends, chip in for rent, and sometimes act as safety nets for the poor in the event of a late welfare cheque, robbery, or some other disaster.

The downside of the domestic network arrangement is that it is difficult for individuals, through hard work or good fortune, to become upwardly mobile. To disentangle oneself from the network would mean withdrawing one's resources from others in need. I saw a similar situation within Australian Aboriginal communities. In a society that was expected to share, your food pantry, refrigerator, and other belongings were always available to relatives and friends. Any aspirations to "get ahead" were easily frustrated in such an environment.

Miller (1986) further points out that these circles of domestic networks intersect with deviant social circles primarily engaged in hustling of different kinds, which she calls "deviant street networks." It becomes easy to understand how involvement with drugs, prostitution, and a variety of crime are almost inevitable consequences. It is also easy to see why the criminal justice system is completely ineffective, and why these women hold it in disdain.

Recent work on child abuse also suggests that girls are more likely to be victimized than boys. Moreover, Cathy Widom (1986) notes that abused or neglected females are more likely to have records of adult crime. Interestingly enough, men with abuse backgrounds are more likely to commit violent crimes as adults, but with women who have suffered abuse, the link is not specifically with violence. *Females are more vulnerable, both in their families and in the agencies that respond to their difficulties.* They run away from home, only to find that the streets are also unsafe. They use the only commodity they have to trade in a society where men are ever willing to buy.

A Superior Justice System Response to Marginal Females in France

One might sympathize with judges and social workers who must choose between sending girls back to dysfunctional families or using an institutional facility. However, a case that I witnessed in France illustrated a more flexible approach. The fourteen-year-old wished to take a hairdressing course, the mother disapproved, the girl ran away and stole food. In almost all juvenile cases in France, the youth will appear in the judge's office *the same day of police contact*. The judge must decide if a trial is appropriate. In this case, the judge predictably brushed the offenses aside and concentrated on the basic problem. I interviewed the girl in a group home, where children could leave very easily. The judge did not attempt to impose a solution. The social worker was to attempt family reconciliation, and the girl could go home at any time, but she could clearly stay in the group home while things were being resolved. If the girl had been older, sixteen or so, the judge might have considered establishing the girl independently in an apartment, but fourteen was rather young.

What impressed me was that the French girl viewed the judge differently from the way girls view the system in North America. She (1) had considerable input into the decisions, (2) saw the judge as flexible but guaranteeing food and shelter, and (3) was aware that she could call upon "her" judge in the future. Without going to a trial, French judges cannot impose incarceration. In 80% to 90% of the cases, the judge foregoes trial. Thus, the relationships between judge and children are almost always seen as helpful, from the standpoint of the juveniles.

But certainly, I thought, some girls pose more serious problems. Therefore, I found a residential facility for really "difficult" girls. I was surprised to learn that 40% of the girls connected with this residence were living in apartments independently, so they could attend specialized schools or work in a variety of settings. In the residence itself, the girls each had keys to their rooms, but the staff did not. In response to my question, "Can they go home on weekends?" the answer was, "Of course, but *we* won't pay the train fare every week." When the staff was organizing a bike ride, I noticed that no one was counting noses. The response was, "they will be able to find their way back." I was concerned that they might run away; the

French staff did not recognize this as a problem. Preventing girls from leaving was simply not their concern. Running from a residence or not obeying a judge is not a crime. It can be annoying, and the judge will probably be unhappy the next time the juvenile wants help, but punishment is not an alternative. Of course, girls have to obey the rules of a residence or *they will not be allowed to stay*. These girls had more control over their destinies than their North American counterparts.

In North America, judges and others simply impose decisions on juveniles. The clients of the system often feel powerless. The logic of the American mentality, in contrast to the French, was expressed by Judge Milligan, representing the National Council of Juvenile Court Judges, when he argued in Congress that the current legislation allows a child to decide for himself whether he will go to school, whether he will live at home, whether he will continue to run, run, run away from home, or whether he will even obey orders of your court (Chesney-Lind, 1988:p. 158).

French judges are also concerned about school, running away, and where children live, but *it is not a crime to disobey administrative rules*. The judge can scold and complain, but punishment can only be justified if there is another actual crime. The French practice lets girls explain their situations. When I asked one judge what she would do if a girl refused to follow the judge's recommendation, she replied, "My choice may not have been the best either, but I will still be here, ready to help, while the girl is working through her problem." But supposing, I asked, the girl is potentially suicidal? The judge responded, "There are risks in helping young people make their decisions versus imposing our own, but in the long run we accomplish little if the juvenile isn't willing."

The system is certainly paternal (or perhaps maternal), but it uses strategies that increase the likelihood of rapport between juveniles and judges, increase the possibility of genuine help, and decrease the likelihood of girls being victimized a second time by the agents of social control.

SELECTING APPROPRIATE EXPLANATIONS OF FEMALE CRIME

None of the current theories, including those offered by feminist scholars, are particularly satisfying when it comes to answering basic questions. For example: (1) some sociologists argue that crime is "normal" in society. If so, why do women commit fewer crimes? (2) The disadvantaged usually commit more crimes than the advantaged. Women seem to be disadvantaged but are less criminal, no matter how we measure it.

Another debate concerns whether or not theories should be "gender neutral," which assumes that males and females respond to similar factors. Doug Smith and Ray Paternoster (1987) tested some of the conventional theories to see if they predicted marijuana use among males and females. They concluded that the factors that influence marijuana use are similar for males and females. They suggest that the sex differences in the volume of deviance reflects *differential exposure* to common factors that precipitate deviant behaviour. Thus, Smith and Paternoster would favour "gender-neutral" theories of crime, as suggested by other scholars (Canter, 1982; Figueira-McDonough and Selo, 1980). They find "gender-specific" theories, which emphasize one set of factors to explain the deviance of males and another to account for the deviance of females, to be based on the doubtful assumption that men and women are influenced by different underlying processes and motivations. Such an approach would perpetuate the sterile sexist origins of theories of deviance.

Some might respond by asking: can you have a gender-neutral theory if neither the social order nor the structure of crime is gender neutral? There are also times when it is difficult to know if you are being gender neutral or gender specific. For example, one extension of power control theory (Keane, Gillis, and Hagan, 1989) argues that boys are more willing to take risks than girls. Therefore, contact with police may deter girls but amplify deviance for boys. Being identified by an agency of social control is embarrassing, given the socialization of girls, but the same experience may enhance status for boys, given their socialization. Does this indicate similar or distinct processes?

CONCLUSION

At present, there is a healthy debate over the explanations of female crime. The simplistic theories of the past have given way to a broader range of issues, which have been stimulated by feminist thinking. The lack of agreement is not only healthy but introduces new directions. Compared to the many decades we have been working on male crime, systematic and critical thinking from a feminist perspective is very new, and perhaps we are still not asking the best questions.

CHAPTER 16

DRUG CRIME: ITS CREATION AND THE CONSEQUENCES

The source of every crime is some defect of the understanding, or some error in reasoning, or some sudden force of the passions.

Thomas Hobbes

THE PHARMACOLOGY OF DRUGS

Supposedly, decisions regarding the criminality of drug use are related to the damage that the drugs do. This is not the case, otherwise tobacco and alcohol would be the first on any list of forbidden substances. However, potential damage is cited as a reason for making a specific drug illegal. Let us use cocaine as an illustration. We have all heard the debate over pregnant mothers who use cocaine. In some places, such mothers have been treated as criminals and their children taken from them at birth. What is the evidence against the use of cocaine by pregnant mothers? If you wish get attention at your next social gathering, simply state that there is no evidence available that shows that cocaine use during pregnancy hurts the fetus. You will probably get a variety of disagreements, but let us look at the state of current knowledge.

Cocaine-using mothers are almost invariably tobacco smokers, alcohol users, and have poor nutritional practices. The illnesses of children of such mothers are all related to tobacco and alcohol use. We know that mothers who smoke during pregnancy are more likely to produce children with medical problems. Even if smoking mothers quit during pregnancy, if they resume smoking while the children are small, these children will have more medical problems than children raised by non-smoking parents. Since cocaine-using mothers are almost inevitably smokers and drinkers, how does one separate out the distinct impact of cocaine on fetuses? We need to find a reasonably large population of pregnant mothers who do not smoke or drink, keep in top physical shape, eat nutritious foods, are never around others who smoke, follow the medical advice of their obstetricians, have supportive husbands who contribute to their psychological well-being, and then, in addition, use cocaine regularly. Such pregnant mothers are very rare.

I am not advocating the use of cocaine. Personally, I favour healthy lifestyles; however, the reader should be aware that the societal demand to punish, stigmatize, and exclude users of certain substances is *not based on pharmacological evidence*. Cocaine-using mothers are usually poor, black, on welfare, unmarried, and less able to resist demands of the society that they be punished. Upper-class women who smoke and drink during pregnancy are dangerous to their children. They may be scolded by their doctors and others, but they do not receive the attention of the police and other criminal-justice agencies. The examples illustrate the difficulty of determining the pharmacological damage of various drugs, but they also demonstrate that such evidence plays a secondary role in drug policy. Instead, hypocrisy characterizes North American drug policy.

Addiction — Pharmacological, Psychological, and Social Aspects

"Junkies" have been viewed as fools who toyed with irresistible pleasure and got "hooked." Some researchers working with animals argue that there is a natural affinity for the pleasure drugs produce. In experimental settings, rats and monkeys consume large amounts of opiate drugs with little encouragement. If opiate addiction is so powerful, then it cannot be cured or even prevented. It is like sex or hunger. But supposing the experimental animals' affinity for opiate drugs existed precisely *because they were isolated in laboratory cages*. Who wouldn't want to be stoned during a life of solitary confinement? Alexander, Hadaway and Coambs (1988) decided to compare opiate consumption of rats in radically different environments. "Rat Park" was spacious, pleasant, with peaceful forests painted on the walls. Tin cans and other "toys" were strewn about the floor. It was also friendly; the 16 to 20 rat groups were coed. The other environment was the traditional laboratory cage, where individual rats could not see or touch one another. The rats were offered opiates in three ways, analogous to the ways they become available to people. In the *Easy Access* procedure, the drugs were freely available, but rats in both environments avoided the narcotic solution. The impact of the environment could not be tested.

In the *Seduction* mode of presentation, the narcotic solution was sweetened, and the pure tap-water was not. Since rats have a powerful sweet tooth, the experimenters gradually (and diabolically) increased the level of sweetener in the narcotic solution. Rat Park rats resisted the narcotic solution very successfully, but the rats in steel cages drank plenty of it. Finally, in the *Kicking-the-Habit* procedure, the rats were given nothing but the narcotic solution for 57 days, long enough to make them physically dependent. Then the two sets of rats were given free choice between water and the narcotic solution. The rats in Rat Park again resisted the narcotic solution, while the caged rats continued to drug themselves.

Like humans, rats are gregarious, active, and curious. The experimenters suggest that in a "rich" environment, rats (and people) resist narcotic use, because it interferes with playing, eating, mating, and engaging in those active behaviours that make life rewarding. Chein and his colleagues (1964) noted that in areas where heroin is freely available, most people simply ignore it. Those who use it often suffer from other problems and have painful self-concepts. Richard Stephens (1991) confirms this line of thought, and notes that the use of heroin and other drugs is an allegiance to a way of life as much as an addiction to a specific substance.

The "Once an Addict, Always an Addict" Myth: Environmental Conditions and Policy Implications

Much evidence explodes the popular myth of inevitable and irreversible addiction. People can, and do, leave drug dependence behind, even in the case of what appears to be one of the most addicting, tobacco. American soldiers in Vietnam had access to large amounts of heroin, combined with a decidedly unpleasant environment. This may have increased the likelihood of regular heroin use; but only twelve percent of these regular heroin users relapsed to addiction within three years of returning to the United States (O'Brien, et al., 1980). Over ninety percent of those who become physically dependent on hospital medication do not crave opiates upon recovery from their illness and release from the hospital.

The policy implications of the logic presented above should be obvious: we should be striving for interesting, fulfilling, and rewarding lives for all members of society. Instead, we have experienced a decade and a half of policies designed to take those who have had the most barren experiences and stigmatize and exclude them even more.

TRENDS IN DRUG USE

The popular press tells us that illegal drug use is out of control. The Addiction Research Foundation of Ontario has made comparisons with U.S. studies (Johnston, O'Malley, and Bachman, 1988). Compared to Americans, Canadian youth are more likely to drink (81.2% vs. 51.7%), slightly less likely to use cannabis (12.2% versus 19.7%), and half as likely to use cocaine (2.1% versus 4%) (Adlaf and Smart, 1991). However, these comparisons are for 15- to 24-year-old Canadian youth and 12- to 17-year-old Americans. High-school seniors in Ontario and the U.S., have similar patterns. Canadian seniors are slightly more likely to report drinking during the past twelve months (88.3% versus 85.7%), less likely to report cannabis use (31.9% versus 36.3%) and cocaine use (6.9% versus 10.3%).

However, there is some evidence that there is under-reporting, both in the U.S. (Bachman and O'Malley, 1981; Johnston and O'Malley, 1985) and in Canada (Smart and Jarvis, 1981).

Summarizing seven surveys of students in six Canadian provinces is somewhat complex, but there appeared to be increases in alcohol use from the early 1970s to the late 1970s, and a general decline in the 1980s (Adlaf and Smart, 1991). For cannabis use, there is a well-defined, downward pattern beginning in the late 1970s. Despite the high concern regarding cocaine, there is no significant upward trend among adults, and a downward trend among students (Smart and Adlaf, 1992)[1]. The West Coast region shows a somewhat higher-than-average prevalence of use (Chamberlayne, Kierens, and Fletcher, 1988) and students from Prince Edward Island the lowest.

Contrasting 1977 with 1989, Adlaf and Smart (1991) note significant reductions in the prevalence of ten substances among Ontario students: tobacco (30% to 23%); alcohol (76% to 66%); cannabis (25% to 14%); glue (4% to 2%); solvents (7% to 3%); medically-used barbiturates (6% to 2%); and so on. In 1989, almost one third (29.2%) used no drugs, versus 17.6% of students in 1977. This refutes the speculation that declines in the use of one drug are replaced by the use of others.

The Discrepancy between Drug Use, Convictions, Media Coverage, and Policies

Crack use among male students declined significantly between 1987 and 1989, but it remained unchanged among female students (Smart and Adlaf, 1992). Crack-users were also more likely to use stimulants, tranquilizers, heroin, glue, and PCP. They were generally heavier users of almost all drugs. These patterns suggest that focusing on a "killer" drug misses the point. A minority of our population, youth as well as others, search out chemical highs. While many others use drugs occasionally, usually as part of a social setting, they rarely become dependent and do not suffer much harm. The greatest health risks to this population still come from the highly addictive and dangerous legal drugs, alcohol and tobacco. Although the perception of a drug "epidemic" among the general population is overstated, and cocaine use is relatively rare compared to alcohol, tobacco, and cannabis, cocaine use is prevalent among certain high-risk groups (Smart and Adlaf, 1992). "Street" youth use more cocaine, crack, alcohol, and other drugs than normal youth. They probably use tobacco more. Unlike students and adults who use drugs for social or recreational reasons, do street youth use them to cope with problems? Are they like the rats imprisoned in steel cages? The "problem" is not a specific drug, but rather the circumstances that leave youth adrift in the community. A repressive drug-enforcement policy does not alleviate the conditions that encourage young people to turn to drugs, legal or illegal. Nor will it reduce the crimes that are an obvious byproduct of such situations.

---

[1] A 1993 survey indicates a possible change in this downward trend.

It would be nice to believe that factual information would have some impact on the media or our politicians. However, we are constantly told that drug use is becoming an epidemic, and that young people are out of control. Politicians continue to pander to a misled population. Thus, it is not surprising that cocaine *conviction* rates have increased five-fold in Canada between 1980 and 1988, despite declining use (Smart and Adlaf, 1992). Enforcement agencies are influenced by the perceptions of those in authority, and by the "needs" of those in charge of agencies to find an "enemy" against whom they can use their resources. This may not be a deliberate strategy, but "drug crimes" are created, to a large degree, by the actions of those in authority. Other crimes against property and against individuals are spawned partially as a result of the creation of the "drug crimes." When Holland deliberately decided to decriminalize some forms of drug use, there was a reduction in other types of crime (Leuw, 1991; Grapendaal, 1991).

One of the consequences of the increasing conviction rates for cocaine offenses is the increase in the load on our prison system. In 1988, three times as many cocaine offenders received sentences of more than two years, compared to 1983 (Smart and Adlaf, 1992). There is also a striking geographic variation for cocaine convictions in 1988. Half of them were in Québec, 30% in Ontario, and 11% in British Columbia, with only 9% for the rest of Canada.

THE FORMATION OF DRUG POLICY IN CANADA, ENGLAND, AND THE UNITED STATES

Scientific evidence and rational thinking had little influences on drug policies. Historical factors provide better explanations. Drug strategies in the U.S., England, and Canada were influenced by somewhat different forces and, in the case of the U.S., *neither* public opinion *nor* medical opinion played an important role.

U.S. Drug Policies and Moral Entrepreneurship[2]

Drug policies in the U.S. were heavily influenced by officials of the Treasury Department, who wished to expand their influence. The U.S. Federal Narcotic Laws were originally, in theory, revenue measures. The *Harrison Act* was passed in 1914 to make the process of drug distribution a matter of record. There was no intent to deny addicts access to legal drugs, or to interfere with medical practice. The act stated that a registered physician would be able to administer drugs "for legitimate medical purposes," as long as they were "prescribed in good faith." Thus, the *Harrison Act* did not make addiction a crime, nor did it forbid doctors to prescribe drugs for addicts. It simply required that the handling of drugs become a matter of record.

---

[2]Although many sources provide a history of drug legislation, my main source for the U.S. has been Lindesmith, 1965.

Court decisions, however, influenced policy. In 1915, a U.S. Supreme Court decision (Jin Fuey Moy case) ruled that possession of illegal drugs by an addict was a crime. A new category of criminals had been created. This decision meant that a medical doctor was the only legal source of drugs left to the addict. Future court decisions against doctors eliminated that source. The Webb case in 1919 and the Behrman case in 1922 involved physicians who prescribed large quantities of drugs to addicts. These cases concluded that a physician may not provide narcotics for a drug user, "to keep him comfortable by maintaining his customary use." This made it almost impossible for a medical doctor to claim that he had acted in good faith.

In 1925, Dr. Charles Lindner received an addict in a state of partial withdrawal. He provided four tablets to be used at her discretion. She was a police informer who reported the incident, and Dr. Lindner was prosecuted. Lindner was convicted by a lower court, but after prolonged litigation, which cost him $30,000 and caused him to be without a medical licence for two years, the decision was overturned by the U.S. Supreme Court. This important decision established two principles. First, drug addiction should be viewed and treated as a disease, and secondly, a physician acting in good faith could give an addict a moderate amount of drugs to relieve withdrawal stress. However, the Treasury Department and its subsidiary, the Federal Bureau of Narcotics, which was established in 1930, acted as if the Supreme Court decision had never taken place. The risk of arrest was present for any physician who attempted to treat drug addicts. Very few physicians cared to risk their careers by challenging the practices of the Federal Bureau of Narcotics.

The lower courts in the United States influenced the punitive pattern for dealing with the drug problem, and the medical profession in the U.S. saw no reason to support its members. Since drug addicts are typically poor, low in status, and a nuisance, there was little inclination to risk a career. Physicians of integrity continued to be arrested. The claim that drug addiction was a disease, according to the Supreme Court, seemed to have no impact on the lower courts. Two 1936 cases illustrate the situation. Three physicians were asked by the city of Los Angeles to take over the treatment of addicts who were former patients in that city's narcotics clinic. All three doctors were then convicted in federal court for violations of the narcotic laws. While the conviction of one was reversed, the appeals of the other two were rejected. One of the ironies in this trial was that the stool pigeon who testified in court admitted that he was being regularly supplied with drugs by government agents, as was the informer in the Lindner case. Although this practice has been deplored, government agents continue to supply helpful addicts with drugs.

Harry Anslinger: Moral Entrepreneur Extraordinaire

The person who founded and directed the Federal Bureau of Narcotics, Harry Anslinger, had a definite image of drug addicts. They were bad people, clearly criminal, and should be prosecuted. He was the most influential person in the United States, possibly in the Western world, in terms of moulding drug policy.

Laws do not come into existence because they are "needed" or "wanted." Rather, rules are created when people are afraid, concerned, or have something to gain. (Becker, 1963: Ch.8) Someone takes the initiative of translating that fear or concern into a law or rule, which then becomes the norm for the society. These moral entrepreneurs are of two types: *rule creators* and *rule enforcers*. Some people create the rules, such as those who campaign to get legislators to pass laws; others, such as the police, enforce them. Some rules are rarely enforced, or enforced selectively. Moral entrepreneurship is not automatically bad. I would be happy to outlaw power boats on lakes in the National Parks and many other areas as well, feeling that pollution and noise detract from an appreciation of the outdoors. We have moral entrepreneurs for the pro-choice movement; others might campaign against smoking. Someone attempts to sell her version of morality to the general public. Harry Anslinger had his version of morality, and, using the Federal Narcotics Bureau, he sold his version to the legislators and the authorities.

This principle was illustrated by the *Marijuana Tax Act* of 1937. The Bureau provided the necessary feeling of urgency and alarm to get the legislation passed. They held themselves up as experts in the area of drugs. The Bureau prepared the wording of the bill and provided the principal witnesses at the hearings of the Congressional Committee considering the bill. Marijuana smokers sent no delegation. The only potential obstacle was the objections of the Hemp Seed Oil and Bird Seed industries, but these were neutralized by minor changes in the bill, which swiftly became law (Cohen, 1966: 35).

Britain: Using the Medical Profession

In Britain during this same period, a similar dispute arose between enforcement authorities and British physicians, concerning the physician's right to prescribe drugs for addicts. The Rolleston Committee was established, and, after extensive testimony from medical personnel with specialized knowledge, the committee recommended that doctors be permitted to treat addicts as ill persons. When this report was published in 1926, it became the official interpretation of the *Dangerous Drug Laws* of 1920.

In reality, the English and U.S. legislation were similar. It was legal for a physician to provide drugs for medical purposes, and the drug addict was defined as a person in need of medical care, rather than as a criminal. The dramatic differences in the way the drug problem has been handled in England and the U.S. is not based on legislation, but on the behaviour of certain agencies, such as the Federal Bureau of Narcotics.

In the 1950s, the U.S. pressured the United Nations to demand an international ban on the use of heroin. In 1955, Britain complied, but opposition from the medical profession led to a gradual shift towards a compromise pattern utilizing public clinics (Boyd, 1991). More intrusive controls and policing followed. The number of known addicts grew in England, and government policies of the last few decades have been controversial. However, one thing is very clear: the illegal drug problem in England is nowhere near as severe as in the U.S.A.

Canada: The Bias Against Asians

Shirley Small (1978) points out that the first anti-opium legislation was passed in 1908, as a result of Mackenzie King's investigation on the use of opium in Vancouver. As Deputy Minister of Labour, King was sent to supervise the compensations to be paid the Chinese and Japanese after the anti-Asiatic riots of 1907 in Vancouver. Much to his surprise, he received claims from Chinese opium-manufacturing merchants whose stock had been destroyed. One could purchase opium over the counter, in spite of a provincial law against it. King submitted his report, and the *Opium Act* of 1908 was passed with little discussion. Not surprisingly, the type of opiates used by the Chinese became illegal, but opiates in medicine, with the ingredients on the label, were legal.

King soon acquired the reputation of being a specialist on opium. He read alarmist testimonials concerning drug abuse during debates in the House of Commons. Public concern became apparent in the 1920s, and harsher penalties for drug users were being demanded. *Maclean's* magazine ran five sensationalist articles in 1920, written by Mrs. Emily Murphy, a juvenile court judge in Edmonton. Her book, *The Black Candle*, expanded on these views in 1922.

The opiate users were primarily Chinese, and the early legislation was directed against them. The House of Commons debates in 1907 and 1908 illustrated the antagonism Canadians displayed towards Asian immigration. Each article in *Maclean's* magazine written by Judge Emily Murphy included a cartoon caricature of a Chinese opium smoker, slanted eyes closed, with puffs of smoke coming out of each ear. Small quotes Murphy as follows:

> It is hardly credible that the average Chinese pedlar has any definite idea in his mind of bringing about the downfall of the white race, his swaying motive being ... greed, but in the hands of his superiors he may become a powerful instrument to this very end ... whatever their motive, the traffic always comes with the Oriental, and ... one would, therefore, be justified in assuming that it was their desire to injure the bright-browed races of the world ... Some of the Negroes coming into Canada ... have similar ideas, and one of their greatest writers has boasted how ultimately, they will control the white man (Murphy, 1922: 186-189).

A few objected to the growing tide of prejudice. Small quotes a portion of a speech by Senator J. H. Wilson, a physician who strongly objected to making addiction a crime. A political decision was being made when the Chinese, rather than the medical profession, were singled out as offenders.

The indiscriminate use of opium is a very deleterious habit, yet there is no justification for making the use of it a criminal offense. This habit is principally among the Chinese. Have we the right to make criminals of people, because they have learned the habit in their younger days and now desire to continue it? They give no offense except by injuring themselves. Much of the habit of using opiates, morphine or cocaine has been brought about by its indiscriminate use as authorized by physicians. ... Why not punish the physician? (Small, 1978: 32)

Some medical doctors insisted on the treatment of drug addicts as persons who were ill, but the general public assumed that addicts were dangerous persons. Authorities were allowed to harass Asians, while treating medical doctors, druggists, and other "honest citizens" quite differently.

The Role of Law Enforcement Interests in Shaping Drug Prohibition

Organizations tend to expand. Bureaucracies seek new worlds to conquer, new ways to be of service. Universities, industrial firms, and government bureaus utilize the equipment and expertise they have, to convince the powers that be that they should be given new tasks and expanded roles to play. Law enforcement agencies fit into this picture. In Canada, the Division of Narcotic Control was a branch of the Department of Health in 1919. The first two men to occupy the position of Chief of the Division acquired the status of experts on narcotics. Like Anslinger in the U.S., it was difficult to challenge their views. Colonel C. H. L. Sharman, who headed the Division for eighteen years until 1945, had his version of reality. There were three types of addicts: 1) medical addicts suffering from painful disease, 2) professional addicts, usually doctors and nurses, and 3) criminal addicts or members of the underworld (Small, 1978). Although professional addicts used drugs illegally, they neither deserved nor received criminal treatment.

Small also points out that the RCMP was facing a precarious existence during this period. It had been criticized for its role in labour disputes, such as the Winnipeg General Strike. Fortunately for the survival of the RCMP, there was a new world to conquer. They convinced others that they could wage a war on drugs and, incidentally, save their jobs. Just as Harry Anslinger expanded his power and influence in the U.S. by finding a convenient enemy, the Mountie drug squads became leaders in the moral crusade in Canada. Their enthusiasm continues to this day.

One might deplore the nature of the leadership provided by the U.S., but there was also an American impact on those countries with more progressive social programmes. Jorgen Jepsen (1988) laments the pressures for international solidarity and cooperation in drug-control practices, which are heavily influenced by American thinking. He worries that even the Scandinavian countries can be caught up in "magical thinking and unrealistic, but powerful moral imperialism" (p. 11).

Differences Among Canada, Britain, and the U.S. in Responding to Drugs

In a sense, England went the medical route, the U.S. went the law-enforcement route, and Canada followed a path somewhere in between. This is a vast over-simplification, and Canadian scholars have recently produced considerable sophisticated and detailed analyses of early and recent drug policies (for example, Giffen, Endicott, and Lambert, 1991; Blackwell and Erickson, 1988). Canada's early entry into drug prohibition may have influenced the U.S. in the period prior to the formation of the Federal Bureau of Narcotics (Erickson, 1992). My argument that Canada has been less repressive than the U.S.A. is illustrated by the handling of a documentary film done by the National Film Board of Canada in cooperation with the police. The film used drug addicts as actors, won a National Film Award and, in 1948, was taken to the United Nations in New York for a showing before the Division of Narcotic Drugs. The U.N. Bulletin called it "the best technical film relating to the control of narcotic drugs which has yet been shown to them. The enlightened treatment of the problem of the drug addict must receive specially favourable criticism." Mr. Anslinger, however, was not pleased, and attempted to prevent it being shown in the United States. He was generally successful. One showing was cancelled, despite great interest, because Anslinger did not feel it was appropriate for the susceptible minds of the people in this group: the American Psychiatric Association (Lindesmith, 1965: 252-254).

The hegemony of the United States in the United Nations enabled Anslinger to become influential internationally. This made it more difficult for enlightened approaches to be adopted at the international level. However, research agencies and government organizations in other countries, such as the Home Office in England, have maintained a more objective approach. Here in Canada, the Addiction Research Foundation in Toronto has consistently produced well balanced research.

The Le Dain Commission (Commission of Inquiry into the Non-Medical Use of Drugs) also produced four reports in the early 1970s, which were more enlightened than the official practices of the Canadian government and in marked contrast to the punitive policies of the U.S. government. In its final report, the commission recommended against any further extension of the criminal sanction. "We should gradually withdraw from the use of the criminal law against the non-medical user of drugs rather than extend its application" (Commission of Inquiry into the Non-Medical Use of Drugs, 1973: 129). One of the commissioners, Marie-Andrée Bertrand of the Université de Montréal, has long favoured a controlled, legalized sale of opiates to drug-dependent persons (Erickson and Smart, 1988), a view that has come to represent a majority position of North American criminologists. The majority of the commission, however, favoured the treatment approach of methadone maintenance over heroin maintenance, in most cases. Despite the positive reception given the work produced by the Le Dain Commission in the academic world, the formal reaction to the commission's legal recommendations, in terms of legislation and policy-making in Canada, was negligible (Erickson and Smart, 1988; Giffen and Lambert, 1988; Giffen, Endicott, and Lambert, 1991: ch 18.). No government wants to "concede that the line between legal and illegal drugs is a rather arbitrary by-product of our social history, rather than a matter of moral consequence" (Boyd, 1991:11).

Two Ways of Conceptualizing Differences Between Canada and the United States

The *cultural lag* model assumes that the differences between the two countries are only a matter of degree; it is simply a matter of time before Canada imitates the pattern of its larger neighbour. The media favour this argument (Erickson, 1992). Each drug bust, each case of drug-related violence or cocaine overdose indicates that we are destined to achieve American levels of urban disorder and decay. The *distinct society* view holds that the two countries are fundamentally different in values, culture, and social institutions. Canada values social order over individual rights and places greater faith in the discretion of legal authorities. The broader social net in Canada may have helped reduce levels of poverty and deprivation, and may provide less fertile ground for drug use. I hope this second view will prevail.

The Resurgence of Prohibitionism: From Malign Neglect to Renewed Repression, 1986-1992

Despite the apparent decrease in drug use in both countries in the 1980s, Pat Erickson (1992) notes that policies became more punitive by the middle 1980s. In 1986, when the American President, Ronald Reagan, declared a new crusade on drugs, Prime Minister Brian Mulroney followed suit two days later, when he departed from a prepared text. Government officials were caught off guard. As one high-ranking official noted, "when he [the PM] made that statement, then *we* had to make it a *problem*." Drug professionals attempted to respond to new government initiatives by emphasizing prevention and treatment and by including alcohol, legal drugs, solvents, and even tobacco in their efforts.

A number of factors encouraged the renewal of prohibitionism and repressive strategies. The American media portrayed cocaine as a "demon drug," representing it as a highly dangerous and addictive drug (Akers, 1991). Evidence that demand for cocaine and cocaine derivatives was declining (Bachman, Johnston, and O'Malley, 1990) had little impact on the need of the media to sensationalize and distort this issue. The "borrowed" drug panic about cocaine was imported from the U.S., and helped to justify further repression, even though evidence from Ontario showed a decline in cocaine use among students after 1985 and a stable level of use among adults (Erickson, 1992). While Canadian journalists produced "scare" stories, a more balanced view was provided by David Suzuki's *Nature of Things* special on CBC, "Dealing with Drugs."

Like the U.S., Canada usually ignores most of its drug professionals when developing policy. Researchers at the Addiction Research Foundation favour harm-reduction strategies and including drugs like tobacco and alcohol in the "drug problem." Compared to the U.S., Canadian professionals probably have a greater impact on the thinking of those who influence public policy than their American counterparts. Thus, Canada may be more likely than the U.S. to adopt some of the strategies used in Holland, Australia, and elsewhere, which focus on health factors rather than on simple prohibition. Let us now turn to some strategies that might be incorporated into future policies.

Reducing Drug Use by Aiming at a Broader Target

There are links between legal drug habits and illegal substance abuse. The logic for the argument presented here is borrowed primarily from empirical work done by Canadian alcohol and drug researchers (Popham, Schmidt, and de Lint, 1976; Schmidt and Popham, 1978; Whitehead and Smart, 1972). The distribution of alcohol use is one in which most drinkers are light users, fewer consumers are moderate users, and even fewer are heavy users. It is impossible to draw a clear line between *abusers* on the one hand and *normal drinkers* on the other. The distribution of alcohol consumption is characterized by the curve as described by the solid line in Figure 16.1.

Drug use also fits the pattern described above. Minor offenders are common; as drug abuse becomes more serious, offenders are less common. If we lump all sorts of drug use together, it seems that many people drink coffee and ingest the occasional substance that is not very healthy. Relatively few, however, are hooked on heroin or alcohol, or smoke six packs of cigarettes a day. While the news media call attention to specific exotic substances from time to time, the general phenomenon of drug abuse remains fairly stable: minor abusers are common, serious abusers are rare. However, we respond to the serious abusers and ignore the minor abusers. While this seems reasonable at first glance, the *shape* of the curve described by the solid line remains constant. One cannot chop off the right side of the curve. With cigarette smoking, for example, marginal smokers have quit and heavier smokers have cut down on the amount they smoke. The curve is a *smooth* one, but it has been shifted to the left. In other words, a successful *uniform* response to all substance abuse is accompanied by decreases among moderate *as well as* heavy users. It also suggests that there are common factors that influence all drug use, and thus one might conclude that a *single* sort of prevention strategy is possible.

Who are the logical targets for bringing about change? Typically, we assume that the real problem lies only with a particular group of bad people. These heavy abusers require our immediate attention. The rest of us are minor abusers of drugs

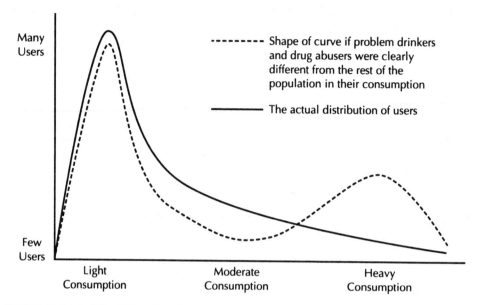

FIGURE 16.1 The Distribution of Drug Use

from time to time; but because our acts are less serious, they can be conveniently ignored. Instead, public outrage is directed towards that special group of extreme individuals who are serious abusers. We direct programmes and laws against the minority of serious trouble-makers rather than towards the majority of minor offenders.

Focusing on "Leisure" Users Rather Than "Deficit" Users

Pat O'Malley and Stephen Mugford have written extensively and perceptively on this issue. They note that some people use drugs to escape from a reality that is unpleasant: poverty, lack of social support, low self-esteem, lack of coping skills (1991). Such "deficit" users tend to become addicted. "Leisure" users go to parties and use a mixture of legal and illegal drugs. The use of most substances tends to be episodic, and illegal drug use is embedded in a wider network of social activities that are not dominated by drug use. In fact, the social activities limit the use. These social users account for the fact that there are many users of any drug, but few of these dabblers and nondependent users come to the attention of authorities. In addition, noticeable harm from leisure use is uncommon, as Reginald Smart (1986) notes in his study of "leisure" cocaine users.

Actually, drug users should be seen on a continuum rather than as one of two types. Most social drinkers handle alcohol, a very addictive substance, without great difficulty, but some become alcoholics. Some emphasize the addictive qualities of the substance, but those with a sociological perspective see social success and integration into social groups as much more crucial. Unemployed and less successful drug users who fall into the "deficit" category abandon the struggle for monetary and career success, and escape into the drug world. Leisure users, on the other hand, such as those studied by Patricia Erickson and others at the Addiction Research Foundation (1987), retain conventional goals in the larger society while seeking excitement and pleasure in innovative ways.

Leisure users are more numerous than deficit users, and represent a normal element in a society that has a "work hard, play hard" ethic. On the one hand, work and production are important: there is dedication to delayed gratification, careers, and devotion to enterprise. On the other hand, marketing campaigns offer glossy images of glamour and sex, promising gratification of all desires. Paragons of industry during the day sometimes indulge themselves at night. They are "straight by day and swingers by night" (Bell, 1978:*xxv*). These are not deviants so much as normal people responding to work stress and seeking excitement. A consumer-oriented society offers pleasure in a variety of forms. Some are usually safe and healthy, such as tourism, hiking, bird watching, etc. Others are more dangerous, such as mountain climbing, hang gliding, sky diving, and consuming alcohol while on a hunting trip. Still others are illegal. These leisure users and consumers of pleasurable products generate a constant demand for a variety of drugs, legal and illegal. Keeping in mind the skewed curve in Figure 16.1, this large population of leisure users is the primary target for the reduction of drug consumption, which obviously includes tobacco and alcohol.

As the Rat Park experiment described above suggests, an impoverished social environment may increase the search for alternatives. The search for excitement takes many forms. This may be heroin in Hong Kong, marijuana in California, alcohol or cigarettes among juveniles in Mormon communities, or bungie jumping at West Edmonton Mall. Control strategies might differ for various drugs, but our most profitable targets would be those that involve *the largest number of people*. By contrast, our current policies chose heavy users, targets that involve small numbers of people.

The Curve with Two Humps

If one looks at the dotted line in Figure 16.1, instead of the solid line, the shape of this curve might describe reality *if* the heavy drug abusers were more numerous than moderate users, and could be clearly distinguished from the rest of us. The dotted line describes a curve with two peaks, abusers on the right side of the chart, leisure users on the left. Belief in this bi-modal curve leads to a distorted world-view. Most of us have no trouble with the peak on the left; paragons of virtue are rare, but most of us commit indiscretions that are not serious. The *real* problem, for those with this distorted view of reality, is with those who represent the smaller hump, the abusers. They need special handling. We can tolerate the large group of leisure users on the left but must take action against the abusers on the right. The basic flaw in this argument is with the shape of the curve; the *solid* line represents reality, not the broken line with two humps, and it is difficult to change drug use by concentrating on the few. One must move *the entire curve to the left*.

Most drug policies are ineffective because they are based on the mythical two-humped curve. Programmes designed to change abusers are common, but an *effective* policy must alter the entire curve. Thus, programmes that reduce the consumption of *commonly* used substances, such as tobacco and alcohol, would move the entire drug using curve to the left. Thus, I oppose free drinks on airlines. We do not give out free marijuana, why free booze? Should Air Canada be a drug pusher? When people pay for their drugs, they consume less. Free booze (cigarettes, etc.) increases consumption and moves the skewed curve to the right. Similarly, we allow drugs as business expenses, as part of entertainment. Heroin, cocaine, and marijuana are not included, but alcohol, tobacco, and the services of prostitutes (disguised in various ways) are allowed. I am not so naïve as to believe that corporations will stop providing the last three items, but at least the taxpayer should not subsidize them. Small reductions in drug use among large numbers of people makes more sense than efforts to change smaller, select groups. By contrast, the focus on the latest "demon" drug discovered by the media in their search for something spectacular has little impact.

Reductions in drug use have taken place in North America in the cases of alcohol and tobacco. Canada has used taxes more effectively than the United States. Our tobacco prices rose 158% between 1979 and 1991 and teenage smoking fell by two thirds. The U.S. tax rate on tobacco remains the lowest of all industrialized countries. The June 1993 issue of the University of California at Berkeley *Wellness Letter* notes that a 10% increase in the price of cigarettes reduces consumption by 4%, even more with teenagers. Despite increases in the U.S. federal tax, it represents a far smaller proportion of the cost of cigarettes than it did in the the 1950s. Tobacco lobbies, particularly in the U.S., are powerful and their goal is to increase drug use. Canada has done better than the U.S. at moving the drug-using curve to the left, but it is tough going when the biggest drug pushers in the world are on your border and supported by their government.

STRATEGIES: DECRIMINALIZATION, LEGALIZATION, OR STATE CONTROLS

It would be difficult to design a more destructive process than the current one, especially as practised in the U.S. Illegal drug distribution is very lucrative and legitimate business are obviously excluded; this profitable business is reserved for criminals. In addition, it is more profitable for the most ruthless criminals. One might shame tobacco companies who hold smoking contests among children in developing countries, in order to gain future customers, but publicity and shame has little impact on criminal drug lords. We invite corruption, of police forces and entire governments. We place legitimate police forces in hopeless situations. It would be difficult to devise a more disastrous strategy.

The outcomes of various policies are difficult to anticipate (O'Malley and Mugford, 1991). When there was a strong attempt to eliminate marijuana, prices increased, which raised profitability so that more determined and violent criminal gangs replaced a more casual "hippy" distribution network. Crops of more potent strains of marijuana, such as *sinsemilla*, provided crops with higher value for their volume and replaced the bulkier, lower-grade version.

The illegality of a drug is said to increase the likelihood of theft to obtain money for that drug. However, a Toronto study showed that most cocaine users bought drugs with their own money, others were given drugs, and the third-most-frequent strategy involved selling drugs to obtain cocaine. Only 10% used other crime to obtain money to purchase cocaine (Erickson and Weber, 1992). Erickson and Weber, along with other researchers, found a typical drop-off of cocaine use after a period of higher use. In other words, if cocaine were available through legal channels, it might reduce some secondary crime, but it is possible that this problem has also been overstated.

Holland is unique, in that policy-makers and drug researchers work together. Amsterdam may shock some North Americans, with a highly visible retail market for hard drugs operating as part of a deliberate policy (Grapendaal, 1991). This compromise is less damaging than the U.S. pattern. Despite complaints about noisy and unhygienic drug users who sleep and urinate in doorways, there are promising signs in Holland. Very few "new" young users become involved in a junkie lifestyle (Grapendaal, 1991). Dutch drug users commit less property crime than their counterparts in the U.S. and Great Britain, and most Amsterdam addicts lead a deviant lifestyle with fewer harmful consequences for themselves and others. The accessible retail drug market provides a portion of hard drug users with a source of income without having to commit property crime. The importance of this gain is usually lost on policy-makers with a moralistic rather than harm-reduction orientation. An additional gain comes from the decreased danger for police who work in these areas of the city.

A Harm Reduction Drug Policy

Many Canadian drug researchers favour policies that focus on the reduction of harm (Single, 1991; Boyd, 1991). Ideas from Stephen Mugford in Australia (Mugford, 1991; O'Malley and Mugford, 1991) fit this pattern. Mugford distinguishes among the different types of harm. Any progressive policy should attempt to reduce certain types of harm more than others. We should protect people from passive tobacco smoke, and warn smokers of the risk of their behaviour. Similarly, we should prevent heroin users from stealing to support their habits, and warn them of the risk of continued use. On the other hand, in a society that vigorously markets pleasure-producing commodities indiscriminately, it makes little sense to outlaw smoking or heroin use when the harm is to the user. Forgoing prohibition strategies, however, does not imply approval of drug use.

Drugs need to be assessed in terms of their harm, to individual users and to others. Alcohol, tobacco, and cocaine are higher on that scale than opiates. If opiate use is relatively stable, the effects are typically constipation and a reduced sex drive. A lifelong dependence on opiates is consistent with social productivity comparable to a lifelong dependence on tea or coffee (Boyd, 1991:5-6). Thus, we should discourage (not prohibit) those that are more harmful. Similarly, some modes of use, such as injection, which is involved in the spread of AIDS, should be discouraged over less harmful modes of use, such as oral ingestion.

While Mugford and O'Malley oppose prohibition, they also disapprove of complete legalization. True, the ban on heroin has generated a black market, soaring prices, corruption, needle-sharing, and accelerated property crime to support habits; but complete legalization, as in the cases of alcohol and tobacco, is also bad. The extensive availability and the locations and contexts in which it is accepted, in fact encouraged, have led to a tremendous toll in death and health. Commercial merchants of death would probably succeed in increasing sales if they were given a broader selection of harmful products. Thus, to give the distribution of cannabis, heroin, and cocaine to the tobacco companies would mean that it would be vigorously pushed, along with tobacco, to teenagers in the Third World. Prohibition is too severe, but legalization, as it currently applies to tobacco and alcohol, is too soft. It appears that high profit for sellers and high damage for society is related to *both* prohibition and open legalization.

This does not mean banning alcohol and tobacco, but we could remove advertising, raise prices through taxes near to, but not over, the point at which substantial black-market alternatives would appear, and rigorously enforce age limits on purchase. With illegal drugs, one needs to move away from prohibition without causing a flood of use. Mugford and O'Malley would advocate *normalizing the user*. The addict should not be cast out of the society. "Junkies" are only a minority of drug users, and should not be pushed further towards harmful patterns and social irresponsibility. The Dutch, as noted above, have tried to normalize their users, expecting them to have normal rights *and* display normal responsibilities.

However, we should *not normalize drug use*. It is unwise to rely on the market, since commercial forces glamorize, make drug use acceptable, and influence peer groups to be like the "Marlborough Man" or some other "hip" or "cool" person. While junkies on illegal drugs are viewed as bums, junkies on legal drugs are portrayed as beautiful, sophisticated, virile, and having dazzling smiles. Government-supported advertising showing heavy tobacco and alcohol users as having diseased gums, bad breath, lousy complexions, etc. would be more appropriate. Attractive advertising for *all* drugs should be banned, while educational and disuasive advertising would be encouraged.

Harm reduction would make safer options more available than dangerous ones. Coca tea might be available more readily than cocaine, which in turn would be more available than "crack." Safer routes of administration would be encouraged over hazardous ones, such as opium for smoking rather than morphine for injection. The cultivation, possession, and private sale of *small* amounts of cannabis would be decriminalized. Heroin would be available through a variety of prescription or licensing arrangements, but without incentives for new users (O'Malley and Mugford, 1991).

Don Weatherburn (1992a) feels that some of Mugford's proposals are less convincing, which led to a useful debate in the *Australian and New Zealand Journal of Criminology* (Mugford, 1992; Weatherburn, 1992b). A detailed discussion of different drug policies is not possible here, but one can ask a broader question: are governments sincere in their desire to develop drug policies for the social good? I would like to believe that Canadian officials are sincere, if at times misguided. However, I share Mugford's view that hypocrisy characterizes drug policy in the United States.

Hypocrisy as a Major Barrier to Reasonable Drug Policies

While promoting a prohibitionist policy at home and pressuring other countries to do the same, the U.S.A. is the largest exporter of tobacco, the source of the largest single set of health care problems. The tobacco industry has successfully kept taxes lower than any other industrial country, guaranteeing a major smuggling racket into Canada and providing lucrative opportunities for crime. While the U.S. government claims these exports are made by private companies, American trade negotiators have systematically threatened Japan, South Korea, Taiwan, and Thailand with retaliatory tariffs on these countries' exports if markets were not opened to its tobacco firms (*The Economist*, 1992). Increasingly worried about the success of health advocates in North America, and recently in Europe, tobacco companies are looking for markets elsewhere, with strong government support. Pressured by the tobacco lobby, the government displays further hypocrisy in failing to stop harmful advertising directed at children. Since 1988, RJR Nabisco has promoted Camel cigarettes with a sunglass-clad, macho-clothed, bulbous-nosed cartoon camel named Joe, designed to appeal to younger male smokers. The campaign clearly worked. Efforts to develop addiction among children, strategies long used in North America, have been successful in other countries. Some marketing strategies target urban blacks, others focus on young, poorly educated women. The press obtained a letter from an RJR distributor that urged concentration on convenience stores "in close proximity to colleges, high schools or areas where there are a large number of young adults" (*The Economist*, 1992).

In Canada, Imperial Tobacco launched a programme to push the Tempo cigarette with advertising aimed at the 18- to 24-year-old market. Civil suits brought a number of documents to public notice, including some produced by Imperial's "Creative Research Group." One goal was to offer products "which could delay the quitting process" (Boyd, 1991:189). The tobacco industry in Canada also hires influential people. Bill Neville, chief of staff when Joe Clark was prime minister and member of Brian Mulroney's election campaign committee for 1988, has been president of the Canadian Tobacco Manufacturers' Council since 1987.

The hypocrisy of the U.S. government is particularly blatant in dealing with hard drugs, although probably not as damaging in terms of world health as their support for tobacco sales. Space does not permit elaboration here, but the illegal activities of various U.S. agencies have been reviewed in both the popular press and scholarly publications. These include: laundering of drug money through a bank in Sydney, Australia for the purpose of funding clandestine and illegal activities, the selective crackdown on drug cartels and dictators in exchange for political favours, the gap between rhetoric and action for helping those affected by drugs, and the deliberate sabotaging of one U.S. drug enforcement agency by the committee chaired by then Vice-President Bush (Boyd, 1991; Herman, 1991; Johns, 1991, 1992).

Counter-espionage activities involve choices that compromise morality, but the flagrant inconsistency between the public claims and actual behaviour of U.S. officials makes it impossible to develop a credible drug policy. It also makes it difficult for Canada and other countries to develop enlightened strategies, because the U.S.A. plays such a prominent role in the international drug scene.

CONCLUSION: DRUGS AS SYMPTOM RATHER THAN CAUSE — THE CASE OF STREET KIDS

Early in this chapter, I suggested that people with fulfilling lives are less inclined to use drugs. It is not always possible for policy-makers to provide people with fulfilling lives, but there are certain target populations that can be helped. Marlene Webber (1991) has studied youths living on the streets of cities in Canada. Many of these young people have experienced neglect and abuse, including rape and incest. The troubles they face can be overwhelming, and it is not surprising that they turn to drugs to "kill the pain." The same pattern applies to poverty-stricken countries where children rummage through garbage heaps to survive, but also use their meagre resources to buy marijuana. The reduction of pain among children would clearly be among our most potent weapons in the "war on drugs."

THE MAJOR SOURCES OF CRIMES OF VIOLENCE

I am sure that half of my patients are not dangerous and could be safely released, but I'm not sure which half.

Psychiatrist P. D. Scott

WHICH VIOLENT CRIMES SHOULD WE STUDY?

When we think of crimes of violence, murder, robbery, rape, and assault come to mind. We are less likely to think of family violence, which involves child abuse, sibling attacks on each other, and spousal abuse. However, family violence is more frequent and more lethal than those crimes we traditionally associate with violence. Most of us also give little thought to corporate violence, or actions taken by large organizations that do damage to others. Again, the damage done by corporations, and governments clearly outweighs the damage done by conventional criminals. This chapter focuses on violence that does the greatest damage. The most lethal instrument in North America is the automobile. This book neglects the serious offense of drunk driving, and concentrates instead on deliberate actions taken by individuals that knowingly injures someone. Usually, those who deliberately cause someone else to die are called murderers. Should that label be attached to executives of the Ford Motor Company?

Corporate Violence: The Case of the Ford Pinto

According to one author (Dowie, 1977), exploding gas tanks on the badly designed Ford Pinto caused over 500, possibly 900, deaths by burning. These deaths would not have occurred with a properly designed automobile. The Ford Motor company knew about the danger and calculated that about 180 burn deaths, 180 serious burn injuries, and 2,100 burned vehicles would result. They calculated their costs to be about $50 million. However, if the company spent eleven dollars per vehicle to correct the problem, it would cost $137 million. The decision to accept the deaths and injuries was an economic one. The unusual aspect of this case is that it led to a charge of reckless homicide and a court trial (Cullen, Maakestad, and Cavender, 1991). Ford was acquitted of the charges, but it helps us view corporate violence in a new light.

The Ford Pinto case is not unique. It is difficult to assess guilt and intent among corporations, but General Motors was in a similar situation. Since 1973, more than three hundred people have been killed from burning gas tanks in GM pickup trucks. Safety engineer George Carvil warned GM in 1970, and recommended moving the tank inside the frame rails (*Time*, November 30, 1992). The company acknowledged the problem in 1983, and has paid $200 million in settlements. The gas tank was moved to a more protected position in 1988. Criminal charges have not been laid against GM, but there are clear parallels with the Ford situation. Some corporate decisions *knowingly* risk the lives and welfare of others in order to make a larger profit.

The Costs of Corporate Violence

Charles Reasons, Lois Ross, and Craig Paterson (1981) point out that workers in Canada are at greater risk from their employment situation than they are from "conventional" criminals. We think of crime as involving an easily identifiable victim and offender. When a company exposes workers to toxic substances, leading to their deaths, the company is not criminally liable, although they might be charged with violating health and safety regulations. Reasons and his colleagues describe a case involving Quasar Petroleum, which was found guilty of violations of safety regulations resulting in the deaths of three men. The company did not provide respiratory protective equipment and an external gauge on an enclosed tank. The men had to go inside the tank without protective equipment, and were overcome by the fumes (1981: 6-7). Nor had the company trained the workers concerning the hazards and the need for such equipment. The company was fined $5000. While the company did not intend to kill these men, it created the conditions by violating the law. Reasons and his colleagues argue that armed robbers do not intend to kill victims, but their actions create the conditions for such violence.

We have a growing literature on the illegal behaviour of large corporations (Ross, 1980), but the public rarely sees these activities as "real" crimes.

Although illegal and dangerous behaviour by corporations is rarely successfully challenged in the courts, strategies using reintegrative shaming may already be working. In the past, illegal and hazardous activities have largely been sheltered from shaming. Decisions leading to death and danger were easier to hide in the past, and fellow executives may have supported each other. Today, business publications such as *Fortune* magazine discuss company lawlessness (Ross, 1980), and friends and families are more aware of corporate decisions that hurt others. Even if the criminal justice system is ineffective in dealing with corporate criminals, stripping away the shelter of anonymity from individual business leaders may make them vulnerable to shaming. If criminology is concerned with illegal acts that do great damage, then focusing on those in positions of power makes considerable sense. Not only might such people be susceptible to reintegrative shaming, they are also relatively good candidates for rehabilitation. Although they may not forego all of their illegal activities, the possibility of reducing their most harmful behaviour is more promising than attempts to change conventional criminals. Let us now turn to more conventional violence.

SUBCULTURES OF VIOLENCE

Explanations of violence typically focus on individuals, but some look at cultures or subcultures in which norms prevail favouring, or at least permitting, violence. Wolfgang and Ferracuti (1967) pioneered such ideas, and concluded that homicide should be viewed within a cultural context. They found that homicide was most prevalent among relatively homogeneous subcultural groups in most large urban communities. Some rural areas also shared similar characteristics. Ideas such as *anomie* are not appropriate here. Neither the killers or their victims are alienated or marginal members of their subcultural groups. Rather, they are well integrated into a group of people who accept violence as the norm.

By distinguishing groups with high murder rates, Wolfgang and Ferracuti identified subcultures of violence. In some settings, a man jostling another may provoke a challenge. Derogatory remarks can be interpreted differently in some gatherings. Men are expected to defend their names and honour from any slurs or aspersions on their manhood, and quickly resort to physical combat. Carrying knives or other weapons is considered normal under these circumstances. In such settings, violence is not the result of *deviant* behaviour. Rather, *conformity* to *these* cultural norms and to *this* set of values leads to violence. In these settings, it is not always easy to distinguish offenders and victims. In data from Philadelphia, Wolfgang and Ferracuti note that 65% of the offenders and 47% of the victims had arrest records. While we sometimes think of murders being committed against innocent and uninvolved victims, in fact both offenders and victims are often committed to the norms of a violent subculture. The specific outcome as to who gets killed may be due to circumstances rather than intent. Sandra Ball-Rokeach (1973) argues against the subculture-of-violence hypothesis. Her study of violent and non-violent inmates in a Michigan prison found little relationship between values and self-reported violent behaviour, and only a weak relationship between attitudes regarding the approval of violence and behaviour. Thus, the potency of these subcultural values regarding violence may be overrated. While Wolfgang and Ferracuti emphasize subcultural norms, the dynamics of collective behaviour, where one event leads to another, as reviewed earlier, may be more important than static cultural norms.

Despite these reservations, the idea of a subculture of violence may be relevant to Native populations in Canada. Repressed aggression may characterize some Native people who do not attack outsiders, but may respond violently to peers in bars or other settings where alcohol leads to a reduction in inhibitions (Campbell, 1973; Thrasher, 1976). Some working conditions have groups of young males working and living together without the restraining influence of wives and children. In some settings, such as lumber camps, mining communities in the North, oil-rig crews, etc. where males make up the vast majority of the population, chauvinistic, individualistic norms characteristic of a subculture of violence could easily arise. Such subcultures have been identified in Canadian prisons (Mann 1967), and they appear in prison subcultures in other parts of the world.

Wolfgang and Ferracuti have stated their core ideas in a series of propositions, which are summarized and simplified here:

1. No subculture can be totally different from, or totally in conflict with the society of which it is a part. A subculture of violence is not that alone but, instead, shares most of the cultural elements of the large society.

2. To establish a subculture of violence, actors sharing those basic values do not have to express violence in all situations. Each insult does not have to lead to a fight. Although each member may express a *willingness* to fight, sometimes threats, negotiation by others, and other mechanisms are used to avoid actual battle. However, weapons are carried and displayed to maintain the values of the system.

3. The ethos of violence is most prominent in a limited age group, males from late adolescence to middle age.

4. The formation of these subcultural norms probably involves differential learning, association, and identification. In other words, these ideas are compatible with other explanations of crime.

5. Violence is not viewed as illicit or inappropriate conduct, hence there is little guilt about aggression. Psychiatrists who diagnose such offenders as psychopathic, assuming that a lack of remorse indicates abnormality, miss the essence of the subcultural norms. These men *must* respond in certain ways. It is simply bad luck if someone gets killed.

Rape and Subcultural Factors

Recent work on rape has produced a wealth of insights, but an older study by Menachim Amir (1971) fits with the subcultural argument. Amir is considered sexist by many critics, for viewing rape as a sexual act, whereas most scholars would view rape as violence and as a display of power. He also suggests that women sometimes contribute to the possibility of rape. Despite these criticisms, the study is informative.

The image of rapes being committed primarily by strangers who drag women into alleys is not supported. In fact, the most brutal rapes were between neighbours and acquaintances. The setting is likely to be the woman's apartment. Another common belief is that alcohol use is common, but only about one third of the cases in Amir's study involved drinking. Brutal acts were involved in about one third of the cases, but how does one interpret statistics that half did not resist? Assessing the impact of verbal coercion is difficult.

Were the victims innocents? This is another place where Amir gets on shaky ground. One fifth of the victims had prior arrest records, but half of the rapists had records. Another fifth of the victims had "bad reputations." Should the victims be seen as responsible for their victimization? Amir says no, except for about 19% of the cases. This issue is central to a subculture-of-violence argument. To what extent do attitudes and values about what women mean when they say "no" influence the incidence of rape? Are factors operating at the individual level, as distinct from the cultural level? There have been cases of women who decided to enter rape charges after changing their minds after the act, but using official records does not allow researchers to determine the frequency of such incidents, nor can we determine if this is an individual act of revenge or influenced by cultural factors.

Although analyses of individual characteristics are revealing, both subcultural factors and routine-activity theory provide insights into the conditions and settings that increase the likelihood of rape, thereby providing useful suggestions for policy changes. For example, Ruth Peterson and William Bailey (1988) found that relative inequality and other aspects of social disorganization were also related to rape. Pockets of deprived people within a wealthy society breed violence, including rape. Amir argues that a lower-class subculture of violence is the primary source of rape. It takes place disproportionately among lower-class, minority, chauvinistic, urban youth, where similar subcultural elements encourage other violent crimes. Attitudes and values conducive to the use of violence are extended to sexist attitudes, which view females as sexual objects. While feminists are not fond of Amir's study, a more legalistic and individualist approach may not be as useful in the long run as a strategy that attempts to change subcultures.

Guns and a Subculture of Violence

One of the debates that profits from comparison between the U.S. and Canada is gun ownership. Canadians have fewer guns in the home, and find it more difficult to purchase handguns. Canadian cities, such as Vancouver, have fewer handgun deaths than similar U.S. cities, such as Seattle (Sloan, Kellerman, and Reay, 1988). Some hypotheses suggest a less violent general culture in Canada, independent of the use of handguns. Others see handgun ownership as an indicator of, and contributing factor to, the subculture of violence. A private firearm is six times more likely to be involved in a firearms accident than to be used in deterring a crime, but some scholars question the methodology and conclusions of many of these studies (Wright, 1991:453). Gary Kleck (1988) argues that 1,500 to 2,800 felons were killed in the act of committing a crime annually by gun-using civilians in the U.S., far more than are killed by the police. Is this good? Others view the 300,000 times a year that civilians use guns against criminals as evidence of a violent culture. Clearly, guns are more lethal than knives, and guns of larger calibres are more lethal than smaller calibres (Barlow and Schmidt, 1988). The debate over gun legislation will go on, but requiring gun owners to take training courses, and diligent licensing and recording of certain types of weapons have more advantages than disadvantages. Like the debate over the amount of violence in the media, compromises with individual rights may not yield great gains, but like seat belts and safety glass, some restrictions could lead to modest reductions in deaths.

The Anatomy of a Motorcycle Gang

In his book, *The Rebels: A Brotherhood of Outlaw Bikers* (1991), Daniel Wolf provides unusual insights into an outlaw motorcycle club in Edmonton, Alberta. He spent three years riding with the Rebels (their real name), and then gained permission to study them systematically for his doctoral dissertation in anthropology. Some anthropologists are criticized for "going native" and losing objectivity. Wolf, however, began as a "native," including sharing the lower-working-class background of other bikers.

Why does the lower working class produce candidates for a biker subculture? The worker is a cog in an impersonal machine, an anomic world with little psychological pay-off in the way of life-expanding experiences (p. 31). Work does not excite him, but on his motorcycle he creates the highly romanticized image of the hero, or rather, anti-hero. Speed spiced with danger satisfies his quest for thrills, and the machismo image provides a new basis for self-esteem. The biker uses his possessions to create an identity or social position. The motorcycle represents a departure from the rational, secure, and sensible (p. 32). He adopts attitudes and behaviours centring on independence, toughness, impulsiveness, and masculinity. Becoming an outlaw biker, however, requires a lengthy socialization.

For the outlaw biker, there is only one motorcycle, the Harley-Davidson "Hog." Japanese two-wheelers are not considered motorcycles, but "rice-burners." Anyone can handle a Japanese bike; he is a "ricer" and lacks the mechanical skill and commitment characteristic of a "true" biker. Riding "Jap Crap" is not respectable; it does not make a statement about personal freedom, macho self-reliance, and daring. For a true biker, the Hog is the basis of his lifestyle. The ricer regards his motorcycle as he does his Maytag washer. The true biker personalizes his Hog by rebuilding, customizing, and virtually redesigning it.

The dress of leather vest, jeans, and cowboy boots is part of the aura. "The pretty yellow and orange rain suits are strictly for candy asses who ride riceburners" (p. 52). Bikers face accidents with a cavalier attitude. "At one hundred miles an hour ... if you hit a half-brick on the road you won't stop rolling for two days. ... It's only a fatal twitch away, and your fate is finally in your own hands! ... That's better than sex, drugs, anything you name" (p. 54).

Of course, social rebellion does not go unpunished. After refusals by insurance companies, restaurants, and campgrounds, and hassles by police, he grows contemptuous of a world that pays tribute to personal freedom, but punishes those who are different. Some find the hassles too great and abandon the biker role, but others move further into psychological allegiance with the outlaw-biker subculture. Harassment from outsiders can result in greater solidarity for those in the group (Cohen, 1955). The biker wants to socialize, discuss, exchange information, and share the mystique. This eventually leads to the doorsteps of an outlaw club.

Socialization and social interactions are more complex than we had thought, as illustrated by the relationships with women. Chauvinism is the norm, but women relate to the club in different ways. "Broads" are casual and usually temporary, "Mamas" maintain an affiliation with the club as a whole, while "Ol' Ladies" have established relationships with individual members (p. 132). Interestingly, members' personal ties with women are the major threat to the internal cohesion of an outlaw motorcycle club. The club demands almost complete allegiance, but many women do not share this allegiance. Marriage frequently means leaving the club. As one biker said, "There are no biker weddings, only ex-biker weddings."

Sharing similar attitudes brings bikers from different areas together under certain conditions, but the common bonds of biking are completely overriden when inter-club rivalry dictates warfare. From the outlaw-biker viewpoint a club did not exist unless it openly wore "colours," and its existence was automatically terminated when it lost those colours, often at the hands of a victorious club. One detects pride in Wolf's description of the Rebels' successful rivalry with other clubs. The colours of other clubs were draped upside down on a wall in the clubhouse, all seized from clubs that they had "taken off the road." Wolf argues that territoriality was both necessary and inescapable. Ironically, there is more violence when territorial dominance breaks down. The Rebels' dominance in Edmonton, allied with other clubs at times, and unofficially sanctioned by the police, kept Edmonton more peaceful than Calgary, where gang rivalries led to bloodshed and deaths.

Why do motorcycle gangs persist? Wolf portrays the Rebels as a product of urban industrial society, a collective social response to the conditions of alienation as experienced by young, working-class men. They form a subculture in opposition to, and sometimes in criminal conflict with, the social norms of mainstream North America. They create an opportunity for meaningful participation at personal and social levels. The man who "earns his colours" becomes a member of an élite, which struts with a high profile. (One can imagine the same type of psychological strutting from a politician, athlete, successful businessman, academic, or student who has received an award.) At the personal level the biker is part of a tightly knit social network, a brotherhood. He is not antisocial or fleeing from commitment. He is an organization man.

War and the Creation of Violent Cultures

The borderline between subcultures and the total culture of a society is debated by many criminologists. If the subculture differs considerably from the dominant society, conflict with the majority of the population and with the agents of social control is likely. On the other hand, if the larger culture is permeated by violent norms, different strategies might be appropriate to reduce violence. Dane Archer and Rosemary Gartner (1976) address the larger issue of elements that pervade an entire society. They, along with others in the past, argue that wars contribute to violence, not just during the wars themselves, but afterwards.

The idea that war might increase domestic violence is not new, but Archer and Gartner test a number of different hypotheses, using 110 nations with data on wars and homicide rates. Such data are complicated, problematic, and difficult to interpret. During major wars, crime rates are lower because young males leave the civilian population for the military, convicts are released prematurely to enter the armed forces, those arrested are convicted and imprisoned less, etc. On the other hand, crimes might increase because families are disrupted, blackouts create criminal opportunities, etc.

After a war, there are factors that might lead to a reduction of violence. Young men killed in action would remove from the population those most likely to commit violent crimes in post-war years. Law enforcement agencies return to normal manpower levels. But the return of young males might increase violent crime. In an attempt to sort out these arguments, Archer and Gartner identify seven theoretical models that attempt to explain the impact of war on homicide. I discuss only four.

1. The Social Solidarity Model
Wars increase solidarity and thereby reduce homicide rates. The social solidarity

model suggests that crime rates would decline during wartime and return to pre-war rates after the war.

2. The Social Disorganization Model

Wars disrupt the established order of societies. Thus, this model suggests that more homicide would occur in countries that suffer disintegration of the economic, political, and social systems after a war. Homicide would increase among defeated nations.

3. The Catharsis Model

Wars substitute public violence for private violence. The catharsis model predicts that homicide would decrease during and after a war. The impact depends on how long the cathartic effects are thought to last. The model also suggests that societies that experienced the greatest violence would have the greatest catharsis, and thus, experience post-war decreases in violent crimes.

4. The Legitimation of Violence Model

Wars influence homicide, through the reduction of inhibitions and the legitimation of violence. Social approval of violence as a way of solving problems reduces inhibitions against taking human life. Wars legitimate killing people. The model predicts increases in homicide in post-war societies among both veterans and non-veterans.

The 110-nation Comparative Crime Data File, with rates of various offenses for 1900-1970, enabled Archer and Gartner to examine many "nation-wars." There are gaps in the data, and my summary oversimplifies the sophisticated analysis and presentation. The tables that follow look at changes in homicide rates after wars, and note decreases, no change (less than 10%), or increases.

Table 17.1 shows the post-war homicide-rate changes in combatant nations and in nearby nations not involved in the fighting. For the combatant nations, six nation-wars were followed by decreases in homicide rates. This included Canada after World War I and the U.S. after World War II. Four nation-wars resulted in changes of less than 10%, including Canada after WW II. Seventeen nations were in the third category, which showed a distinct increase in homicide rates after the two world wars. Clearly, increases were more common than decreases. By contrast the non-combatant nations showed more decreases in homicide than increases. However, if we were to limit our arguments to Canada, England, and the U.S., decreases were just as common as increases. We would be misled. The social science research done on English-speaking societies might be much less universalistic than many of us would like to think.

Would the Vietnam War and others differ from the World Wars? In Table 17.2 the same pattern appears. Combatant nations displayed increases in homicide rates, while noncombatants exhibited decreases.

Table 17.1 Homicide Rate Changes in Combatant and Noncombatant Nations after WWI and WWII

Decrease %		Combatant Nations No Change < 10%		Increase %	
Canada (I)	-25%	Canada (II)	6%	Germany (I)	98%
U.S. (II)	-12%	England (I)	-5%	Italy(I)	52%
+4 others		+ 2 others		U.S. (I)13%	
				England (II)	13%
				France (II)	51%
				Italy (II)	133%
				Japan (II)	20%
				New Zealand (II)	313%
				Norway (II)	65%
				+ 8 Others	

Decrease %		Control Nations (Noncombatant) No Change		Increase %	
Norway (I)	-37%	Ceylon (I)	8%	Finland (I)	124%
Ceylon (II)	-19%	Chile (I)	-3%	Thailand (I)	112%
Chile (II)	-67%	Netherlands (I)	-2%	Sweden (II)	14%
Switzerland (II)	-42%			+ 2 others	

Source: Archer and Gartner (1976)

Table 17.2 Homicide Rate Change for Vietnam and 11 Other Wars

Decrease %		Combatant Nations No Change < 10%		Increase %	
India (1962 Sino-Ind)	-14%	Australia (VN)	7%	New Zealand (VN)	50%
Israel (1956 Sinai)	-58%	Korea (VN)	6%	Thailand (VN)	14%
+ 2 others		Philippines (VN)	9%	U.S. (VN)	42%
		Japan (1904 -Russo)	-9%	Israel (1967 - 6 day)	14%
		Japan (1932 -Manch)	-8%	Japan (1984 Sino)	15%
		+ 5 others		Jordan (1967 - 6 day)	35%
				+ 2 others	

Decrease %		Control Nations (Non-combatant) No Change %		Increase %	
Burma (VN)	-17%	Thailand (1932 Manch)	7%	Canada (VN)	11%
Indonesia (VN)	-23%	Ceylon (1962 Sino-Ind)	-4%	England (VN)	23%
Japan (VN)	-23%			Taiwan (VN)	37%
France (1896 Italo-Eth)	-22%			Ceylon (1965, 2d Kash)	11%
Turkey (1956 Sinai)	-33%				
+ 4 others					

Source: Archer and Gartner (1976)

Table 17.3 compares combatant nations that had many battle deaths with those that had few. Those nations that saw "more" war; that is, suffered more battle deaths, showed the greatest post-war increase in homicide. This is clearly incompatible with the catharsis model.

Table 17.3 Post-War Homicide Rate Changes

Nations with *Many* Battle Deaths		
Decrease	**No Change**	**Increase**
Finland (II)	Canada (II)	Australia (II)
Hungary (I)	England (I)	Belgium (I)
U.S. (II)	France (I)	England (II)
	Japan (1904 Russ)	France (II)
		Germany (I)
+ 4 others		Italy (I)
		Italy (II)
		Japan (II)
		Netherlands (II)
		New Zealand (II)
		Norway (II)
		U.S. (I)
		+ 5 others

Nations with *Few* Battle Deaths		
Decrease	**No Change**	**Increase**
4 nations	7 nations	7 nations

Source: Archer and Gartner (1976)

Table 17.4 looks at nations with many battle deaths separately for victorious and defeated nations. The social-disorganization model predicts that homicide increases would be confined to defeated nations, but victorious nations also experienced increased homicide rates. As Archer and Gartner continue their analysis, they examine other combinations to test the different models. Non-combatant nations show more decreases in homicide. Nations with good or poor post-war economies display similar patterns, and post-war increases in homicide occur for women as well as men. To summarize, only the legitimation-of-violence model is consistent with the frequent and pervasive post-war homicide increases in combatant nations. The other models are rejected. Sanctioned killing during war has a residual effect in peacetime. It is tempting to generalize this argument to other authorized violence, such as capital punishment. Do nations that use violence as a way to solve problems contribute to further violence?

Table 17.4 Homicide-Rate Change by Number of Battle Deaths: Victorious and Defeated Nations

Victorious Nations with *Many* Battle Deaths		
Decrease	**Unchanged**	**Increase**
U.S. (II)	Canada (II)	Australia (II)
	England (I)	England (II)
		France (II)
		U.S. (I)
		+ 7 others

Defeated Nations with *Many* Battle Deaths		
Decrease	**Unchanged**	**Increase**
Finland (II)		Bulgaria (I)
Hungary (I)		Germany (I)
		Hungary (1956-Russo)
		Italy (II)
		Japan (II)

Source: Archer and Gartner (1976)

Harold Pepinsky and Richard Quinney (1991) would respond to that question with a resounding "Yes." Many criminologists, including those who are somewhat conventional in their orientation, share a growing consensus that coercive social control cannot reduce violent crime or solve social problems. War is one of those unsuccessful attempts to solve problems with violence.

FAMILY VIOLENCE

Only recently has much attention been given to the family as a major source of violence. In 1991, 34% of the murders in Canada were committed by family members, 53% by an acquaintance, and 13% by a stranger (Wright, 1992). For female victims, 54% were killed by family members, 38% by an acquaintance, and 8% by a stranger. If we are interested in policies to reduce violent crime, the family should be a major focus of our attention. There are disagreements regarding the nature of the impact of family violence on the behaviour of children and on violence in general (Walker, 1984; Kincaid, 1985; Pagelow, 1984; Straus, Gelles, and Steinmetz, 1980; Fleming, 1979; Schechter, 1982), but it is not necessary to resolve all debates to pursue the logic presented here.

Since the proportion of spousal murder is higher in Canada than it is in the U.S. (Silverman and Kennedy, 1993:69), family violence is particularly relevant to us. In the early 1960s, murderers were more likely to be spouses and lovers than friends or acquaintances. By 1990, friends or acquaintances accounted for the highest proportion of murders. When spouses and lovers are combined with "other family," these family murders exceed those by friends and acquaintances, except during the most recent years. Murders by strangers, which generate the most fear and lead to the greatest demand for increased punitiveness, have not shown any systematic increase in the past thirty years. Focusing on family violence, instead of strangers lurking in the shadows, makes good sense if we are serious about reducing violence.

Emphasis on immediate, short-term strategies preoccupies policy-makers with serious offenders. Unfortunately, such efforts rarely have much positive impact on future violence. There is a tendency to focus on those *persons* who commit violent acts, rather than on the *conditions* that give rise to violence. It is difficult to legislate against violent crime, but structural changes that would decrease conditions leading to violence are amenable to legislative change. What changes would have the greatest impact?

The Distribution of Violence

Serious offenses are less common than minor ones (O'Brien, 1985). Such a distribution is shown by the curve indicated by the solid line in Figure 17.1, where I have attempted to diagram the frequency of violent acts committed by the total population, charted against the seriousness of each violent act. The horizontal axis goes from "not serious at all" to "very serious"; the vertical axis shows the number of people in that category. For the solid line, the single hump of the curve towards the left suggests that many people commit minor acts of violence. Most people occasionally spank their children; many children get into minor fights. There are only a few angels on the extreme left of the chart who are perfect. It is a rare person who does not step on insects or kick vending machines when they lose their money. Towards the right of the curve are people who are violent. The main point is that the curve tapers off to the right; extreme behaviour is much less frequent.

The *broken line* in Figure 17.1 has two humps. If extremely violent persons were clearly unique and numerous, they might fall under the hump to the right. Most of us have no trouble with the peak on the left; the paragons of virtue are rare and most of us commit indiscretions that are not truly serious. The *real* problem is with those under the peak to the right, who are more dangerous, and therefore require special handling. The basic flaw in this argument is that the *solid* line represents the correct shape, and it is difficult to have much impact on the total violence curve by concentrating on the few. By now, the reader has certainly recognized that the logic is the same as that used in the chapter on drugs.

Typically, we assume that the problem lies with a particular group of violent individuals who require our immediate attention. Others commit minor acts of

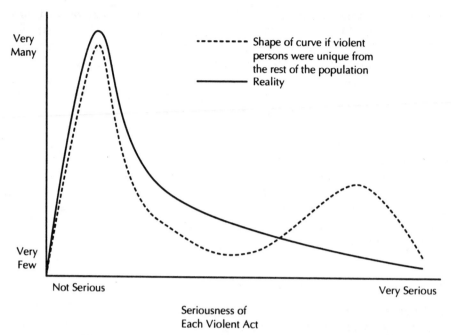

FIGURE 17.1 The Frequency of Violent Acts Committed by the Total Population, Charted Against the Seriousness of Each Violent Act*

*Basic idea from Whitehead and Smart (1972).

violence from time to time, but because their acts are less serious, and, taken individually, of little consequence, they can be conveniently ignored. Public outrage is directed at extreme individuals who commit serious crimes. Moral outrage must be distinguished from effective public policy. Programmes and laws directed against the *minority of serious* trouble-makers, rather than towards the *majority of minor* offenders, has little impact. However, modest changes for many *minor* forms of violence would eventually influence the extreme and dangerous behaviour of the few, if we could change the *conditions* that influence violent behaviour in general. There is no distinct target population; serious offenders are simply at one end of a *smooth* continuum. Present policies make a few people the target of some anti-violence strategy. However, the *shape* of the curve remains constant; efforts directed towards that small population on the right of the curve will have little impact on the *entire* curve. The only way to reduce violence is to move the entire curve to the left.

A similar logic fits family violence. Instead of concentrating on extreme cases, policies should emphasize conditions that influence all cases. Women trapped in certain types of family situations are more likely to experience violence (Tong, 1984; Atkins and Hoggett, 1984; Brophy and Smart, 1985). Economic factors that make it difficult for a woman to leave a dangerous family situation contribute to the potential for violence. Thus, social policies giving women more economic independence would reduce the frequency of conditions that lead to violence (Hackler, 1991).

Family Violence and Future Criminality

Evidence that physical violence in families can influence subsequent criminal careers should be approached cautiously. Since the family should provide love, supportiveness, and moral training, it is hard to view the family as an institution that teaches violence (Steinmetz and Straus, 1974). In addition, much family violence is seen as legitimate, as in parental use of physical punishment or the high rate of pushing, shoving, slapping, and throwing things (Gelles and Straus, 1979). The acceptance of this violence as normal blinds us to the possibility that it might train children to be violent, and might also contribute to criminal behaviour.

White and Straus (1981) explore the way children are socialized into violent behaviour, and conclude that such behaviour is *transferrable* from one setting to another. Child abuse, then, especially when it is a part of an erratic punishment pattern, gives victims guidelines for future behaviour in other settings. In the Montréal Massacre of December 1989, a young man, Marc Lépine, who had been abused as a child, murdered fourteen female engineering students at l'École Polytéchnique. Perhaps it is an oversimplification to claim that he transferred his family experience to his hatred of women, but it is compatible with the evidence that violence in the family becomes a model for violence outside the home.

The Consequences of Parents Hitting Children

The family is the setting where rules are first learned and reinforced. Children learn that they (or the mother) can be physically punished "if they deserve it." These rules can be applied to settings outside the family. In their national study of family violence, Straus, Gelles, and Steinmetz, (1980) found that the more husbands and wives were hit as children, the greater the rate of violence towards their spouses. According to Lincoln and Straus (1985: Ch. 10) the more children are hit by their parents, the more these children hit their brothers, sisters, and parents. Sibling violence may be more frequent than other family violence, but it is the least likely to be reported to authorities (Pagelow, 1989).

Cathy Spatz Widom (1989a) used a sophisticated cohort design that compared 908 cases of physical and sexual abuse and neglect cases with those of a matched control group of 667 individuals with no official record of abuse. Overall, 29% of those who were abused as children had adult criminal records, in comparison with

21% of the controls. The abused individuals were more likely to be violent offenders, but this was true for males only. A Canadian study found that children who
had been beaten were also more likely to injure themselves (Ross, 1980).

Admittedly, the evidence is less clear-cut because of the complexity of disentangling causal factors (Pagelow, 1984; Pagelow, 1989; Widom, 1986; Widom
1989b). In an extensive review of the literature, Cathy Spatz Widom (1989b) suggests that abusive or neglectful experiences may not lead directly to future violence. "Being abused as a child may increase one's risks of becoming an abusive
parent, a delinquent, or an adult violent criminal. ... However, the pathway is
neither straight nor certain" (p. 184). The damage may be more subtle, and appear
as emotional damage. In this chapter, I err on the side of uncritical acceptance of
the transmission of violence, but for policy purposes this may be reasonable.

Government Response Towards Family Violence

When Margaret Mitchell, Member of Parliament in Canada, told the House of
Commons a few years ago that one out of ten men regularly beats his wife, there
were guffaws from some of the male Members. Obviously, an initial task is to convince male-dominated policy-making bodies that a problem exists. There is also a
tendency to make the battered wife the focus of attention. The battered woman is
given "therapy" and shown how to "identify tensions in the marriage relationship" (Tierney, 1982), as if she, rather than the male-oriented values that influence
social inequality, were the problem. The wife-beating problem can be medical-
ized, professionalized, individualized, and de-politicized (Conrad and Schneider,
1980) while ignoring conditions that increase the likelihood of family stress.

Another element in this strategy, perhaps unintended, is that militant feminist
groups that emphasize basic change can be "cooled out" by supposedly sympathetic social service agencies and government projects willing to sponsor programmes that focus on a specific identifiable problem. Feminist movements must
rely on governments to keep specific programmes, such as shelters for battered
women, operating; however, traditional, male-dominated political structures may
have goals that are antithetical to militant movements (Tierney, 1982). The practice of "funding and defanging" them through manipulating funding, influencing
hiring, and guiding referrals keeps some of these feminist groups more "manage-
able" (Burstyn, 1987: 21-22).

Using Child Support Payments to Move the Violence Curve to the Left

Many mothers appear in family court because a former husband has failed to
make child-support payments. The father may also be facing financial difficulties.

He tries to visit his children; the mother resists because he has not made payments; a fight ensues. If the state took on the task of paying child support and collecting from the husband, the situation could be quite different. Once child support is awarded, the state could guarantee those payments, providing better protection for children. Collecting payments from the father becomes a separate issue, which does not have to effect the family. An unemployed father might have difficulties, but this is between the court and the father, *not between the mother and the father*. Divorces already involve stress. By making the mother as independent as possible, we minimize the negative impact on the children. Chasing a former husband through the courts to recover overdue child-support payments is a poor way for a divorced mother to use her time or finances, and can lead to retaliation when the mother attempts to deny visitation rights to the father.

Our present situation penalizes the weakest and most vulnerable people. Economic factors frequently make it difficult for a woman to leave a potentially or actually violent situation. Whether it is during a marriage or afterwards, society has a vested interest in enabling women to act independently when faced with stressful conditions. At present, we focus on families who are *currently* displaying serious violence. In reality, there is a continuum of family violence, from serious to minor, as represented by the skewed curve in Figure 18.5. The target group is always unclear, so a truly effective strategy would include many who are marginal. Universal plans have an impact on many families, including those with severe problems.

Family Violence and Native Families in Canada

Empirical data on violence in Native families in Canada is scarce, but there was a doubling of the murder rate for Canadian Indian offenders from 1961 to 1990. Murder is probably the best indicator of general violence over time. Changes in reporting practices have probably influenced crime statistics on sexual assault, child abuse, and wife-battering. Murder represents the most visible tip of the iceberg, but it is a mere tip. Thus, I suggest it indicates that violence has increased among Native families from 1961 until the late 1970s. If violence is of concern in the population in general, it is much more serious among our Native population. Since violence among marginal families today leads to children being violent in the future, improving family conditions for Native children should be of the highest priority. All of the points made above with regard to economic equality, and other factors that make women vulnerable, apply even more to Native women. Few areas of public policy have greater potential for reducing crime in the future.

The recent increases in homicide in Canada may be primarily because of the increases in Native homicides. Although the Native population is small in Canada, if we were to remove the Native homicides, the increases for the rest of the population are minimal. Similarly in the U.S., where Blacks make up a larger portion of the total population, if one were to remove Black homicides, increases for the rest of the populations are less apparent. This fits with a major theme in this book: *violence in recent years has increased most dramatically among members of those groups who have been marginalized by society rather than among members of the dominant society.* Policies that would improve the lot of marginalized people would probably contribute more to the reduction of violent crime than the repressive tactics that have been favoured in North America during the past two decades.

Can Government Policy Make a Difference in Violent Crime?

Government intervention reduces wife abuse. For example, the family allowance contributes toward the financial independence of women. In a small but possibly long-range manner, stresses that lead to other forms of violent crime would be reduced. Women raising small children either without a husband or with a non-supportive husband are vulnerable. Policy-makers overlook the criminogenic potential of such family conditions. By simply providing a woman with the means to move away, circumstances conducive to violence might be avoided. Some of these changes may already be occurring in North America (Ursel, 1991). When Straus and Gelles (1986) reported a decrease in child and wife abuse between 1975 and 1985, there was a mixed response from official agencies, since they had witnessed an increase in such cases. Broad-based social concern leading to a variety of programmes could make women seek help instead of enduring beatings. This would mean more contact with agencies, but also a decrease in actual beatings. When a society mobilizes, there is the potential for positive change. Broad-based programmes that make modest contributions to the quality of family life for many families are often overlooked in favour of those programmes that focus on the violent few.

GENERALIZING EXPLANATIONS OF VIOLENCE: RAPE AS AN ILLUSTRATION

There are different explanatory factors for different types of violent crime, but there is also extensive overlap in causal factors. The skewed curve in Figure 17.1 suggests that societies (or communities or neighbourhoods) that have high rates of one type of violence also have high rates of others. The conditions that lead to wife-battering and child abuse also lead to murder. Therefore, *Four Theories of Rape in American Society*, by Larry Baron and Murray A. Straus (1989), reviews theories that apply to violent crime in general. The book does not attempt to explain sexually violent men; instead, it tries to understand sexually violent societies. The four theories are summarized as follows:

- A test of a *gender inequality* explanation of rape looked at differences in economic resources, political power, and legal rights between men and women, that is, measures of patriarchal social organization. Indicators include average incomes, percent of women in administrative positions, percent of loans by the Small Business Administration granted to women, percent of women in each state who hold political office, judges positions, etc., and the passage of state legislation effecting women.

- A test of a *social disorganization* theory of rape used measures such as divorce, lack of religious affiliation, households headed by males with no females present, and female-headed households with children. This theory draws from the traditional Chicago school of social problems, which focuses on factors that disrupt societies, such as migration, marital problems, and cultural heterogeneity.

- The *legitimate violence* theory is the same as the argument put forward by Archer and Gartner in their study of wars. The approval of non-criminal violence spills over into tolerance of rape and other forms of criminal violence. Indicators of this concept include watching violence on television, violent-magazine circulation, National Guard enrolment and expenditures, hunting licences per 100,000 population, physical punishment in schools, lynchings per million population, prisoners under death sentences, and executions per 100,000 homicide arrests.

- The *pornography* theory was tested by size of the circulation of sexually explicit magazines like *Playboy, Hustler, Penthouse*, etc. In fact, most feminists are not particulary concerned with erotica or sexually explicit materials, but rather with images of violence and degradation, but this distinction is not made in the Baron and Straus study.

The concluding recommendations in Baron and Straus make sense for the reduction of rape and, indirectly, for all types of violent crime:

1. We need equal rights for women, economically and otherwise. Sweden illustrates what can be accomplished in recent decades.

2. The demoralizing and brutalizing conditions of poverty and economic inequality should be eradicated. Northern European countries have done fairly well in this regard. Canada could too.

3. The stress of urban life can be reduced by strengthening family and community ties.

4. Male gender roles can be restructured to emphasize warmth, equality, and supportiveness rather than aloofness, dominance, and violence (1989:193-194).

CONCLUSION

Effective violent-crime reduction requires broad changes in the structure of society. The law-and-order mentality, which has emphasized increased punishment for the past dozen years, will not only fail but will contribute to greater violence. A couple of decades ago, the violence chapter of a criminology text would have focused on murderers, rapists, robbers, and other such nasty individuals. Instead, this chapter has focused on a broader argument appropriate to some of the major sources of violence: corporate activities, broader cultural elements, and family violence. Because of space, I neglected one other major source of violence, drunken driving. This presentation will not satisfy those who think criminology should focus on conventional "real" criminals. Policies that take into account points reviewed above would, in the long run, be more likely to reduce murder, rape, robbery and the like.

We can also identify practices that are clearly *ineffective*. There is little the criminal justice system can do to reduce violent crime. Police and courts might become more involved with domestic violence, for example, but their potential effectiveness is limited. John Conrad (1985) tried to assess the potential impact of the criminal justice system on violent crime, and found that a substantial number of violent delinquents terminated their careers before they reached adulthood. However, most recidivists will again commit violent crimes, and the justice system does not deter such offenders. In addition, 73% of the sample could not have been prevented from committing their offenses by an incapacitating sentence. By the time crimes come to the attention of officials, it is too late.

Any real decrease in violence will require changes in the way we do business, the way we resolve disputes, and the way we organize family life. While the criminal justice system is less consequential for preventing violent crime, it might be used to expose offenders to "reintegrative shaming," as advocated by John Braithwaite in previous chapters. We can shame Ford Motor Company executives when they hide behind business practices and deliberately produce a dangerous automobile. We can shame people who advocate violence as a way of solving disputes. We can also reduce many of the stresses that lead to family violence, while shaming family members who use violence. However, as Braithwaite reminds us, we must also reintegrate those who have done wrong. We must congratulate General Motors for emphasizing safety in their recent advertising; and if they recall the five million trucks and move their vulnerable gas tanks to a more protected position, we should sing their praises. We must applaud family members who resolve issues in a nonviolent way. The reduction of violent crime requires policy-makers to have a broader vision than the "get-tough" strategies that have failed for years.

CRIMES FOR PROFIT AND OTHER REWARDS

Earth provides enough to satisfy everyman's needs, *but not for everyman's* greed.

Gandhi

A FUNCTIONALIST ARGUMENT FOR CORRUPTION AND ORGANIZED CRIME

One of the traditional ways of explaining property crime was to use a concept referred to as *functionalism*. Instead of asking about the nature of things, one focuses on *what things do*. That is, what function does something have? This perspective is no longer very popular, but it has heuristic uses and influences criminological explanations.

Robert Merton (1968) distinguished between manifest (intended) functions and latent (unintended) functions. The manifest function of parole is to reduce time spent in prison. However, if judges assume defendants get parole and do not serve the full sentences, the latent, or unintended, function of parole might be to create longer sentences. Judges could decide to "compensate" for the fact that they were sure offenders were going to be released early.

Merton looked at the functions (some of them latent) of the political machine. The borders between political crime, organized crime, and powerful members of the economic elite are admittedly blurred in this discussion, and I will not attempt to disentangle them.

Barriers to Legitimate Goals in Democratic Societies

Merton poses two questions:
1. Is society organized so that it is difficult, if not impossible for legitimate tasks to be completed? If so, is a political machine necessary to fulfil legitimate needs,

thereby giving rise to illegitimate tasks? That is, are most societies organized in a manner that makes necessary tasks difficult to accomplish?

2. Are there certain distinctive subgroups within a society whose needs are unsatisfied, thus leading to political machines that meets those needs?

These two issues appear to be related to the structure of American and Canadian democracy. In democracies, there is a lack of highly centralized power. Governments have a check-and-balance system. Power is decentralized even on the local scene. There is rarely a single "boss" who can really act when something needs to be done. The mayor of Edmonton may wish to devote more resources to public transportation, but power in many city governments is distributed among many people. Thus, political action requires compromise.

Imagine a Canadian city that wishes to sell sand to a U.S. city, but cities cannot engage in international trade. There may be tremendous barriers to accomplishing a sensible and legitimate task. Imagine that you want to dam a river in the north. This might raise the water level, produce electricity, and provide irrigation in one province, but it might flood farmers in another province. Let us also assume that the dam would lower water downstream, reducing muskrat population and annoying Native people who trap the muskrats for their fur. Even if the overall project were very desirable and the gains outweighed the losses, many governments would be involved. Public figures and civil servants come and go. Political power is dispersed among federal, provincial, and local authorities. Tenure in office is limited in democracies. Usually there is no overall powerful leader. If you were a legitimate person who wished to build this dam, which would be a boon to society, you might find yourself frustrated. Enter the political "boss."

This individual has "influence." He has ways of convincing members of legislative bodies, ministers, local governments, etc. Even if there are elections with new people in power, the "boss" can deliver enough votes, persuade enough people, and manipulate enough situations to enable you to build your dam. Naturally, there would be a price. As an upstanding Canadian you would not think of paying a bribe, and you only want to do something that is perfectly legal. Merton suggests that the difficulty of getting legitimate jobs done in democratic societies gives rise to an illegitimate system that can overcome these barriers. North America is not unique. Bribes, payoffs, and the like are endemic to many societies. In eastern Europe one of the major weaknesses in the communist system was its inefficiency and corruption. Merton would probably agree that the inability to do the jobs well through legal channels was a major factor in creating corruption.

The second point made by Merton is that certain subgroups are not well served in democratic societies. If you are an immigrant, and someone who speaks your language greets you after you clear Customs and offers to help you get established, would you not be inclined to cast your vote for the person recommended by your benefactor? If the official bureaucracy works poorly, a more humane system could easily arise. Imagine that you are a member of a minority group that faces prejudice. The political machine may be more sensitive to people in the local community and neighbourhood. The precinct captain humanizes and personalizes all manner of assistance — food baskets, jobs, legal advice, scholarships for a bright kid. There is no need to fill out application forms. No middle-class social worker will snoop about your home. When your kid gets in trouble with the police, you want help, not justice, and the representative of the political boss has the power to help. There is no loss of self-respect. The precinct captain only wants your vote.

Thus, the political machine performs a function for diverse subgroups. Deprived classes may be among the subgroups that are helped. Similarly, business, primarily big business, is served by the boss. Business does not want open competition. It prefers a predictable economic czar rather than unpredictable legislative control, which would permit public scrutiny. Just as the Oil King or Lumber King performs integrating services for legitimate business, so does the Vice King provide similar services for prostitution and gambling. Just as business eliminates competition, so does the racketeer.

When we look at the formation of the Canadian Pacific Railway or the history of the Hudson's Bay Company in Canada it is not difficult to find illustrations of dishonest activity. Compared to the U.S., Canada's power elite is more concentrated. The need for an outside political boss may not have been as compelling. Canadian leaders probably had little difficulty convincing themselves that their activities benefited the country as well as themselves. If someone could say that what was good for General Motors was good for the U.S., I suspect Van Horne thought that what was good for the Canadian Pacific Railway was good for Canada. At any rate, the captains of industry in both Canada and the U.S. might find engaging in corrupt activities an inevitable part of their business.

Merton asks if it makes sense to talk of the "evil" political machine. Does it provide social mobility for certain underprivileged people, who have little access to conventional and legitimate means? In economic terms, it is difficult to distinguish between legitimate, illegitimate, and undesirable goods and services. Prostitution is big business. Prostitutes outnumber doctors. One might argue that if it were organized legally and efficiently by governments, as in Hamburg, Germany, it would be less damaging to society. It is difficult to assess the consequence of gambling when it is organized illegally, rather than by the Canadian Legion and the churches. During the Duplessis period in Québec the government broke laws, but did it also provide services? Do corrupt systems provide services better than honest ones at times? Seen from a functional perspective, one might understand why reform campaigns are typically short-lived. Merton summarizes his argument as follows:

> Any attempt to eliminate an existing social structure without providing alternatives for filling needs previously filled by the abolished organization is doomed to failure . .... To seek social change, without due recognition of the manifest and la-

tent functions performed by the social organization undergoing change, is to indulge in social ritual rather than social engineering (Merton, 1968:135).

This functional argument has generated many criticisms. It assumes that everything that exists performs some function. This becomes a tautology. If something were dysfunctional, one might argue that it would soon cease to exist. Despite weaknesses, however, the above argument leads to some thought-provoking issues. It suggests that democracies, or dictatorships for that matter, must be fairly well run if they are to operate without the type of corruption and crime that characterizes much of the world.

Can the Functionalist Argument Be Generalized?

A Case of Ineffective Government: The Rise of the Mafia

Explanations of the Mafia, organized crime, and political crime differ. One approach would emphasize the characteristics of criminals and their organizations, viewing them as cancers that invade and destroy healthy societies. By contrast, a functionalist approach would see deficiencies in the society, which would lead to new organizational structures arising to deal with these deficiencies. The description offered here fits the latter explanation.

In the 1860s and earlier, local organizations in Sicily served as an intermediary force between powerless peasants and the wealthy, local feudal lords who owned estates (Cavan and Cavan, 1968: Ch. 6). Government was remote and ineffective. Tax collectors and police were viewed by the peasants as predators. Informal structures, Mafias, at the local level arose to fill the gap in authority. Originally, the term *Mafia* referred to a sign of bravado. Men settled disputes without reference to the authorities. A theft was a personal insult. The thief held his victim in contempt. These values were supported by *omerta*, a conspiracy of silence towards law-enforcement officers. It also required absolute obedience by younger persons.

Different Mafias might function independently in the same area. One might control the water from the local spring, another the marketing of a specific product. Frequently, alliances developed. Leaders were men of natural ability. Often, they were humble, courteous, reliable, but also firm and ruthless as disciplinarians. Once a part of a Mafia it was very difficult to withdraw or become a member of an opposing group. A young cousin of a Mafioso joined the police, and was later killed by family leaders to remove the stain on their honour. Some of the functions of Mafias would normally have been performed by an effective government.

Would the evolution of Mafias fit a functionalist argument? One could argue that these structures arose to fill societal needs. It is also possible that, once having come into being, organizations take on a life of their own. In the past, the Italian government has had little luck in eliminating Mafias. At times, the government has even cooperated with them and turned to them for political support. In the 1990s, the Italian government appears to be making strenuous efforts to destroy them , but the functionalist approach provides a warning — if legitimate governments do not serve the needs of society effectively, illegitimate structures will arise.

In parts of South America, wealthy drug lords are providing housing and other services to the poor. It would be a mistake to see this as a natural response to societal needs, but drug lords may be filling gaps left unfilled by governments. The Mertonian argument suggests that, as illegitimate organizations perform useful societal tasks, they will be particularly hard to eliminate.

The Criminal Tribes of India

When the British arrived in India, they found themselves dealing with "criminal tribes" (Bose, 1956). In these groups, crime was a central part of their livelihood. These crimes were directed against outsiders, were carefully planned and organized by the local council, and were for financial gain only. If the elders were given a contract to murder someone, it was not because of anger or insult. It was business. Some writers believe the origin of these criminal tribes was in organized bands of "thugs," a word that is now part of English (Biswas, 1960; Curry 1932). The British government recognized these activities as evolving into part of tribal cultures, rather than as the work of gangs of marauders who did not have any particular social or cultural background. The result was that part of child training included stealing and other types of crime.

Sex inside the tribe was regulated, but prostitution outside was acceptable to get money and information on sources of wealth. Thus a prostitute would follow different rules within her own group. This principle applied to other crimes as well. One did not steal from "your own people." The British found it difficult to change the situation. When jobs were provided, men said that it was more rewarding, monetarily as well as psychologically, to pick pockets than to work in a factory.

Let us again pose the question: Do these tribes perform a function? We might ask, functions for whom? From the standpoint of the total Indian society, the rest of the population would have functioned quite well without the criminal tribes. From the standpoint of the criminal tribe itself, perhaps crimes could be viewed as functional; but if the authorities decide to eliminate this source of trouble, crime would become dysfunctional. It is also difficult to explain this pattern of crime as the product of an ineffective government or society.

Picking Pockets in the Paris Subway

In the past decade, a pattern of picking pockets has evolved in Paris. A group of youngsters, often Gypsies, surrounds someone and pushes a map into the victim's face. Others quickly steal wallets, and then all scatter.

It appears that these thefts may have evolved out of an earlier, non-criminal activity — begging. In 1976, I followed a youngster of ten or eleven in the Paris subways for over an hour. He held a card that had the traditional plea for money, "My father is dead, my mother is sick, etc." Parisians rarely read the sign, but since the one-franc piece was the normal coin given to the beggar, I found it easy to estimate the "take." He was earning about $45 an hour.

If other children in a Gypsy family are doing as well, and mother is also sitting in the subway with a chalked message on the floor that reads, "My husband is dead, my children are sick, etc." the family is probably earning a good income. The incentive to shift to normal work would not be there. One can see how begging can develop into a stable pattern; however, explaining the more recent shift into picking pockets is more difficult. From a rational standpoint, it is difficult to see that the shift from begging to theft would be more profitable. Was begging too dull, so that these children decided that picking pockets was more exciting? Did adults who socialized them believe stealing would be more profitable than begging? From a functional perspective, it is difficult to see either begging or picking pockets as performing a function that is handled badly by government. It is also difficult to explain why begging gave way to stealing wallets, which naturally brings a strong official response.

Criminal Organizations in Japan: The Yakuza

Many of us think of Japan as being more orderly than North America and Europe. Furthermore, if one considers the theories offered in this chapter and earlier in the book, it is somewhat puzzling that criminal organizations, such as the yakuza, persist in Japan. These organizations control gambling, prostitution, and a variety of other illegal activities. Usually a single group controls these activities, and occasionally there are power struggles among them. These organizations sometimes have links with legitimate leaders in business and politics. They are known to the police, and their relations with the authorities follow traditional customs. Does a functionalist argument fit? Do yakuzas fill some niche that has been neglected by government? As we look at crime in different countries we might find that theories developed in North America are quite limited.

CONVENTIONAL STREET CRIME

Greed has been viewed as the major motivating factor for many crimes. This is a vast oversimplification, but it forms the basis of much criminological research. Crime represents a rational quest for a supposedly universal goal, which people seek in a variety of ways. In a modern society, that means money and all of the goods, services, privilege, and prestige that money can buy. Explanations such as the routine-activities theory take these motivations for granted, as does opportunity theory. These theories look at situations.

Another strategy, or formula, for explaining property crime is to look at characteristics of the criminal, such as age, gender, race, ethnicity, socioeconomic status, and education. This strategy could be subdivided into characteristics that are more individual or more social. Researchers can focus on individual characteristics or on the way individuals interact with aspects of the society. Still another formula is to see crime as irrational, the manifestation of mental, or at least emotional, illness to the extent that rational thought has been suspended.

Stealing: Rational Behaviour or Getting One's Kicks?

Serious Thieves in Toronto

Gordon West (1978) notes that these youths lacked acceptable employment opportunities. When this was combined with access to thieving, they claimed they made a rational choice to steal. The restraints of a spouse, a good job, or self-concept, variables discussed in control theory and other conventional theories of crime, could inhibit this pattern, but serious thieves lacked such restraints. West distinguishes "serious thieves" from "professional thieves" in that they do not have highly developed skills, such as safe-cracking. They are non-migratory, make much less money, can rarely "fix" cases that come to the attention of the police (Sutherland and Conwell, 1937), and as a result spend much more time in jail than the professionals.

From West's perspective some professionals may achieve the success described by John Mack (1972) as "able" criminals in Scotland. Mack argues that a small number of very skilled and capable criminals steal successfully and are never caught. However, successful professional thieves are few in number and rarely appear in court. The serious thieves studied by West are not in the same league. They are young, averaging 18.8 years, and figure prominently in the official court records. They specialize in shoplifting, burglary, vehicle theft, and fraud. Rather than being "irrational," committing theft for "kicks" or symbolizing rebellion, etc., these serious thieves organize their activities efficiently along business lines, to maximize profit.

West presents an image of stealing that is compatible with: 1) opportunity or strain theory (these young men from lower-class backgrounds aspire to wealth, but have less opportunity to achieve it); 2) control theory (the social bonds to others are not as strong); and 3) differential association (there are others around who favour stealing). These conventional theories suggest social policies that appeal to fairly rational thinking on the part of potential criminals. Thus, it is important to know whether assumptions regarding rationality fit the descriptions and explanations applied to property offenders.

The Seductions of Crime: Shoplifting, Joyriding, Burglary and Other Sneaky Thrills

In a book with the provocative title *Seductions of Crime: Moral and Sensual Attractions of Doing Evil*, Jack Katz (1988) argues that these rational strategies are inadequate, because they do not capture the essence of the experience from the standpoint of the criminal. Crime cannot be explained without knowing what it means to the actor. Conventional criminology assumes that criminals want to acquire money or goods, get revenge, satisfy sexual urges, get high on drugs, and the like. Katz feels that criminologists, whether they are using quantitative or qualitative techniques, impose their own interpretation on what is going on in the mind of the criminal.

Material needs are often insufficient to account for the fleeting fascination with theft. Albert Cohen (1955) and many others suggest that much crime is fun. When a youth steals a hat and then goes into store after store exchanging one hat for another, it would be hard to say that he had a great desire to have a hat. But it certainly makes him seem daring in the eyes of his peers. Katz used self-reports of students in his criminology courses to construct his ideas about the sneaky thrill of shoplifting, experiences that were not utilitarian and practical, but "eminently magical" (1988:54). He emphasizes the reports of his female students. One student was fascinated with nonacquisitive burglary.

> When she was 13, she would enter neighbours' homes and roam around. Somehow being in a neighbour's house without express permission made the otherwise mundane environment charged. ... She found that a familiar kitchen or living room was magically transformed into a provocative environment. The excitement was distinctly sensual (69-70).

Katz notes that girls "seem seduced by items of makeup, jewellery, and clothes: things used to cover-up the naked female self, ... to make the self dazzlingly attractive to a world blinded to the blemishes underneath" (71). In general, Katz downplays rational and practical elements. Much research shows that girls steal cosmetics, and while Katz sees this as sensual and seductive, others view such theft as rational.

Robbery: Rational or the Pleasures of Doing Evil?

Katz argues that "distinctive sensual dynamics" emerge and must be understood. Doing evil has authenticity, an attractiveness that uplifts, excites, and purifies. He argues that each crime has its own distinctive appeals.

Robbery is often classified with violent crimes, but some argue that banks are robbed because "that is where the money is." However, Nettler (1982) and others, in addition to Katz, have done cost-benefit analyses to show that monetary gain as the principal reward cannot account for robbery, or for most other property crime. Nettler captures the pleasure of theft by quoting from Willie Sutton (1976), an intelligent and persistent bank robber.

Why did I rob banks? Because I enjoyed it. I loved it. I was more alive when I was inside a bank, robbing it, than at any other time in my life. I enjoyed everything about it so much that one or two weeks later I'd be out looking for the next job. But to me the money was the chips, that's all. The winnings. I kept robbing banks, when, by all logic, it was foolish. When it could cost me far more than I could possibly gain (Nettler, 1982:96).

Katz would also agree that robbery is risky and, from a rational standpoint, a dangerous, difficult, and not particularly lucrative way to make a living. Those who persist spend time in jail and face considerable risk, but Katz argues that the sensual attraction is the excitement, the thrill, the pursuit, and the satisfaction of forcing others to bow to their will. In a section entitled "Constructing Subjective Moral Dominance" Katz describes how the robber creates "*an angle of moral superiority* over the intended victim" (p. 169). Different types of robberies provide different rewards, including the pleasure of ridiculing and humiliating, as well as ripping off, the victim.

Although Katz offers some stimulating ideas, Erich Goode (1990), in reviewing the book, asks a number of questions. "How does the author know this? Where is his evidence? Is a different interpretation possible?" (p. 10) Researchers who have worked more directly with offenders create different images. Fred Descroches (1991) interviewed bank robbers in Ontario, and found that the modern bandit is typically a man who works alone, stands in line with customers, does not carry a weapon, uses minimal disguises, discreetly passes a note to a single teller, and walks out with $1500 to $2500. Some bandits walk around for hours, trying to decide whether or not to commit a robbery. Sometimes they walk away or just as compulsively do the robbery with a minimal amount of careful planning. Are these relatively inept individuals who vacillate over decisions? Or, as Katz would suggest, daring men, open to anything, prepared for anything, and deliberately looking for excitement?

Montréal has a tradition of robbery that is unique in Canada (Gabor, et al., 1987).

"In Canada, the French Canadian minority is overrepresented in armed robbery in a significant way. ... Québec accounts for 60 percent of all armed robberies in Canada while having only a quarter of Canada's population" (Gabor and Normandeau, 1989:274).

In the U.S., the Black minority is overrepresented in most crime categories, but even more so in robbery. Although Katz tells us that looking at age or ethnicity is not the way to go in explaining crime, conventional thinking would reasonably ask why French Canadians and Blacks are more likely to commit certain crimes. Even if we are sympathetic to the "seduction-of-crime" argument, why is it that French Canadians find it more satisfying to humiliate victims than English Canadians? Why do Blacks search for thrills and dangers in the excitement of pursuit, and in the domination of others? Conventional criminology has been criticized for its mundane habit of looking at "background" variables and correlating them with crime; but if we are to abandon this traditional line of inquiry, are we left to conclude that French Canadians and Blacks are more evil than others? That their happiness comes in hurting and humiliating others? Clearly, Katz would not make such an argument, but a more conventional argument for French Canadians and Blacks is made by Gabor and Normandeau.

> Both groups were going through considerable upheaval during the 1960s; a fact that may explain the intensification of their participation in robbery at that time. Both groups faced political oppression and exclusion from the economic elite. Both have faced the humiliations accorded those considered inferior in status (1989:274-275).

On the other hand, Gabor and his colleagues (1987) describe elements that are compatible with the argument made by Katz. Most of the robbers did little planning, while others made elaborate preparations. Some decided spontaneously to commit a robbery. Younger robbers liked the thrills, status, and feelings of power. One boy said:

> It's funny to see the expression of people when they have a .38 in their face. Sometimes I went home at night I thought of it and laughed. ... Maybe I was just fascinated ... (Gabor and Normandeau, 1989:277).

Still other robbers told Gabor that they had a code of ethics. They excluded certain targets, such as small businesses in which the owners themselves were struggling to make a living. Such reasoning seems strange for evil, daring, excitement-seekers. Most explanations do not fit all people or all situations. Perhaps some people do find magic, beauty, excitement, and gratification in doing evil, as Katz would argue, but many other criminals do not.

Roger Caron may be one of those persons who found magic and satisfaction in crime. In his book, *Go Boy*, Roger Caron describes some of the brutalizing aspects of imprisonment, and with its publication Caron became a well-known personality. One might assume that Caron's new-found fame as a writer and sought-after speaker at various functions would alter his pattern of criminal behaviour. Two more popular books appeared: *Bingo!* and *Jojo*. His latest book, *Dreamcaper*, features an old con who finally gets parole and decides to pull off his last big job. The book includes daring and ingenious escapes, a brilliantly executed heist, nasty and vindictive police, and the idyllic tropical setting where the successful criminal retires. Caron himself, of course, hoped for such criminal success, but in fact was a dismal failure. Ironically, the hero of *Dreamcaper* said, "all convicts suffer from defective reasoning; they never seem to learn from experience." About the time the book was published, Roger Caron was arrested for armed robbery. Few criminals had better chances for rehabilitation. Caron was clearly a failure as a crook; and even though he was a success as an author, the seduction of crime seemed to be too great.

Although this chapter is primarily on property crime, some studies of violent offenders fit with discussions of motives and viewing situations through the eyes of the criminal. In her study of rapists, Diana Scully (1990) offers explanations at two levels: one that depends on characteristics of individuals, and another notes that societies create different situations. In the latter argument, she claims that there is more rape in those societies that are patriarchal, produce great power and opportunity differences between men and women, and are generally more violent. That is, the nature of the society influences the amount of certain crimes. At the individual level, Scully notes that, in their interviews, convicted rapists could be distinguished between *admitters* and *deniers*. Those who admitted their rapes attempted to rationalize their behaviour as being abnormal and influenced by conditions beyond their control, such as being drunk. They accepted the fact that what they did was terribly wrong.

However, those who denied that their sexual contact was actually rape distorted both their own and the victim's experiences. They argued that the victims asked for it and enjoyed it, and therefore it was not really rape. This study illustrates the problem of developing explanations based on the categories of crime, and the need of combining explanatory levels. Regardless of the type of crime we are trying to explain, it is unlikely that an explanation that takes only one dimension into account will be adequate.

Choosing Between Explanatory Models of Street Crime

A number of questions come to mind. Are these scholars looking at the same type of people? Do they begin their research with preconceived ideas? If, as Katz would argue, crime is explained primarily by the pleasure it yields, then clearly some countries are enjoying it much more than others. Why are Americans getting so many kicks out of crime, compared to Japan? Why do Canadians find evil so much more pleasurable than northern Europeans, who have lower crime rates? Conventional criminologists have gathered facts about different amounts of crime by gender, race, social class, country, etc., but if pleasure explains crime, why do males, blacks, lower-class people, etc. find crime more seductive than others?

Do peer pressure, collective behaviour, group dynamics, and those factors reviewed earlier explain compulsive theft and robbery better than the arguments offered by Katz? Do the ecological models, including routine-activity theories and other approaches emphasizing opportunities, offer more adequate explanations of burglary than the motivation of thrills? Is it also possible that the pleasure described in doing crime is partially a reconstruction of realities after the fact? In earlier chapters, we noted that people can use cognitive dissonance to convince themselves that they had reasons for doing what they did. Qualitative research has clearly enriched our thinking, but it would be a mistake to believe that this work automatically provides clear and adequate explanations that can now replace the emphasis on evidence.

How Specialized Are Property Offenders?

Despite the wealth of research that concentrates on a particular type of offender, most property offenders are not particularly specialized. Shover (1991) has summarized the literature for burglary, and concludes that those who think of themselves as burglars not only engage in a variety of other crimes but increase their versatility with success. The issue of specialization is important for policy decisions. If unique explanations are required for each type of crime, it would be difficult to develop societal responses that would be effective. While acknowledging different causal factors for violent crime and property crime, how different are white-collar offenders from other greedy people? Do our theories cover a broad spectrum of those who lie, cheat, and steal, including white-collar criminals?

WHITE-COLLAR CRIME

In 1939, Edwin H. Sutherland introduced the term *white-collar crime* in his presidential address to the American Sociological Society, and criticized criminologists for the narrowness of their thinking about crime. Poverty, broken homes, and the traditional variables did not explain some of the most common and costly crimes. As criminologists looked beyond the lower classes and street crime, they discovered that crimes such as income tax evasion were very frequent and costly, but rarely studied as crime. The borderlines of white-collar crime differ, depending on a number of considerations. When an officer of a large corporation has insider information that would enable him to profit over others, it is a criminal offense to use that knowledge for personal gain. However, if a cab driver overhears a conversation, borrows money, and makes a killing on the stock market it would not be a crime. White-collar crime refers to the abuse of power and privilege, and there is considerable agreement that modern, democratic, free-enterprise societies must strive for a reasonably level playing field if our headlong striving after material wealth is to be pursued in an orderly fashion.

Recording and enforcement is also more problematic with white-collar crime. A former premier of British Columbia was considered an "insider" because of his holdings and his involvement in a certain company. When a phone call came to his office with devastating financial news about the company, was it just a coincidence that he sold his stock in the company a few moments later? At any rate, this former premier was acquitted in the B. C. courts.

In monetary terms, white-collar crime is of greater consequence than conventional crime. John Irwin and James Austin (1987) summarize these costs in the U.S.. The total for all street crimes in a year is about $11 billion. The U.S. spends more than four times that amount ($45.6 billion) on the criminal justice system to fight property crimes. The medical costs related to tobacco smoking are around $50 billion a year, and the cost of white-collar crime is about $200 billion per year. Although many white-collar criminals argue that they do not "hurt" people, because they steal from the government or a large company, the same argument can be made for some safe-crackers. Harry King (1972) claimed that he kept insurance companies and safe companies in business. He specialized in large corporations, which could easily absorb the expenses he created for them. The public is beginning to realize that the Principal affair in Alberta, which led to the loss of life savings for thousands of persons, caused more pain and damage than most burglaries.

Being able to utilize an organization, such as a corporation, provides greater rewards for the criminally inclined (Hagan and Parker, 1985). report a similar pattern. Securities violators who use organizational resources commit crimes that involve more victims. When a president of a corporation presents a bank with false information, as a way of defrauding shareholders, for example, he is more likely to be believed than a person acting alone. Organizations, and those who speak for them, are seen as more trustworthy than individuals. Thus, Hagan (1992) argues that people in organizations such as corporations have tremendous advantages over individuals and this leads to greater criminal gains than for persons acting alone. Hagan concludes that the social organization of work itself is criminogenic in the world of the modern corporation. Later I will return to crimes of the powerful, but for now it is appropriate to emphasize that white-collar crime is a major part of our crime problem and deserves more attention from policy-makers than it currently receives. Explanations of white-collar crime are compatible with conventional theories. Why powerful people steal is no mystery. What requires more attention is why societies respond less vigorously to this type of crime.

THE LIMITATIONS OF EXPLANATIONS FOR PROPERTY CRIMES

A number of perspectives provide plausible arguments of property crime, but none is adequate as a reasonably complete explanation. Despite the variety of "new" theories that arise from time to time, such as the work by Katz on the seductions of crime, we still find that background factors, information about types of people, neighbourhoods, situations, and even nations, are needed. This is not the same as explaining crime, but any useful theory of crime must be compatible with the facts.

A Dutch study, based on interviews with 106 burglars, suggests that elements found in a variety of theories all seemed to be relevant (Netherlands Ministry of Justice, 1991). The burglars wanted to be accepted by peers, but they also needed money to buy drugs. Once involved in burglary, it was hard to quit: they became dependent on the money, the drugs, and being part of the criminal subculture. At the same time, they expressed dislike for what they were doing. Many were addicted to drugs (43%), gambling (23%), or alcohol (18%). Clearly, differential association, subcultures, and other theories were relevant. In addition, there are potential problems of methodology. In the interviews, were they making excuses or rationalizing? Ecological factors were also apparent. They preferred to steal from detached, single-family houses, preferably those on street corners, usually in the burglars' hometowns but not in their neighbourhoods.

When Louise Biron and Carol Ladouceur (1991) interviewed twenty-five teenage burglars in Montréal, they also found that a combination of factors seemed to be operating. Perhaps we cannot develop a distinct explanation for property crimes. The facts surrounding property crime considerably, depending on circumstances, and therefore, the number of variables that interact make prediction especially difficult. Opportunities for property crime can also change through technology, such as credit-card fraud, or the way people travel, such as theft from the luggage of air travellers. Thus, finding theories for property crime that lead to intelligent policies may be particularly challenging.

Changing Technology, Changing Crimes, and Changing Explanations

Obviously, changing technology and changing organizational activities will lead to new crimes and problems that had not been anticipated. A small sample of these situations may illustrate why criminologists will have a difficult time developing satisfactory theories to explain them.

Finland is becoming a target for criminals from Russia (*Maclean's*, August 3, 1992: 20). Finnish police have arrested dozens of underworld members who entered Finland posing as refugees. They typically steal electronic goods, designer clothes, and luxury cars and smuggle them back to Russia, where confederates sell the contraband on the black market. One Finnish civic leader said it was better under the Kremlin dictatorship. "The Iron Curtain kept the criminals on the other side of the border."

David Slatter was settling into his seat on the Air Canada plane in the Miami airport, when he glanced out the window and saw an airport ramp worker unzip his bag on the conveyor belt (*Globe and Mail*, February 29, 1992). He complained to a stewardess, but Air Canada would not delay the flight. When Mr. Slatter arrived in Toronto his $1300 camera was gone.

Airport baggage theft illustrates the changing opportunities for property crime in a modern society. In some situations a variety of protective techniques arise, and there is a competition in innovation as thieves and victims develop new strategies. In addition to the technological changes and opportunities for theft, the way human groups are organized will influence crime. In Canada, baggage handlers are members of the International Association of Machinists and Aerospace Workers, and theft from baggage in Canada appears to be low. By contrast, in Miami, where Air Canada contracts with Dynair Services to handle baggage, there had been many complaints. An investigation showed that 70 of Dynair's 350 workers had arrest records. Obviously, the subcultural norms among a group of workers can influence theft rates. Although I do not have direct information, the baggage handlers in Canada may share group norms and attitudes that would condemn an individual worker who stole from clients. In other organizations, such as some longshoreman unions, theft from cargoes was seen as normal and acceptable. Anyone who ships a vehicle from Europe knows that the car keys will be given to supposedly responsible people, but anything left in the locked trunk will probably be stolen. At the same time, the thieves have their rules — the valuable spare tires are rarely taken. Understanding the way subcultural norms develop among groups of employees might help us to understand, and deal with, theft in a specific setting, but it is not clear how well such a strategy would transfer to other settings.

Employee theft accounts for a considerable proportion of the thievery in North America. Therefore, it is reasonable to ask what strategies would best reduce this type of crime. Taking action against employee theft is difficult, and the criminal justice system will have a trivial impact on the problem. Mr. Slatter, who lost his camera, filed a complaint. Two detectives flew to Toronto with pictures of several airport workers, and Mr. Slatter identified the culprit. When Slatter returned to Miami to testify, he said he only saw the ramp worker unzip the bag. That didn't prove he had stolen the camera. The prosecutor dropped the case. Mr. Slatter never saw his camera again.

CONCLUSION

Various crimes were chosen to illustrate the difficulties in using descriptions of what crooks do to create explanatory arguments. Many perspectives offer plausible arguments, but none provide precise theories. Perhaps this is an unreasonable goal. When we look at the range, variety, and ingenuity of crimes, one might assume that there is no hope; it is simply a terribly corrupt world. But there are degrees. Some countries, some communities, some families are less involved with crime than others.

Many years ago, I carelessly left my wallet in a phone booth while going for change. It was gone when I returned; however, I later received an envelope, stamped with double postage, containing all my credit cards and other papers. Even thieves have principles, and this thief had clearly not abandoned all societal values. The point I wish to make is that significant reductions in property crime will only result if almost everyone has reasonable access to basic needs, feels tied in to the norms of society, and has strong internal inhibitions against stealing. There are countries, neighbourhoods, work groups, etc. where such conditions and values are widespread. Developing a non-deviant "climate" is not an impossible task for human groups. Policy-makers should also be aware that the increased processing of cases by the criminal justice system will have little impact on creating such a society.

CRIMINALIZING SEX

He who marries his daughter to an old man makes a prostitute of her.

Hebrew Proverb

SEX IN PUBLIC PLACES: AN ILLUSTRATION OF AN "ORDER MAINTENANCE" PROBLEM

One might assume that homosexuality would no longer be a topic for criminologists, but sex in public places is still an offense and brings a response from the police. Criminologists find it useful to look at activities that might better be defined as requiring "order maintenance," rather than crime control. There are a number of crimes, such as drug use, prostitution, or homosexual activities in public toilets where the victims are unclear, and where one might question the response of the criminal justice system.

Fred Desroches (1991) notes that, in the past several years, police in Canada have invoked a crime-control model of enforcement in response to complaints of men using public washrooms for sexual purposes. Public toilets that are frequently used for homosexual encounters are often referred to as "tearooms" (Humphreys, 1970a). Using the crime-control model results in the arrest and charging of numerous "tearoom" participants. Desroches studied the police response to the situation in five Canadian urban areas. Although successful in apprehending offenders and getting convictions, the police have been criticized for their use of intrusive surveillance techniques. The publication of accused persons' names by local newspapers and the resulting loss of jobs, break-up of families, and the suicide of one offender, have raised questions over the appropriateness of police investigative practices. Desroches suggests that there are alternatives that are equally effective, less intrusive, more humane, and less costly than an aggressive arrest-and-charge crime-control strategy.

Of the five settings studied, there had been complaints in four, and in the fifth, the store security requested police involvement. The places included a public park, the basement of a theatre, three shopping centres, a department store, and the basement of a shopping mall. Between 27 and 62 men were arrested in each setting. Videotape was used in three places, and direct surveillance through air ducts in the other two.

The police in all five communities estimate that only 10% to 15% of the men used the washrooms for legitimate purposes. One officer said, "Given the percentage of legitimate usage, we may as well have taped everything." Although police attempted to use a separate tape for each offence, sexual activity sometimes occurred so quickly that as many as six offenders appear on a single tape. In each setting, the police terminated operations when they had a high proportion of repeat offenders.

Police in one community postponed their arrests until after Christmas, so that family holidays would not be destroyed. In general, most of the men who were contacted asked to talk about their situation. They were quiet on the first visit to pick up their summonses, but on the second visit they wanted to talk. Some hadn't told their wives, some had.

Did the operation achieve deterrence? Routine observations in the same settings covered by the police operations indicate that the activity has increased to its former level. Desroches argues that instead of a *crime control model* this situation should be viewed as an *order-maintenance problem*. Tearoom behaviour constitutes a low level of threat to society. Alternative strategies for security forces at universities, department stores, and shopping malls could include issuing trespassing notices to men observed lingering about public lavatories. Men can be identified and charged with trespassing if they return. There is reason to believe that cautions would work, at least for some of the men. In addition, the environmental design of areas should be considered. Tearoom participants prefer places rarely used by legitimate users. The location of restrooms can make a difference.

Considering the devastating impact of certain types of police action in the case described above, it is important to scrutinize the actions of agents of social control. Just as we are concerned about the damage done by crime, we should be concerned about the damage done by enforcement procedures.

Why Do They Do It? Laud Humphreys: Tearoom Trade

Since the consequences of these arrests were so disastrous, the reader might well be puzzled why these men used public restrooms instead developing homosexual relations in private. A unique study by Laud Humphreys (1970a; 1970b) provides some insights into the frequency and magnitude of this type of crime. I deliberately use the word *crime* because, in the eyes of the law, and from the perspective of shopping-mall managers, this is unacceptable behaviour and punishable under the *Criminal Code*.

Rarely can criminologists observe criminal behaviour directly, but the fear and suspicion of tearoom participants produces a mechanism that makes observation possible. A third man (usually one who obtains voyeuristic pleasure from the job) serves as a lookout, moving back and forth from door to windows. This "watchqueen" coughs when a police car stops nearby or when a stranger approaches. He nods affirmatively when he recognizes a man entering as a "regular." Laud Humphreys played the watchqueen role while observing hundreds of acts of fellatio.

Some of the tearooms were the scenes of a great deal of activity. These were usually located in parks on an island of grass, with roads and parking close by. The getaway car was just a few steps away; children were not apt to wander over from a playground; straight people rarely stopped there; the women's side was rarely used. Participants assured Humphreys that it was not uncommon for one man to fellate as many as ten others in a day. Some waited their turn for service. After leaving a place, Humphreys remarked to one man, "Kind of crowded in there, isn't it?" "Hell, yes," he answered, "It's getting so you have to take a number and wait in line in these places!" (Humphreys, 1970b).

Since Humphreys wanted to know more about men who take such risks, he engaged some in conversation outside the restrooms and eventually gained a dozen respondents who were interviewed. In addition, Humphreys noted licence numbers of cars. To learn more about these men, the researcher faced an ethical concern. How could these covert deviants be interviewed? During this period, Humphreys was also working on a health survey. With permission from the survey's directors, he traced the addresses of the men he had observed, by means of the licence plates, and added them to the larger group to be interviewed as part of the health survey. After a year, he changed his hair-style, attire, automobile, and glasses, and interviewed these men in their homes. They did not realize that he had observed them engaging in fellatio in a restroom over a year earlier. The ethics and risks involved have been the focus of other debates, but I will avoid that topic here.

Most of the men in Humphrey's study were married and living with their wives. Most of those marriages appeared to be stable, and the wives were unaware of their husbands' secret sexual activity. Indeed, the husbands choose tearooms to avoid such exposure.

Interviews from the health survey suggest that the tearoom participants are not particularly different from others. Some feel that their frequency of intercourse with their wives is somewhat restricted, because the wife objects to birth control devices. But how does one make the transition from normal to deviant sex? What is the nature of the tearoom experience that makes it so common, compared to other homosexual experiences? And finally, what makes a man shift from getting a blow job to giving them?

As Desroches (1991) found two decades later, participants tend to be strangers. Humphreys noted that they rarely spoke. Barring unusual events, an occasionally whispered "thanks" at the conclusion of the act constituted the bulk of the communication. But silence was not just the means to protect privacy; it guaranteed anonymity and assured the impersonality of the sexual liaison.

> Tearoom sex is distinctly less personal than any other form of sexual activity. ... There is less emotional and physical involvement in restroom fellatio — less, even, than in the furtive action that takes place in autos and behind bushes. ... In tearoom stalls, the only portions of the players' bodies that touch are the mouth of the insertee and the penis of insertor; and the mouths of these partners seldom open for speech (Humphreys, 1970b:13).

One might ask how such activities take place without attracting the attention of the public more often. While visiting a scenic Canadian city, my wife stopped to use a public restroom before we wandered through a forested area. A few days later, I was walking through the same area with a plainclothes policeman, and one of his tasks was to warn homosexuals that a gang of youth were attacking "queers" in this same wooded area. It did not dawn on me, as I was walking with my wife, that the strollers in the woods were predominantly male. Later, when the policemen and I introduced ourselves, most of the men claimed to be "out-of-town visitors," but the warning about the youth gang was passed on. Those who were willing to talk told me that the restroom my wife used earlier was a tearoom, which was news to my policeman colleague.

Most of us are concerned with the question, "why do they do it?" A current debate about genetic make-up suggests that there is a biological base for homosexuality. However, there are some obvious sociological components that suggest both learning and situational factors. One component concerns the "aging crisis." Some participants are seen as "trade," those men who make themselves available for acts of fellatio but who regard themselves as "straight." They do not reciprocate. In most cases, fellatio is performed by an older man upon a younger man, but references to the aging crisis were common.

> Well, I started off as the straight young thing. Everyone wanted to suck my cock. I wouldn't have been caught dead with one of the things in my mouth! ... So, here I am ... with grown kids ... and the biggest cocksucker in [the city]! (Humphreys, 1970b:16).

It is important to dispel the idea that men who engage in homosexual acts may be typed by any consistency of performance in one or another sexual role.

> Undoubtedly, there are preferences: few persons are so adaptable, their conditions so undifferentiated, that they fail to exercise choice between various sexual roles ... Such preferences, however, are learned, and sexual repertories tend to expand with time and experience (16).

Many of the men in this study considered themselves "normal" men simply looking for orgasms, when they first discovered the tearoom activity. As people engage in heterosexual relationships, their repertories also expand. Activities and positions that may not have been enjoyable initially often become defined as pleasurable.

Extending the Argument to Theft and Other Crime

This "socialization" argument could be expanded to crime in general. Sutherland's differential association suggests that crime is learned in group interaction with significant others. Humphreys suggests that individuals interacting with *strangers* can also learn deviant behaviour. Men find themselves in learning environments that provide new definitions of sex. Peers acting as coaches help and encourage us but, in addition, we work out our own adaptations to situations. Humphreys argument fits gradual involvement in a wide range of deviance. Circumstances matter. At an early age, one might discover the tearoom as an adventure. Later, the aging crisis makes the "straight" participant in the tearoom trade reconsider roles. Applying the same logic, the trusted employee would not think of stealing at first, but times get tough, opportunities become available, and "borrowing" from the company becomes an alternative.

In most of the theories discussed earlier, I emphasized individuals operating in small groups within larger social settings; however, as individuals, humans are imaginative and can operate covertly in response to surrounding circumstances. To paraphrase Humphreys: criminal preferences are also learned, and criminal repertories tend to expand with time and experience. This process can be covert rather than subject to the scrutiny of peers or others. Sociologists naturally think in terms of social networks and may overlook the creativity that *individuals* express in creating their own social reality.

The qualitative research referred to in previous chapters (Katz, 1988) may also make more sense in these types of situations. If armed robbers get a thrill out of their dangerous games, one can see how the men in the tearooms described above would take risks that do not make much sense from a rational point of view. My dissatisfaction with using excitement as the motivating factor in crime, or in tearoom activity, is that there should be *precursors* that indicate why some pursue the thrills and others decide that the risk is too great. I am inclined to see these precursors arising out of social interaction. What other factors influenced these tearoom participants that would sway them to move towards a pattern of deviant behaviour?

The Making of Marginal Men

George was considered "trade" in the tearoom business, and like most of those who played the "straight" role, was married. His appearance and mannerisms were masculine. At twenty, he married a Roman Catholic girl. They had seven children, and his wife objected to any type of birth control other than the rhythm method. "How often do you have intercourse?" Humphreys asked, as part of the social health survey. "Not very much the last few years. It's up to when she feels like giving it to me — which ain't very often."

Cooking hamburgers on an outdoor grill, George was relaxed. He mentioned how much he enjoyed his children, but there were strains with his wife, who did not like to go places with the kids. "She's an A-1 mother ... but don't cross her! She gets aggravated with me ... We fight all the time ... Mostly we argue about the kids. She's afraid of having more. ... I won't suggest having sex anyway — and she doesn't want it anymore" (1970b: 18). Whatever causes George to turn from the marriage bed, the alternative must be quick, inexpensive, and impersonal. Any personal, ongoing, or expensive affair would threaten a marriage that is already shaky, and jeopardize the man's standing as a father. There is little indication that these men seek homosexual contact as such; rather they want orgasm-producing action.

George was affable and at ease during the interview. A year earlier, he was nervous and cautious in a tearoom, engaging in furtive sex. For him, the aging crisis would also be an identity crisis. Only with reluctance will he turn to the insertee role. His socialization into homosexual activity may have taken place in a world where it was permissible for young males to accept money from a "queer" for getting blown. Nor did George have a network of friends in the tearooms to help him adapt to change. Marginal to both heterosexual and homosexual worlds, these men shun involvement in the gay subculture. When asked how many close friends he had, George answered: "None. I haven't got time for that." At the end of the interview, he urged Humphreys to stay for supper. "I really wish you'd stay awhile. I haven't talked to anyone about myself in a hell of a long time!" (1970b:19).

Humphreys describes four types of tearoom participants. In addition to "trade," he discusses "ambisexuals," who seem to enjoy sex in a variety of forms, and "gay guys," who correspond most closely to society's homosexual stereotype. The last type, the "closet queen," differs from trade in that they are more likely to be unmarried and even more isolated. Some may have entered the tearoom trade as straights, while others were attracted to other men.

> I can't remember a time when I didn't find men attractive. ... I used to have terrible crushes on my gym teachers, but nothing sexual ever came of it. I just worshipped them, and wanted to be around them all the time. I had coitus with a woman when I was 16 — she was 22. After it was over, she asked me what I thought of it. I told her I would rather masturbate. Boy, was she pissed off! I've always liked older men. If they are under 30, I just couldn't be less interested. ... The trouble is that they always want sex — and sex isn't really what I want. ... I just want to be loved by an older man. (1970b:24).

Other closet queens prefer young boys, and this involvement obviously raises community concern. Reports of molestations usually suggest these types of offenders. Although tearoom participants as well, many closet queens also want a personal relationship. One man, an alcoholic whose intense self-hatred seemed always about to overflow, spoke of his loneliness and endless search for love:

> I don't find it in the tearooms — although I go there because it's handy to my work. But I suppose the [hustler's hangout] is really my meat. I just want to love every one of those kids! (1970b:25).

Later, this man was murdered by a teen-ager he had picked up. It is tempting to look for psychological explanations for the preference of some closet queens for young boys, but there are clear situational factors. They fear exposure and the stigmatization that might result from overt participation in the gay subculture, but their involvement with youths is obviously dangerous for others, as well as themselves.

Marginality and Criminality

We may have a theory that explains why men use tearooms, but marginal men (or women) are more prone to other forms of deviance and crime. Control theory suggests that bonds with conventional others inhibits crime and ties to deviant peers increases the likelihood of crime (Linden and Hackler, 1973). Some of the men studied above had social bonds with their children, which would inhibit deviance. They were not connected with deviant peer groups, but neither were they strongly bound to conventional society. While marginality may not lead people into deviance automatically, there may be a parallel between some types of crime and the lonely and isolated men who slip off the freeway for a few moments of impersonal sex in a toilet stall. Before Marc Lépine killed fourteen women at the Université de Montréal, was he a marginal person? Do child molesters have rich and successful lives? Are children who abuse their siblings isolated from rich human relationships? Some ethnic groups have been marginalized, such as Blacks in the U.S. and Native peoples in Canada, and they experience more crime. A meaningful crime reduction strategy would advocate social policies that improve family life (including gay family life), provide social networks among lonely individuals, or afford some measure of success to those who experience little of it. In other words, reducing marginality reduces deviance and marginality may be one of the precursors, not only of tearoom activity, but of crime in general.

It is unfortunate that we cannot borrow practices from other societies that might, in fact, improve social relationships. For example, adolescent males receive extensive sexual instructions from older women and widows in some Polynesian communities (Marshall, 1972). The experience of mature lovers is passed on to youths, and helps them to become skilled and considerate lovers. Such a practice would hardly get the endorsement of Home and School organizations in Canada. On the other hand, sex education in the schools might contribute to better-quality relationships in the future, and hopefully, less need for the tearooms.

Other government policies would have a more direct impact on marginality. When teenage girls give birth, the likelihood that they will have marginal lives and their children will be criminal increases, considerably. Crime reduction would be greatly enhanced by minimizing the number of teenage mothers. In some countries, the drug RU486, sometimes referred to as the abortion pill, is available. Its use, along with other practices, makes it possible to avoid teen-age pregnancies almost completely today. Sweden reduced such pregnancies approximately sixteen-fold between 1959 and 1979. These ideas may seem to stray from the ideas presented in *Tearoom Trade*, but what makes people choose either tearooms or crime can often be traced to societal conditions that create marginality.

PROSTITUTION

The Myth of Legality[1]

Prostitution is technically legal in Canada, but it is almost impossible for a prostitute to work without violating laws. If she were to service customers regularly in the same room, in her home or in a hotel, the premises could be defined as a "bawdy house," and violate the *Criminal Code*. Even a parking lot can be defined as a "bawdy house." Cooperation with someone else, not necessarily a pimp, could lead to a charge of "procuring" or "living on the avails." Vagrancy statutes were used to control prostitutes during an earlier period (Backhouse, 1984; Lowman, 1991; McLaren and Lowman, 1990; McLaren, 1986), and in the 1980s, municipal by-laws in some cities curtailed street prostitution. In 1983, the Supreme Court of Canada ruled that by-laws of this nature were not within the jurisdiction of cities, because this was criminal law, an area that is within federal jurisdiction. In 1985, new legislation was enacted, creating the offense of "communicating for the purpose of prostitution," usually referred to as soliciting. However, to see prostitution as not being against the law "is a legal fiction, since every avenue of its expression (save the transaction) contravenes other laws" (Brannigan and Fleischman, 1989: 91).

Public interest in prostitution has varied over time. For long periods, the activity was localized, the situation was accepted, and the public did not express great concern (Lowman, 1991). Since the 1970s, there has been more interest, and a variety of lobby groups have been advocating action, usually to eliminate prostitution; but other groups have formed that represent the prostitutes themselves, such as POWER (Prostitutes and Other Women for Equal Rights), CORP (Canadian

---

[1]This brief survey borrows heavily from the work of John Lowman and Frances Shaver. Their review articles, noted in the bibliography, provide a more extensive introduction to the topic.

Organization for the Rights of Prostitutes), and DANS LA RUE. The American organization COYOTE (Call Off Your Old Tired Ethics) may be better known in the media.

Police are in a no-win situation when it comes to enforcing or ignoring legislation. They realize that prostitution will not disappear, but various lobby groups pressure them to do something. Those pressures will not be consistent. A Crown Attorney told John Lowman (1989: 211) that they had been able to turn a blind eye to some of the realities of prostitution. Wearing blinders is practical, since no politician will speak publicly on behalf of red-light districts. Church groups and others would be up in arms, so there is a balancing act between a variety of conflicting interests. The lawmakers would have to come down firmly: either outlaw prostitution altogether or identify locations and settings where it can take place. The former makes little sense, and the latter would require courage and long-range vision. On the other hand, policies can influence where the sex trade takes place. When sex-trade cabarets in Vancouver were closed in 1975, it led to an expansion of street prostitution (Lowman 1989).

Causes and Background

Erin Van Brunschot (1991) uses a pathology/rational choice dichotomy suggested by Gus Brannigan as a means of organizing "causes" of prostitution. The "pathology" category includes prostitutes who are dysfunctional in some way, possibly as a result of abuse or neglect. Unfortunate family backgrounds may contribute to psychological problems and personality disorders. "Rational choice" focuses more on present needs, such as money, and the belief that the prostitute is acting rationally, given the circumstances. The pathology view places more emphasis on background factors, while the rational-choice perspective places more emphasis on (foreground) current, situational factors.

Different explanations of prostitution parallel explanations of crime. Lowman (1988) reviews these perspectives in six different categories. I will deliberately neglect the "prostitution-as-atavism," "psychopathology," and "sex-as-genetic-imperative" orientations. These three categories reflect certain negative individual biases that contribute little to a genuine explanation of prostitution. The "undersocialization/social-disorganization" approach also focuses on the individual, but one who was moulded in an undesirable environment.

The "functionalist" perspective will also be familiar to the reader from the chapter on property crime. This position suggests that prostitution performs a *function* for the society (Davis, 1937). It solves contradictory expectations arising out of the double standard for men and women: females should follow a code of premarital chastity and postmarital fidelity, while premarital and extramarital sex are tolerated for men, supposedly because of their stronger innate sex drive. Thus, the prostitute becomes the protector of family stability. This view exposes the double standard, but it also tends to reinforce the status quo. In addition, when Davis assumes that prostitution serves the "latent function" of guarding marriages, he accepts the now-questionable belief about differing sex drives. We might ask, "functional for whom?" Prostitution may be functional for the male customer, who is viewed as a victim of his uncontrollable sex drive (unless channelled by prostitutes). At the same time, he is immune from sanctions because of the important social functions he performs. By contrast, the prostitute is powerless, less useful than the man, of marginal status, and an appropriate target for control mechanisms. Thus, if the needs of society are equated with the needs of men, then, indeed, prostitution might be functional.

Lowman (1988) and many researchers favour aspects of the "feminist" perspective, which focus on the patriarchal power structure of society. There is no single feminist perspective (Brock, 1984), but there are some common themes. Women are conditioned into being subservient to men, to be owned by men and transformed into commodities to be bought and sold.

Brock distinguishes three main types of feminism. *Liberal feminists* assert the right of a woman to retain sovereignty over her own body; decriminalization secures that right in the short term. The long-term goal is to change gender roles, so women are no longer subordinate. *Radical feminists* condemn prostitution as the ultimate example of male power, but pledge support to prostitutes as a necessary part of "sisterhood." *Socialist feminists* focus on the way the political and economic realities of capitalism shape patriarchy. The policy initiatives covered in this chapter draw on elements of various feminist perspectives.

Focus on the Individual: The Badgley Report

The Badgley Committee (Committee on Sexual Offenses Against Children and Youth, 1984) initiated considerable work on prostitution in Canada, with particular attention to youth (Lowman, 1988; Lowman, 1991). Young prostitutes share characteristics of many young delinquents. Many had run away from home or had been thrown out. The Badgley Committee reported 52% of the females recall home life as characterized by continual fighting or arguments. In Vancouver, 65% of the prostitutes interviewed in one study reported family violence (Lowman, 1984). The majority of prostitutes were from the lower social strata. For the Badgley Committee, the logical way to deal with young prostitutes was to criminalize their behaviour, so they could be given "help." Like other young deviants, they were to be arrested and held so that they could be rehabilitated. Lowman (1987) is one of those who questions this logic.

Some obvious factors influence the choice of prostitution, if, in fact, there is a choice. Youth are part of the age group with the highest unemployment. They are not eligible for welfare. Prostitution provides a feeling of autonomy and financial independence. But the factors which lead a person into prostitution, are not that obvious. Diana Gray (1973) presents a picture that is not in keeping with other studies but offers different insights.

Turning Out and Seeking a Pimp

In keeping with other studies, Gray found that parental ties and attachments were weak for teenage prostitutes. They did poorly in school and expressed little expectation of a happy marriage. Their families provided little that they wished to imitate. None of this necessarily leads directly to prostitution, although it makes girls vulnerable. These girls had sex rather early, but Gray did not discover incest or any particular promiscuity or activity that distinguished them from others of their social-class background.

What *was* different for these girls was knowing someone who was in the sex trade, a point also made by Van Brunschot (1991:111) in Calgary. Sometimes it was a relative, at other times a friend. They were curious and sought out persons who "were in the life." There were attractions that were social as well as material. It was a way to be important, to be admired. Social rewards were recognized as readily as material rewards, even prior to their entry into prostitution. They were also aware of the negative side, such as having sex with the customer, arrest, and venereal disease. From a middle-class vantage point, it is difficult to see the attractions of prostitution; but if life is boring and living conditions are unstable, the fast life may have its appeal.

This study differs from others, in arguing that these girls *sought out pimps* so they could make it big on the stroll. Most of them turned their money over to the pimp and were satisfied with the way it was handled. They received social reinforcement from their "man" when they were able to provide him with large sums of money. Relationships with the pimps ranged from impersonally businesslike to shockingly brutal. Gray acknowledges the difficulty in interpreting the meaning of these relationships, but many girls saw the verbal and physical abuses as justified. "We had fights, like we were married — married people have fights. He beat me a couple of times, but not very bad. ... But after our fights he'd just be so lovey-dovey" (p. 416). Clearly, these girls did not think very highly of marriage.

Gray argues that the girls seek out their male partners, and consider them essential for success on the stroll. "If you want to make something of yourself out there in the fast life, you got to get a for-real man" (p. 417). They believe they need a man to "take care of business" and give them social status. "I always managed to get with a different guy ... who was more important, who had more strength ... They have to have respect for another man's woman ... When I got with James, that was the top. Nobody messed with me at all."

Feminists, understandably, should be annoyed with these girls' acceptance of male domination, and all of us should be dismayed at their acceptance of violence as part of "family" life, but Gray calls attention to the need for acceptance, status, and relationships with others in some kind of world, even though that world is loaded with negatives.

Van Brunschot's study in Calgary (1991) does not support Gray's argument completely. Juveniles had no choice; they *had* to have a pimp to work, and were pressured both by other women and the pimps (p. 119). However, smart pimps avoided the juveniles because they were "heat scores," they attracted the attention of the police (p. 121). The Badgley Committee felt that pimps kept girls in a sort of slavery and encouraged drug use to keep the girls dependent. Lowman (1987) feels the evidence is less clear. However, the Committee found that drug use was not as endemic as they had anticipated (Committee on Sexual Offenses, 1984: p. 1021). It is also not clear what pimping means. Melanie Lautt (1984) describes the *modus operandi* of pimps on the Prairies. Can a prostitute have "friends" or a lover? In Vancouver, (Lowman 1991) organizers of local prostitutes' rights groups estimate that about half of the city's prostitutes do not have pimps but pimps may be more in evidence elsewhere, in Montréal, for example (Shaver, 1992).

Focus on the Structure of Society: The Feminist Debate and the Fraser Report

Many studies of a historical nature fit into the feminist argument about the consequences of a patriarchal society. Poverty-stricken women in the past century had few alternatives to menial, low-paying positions in agriculture, factories, or domestic service (McLaren, 1986; Backhouse, 1985). In frontier societies, where men outnumbered the women, the incentive for prostitution was even greater. Feminists generally call for the long-term elimination of prostitution, because it represents the exploitation of women; but if women have the right to control their own bodies, they have the right to sell sex (Bell, 1987).

The Fraser Committee (Special Committee on Pornography and Prostitution, 1985) developed a political economy of prostitution, taking into account patriarchal social relationships. They stressed earning power, inequalities in job opportunities, and sexual socialization. Obviously, the main concern is for the reduction of prostitution, but it also leads to some more realistic questions. For example, prostitution is a vital means of subsistence for many Native people in Canadian cities. Should we not be asking how the sex trade can continue, without damaging women or society as much?

Other issues and assumptions are traditionally ignored. In urban areas, there is a contest between the rights of residents and landowners versus the rights of prostitutes to work. This is a one-sided dispute, because the public clearly favours residents and landowners, but is this the case for all disputes? When business, light-rail lines, large buildings, and other developments come into areas where people live, there are disputes. When airports, highways, and oil wells encroach upon farm lands, there are disputes. Governments mediate claims of various parties. Should this be done for those in the sex trade as well, instead of dealing one-sidedly with public nuisances (Lowman, 1989; 1991: 129)? What claims do prostitutes have against the rights of others?

Questions to Ask About the Sex Trade

Frances Shaver (1992, 1988) has asked some fundamental questions that need to be addressed and information that must be gathered before one can develop intelligent policies towards prostitution. Many simply denounce prostitution as dangerous, degrading, and undesirable. Shaver discusses the assumptions behind these positions.

Commercial Sex as Degradation

It is often presumed that commercial sex is cold, impersonal, and impoverished. It dehumanizes sexual relations. Is the quality of purchased sex inferior to other forms of impersonal or recreational sex that do not involve payment? Non-commercial sex is also often characterized by brevity and lack of affection. Blatant sexual bargaining goes on in singles clubs, in the back seats of cars, in the office, and in marriage (1988). While sex can be degrading, so are other human relationships. Many prostitutes have unpleasant encounters with men, but so do waitresses, nurses aides, flight attendants, secretaries, and factory workers. There is simply a great deal of variety in human and sexual relations, and the potential for inferior human interaction or inferior sex exists within both commercial and non-commercial settings.

Commercial Sex as Dangerous

Shaver notes that the vulnerability of prostitutes is due to gender bias and the application of the law, rather than to the commercialization of sexual services. Male hustlers are less likely to be attacked and are much less likely to be victims of "bad tricks" than are females (Visano, 1987; Perkins and Bennett, 1985:238-241). Battered prostitutes need protection just as do battered wives; and before either will bring charges against their abusers, they need to feel safe from reprisals.

Occupational dangers should be viewed in comparison with other potentially dangerous or "dirty" work. Infection is a risk, but this element is also inherent in the work of doctors, nurses, hospital attendants, morticians, domestic workers, and hotel cleaners. Prostitutes have also developed procedures for minimizing other dangers. They have regular medical check-ups, examine their customers for STD (sexually transmitted disease) symptoms, and require them to use condoms. Their organizations distribute "Bad Trick Sheets," describing and identifying dangerous customers (Shaver 1988:85; Shaver, 1992:19). They also learn techniques for avoiding unwanted men. When harassed, one can say "I'm not working tonight," a ploy Shaver often uses during her field work. If this does not work, she can shout down the street: "Hey Jan, this here jerk thinks he can get a blow-job for twenty-five bucks." The would-be harasser invariably moves away.

Prostitutes develop protective routines. They work in pairs, note when and with whom the other leaves; licence plates are remembered; desk clerks are tipped, and are expected to keep an eye on the time and an ear out for the sound of violence. Police practices and public policy could alter the conditions that influence danger. The removal of bawdy-house legislation might permit the creation of safer locales for the sex trade, since street prostitution exposes women to greater risks.

Commercial Sex as Exploitation

Studies of prostitutes that view them within the context of their profession do not describe them as powerless victims or passive partners (Shaver 1988). Like other workers, their exploitation is related to a variety of structural features. For example, the role of pimps needs to be carefully examined. Male prostitutes are rarely pimped and report fewer rapes and beatings than women (Lowman, 1985:35-36; Fraser et al, 1985:379; and Forbes, 1977; Visano, 1987). Exploitation and danger are gender-based, rather than work-based. On the other hand, Van Brunschot notes that far fewer police patrol the male stroll area in Calgary than the female strolls. Thus, *reported* victimization may be less for the males.

Shaver and others also note that it is difficult to determine if a woman is being exploited, in contrast to being served. Legislation fails to distinguish between lover, business manager, or cohabitant. The *Criminal Code* defines as a pimp anyone who lives wholly or in part on the avails of prostitution. Appropriate legislation must differentiate between friend and parasite, and create conditions under which the woman is willing to bring charges.

Strategies for Intervention and Public Policy

Despite the superficiality of my coverage of prostitution, a number of common practices clearly make little sense, while several strategies for intervention should be obvious. This "problem," rather than being unique, has elements in common with the sources of violence reviewed earlier. The long-range reduction of prostitution, and other crime, requires the strengthening of family life and the protection of vulnerable youngsters when families break down. This requires an investment in helping services, rather than controlling functions; but Canada and the U.S., in contrast to northern European countries, seem to prefer the latter over the former.

Those who believe that it is necessary to criminalize juvenile prostitution, so the prostitutes can be saved, may perceive "control" to be the same as "help." Unfortunately, "street kids" in North America rarely see the agencies of social control as a source of genuine help. In contrast, French juveniles with problems normally talk about "my judge" and compare notes with others as to how they were helped. To illustrate, one young prostitute went to her judge in Paris because she was hoping to escape from her pimp, who wished to take her away from the Paris area to another part of France. Putting a girl in custody for prostitution, or for any deviance for that matter, is simply outside the thinking of almost all French juvenile-court judges. Providing help in a variety of ways is within their power and part of what is expected. In this case, the judge provided a plane ticket for the girl to stay with relatives in North Africa for a couple of months, until her pimp left Paris. She then returned to her family in Paris and gave up prostitution. French juvenile court judges are given flexible powers to deal with situations in ways that they feel are sensible.

In Canada, we spend vast amounts on charging, prosecuting, and defending juveniles. Once juveniles are found guilty, we invest heavily in custodial facilities, but are less generous in terms of support services. In other areas, such as France and northern Europe, resources are concentrated on helping juveniles.

The general feminist economic argument, with regard to power and economic clout based on gender, plays a role in prostitution as it does in other crime. Most research notes that those in the sex trade are almost overwhelmingly economically deprived women and juveniles, many of whom have suffered a history of physical and sexual abuse (Larsen, 1992). Similarly, early pregnancies increase the vulnerability of women. Universal programmes, such as a guaranteed annual wage, widespread medical coverage, and low tuition for school and training programmes, are seen as expensive but, in fact, they may be less expensive than specialized programmes that target some individuals while neglecting others. These universal programmes are more crucial to women than men in terms of avoiding the deprived conditions that are often precursors to prostitution.

Some women need physical protection from men at times; thus, shelters for battered women indirectly make women less vulnerable, more able to gain control over their lives, and, to a degree, less likely to be involved in crime or prostitution. If any principle is clear in terms of the reduction of prostitution, it is that tougher laws yield minimal returns. Arresting prostitutes or their johns is an exercise in futility. Stricter criminal sanctions would probably force prostitutes to adopt riskier working styles. As prostitutes move off main thoroughfares onto poorly lighted lanes and side streets, or use hitchhiking, it reduces their ability to screen potential clients who appear to be dangerous. Similarly, if the law is successful in deterring "respectable" customers from frequenting the strolls, the dearth of customers may force prostitutes to accept customers they would otherwise reject.

There is little debate over the fact that prostitution will continue. Some societies manage it better than others. The brothels in Bremerhaven, Germany, appear to be safer places for the women and their customers. The bawdy-house provisions of the *Criminal Code* need to be repealed, so that prostitutes can operate legally in fixed locations (Larsen, 1992). Street life is dangerous, and most prostitutes would prefer to be off the street if they could have enough customers.

The creation of "red-light areas" is naturally controversial, but advantages and disadvantages need to be assessed. In some European countries, local prostitutes are normal components of the neighbourhood and are not seen as disruptive. Tax concessions and compensation to residents and business owners could mitigate some concerns. Local committees of residents, business owners, police officials, politicians, and prostitutes could monitor the prostitution trade and liaise with others to resolve disputes. This has been done in Vancouver, Edmonton, and Ottawa with some success (Larsen, 1992). Committees formed without including prostitutes were less successful.

Pimps could be prosecuted under extortion laws (Lowman, 1991:128), and patronizing juvenile prostitutes should still be illegal; but unless juveniles see agencies as a genuine source of help, enforcement practices need to be carefully assessed. Adult prostitutes might become allies of the authorities in trying to discourage juveniles in this area.

The government could provide some of the services usually offered by pimps. A knowledgeable government agent, possibly a social worker or nurse, or a former prostitute, would have some advantages over other pimps, because of reinforcement from police and other agencies, awareness of medical care, contacts with drug counsellors, etc. While most pimps are attempting to *keep* women in the business, the goal of a government operation would be just the opposite — to encourage women to move into other roles. Failing that, the goal might be to make prostitution more of a "genuine" choice, hopefully safer and non-exploitive (Lowman, 1993). In keeping with this line of thinking, prostitutes would pay into pension plans, unemployment insurance, and the like. Admittedly, this approach is somewhat naïve, considering the status that may come from having a pimp. It is unclear whether a government pimp, could provide status and a sense of belonging, but she could provide more options, not only to make the business safer, but to prepare for an alternative lifestyle.

CONCLUSION

Many activities treated as crimes might better be seen as "order-maintenance problems." These might include homosexual activities in public restrooms, prostitution, drug use (including alcohol and tobacco), driving over the speed limit, and a variety of other behaviours that cause legitimate concern. The criminal law is ill-equipped to respond effectively. As mentioned earlier with regard to drug policies, strategies that minimize harm make more sense than those that try to legislate morality.

The root causes of prostitution are similar to those that lead to crime: children being raised in vulnerable situations, marginal people unable to partake fully in the riches society has to offer, and government agencies and institutions that are clumsy and inadequate as they attempt to aid those who have been marginalized. In our specialized world, we become narrow-minded in our policy responses to crime and prostitution, failing to see that both are part of the same web, which includes other problems.

PART **IV**

RESPONDING TO
CRIME

It is obvious to many criminologists that by the time offenders appear in court, it is difficult to do anything very constructive. The factors that lead to crime cannot be influenced to a great extent by the criminal justice system in terms of prevention. Chapter 20 reviews situations where the system actually increases the probability of crime. The final chapter may be viewed as pessimistic or optimistic depending on whether one feels the authorities will act on certain issues. Clearly, many character- istics of Canadian society are criminogenic, but both the abuse of power and caring for the weak are areas where government policies can make a difference. While crime will not disappear, some of the most damaging crime can be reduced, as demonstrated by a number of countries. Whether policy makers in Canada will uti- lize the knowledge which is available remains to be seen.

HOW THE CRIMINAL JUSTICE SYSTEM INCREASES CRIME IN CANADA

One has to be careful not to award custody of the child to the best lawyer.

Judge Al Catonio

FOCUSING ON PROCEDURES AND MISSING THE ESSENCE OF PROBLEMS

The general theme of this section is that North America has created a criminal justice system that increases crime by focusing on procedures rather than directly on justice. The system is poorly designed to deal with the complex problems that contribute to crime. Although the claim is made by many North American lawyers that the procedures guarantee certain protections and thereby produce justice, another argument is that by creating a litigious system, greater emphasis is placed on winning contests than on doing the best thing for society and for the individuals involved. The U.S., with 744,000 lawyers in 1991, has more lawyers than the rest of the world put together (U.S. Bureau of Statistics, 1992). This represents a lawyer for every 340 persons. Canada's 53,570 lawyers represents a lawyer for every 509 persons (Statistics Canada, 1993), the second highest in the world. It is difficult to distinguish cause and effect. Has North America, particularly the U.S., but also Canada and Australia, created a legalistic society *because* it has so many lawyers, or did the nature of the society *produce* and create many opportunities for lawyers?

The quotation above from Al Catonio, an experienced Family Court judge, illustrates the dilemma for the criminal justice system as a whole. Family courts and criminal courts are constantly faced with *social* issues, even though we deal with them by having judges make *legal* decisions. Frequently, judges are trying to decide what is best for a child. Lawyers representing different sides of the issue differ in their ability and persuasiveness. The setting is a contest where both sides are striving to win. One response to this adversarial mentality is for the court to appoint an additional lawyer to represent the child. This process can be carried to extremes. In one Children's Court in Australia, I was observing a relatively straightforward case involving whether an infant should be returned to a couple. The father had just been released from prison. Supposedly, the main concern was for the child and the competence of the parents. In fact, the self-interest of several different agencies was also involved. There were five lawyers presenting different arguments and representing different agencies, but at no time did the parents testify, nor were they asked for their opinions. The needs of the family were lost in this contest among lawyers. There is a parallel between changes in the juvenile and family courts and the rest of the justice system: the voices of the people affected are often lost, as agencies and other interests vie for influence.

Criminal matters are often connected to social issues involving a web of human relations. These issues have been "legalized." Lawyers argue among themselves and take these debates out of the hands of those most concerned (Christie, 1977). As a result, the clients of the system feel they are left out, and are more inclined to deny legitimacy to the system. Thus, North Americans may feel that justice is not being done; instead, lawyers are doing their thing.

The main causes of crime are in the structure of society itself. The response of the various components of the criminal justice system, at least as it operates now, cannot make a significant impact on criminal behaviour. However, the way the criminal justice system responds can have a long-range impact on the way people view the rules of society. When the system loses credibility and is seen as neither just or effective, it can undermine the willingness of individuals to obey the rules, to have any confidence in the appropriateness of those rules.

Sally Merry (1991) describes the contest between clients of the system and the professionals who run it. She studies "the process of cultural domination exercised by the law over people who bring their personal problems to the lower courts" (p. 9). The problems are important to the people involved, but they are not always amenable to legal solutions. Thus, the clients define their problems one way and the legal professionals another way. My contention is that the continuous expansion of a system ill-suited for resolving problems related to crime is, in the long run, criminogenic.

A Japanese Response to a Potential Crime

A North American husband and wife were working and studying in Japan. They had an argument. The man went out, got drunk, kicked in a garbage can, and damaged a door of an old lady's house. She called the police. Two officers arrived by bicycle and walked the offender to the police station. His Japanese was very poor, and he was belligerent at times. The police called the man's wife, who spoke Japanese. She came to the station, explained that there had been a domestic dispute and the husband went out and got drunk. The police were sympathetic; but since the man was in a high-status position, they scolded him for acting so shamefully. In Japan, people of high status are expected to behave more responsibly than others. They sent the man home in the custody of his wife, and required that he go to the victim's house the next day and apologize, as well as pay for the damages. The apology was particularly important, and since his Japanese was poor and he might say the wrong thing, his wife was to translate. At the old lady's house the next day, the wife translated the apology, and the old lady also apologized for having her garbage can in an awkward place. Clearly there was an attempt to restore the peace, so even the victim made an effort.

Notice that no charge was laid, no judge was involved, there was no court process. Everything was done at the police and community level. In Canada, we might have laid charges, a defence lawyer could have asked for adjournments, and many months later the case might be resolved in an expensive and not particularly satisfactory manner. True, civil rights may not be as secure in Japan, but even serious crimes are often screened out at the prosecutorial level. Getting a conviction is not the goal of the system. Preventing further crime is. As long as the Canadian system is primarily concerned with punishing people, we must pretend that we are very careful about convicting people. In fact, our system convicts a very high percentage of lower-status defendants (Erickson and Baranek, 1982); it simply takes us a long time to do it. In such a system, the need for civil-rights protection is naturally greater. Unfortunately, we may have burdened ourselves with a system that is out of touch with the concerns of society.

The Consequences of an Adversarial System: The Pressure to Win

It is beyond a general criminology book to compare, in detail, the Canadian criminal justice with many other systems in the world. However, I am basically arguing that Canada, perhaps less than the U.S., has developed an *inferior* criminal justice system. Many countries tend to be ethnocentric about their legal systems, believing that they are superior to the systems of others, which they do not fully understand. North Americans are understandably proud of some legal achievements that speak to individual issues such as civil rights. Unfortunately, these accomplishments can lead to the naïve assumption that this creates a system that responds constructively to the myriad of social issues that are so entwined with crime.

Investigating Crimes in Switzerland and France

A comparison with the Swiss canton of Vaud is revealing. There are differences in the various cantons of Switzerland, just as there are in the various states of the U.S., but there are some general characteristics of the law in Vaud that are similar to those in the rest of Switzerland, and also in France. An English scholar, who was familiar with the common-law system of England as well as with the Swiss system, said that if he were innocent, he would prefer to be tried under the Swiss system, but if he were guilty he would choose the common law in England or the United States (Godfrey, 1981: Ch. 16). In Switzerland the guilty were more likely to be convicted and the innocent never brought to trial. The slower, drawn-out process in common-law countries, such as England and Canada, favoured guilty persons with resources. In other words, he believed the Swiss distinguished more accurately between guilt and innocence. Of course, this requires that the preliminary stage of the process, the police investigation, be rigorously fair. In North America, the adversarial system puts pressure on the police to produce charges that stick in court.

During the period of police investigation in Switzerland — the *instruction*, which is directed by a magistrate — the police gather information relevant to both sides of the case. The Swiss police have greater leeway than those in North America. Information that is considered privileged or inappropriate in Canada is permitted in the Swiss canton of Vaud, such as hearsay evidence. Other protections available to suspects are not available in Switzerland. For example, the presumed suspect, the *prévenu*, can be held without charge. The investigation is secret until complete. (While the French system is similar, it differs on this point, and some French magistrates criticize this aspect of the system in Vaud.) When the file, or *dossier*, from the *instruction* is completed, it then becomes available to the defence, who can ask that the police gather more information. In other words, the *juge d'instruction* instructs the investigating police to gather *all* relevant information. The failure to do this job fairly and thoroughly would bring criticism on the people involved.

By contrast, there is a tendency for the police in the U.S., Canada, and Australia to decide on the guilt of a suspect and then continue the investigation to make a strong case. Our system may have more safeguards during a trial, but police investigations are not neutral. There is pressure to build a strong case against the defendant. The police and prosecution are not rewarded for building a balanced case. Prosecutors, can and do withhold evidence from the defence. The defence cannot insist that the police investigate in certain areas, whereas in France or Switzerland, the *juge d'instruction* is obligated to have the police search for evidence relevant to innocence as well.

The adversarial system, which is seen as sacred, places more emphasis on legal tricks and less on the search for truth and justice. When the defence has many resources, skilled lawyers not only protect innocent defendants, they also protect the guilty. A defendant with few resources will be convicted more easily. If the police are wrong, it is very difficult for an ordinary citizen to influence the system.

> In a system and a society which profess to make the individual decision a central
> element of existence, the reality for the accused is that he rarely has a decision

(choice) to take, and when he does, it cannot be viewed as an 'original' decision because it reflects submission to pressure from others and to structural arrangements (Ericson and Baranek, 1982: 217).

Canada has joined the U.S. in creating a criminal justice system that is out of touch with societal needs and is slow, biased against the underprivileged, and favourable towards upper-class defendants, experienced criminals, and those with resources.

The Police and Perceptions of Justice

The police in Canada have been experimenting with "community policing." This is not necessarily new, but the police are getting better acquainted with their neighbourhoods to see if they can "solve problems," rather than simply respond to crime. Such changes should not be viewed as major solutions to crime problems, but the police could become more useful allies to helping agencies as they identify potential problems and become part of a network of agencies that might respond to community concerns.

A less flattering aspect of police activity concerns crimes committed *by* the police. While this plagues police forces in the U.S. more than in Canada, it cannot be dismissed completely in this country. When members of the Los Angeles Police force systematically beat Rodney King, the public had a televised illustration of serious criminal behaviour. When the police are criminals, we can expect this to produce more crime in the rest of society. The moral fabric of the society is torn. Some police officers believe in bending the rules, so that a perceived criminal gets what "he deserves," but the perceived gains rarely outweigh the loss in the sense of justice in the larger society. Although comparative evidence is hard to find, the Japanese and most Northern European police appear to be less criminal than police forces in the United States. As the police in other countries receive the scrutiny they have had in the U.S., this image may change somewhat (Steinhoff, 1991). Fortunately, in Canada the public generally has a good opinion of the police, and Canadian studies suggest that Canadian police forces are less criminal than those in the U.S. (Koenig, 1991; Ericson, 1981; Ericson, 1982). However, to the extent that police commit crimes and violate the law, even when they claim to be getting evidence against "known" offenders, they create conditions which, in the long term, are criminogenic.

THE YOUTH COURTS AS A FACTOR IN INCREASING CRIME IN CANADA

The effectiveness of intervention with juveniles makes a difference on crime in general. The trend in North America is to "get tough on young criminals." This unimaginative approach probably contributes to an increase in crime in the future, because it avoids facing issues that might make a difference. The alienation of youth from the juvenile justice system becomes part of a general alienation from society. While it is unfair to expect the Youth Courts in Canada to do very much in terms of preventing delinquency, they are in a position to make things worse by reinforcing feelings of injustice, lack of care, and lack of opportunity. By failing to expedite the reintegration of young people into the fabric of society, the juvenile justice system, contributes to an increase in crime in Canada.

The critical position taken in this book should not obscure the fact that considerable progress has been made over the last century in developing more effective ways of dealing with youth and families in trouble. My point is that other parts of the world have done even better, and recent decades have not seen a continuation of the longer trend of progress in juvenile justice.

In Canada, Juvenile Courts were usually part of the Family Courts. With the passage of the Young Offenders Act in 1984, these Juvenile Courts became Youth Courts. Prior to 1984, there had been a "welfare orientation" in Juvenile Courts. In her book, *From Punishment to Doing Good: Family Courts and Socialized Justice in Ontario 1880-1940*, Dorothy Chunn (1992) notes that the Family Courts developed a tradition that began recognizing problems and made efforts to help. Until recently, some of the Youth and Family Court judges were not trained as lawyers. A few came from a social-work background. The major contest, well into the early 1930s in Ontario, seemed to be between lawyer types and social-welfare types. But if there was a gradual shift towards helping people up until the 1940s, by the 1970s and 1980s there was clearly a move towards a more legalistic model.

By the 1980s, almost all Juvenile Court judges were trained as lawyers, marking a legalistic trend which continued with more legally trained prosecutors and the increasing appearance of defence attorneys. Duty counsels, defence lawyers who assist anyone who wants help, are found in most large Canadian Youth Courts today. Part of this trend was influenced by concerns that the welfare-oriented system was, in fact, punishing juveniles under the pretence of helping. While there is reason to believe that this happened, it also appears that these abuses were adjusted, over time, through changes in practices in juvenile courts. At any rate, Canadian Youth Courts today resemble adult courts more than they did in the past. At present, many trivial cases appear in Youth Courts, delays and adjournments are common, and juveniles who are not dangerous spend time in custody. These points can be made more clearly with some specific cases.

Case 1

The fifteen-year-old girl was in court for theft. The parents were separated and lived in different cities. The daughter was with neither parent, but lived in a small town with a family who treated her like one of their own. She had been in no trouble in the community and had done well in school. However, she began to date a twenty-year-old. The family did not approve. When the father, who had legal custody, heard of the situation, he drove to the small town, picked up his daughter, and moved her to his apartment in the larger city. The girl did not like the woman who lived with the father, stole $11 from her father's wallet to buy a bus ticket back to the small town, and returned to the family where she had been living. The father swore out a warrant for her arrest for theft. The police picked up the girl, put her in the local detention centre, then brought her to the larger city and housed her in a larger detention centre, pending a hearing in juvenile court on a charge of theft. The social worker who looked into the case found it difficult to recommend any specific action.

In court, the girl expressed her desire to return to the small town. The father, who had legal custody, was concerned about the older boyfriend, even though the girl said she was no longer seeing him. The charge of petty theft remained. Duty counsel (the lawyer for the defence) recommended that the girl plead not guilty, which she did. Therefore, a trial had to be held. But what to do with the girl in the meantime? The judge did not wish to send her back to the detention centre, but the father refused to accept her in his apartment as long as she was pleading not guilty. The session adjourned with the girl being sent back to the detention centre. She turned to the social worker and asked, "Why did I plead not guilty?" After a couple more days in detention, the girl came back, pleaded guilty to the theft before a different judge and was sent home with her father.

I do not know the best way of dealing with family squabbles, but three different stays in detention centres and a criminal record may not be the best way of handling an argument between a father and daughter. We also saw good people doing dirty work; the police, a probation officer, a social worker, and two reluctant judges wishing there were a reasonable way of handling the situation. Unfortunately, the legalism of the system made it difficult to handle this family dispute intelligently. This is another illustration of "stealing conflicts" from those who are in a better position to make decisions (Christie, 1977). The *Young Offenders Act* has encouraged legally trained people to steal conflicts, whereas in the past, perhaps the social workers were guilty of being "professional usurpers" of other people's problems.

Case 2

The boy had been picked up on a Friday evening and held in detention until Monday morning. He was charged with missing appointments with his probation officer, not seeking work, and not living with the family to whom he had been assigned. The Crown prosecutor presented the case from the paperwork she had in front of her. However, no probation officer appeared and there was some confusion as to which probation officer was currently handling the case. The boy's employer had not arrived. (Would having an employer be relevant to the charge of not seeking work?) The boy was staying at home and his mother was in the courtroom, but evidently he was supposed to be staying in another home. There seemed to be some confusion about all three charges. Asked how he pleaded, the boy was confused but pleaded guilty. The duty counsel was also confused. At that point, the judge accepted the guilty plea and adjourned the case until Thursday, when he would decide on the sentence on the basis of a predisposition report. In the meantime, the boy would go back to the detention centre. No thought was given to the possibility that this dangerous criminal could go home with his mother. The mother tried to speak, but the judge cut her off, saying that she would be able to speak on Thursday, at the disposition hearing.

During the break, the distraught mother approached the prosecutor, saying, "I know my boy is a brat, but he shouldn't be shit on like that." After further discussion, the prosecutor agreed to raise the matter with the judge when he returned to the courtroom. When the judge returned, and the prosecutor pointed out that the mother would like to say something about the case, the judge simply repeated that the boy had pleaded guilty and the mother would have adequate time to provide information at the time of sentencing. When the mother stomped out of the courtroom, the judge hurled threats of contempt of court at her departing back as she disappeared through the doors.

In this case, a minor offender had two different stays in detention, at considerable cost to the taxpayer. It is most unlikely that he or his mother will have much faith in the justice, efficiency, or intelligence of the system. But even with skilled people handling such cases, let us look at some structural barriers to an intelligent response. First, in court we insist that juveniles plead guilty or not guilty. They cannot tell their story in their own way. They must conform to the rituals. Second, the prosecutor rarely has any personal background knowledge and usually has limited information, often having only some brief written reports. One prosecutor had to use photocopies that were almost unreadable. Third, the judge is inhibited from exploring confusing situations, or discussing topics not introduced in court. Findings of guilt are separate from sentencing decisions, when, in reality, the two are often entwined. These conditions frequently make a mockery of the Youth Court as a setting for the sensitive handling of complex problems. Fourth, once a situation has been botched, it is hard to correct it. A judge cannot call up a detention centre and say he made a mistake and that the mother will just drop by and pick up the kid.

Better Alternatives for Handling Juveniles: France

Evidence for determining which juvenile justice systems are "better" is not readily available. We simply do not have measures of the impact of systems that can be compared from country to country. However, a majority of criminologists agree that locking large numbers of juveniles up, so they can share ideas with other delinquents, is counterproductive (Krisberg, et al., 1986). Thus, countries that imprison many juveniles are probably doing more damage than good. Using rough estimates, it appears that the U.S. locks up about twenty times as many juveniles per capita as Paris, and the province of Alberta about ten times as many (Hackler, 1988).

At the adult level, the U.S. also locks up more people per capita than almost any other developed country, and Canada tends to be higher than almost all European countries (Pease and Hukkila, 1990). The trend is also frightening. Between 1980 and 1990, the incarceration rate in the U.S. increased 121% (Canadian Centre for Justice Statistics, 1992). Despite the rhetoric concerning the need to "get tough," those countries with high imprisonment rates are illustrations of societies that have failed in their response to crime.

Let us look at France, a country plagued by problems that are not so different from North America, and ask how it responds to juvenile delinquency. A British criminologist and a French juvenile court judge who know both the English and French systems (King and Petit, 1985/86) write that non-punitive responses to the vast majority of young offenders in France seem to avoid the stigmatization, the exclusion from the mainstream of society, and the consequent creation of delinquent subcultures, which characterize the English scene. This is probably even more true in comparison to North America.

The attitudes of the French judges and the way they perform their tasks reflect differences from the North American mentality. Judges in North America often lock up children "for their own good," but the difference between being helped and punished is not always clear to the juveniles. The distinction in France is clear. The judge must either help or punish; the two functions are considered incompatible. Girls are rarely punished. A variety of help is offered, however, including accommodations in residential settings where there is no concern about custody.

If a juvenile spends a night (the legal maximum) in a police lock-up in France, the setting is usually unpleasant. However, the police in France usually try to contact an *educateur* (correctional social worker) the same day a youth is picked up by the police. Prisons are used for detention, with either a wing or a separate section being used for young men under twenty-five. Juveniles are held in a separate portion of this wing. Detention is not provided separately for those not yet proven guilty, thus a sentenced youth would go to the same place. These are not nice places, but when a judge finally uses this alternative, she usually considers the case a failure, after other alternatives have been tried.

There is a wide range of non-custodial group homes in France, but the essential difference from North America is that the juveniles have decided to be there. Such placements are negotiated with a judge, not the result of a decision after a trial. If a juvenile decides to leave a group home, she cannot be punished. The *educateur* may be annoyed, the judge may be displeased, but putting a juvenile in jail for running away is not a choice that is even considered (Syndicate de la Magistrature, 1979). Not following an administrative decision is not a crime, and children can only be imprisoned for committing crimes. If residential placement is to help a juvenile, judges and social workers in France agree that the child must want to stay there. Admittedly, the judge can exert pressure on a youth, but the threat of prison is not an alternative. To understand these different attitudes towards custody, it is necessary to review decision-making at the early stages in the process.

Juvenile Justice Processing in France

The French police do not lay charges; they simply refer the case to the *procureur*, a magistrate who performs a role comparable to our prosecutors. The *procureur* can screen out the case or send it to the juvenile court judge (*le juge des enfants*). Complicated cases or serious crimes go to the *juge d'instruction*, a magistrate who has the responsibility for more detailed investigations. Perhaps 90% of juvenile cases are handled informally in the judge's office. Juveniles who have been dealt with informally cannot be incarcerated. However, if the case is serious or if the child continues to offend, the judge refers the case to trial in the formal courtroom, where two lay judges sit with the *juge des enfants* (the same judge, incidentally) while the *procureur* and defence lawyer present their arguments. After a trial, a juvenile can be sentenced to the juvenile wing of prison, usually for a maximum of a few weeks. Rehabilitative efforts are not undertaken when youths are given punitive sentences, but despite this reasoning, I have seen teachers and social workers making modest helping efforts inside prisons.

Even without using the formal courtroom, the judge has considerable power. She can detain a juvenile temporarily prior to a trial, but this decision is limited to those who are considered dangerous. The numbers in detention are small compared to Canada. In practice, the judges, working from their offices, spend the vast majority of their time offering a wide range of welfare services (Girault, 1984).

The judge can assign a correctional social worker (an *educateur*) to supervise the juvenile, but if the juvenile resists supervision, the judge cannot legally place her in a closed institution, i. e., prison. Of course, judges can harass or coerce juveniles in other ways. For example, they can have the police bring the youth to the office and can use the symbolic position of the judge in a very persuasive way; but unless the juvenile wishes to be "helped," little will be accomplished. Thus, when the judge foregoes a punitive sanction, the focus is on finding alternatives that are likely to gain the cooperation of the juvenile. When the judge decides not to use the formal court machinery, no distinction is made between delinquency and welfare cases; the emphasis turns to meeting the needs of the juvenile. Instead of handing down decisions, French judges concentrate on working out options and arranging services.

Judges discuss placements with juveniles rather extensively. If family ties are positive, arrangements can be flexible, making it easy for a juvenile to keep in touch with parents. Being placed in a residential facility becomes a matter of negotiation, rather than a "sentence." Nor are such placements designed to keep juveniles out of the community.

French judges are expected to be well informed about their cases, have background information, and use it constructively without being biased by it. By contrast, in our concern for the rights of juveniles in North America, we make it difficult for them to tell their story to someone who has the power to help. The Canadian *Young Offenders Act* mandates that a juvenile is not required to face a judge, policeman, or someone else in authority without having a parent, lawyer, or advocate at her side. A Canadian youth, afraid to talk in front of her parents, will have difficulty telling her story in private to the judge. In France, the judge frequently talks to the juvenile without the parents being present. Some French juveniles pointed out to me that the judge was the one person with whom they felt comfortable.

In contrast to French juvenile courts, Canadian courts are relatively unconcerned about adjusting their needs to those of the clients. In southern France, the chief judge in Nice was meeting a family at 6:00 PM on a Friday. The parents would miss work at other times, the judge explained. Our system simply schedules cases; parents and others are expected take time off work or make other sometimes difficult adjustments. Then they may spend only a few moments in court, often without having the opportunity to discuss matters that they felt were relevant.

One juvenile left a residential facility near Paris and went to the court to talk to "his" judge. She was away for a few days, but the juvenile did not wish to talk with anyone else or another judge. The French respect the relationship between juveniles and "their" judges, so the juvenile was accommodated in a residence until "his" judge returned.

Solving Problems Rather Than Making Judicial Rulings

The difference in judicial practices between France and North America is illustrated by the case of a fourteen-year-old girl temporarily staying in a small group home near Paris. She was in conflict with her mother, who wanted her to continue in school; the girl wished to take a course in hairstyling. The girl ran away from home, stole food, and appeared before the judge in his office. The petty-theft charge was immediately set aside, and arrangements were made for the girl to stay in the group home. The social workers were encouraging the girl to go back home and go along with the mother to a greater degree. If the girl were older, for example sixteen, the judge might have considered helping the girl be on her own, but because she was only fourteen, both social worker and judge were encouraging a family reconciliation. The judge was not acting against the juvenile as much as playing an intermediary role between parents and juvenile. Nor was the judge imposing a decision. Hopefully, the family would work it out, but in the meantime, shelter and food were provided. The petty theft charge that brought the girl to court was seen as unimportant.

In Canada, such flexibility would be unlikely. Social services would have to "apprehend" a child. The province would have to become the "guardian." Formal decisions must be made in court, with legal representation from all sides. The Canadian system does not simply provide temporary room and board while things get sorted out. The government bureaucracy cannot provide much support without "taking over."

A French judge was visiting an open-custody group home in Canada, where boys were serving sentences but were able to attend school in the community. One boy was doing very well but was finishing his six-month sentence. Therefore, he could no longer stay in the this "correctional" facility, but would have to be placed somewhere by social services. The French judge asked, "If he is doing well, why can't he stay?" But in our system, juveniles "serve time" in one place under one bureaucracy, but are then transferred to another. The French judge was amazed that a Canadian judge could not order a facility to keep housing a juvenile if the setting seems to be working so well. Bureaucratic needs do not necessarily fit the needs of clients.

The French system has its weaknesses, but it seems better designed to deliver those services that make sense to an individual young person. In Canada, a juvenile is processed by many professionals who have varying degrees of power over her life. In France one person who knows a great deal about the juvenile — the judge — listens to the juvenile and then has the power to provide a wide range of help. If that fails, punishment is available.

Distributing Resources Among Legal and Helping Services

The Canadian system spends scarce resources supporting legalistic rituals, most of which yield a poor return, and fiscal constraints lead to a decrease in helping services. Although the French system is too different from ours to be seriously considered, Melbourne, Australia, uses a legal system much like ours. However, four judges seem to be able to serve three million people, whereas in Edmonton eight judges serve 700,000. The way legal-aid lawyers are trained as public defenders and utilized in Melbourne seems to be a key factor in creating greater efficiency and more intelligent handling of juvenile cases (Hackler, 1992). Within common-law systems in Canada, the U.S., England, and Australia, there are local systems that appear to be more effective. In Canada, for example, Québec uses public defenders and prosecutors in a way that helps them gain experience in Youth Court. This may be one factor that reduces the flow of cases into institutions in Québec. The study of local differences sometimes indicates that minor differences in practices can yield significant differences in outcomes (Hackler, 1991). Alberta has just introduced permanent defense lawyers into the Youth Courts, which could provide gains similar to those achieved in Melbourne.

When court costs go up, we assume this is inevitable and the taxpayer must pay. However, limits on social-service costs are viewed differently. Expenses in this area can be restricted with less public concern. There has been an increase in total legal-aid expenditures in Canada from under $150 million per year in 1981 to over $400 million by 1991 (McPhie and Remedios, 1992). The increase was more marked after 1986. In 1990-1991 there was a 21% increase over the previous year, a constant-dollar increase of 15%. If increased legal-aid representation were actually helping, this might be a worthwhile investment. If, however, it means more adjournments, and increased court, prosecutorial, and police expenditures, it may inhibit the delivery of social services. This concern can be generalized to the overall increase in bureaucratic functions. They crowd out the real tasks that might reduce crime. Experienced lawyer Joe Bovard sums it up very well.

> An overemphasis on the form, rather than the substance, ... can be very detrimental ... One of the government agencies that is responsible for helping young offenders is going to have a week-long seminar on how to fill out the forms that arise under the Young Offenders Act. While they are trying to figure where to put the kid's birthday ... on [a] form, he's out on the street blowing his brains out with a bag of glue (Griffiths, 1987: 91).

A Cause for Optimism: The Adaptability of Local Systems

Despite the barriers to effective action created by some of our bureaucracies, resourceful individuals at the local level often overcome a variety of obstacles. In one small community, an experienced judge and an experienced prosecutor were faced with a man who had been charged with "leaving the scene of an accident." His car had turned over in the ditch, and the driver crawled out of the car and passed out in the tall grass nearby. When the RCMP discovered the car, they did not find the passed-out driver. In court, the defendant had no lawyer and repeatedly made it clear that he was drunk, even when the judge kept assuring him that he had not been charged with drunken driving. Neither the police nor the prosecutor were trying to be harsh, and the judge finally dismissed the case. The system did not try to crush the defendant. The point of this story is that, with experienced personnel who know how things operate, the system can be humanized, can become more efficient, and possibly made more just. A legal-aid lawyer defending this case would have earned more money by asking for adjournments and complicating the matter considerably. I am not arguing against legal aid, but if legal aid were to hire public defenders on a salary, instead of paying them according to the number of times they appear in court, the client and the public would be better served. Our present system is designed to reward inefficiency.

Despite my criticisms of the Canadian criminal justice system, and the juvenile system in particular, I have seen many illustrations of innovative and imaginative individuals making rigid bureaucracies perform more adequately, in terms of activities that might reduce crime. One judge, faced with a request for an adjournment, asked questions that might have "contaminated" his view of the case. Then he refused the adjournment; the case went ahead and was quickly resolved in a very satisfactory manner. Unfortunately, those portions of our governments responsible for criminal justice often make it difficult for creative people to operate effectively.

CONCLUSION

The North American preoccupation with punishing people blinds policy-makers to the progress that has been made in other parts of the world. North Americans seem puzzled by the willingness of Europeans and others to use alternatives to punishment and legal rituals, as a way of responding to criminal behaviour. Fortunetely, the federal government in Canada is giving some thought to change. The Twelth Report of the Standing Committee on Justice and the Solicitor General (1993) to the House of Commons actually stated, "If locking up those who violate the law contributed to safer societies, then the United States should be the safest country in the world" (p. 2). The report went on to say that the U.S. affords a glaring example of the limited impact criminal-justice responses have on crime. This argument has been made by criminologists for years, so it is gratifying that it is finally being heard by Members of the House of Commons. Perhaps things will change if restitution and mediation become part of our response to crime. When victims receive restitution, their desire to punish the offender is greatly reduced. This frees the court to make punishment consistent with the rehabilitative needs of the offender, rather than the animosity of the victim.

Since this book is interested in policies that would eventually reduce crime, juvenile justice seems to offer more promise as a place to introduce change. Although governments seem resistant to changes in Youth Court, many of the professionals who are familiar with juvenile justice see considerable potential for constructive progress. One could spend time criticizing criminal justice at the adult level, but reforms there would probably not have a similar impact on future criminality.

The Canadian resistance to learning from the rest of the world may be connected with our political culture. As long as "getting tough on crime" continues to increase a politician's chance of getting elected, Canada will have difficulty producing political leaders and policy-makers who can contend with our backwardness in this area.

CRIMINOGENIC CONDITIONS: IMPLICATIONS FOR CRIME REDUCTION

When I give food to the poor, they call me a saint. When I ask why the poor have no food, they call me a communist.

Don Helder Camera, Archbishop of Recife & Olinda, Brazil

CHANGING THE CONDITIONS THAT LEAD TO CRIME

Is a high level of crime inevitable in modern society? Should we accept higher levels of crime as the price we must pay for the individualism, freedom, excitement, and material wealth generated by the free-enterprise system? Economists tell us that the human costs associated with increased efficiency are inevitable, but will be balanced by the ultimate rewards that come from "progress" and economic growth. Thus, unemployment, social disruption, and poor people will always be with us. The cartoon in Figure 21.1 suggests that such conventional wisdom is carved in stone, but there are cracks in that stone.

Should we accept the notion that governments can do nothing meaningful about crime? Admittedly, most of the various "wars on crime" are cynical, politically motivated, and ill-founded; in fact, the U.S. has adopted crime-*producing* policies for decades. While there are no grand cures, many countries have adopted strategies that are superior to those used in Canada. Unfortunately, Canada has been influenced by the "justice juggernaut" in the U.S. (Gordon, 1991), which has produced, and probably will continue to produce, ineffective responses to crime. The U.S. sees crime as a decline in individual morality rather than as evidence of flaws in the basic economic and social structure (Gordon, 1991:240). Similarly, many who work in the Canadian justice system say they are serious about crime, but they are largely performing rituals that perpetuate the "justice juggernaut." The politicians, the public, and the media are meeting their own needs, as are those who work for and with the agents of social control. Our responses to crime reflect the needs of politicians to win elections, of newspapers to make sales, and of the general

FIGURE 21.1 Confronting Conventional Wisdom

Source: *Inter Pares Bulletin* 15(1) 1993. Graphics: Michel Lavigne.

population to blame someone else. Space does not permit a review of even a portion of the factors that contribute to crime in Canada. Therefore, only two areas where government action would matter are covered here.

The first is the abuse of power by the powerful. Conventional wisdom argues that there will always be powerful people who will abuse others. Perhaps, but one has to be an extreme pessimist to believe that civilization has never been able to check the lusts of those in power, in a manner that helped the many. The second area focuses on the way societies treat the weakest members. Conservative thinkers may be resigned to "the poor always being with us," but modern industrial societies no longer must accept this as inevitable. We turn first to the abuse of power. Normally, this discussion would be in a chapter on corporate crime as a category of crime. My approach is to treat this topic as a very promising area for the general reduction of *all* crime. That's right, I want to eventually argue that reducing corporate crime will also reduce armed robbery, burglary, and purse-snatching. The steps in this logic are not immediately apparent.

THE ABUSE OF POWER: CORPORATE AND OCCUPATIONAL CRIME

In all societies, individuals differ in their influence. In some societies, those who have influence are given high status, but are also expected to be more honourable than average and to provide help and assistance to those less privileged. Theoretically, that holds for North America as well, but in practice those with power often forget the principle of *noblesse oblige*. Some scholars believe that capitalism has created a situation that increases crime, including crime by corporations. "Corporate crime ... actually does more harm, costs more money, and ruins more lives" than assaults, thefts, and rape (Snider, 1993:1). It "causes more deaths in a month than all the mass murderers combined do in a decade. Canadians are killed on the job by unsafe (and illegal) working conditions; injured by dangerous products ... and robbed by illegal conspiracies that raise prices and eliminate consumer choice" (1993:1).

Other Canadian scholars have documented the harm done by commercial crime in the workplace (Reasons, Ross, and Patterson, 1981). Ray Corrado (1991, 1992) has summarized the impact of political crime, and Gordon and Coneybeer (1991) and Hagan (1992) have reviewed white-collar crime, offenses committed by those in respected positions. The brief illustrations in this chapter merely set the stage for a discussion of appropriate societal responses. First, we should distinguish between occupational and corporate crime.

Occupational crimes are commercial (white-collar) crimes committed by people exclusively for *personal* gain (Coleman, 1985:8). The victims includes organizations, businesses, or government. This would include embezzlement of corporate funds, expense-account fraud, tax evasion, and most computer crime. Perhaps political corruption should be seen as an "occupational" crime.

The occupational crime connected with the business world takes many forms (Francis, 1988). One involves "boiler-room boys," who misrepresent stock over the telephone. Many of these Canadian-run fraudulent operations are international, since avoiding local enforcement authorities often requires moving to other countries. The behaviour of these criminals does not fit comfortably into our criminological theories. Amsterdam was seen as a "good gig" by one boiler-room boy. "All day you sell stocks, and every night most of the guys would go to the red-light district to get laid or just get a blow job" (1988:240). The greed for money is obvious, but are the seductions and excitement described by Katz in an earlier chapter even more significant?

Francis also describes illegal activities involving the Vancouver and Alberta Stock Exchanges, and highlights Canada's role in laundering money from drug transactions. "Canada is a gigantic loophole through which billions of dollars worth of drugs and dirty money pass annually. Canada is a smuggler's and money launderer's mecca. The narcotics business generates an incredible $150 billion a year in cash transactions" (1988:240). Although these types of crimes have not attracted as much attention as violent crime, appropriate explanations are probably similar to other types of crimes of deceit.

In contrast to occupational crime, *corporate crimes* are committed by legitimate formal organizations, through the individuals inside them, with the aim of furthering the interests of the corporation as well as those of the individuals involved. Conspiracies among companies to restrict supplies of goods, and thereby raise prices, to dispose of hazardous wastes illegally, or to deliberately fail to maintain safe working conditions are criminal acts that benefit individuals within the corporation. Corporate crime serves both the organization and the individual criminal, while occupational crime benefits only the individual, but victimizes a variety of others, including different corporations and organizations (Snider, 1992).

The Causes of Corporate Crime

Explanations of corporate crime can be viewed from three overlapping perspectives: 1) the behaviour of individuals, 2) the nature and requirements of the organizations, and 3) the structure and demands of the economic system (Gordon and Coneybeer, 1991:440-444). At the individual level, one asks why executives, owners, and supervisors implement, and sometimes plan, corporate crimes. Why do successful people commit such crimes? Questions of "need" aren't very convincing. Even "greed" fails to provide a satisfactory explanation. "Opportunity" to satisfy wants may be relevant, but many non-criminals have opportunities as well. Earlier, I discussed Sutherland's *differential association* as an explanation of crime in general, including white-collar crime (1949). Corporate leaders commited crimes as a result of learning both techniques and rationalizations from others, that let them override or "neutralize" the moral restraints to violating the law.

Gordon and Coneybeer note that differential association helps us understand *how* crimes are carried out, but is less adequate for explaining *why*. Shifting to the second perspective, which takes into account the requirements of the organizations, one notes that corporations create pressures on executives and managers to "cut corners," to achieve organizational goals for which they will be rewarded (or punished if they resist). The way in which wrongs are done is often complex, making it hard for different supervisors and managers within the system to fully appreciate the implications of some of the illegal actions. Often, middle managers are assured that they have few options. This second perspective expands the explanation somewhat. One can appreciate pressures on the individual managers within the corporation, but why are there demands on the corporation itself? The third perspective, recognizes the structure and demands of the economic system.

Capitalism and free enterprise create certain demands. One of these is the continual pressure to make profits. If one corporation finds a cheap way to dump poisonous wastes into rivers, it has an advantage over a similar company that pays for the safe storage of wastes. There are similar pressures on oil companies to extract oil rapidly. Speed was a factor in the Hibernia oil fields off Newfoundland. Oil-rig owners took shortcuts in safety measures, which led to deaths in the Ocean Ranger disaster (House, 1986). Why are deliberate actions on the part of corporations that lead to death and injury not treated as crimes? One corporate strategy is to describe accidents as regrettable but unavoidable by-products of a system that yields other benefits. Snider (1993) argues that the relationship between the state and corporate interests leads to cooperation in creating misleading public images. Governments are sensitive to projects that might lead to short-term "job creation," even though such commercial enterprises may, in the long run, decrease jobs. (For example, lumbering activities that pollute streams, destroy salmon spawning grounds, may decrease jobs in fishing.) The state also creates agencies, such as worker's compensation, that supposedly helps the worker, but also encourages the continuance of dangerous and criminal practices. Corporations have been able to divert the responsibility and avoid the stigma resulting from deliberate decisions that damage others.

Regulating Corporate Crime vs. Publicizing Unethical Practices

It is difficult for the state to regulate corporations, because the revenues of the state, its educational, welfare, military, and other programmes, are dependent on the profitability of the private sector. On the other hand, some regulations compel industries to take actions in their own interests that they could not take unilaterally. The enforcement of regulations on all companies should influence profits equitably, and a healthier and happier labour force would be able to buy the products being produced. However, when competition also comes from branch plants in other countries, similar regulations are required world-wide. (Snider, 1993:178-198).

The ideological issues vary by countries. For example, the United States seems to have a widespread criminogenic business subculture, which resists enforcement action. Lawsuits constantly challenge the legitimacy of the government to enforce rules. This is less common in Japan, Australia, Britain (Hawkins, 1984; Vogel, 1986) or Sweden (Kelman, 1981). Canadian corporations also have a tendency to resist regulation. The general characteristic of North Americans to resist regulation, and engage in questionable commercial practices, may be part of a general set of values regarding the abuse of power. Therefore, I suggest that we focus on the broad abuse of power, not just criminal activities. Can we publicize behaviour that is unethical, as an indirect way of eventually reducing corporate criminality? For example, corporate executives control their own salaries. This is not criminal, but it is part of a subculture of power abuse which favours a few at the expense of many, and fosters an antisocial climate.

Although publicly traded companies are supposedly owned and controlled by the shareholders, most people realize that a select group of entrenched executives, who control the selection of directors who serve on boards, hold the real power. These directors are often executives in other companies. They vote high salaries for the top executives and generous fees for themselves, knowing that this will also be done in the companies they lead. Shareholders, as well as other employees, certainly would not award these inflated salaries if they had the power to resist. When an armed robber takes money from someone against their will, that is a crime. When executives take undeserved money that the owners (shareholders) of the company oppose, the shareholders are powerless. These self-serving actions on the part of executives are morally similar to other forms of corporate crime, despite rationalizations and justifications.

The argument that these executives display unusual skills and earn their high salaries is not consistent with the evidence.Corporate leaders have built-in guarantees that protect them even when the companies do badly, sometimes due to the incompetence of the executives. If the companies do well, stock options and interest-free loans provide additional wealth. Just as executives rationalize their behaviour when committing clearly criminal acts, a similar logic is applied to this exploitation through the abuse of power. The structure of corporate enterprise creates criminogenic subcultures, and the environment created in the corporate boardroom is antisocial and criminogenic. We should extend our thinking about corporate crime to unethical, but non-crime, areas for two reasons:

1) public policy can change corporate boardroom ethic more easily than actual corporate crime, and

2) prosocial changes in the corporate boardroom would probably lead to a decrease in corporate *and other* crime.

The second point is far from obvious, but there is no clear line between behaviour that is immoral and unethical and that which is criminal. Thus, there is a link between crime and the *subculture of power abuse*. But how would changes in ethical behaviour actually reduce crime? Or specifically, how would prosocial changes in the corporate boardroom lead to a decrease in corporate *and other* crime? The reasoning is the same as the reasoning regarding drugs and violence. I argued that the distribution of drug use resembled a skewed curve and that a meaningful change in hard drug use would require changes in *all* drug use patterns. Violence is distributed the same way; a meaningful change in violence required changes in violent behaviour at *all* levels. The same argument applies to unethical corporate behaviour. Let us lump together all "wicked acts" (Figure 21.2). One might call it a "morality curve."

One could look at the dotted line in Figure 21.2 and say that there are criminals in the corporate and public area who are unique in their wickedness: those who fall under the second hump on the right in the curve represented by the dotted line.

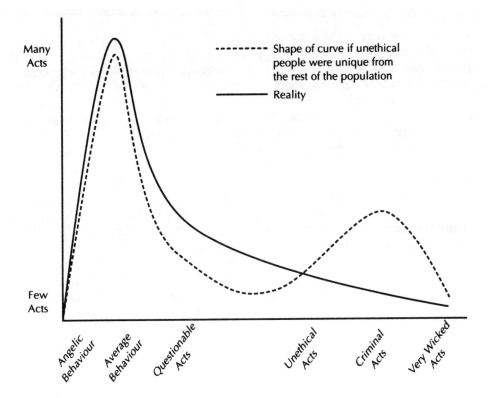

FIGURE 21.2 The Morality Curve: The Frequency of Acts by the Total Population Charted Against the Degree of Wickedness

People like Donald Cormie, of the Principal Affair, and Charles Keating, of the Savings and Loan scandals, were clearly criminals. Some corporate executives would say that they are different from "respectable" businessmen, and different from those who simply abuse their power to award great wealth to themselves and others in similar positions. These others fit under the first lump on the left in the curve. They are the majority. They may not be angels, but they are not really crooks.

This bifurcation of bad and good makes the same mistake I described earlier. It creates a mental set which claims that certain select people should be punished while the rest of us can continue as usual. In fact, the solid line, not the dotted line, represents reality. There is no clear border between those who engage in different degrees of wickedness. The solid line indicates that people who are more wicked are fewer in numbers, but there is no clear distinction between the criminals and the unethical.

As with drug use and violent crime, one cannot change the shape of this curve, but it can be moved to the left or right. In the U.S. in contrast to Norway for example, the morality curve has been pulled to the right in the business sector, as well as in the rest of the society. Corporate executives abuse power more, lawyers cheat more, and average citizens lie about their income tax more. The morality curve in North America spreads out to the right. Not surprisingly, lower-class people and those belonging to certain minorities, who feel neglected, recognize the lack of justice in their society and feel less guilt about burglarizing the homes of others.

Admittedly, I oversimplify the argument, but social life hangs together in an interconnected web of morality. A culture that values honesty and concern for others displays general concerns on moral issues. The situation represented by the dotted line in Figure 21.2, is the myth created by many. It suggests different responses for the bad and the good. Punish those *few* corporate criminals who get caught and ignore the rest. This has little impact on the morality curve. But if the many corporate executives currently abusing their power improved their behaviour, it could move the entire morality curve to the left. Assuming that these leaders have a greater than average impact on others, the spread of higher moral principals among the powerful could eventually have an impact on crime.

Using Public Policy to Decrease Corporate Antisocial Behaviour

Corporations sometimes need government to save them from ruthless competition which is potentially destructive. The competition to pay excessive salaries is influenced by these pressures. Prestige factors make it difficult for executives to accept more realistic salaries. What can governments do? Salaries, and other benefits, should be deductible as company expenses only up to a certain level. It might be a multiple of the lowest salaries paid by the company. An executive salary of thirty times the average of the lowest 20% of the workers might be the limit as a taxable expense. Salaries and benefits beyond these limits would require an explanation in the annual report of the corporation and in a newsletter produced by the Toronto Stock Exchange.

American public companies must reveal the salaries of their CEOs to the stockholders. Until 1993 this was not required in Canada. It could also compile other information: who sits on how many boards of directors? How often did they attend? How much were they paid? What interest-free loans, stock options, and other privileges were they given? Naturally, there would be complaints about privacy; but if you were the owner of a company, or principal of a school, or administrator of a university, you would want to know if your employee is holding a second job somewhere else and is neglecting her current job to earn extra money.

As long as the industrial elite has extensive power over government, it will be difficult to influence tax legislation, or change the practice of the Toronto Stock Exchange; but such changes would be easier to achieve than some of the technical regulations and enforcement that currently exist in safety standards, pollution, and other areas where corporate crime is common. Nor should such changes be unwelcome to all executives. There are many commercial leaders who find that the *intrinsic* rewards of doing a job well outweigh the *extrinsic* rewards, such as obscenely high salaries. Imagine an executive earning $250,000, well respected, performing her job well, who created job security for her workers, reduced pollution and danger in the plant, and had a husband and children who were proud of her. A secure person in such a position might find that extrinsic compensations add little to her quality of life. Nor am I talking about unrealistic idealism. It happens more in other countries. Many take pleasure in their calling, and are not overly concerned about material rewards. Some even have the respect of their business colleagues.

John Coleman was formerly Chairman of the Federal Reserve Bank of Philadelphia, president of Haverford College, and president of the Edna McConnell Clark Foundation in New York City, which gives grants aimed at ameliorating social problems. But he also took time off from his more prestigious roles to work as a garbage man, ditchdigger, kitchen worker, roughneck on an oil rig, hired hand, and correctional officer in prison. He even assumed a different identity to spend time as an inmate in five prisons (Coleman, 1980). Mr. Coleman would be among those influential people who provide valuable role models for leaders who see flaws in the current system of rewards.

In the corporate world the index of "worth" is often measured in dollars. Public policies are needed to reduce the "value" and prestige-enhancing characteristics attached to excessive monetary rewards. North American executives abuse their power, despite the displeasure of their employees and shareholders, to satisfy other than material needs. Conscientious executives might actually welcome regulations that would limit these abuses. Powerful people also have consciences and families that might assess them on a more human yardstick.

Using Reintegrative Shaming to Counter a "Subculture of Power Abuse"

Basically, I am arguing the theme of "reintegrative shaming" described earlier (Braithwaite, 1989). A newsletter put out by the Toronto Stock Exchange, should comment critically on corporate leaders who gouge their corporations and the public. If a tobacco company conducts smoking contests among children in developing countries to get them addicted to nicotine, it is imposible to convict the Chief Executive Officer of the tobacco company. However, he could be identified in the press, along with photographs. If he goes to church, the preacher should refuse to shake his hand, and reject his contribution to the church. In other words, he should be shamed. The families of such individuals should be ashamed of them. Such shame could be a powerful force in changing unethical behaviour generated by the criminogenic subculture that pervades the highly concentrated business elite in Canada. At the same time, business leaders who make genuine contributions and strive to make their corporations more socially responsible should be recognized. Furthermore, executives who abandon their abusive practices and acknowledge the misuse of their positions should be "reintegrated" into the world of honourable persons.

Although powerful people can easily resist technical regulations designed to keep them from harming others, self-esteem is still important to them. Threats to that self-esteem can result in change. Medical doctors who exploit their positions, lawyers who misuse others, commercial leaders who swindle society and professors who abuse students are part of a *subculture of power abuse* that characterizes a portion of the elite in North American society. I would generalize the findings of Hawkins (1984), Vogel (1986), and Kelman (1981) beyond the directly criminogenic business subculture that distinguishes North America from Japan, Britain, Australia, and Sweden. Not only do structural imperatives in North America lead to more corporate crime, they contribute to unethical corporate practices that support leaders who share in this *subculture of power abuse*. A circular pattern develops, which perpetuates itself.

If societal responses are limited to the criminal justice system, few unethical people will be shamed. This will not move the "morality curve" to the left. On the other hand, if we focus on common offenses, such as the income-tax evasion of many wealthy people, we include a much larger number of wrongdoers. The sanctions against income-tax evaders do not have to be severe, nor do they have to involve the criminal justice system, but they should threaten the self-images of these supposedly decent citizens. Professors who accept salaries when they are on sabbatical in order to do research, or dentists who purchase expensive art works for their offices, depreciate them over five years, and then take them home, are illustrations of immoral persons. They are rarely convicted of crimes, but can they be shamed?

Other legal activities could certainly be questioned; accounting practices, for example. Accounting firms sometimes look the other way when crimes are discovered. "Senior executives are embarrassed by the revelation of fraud in their backyard," said Robert Chambers of Toronto-based KPMG Peat Marwick Thorne (*Maclean's*, July 27, 1992). It reflects on their competence. As the London *Times* editorialized, "Accountants are the private police force of capitalism. ... If accountancy is rotten, then that rottenness spreads through the system and confidence is shaken" (*Times*, March 16, 1992). It is unlikely that accounting firms will be disciplined by regulations; but because of the pervasiveness of their role in the business world, exposing unethical accounting practices and naming the people involved could influence the behaviour of accountants and businesses. Actions that have a modest impact on *many* people who commit a wide range of questionable and unethical acts can move the entire "morality curve" to the left. By contrast, actions that have a severe impact on the few people who are on the extreme right of the curve would not move the morality curve very much.

I am not suggesting abandoning the enforcement of rules against corporate crime. Rather, I suggest broadening the criticism and shaming of individuals involved in unethical behaviour. Treating powerful people in society as uniformly venal and selfish is unrealistic, but identifying *individuals* who abuse their power is realistic. Braithwaite and Grabosky (1985) feel that it is worthwhile beginning with the assumption that business leaders think of themselves as upright citizens making a contribution to the society. Perhaps this assumption is naïve, but even if wrong, giving it lip-service may counter the growth of a subculture of power abuse.

To summarize, criminalizing *specific* corporate deviance may help to identify areas of concern, but it will have little impact on the reduction of crime. Enforcing criminal rules has been very difficult and largely ineffective. On the other hand, shaming those who are the models of society might erode the subculture of power abuse and move significant numbers of influential leaders in the direction of prosocial behaviour. The criminal justice approach touches very few. Regulatory law is difficult to enforce. Public-shaming aims at many. *A little success with many has more impact than the rare success with the truly corrupt,* and would move the entire morality curve to the left. When leaders of society are viewed as hypocrites, others can be cynical and feel less guilt about stealing. Leaders can reduce that cynicism. Societies with higher morality should have less crime.

Political Crime and Corruption

Ray Corrado (1992) describes a number of the better-known cases of corruption in Canada, including the scandals involving the establishment of Canadian Pacific Railway, the Duplessis regime in Québec, the Sky Shops affair, and the charges of corruption in the Atlantic provinces. He also states that "the Progressive Conservative government of Brian Mulroney has firmly established itself as one of the most ethically bankrupt administrations in Canadian history" (1992:443-444).

There may be a link between political corruption and corporate crime. When the former Premier of British Columbia, Bill Vander Zalm, sold some of his property under conditions that were questionable, he was not convicted. Four years after another former Premier of British Columbia, Bill Bennett, was accused of insider trading, the B.C. Securities Commission finally scheduled hearings (*The Financial Post*, Jan 9-11, 1993). It is difficult and expensive to convict such people, but in a world with a higher standard of morality, they could at least be shunned.

In Alberta, Members of the Legislative Assembly living in the capital city also received $20,000 or more from apartments in Edmonton they did not need. The former Premier of Alberta, Don Getty, saw no moral dilemma in receiving his salary, even though he would no longer sit in the Legislative Assembly or do any work to earn his salary. He was simply following the practice of former premiers, such as Peter Lougheed, or former prime minister John Turner, who received his salary as a Member of Parliament even though he did not attend.

Actually, I am optimistic about political corruption. Such corruption is less than it was in the past, perhaps because public shaming has, in fact, been used. Few politicians have been punished in the criminal justice system, but many have been shamed. Senator Buchanan of Nova Scotia may have been rewarded by Prime Minister Mulroney with a Senate seat, and possibly avoided accusations of corruption that were levelled in Halifax, but certainly his moral reputation in Nova Scotia has suffered. Even people in the most powerful political positions cannot always fend off embarrassing revelations. The son of former president Bush, George W. Bush, Jr., broke the law in his dealings with BCCI-linked Harken Energy. Two brothers of the president also received unfavourable publicity. Jonathan Bush was barred from selling securities in Massachusetts for violating state laws. Prescott Bush was paid nearly $500,000 for aiding in a takeover of a Wall Street firm by a company reputed to be controlled by Japanese gangsters (*USA Today*, September 4, 1992). The president himself, of course, is always under scrutiny. Income-tax information about the president of the U.S. is normally available. A typical working couple making $53,000 in the U.S. paid about 28% of its 1991 income in federal taxes. Mr. and Mrs. George Bush reported a total income of $1,329,580 and paid only 16%. The press and the citizenry are frequently critical of public figures. In fact, cheating by politicians is trivial, compared to the abuses of corporation executives.

My contention is that public indignation has curbed political crime somewhat, and if John Turner will simply donate to charity the salary he has unethically taken for the past few years, he should be reintegrated into respectable society. The trick is to transfer this strategy to the corporate world. Michael Milken is now free after serving two years of his ten-year sentence. His fraudulent activities did tremendous damage to the social fabric, hurt many innocent victims, and rewarded many other corrupt businessmen. But if Milken repents his criminal deeds, and donates to charity $499 million of the $500-million personal fortune that he obtained from his criminal behaviour, he should be reintegrated into the company of decent people. Other sinners have been saved. Why not John Turner and Michael Milken?

One can generalize this argument to General Motors, for knowingly placing gas tanks in places where they could be damaged and lead to burning deaths. Like Ford, and the Pinto affair, GM knew that people would die, and deliberately failed to make changes because of profit considerations. The strategy of settling damage claims out of court was designed to reduce publicity and was part of a whole set of immoral practices. When a court awarded $100 million to the family of a man who was burned to death, GM's response was predictable: they appealed the case. Chronic lying and denial of responsibility characterizes GM's criminogenic corporate subculture. What is needed, if one follows Braithwaite's logic, is the public shaming of the people responsible, and the public confession of these people, acknowledging their reprehensible behaviour. Mr. Stempel, former CEO of GM, should be stigmatized and shunned. The courtroom is ineffective in changing these criminal tendencies of powerful people. Instead, we have a criminogenic corporate subculture which employs professional liars, in the tobacco industry to argue that cigarettes do not cause cancer, in the auto industry to deny dangerous deficiencies in their vehicles, etc. Ralph Nader would be happy to see people like Mr. Stempel in jail, but this isn't going to happen. An alternate strategy is to make him feel guilty for his sins, admittedly not an easy task; but if Stempel were to repent his evil deeds, he should be reintegrated into the world of respectable citizens.

Others are less convinced that exposés are deterrents to upper-class crooks. "Adverse publicity shows how little is, or can be, done by regulators or police. Exposés do not deter, but actually spur the bad guys on" because it shows how ineffective the sanctioning system is (Francis, 1988:301). This assumes that the actions of the *regulators* are the most important. However, if the opinions of others are important to our self-esteem, then exposés can be important tools, particularly in the reduction of upper-class crime. Deterrence should not be viewed as a narrow legal concept. It must be seen within the context of a complex social world, where citizens make moral judgments. Thus, it is important that upper-class criminals respond to the societal actions against them, not with denial, but with the acceptance that their behaviour was wrong. Whether it is stealing millions, or simply failing to do one's job as a Member of Parliament, being ashamed makes even a mild punishment, or negative publicity, more effective.

CARING FOR THE WEAK AND THE LINK WITH CRIME

Do societies that take better care of their weaker members have less crime? In her 1988 book, Diane Francis agrees with Laureen Snider (1993): powerful people cheat more and at greater cost to society than those who engage in welfare fraud. In recent articles in the *Financial Post*, however, Francis gives the impression that those who engage in welfare fraud are a greater threat to society. I favour her earlier arguments, but my concern is that articulate and influential writers like Diane Francis, reflect the views of influential people. Today we have a "selfish majority," an economically comfortable population which accepts increasing destitution for a growing underclass, and a deteriorating public sector (Hackler, 1993). This encourages short-sightedness and the mistaken belief that private riches and public squalor will adequately serve a modern society (Galbraith, 1992). President Bill Clinton had to appeal to this same contented majority to be elected. In Canada, it is difficult to win elections by appealing to altruism, even though the quality of life for all of us will be related to how well we deal with environmental issues, mass transportation, education, and other areas of *public* concern.

One way to look at the impact of the contented majority on the way a society serves its *total* population is to look at infant mortality rates, that is, the number of deaths of infants under the age of one per 1,000 live births. This is acknowledged to be the best measure for comparing countries in terms of medical care. One might also argue that the infant mortality rate provides a good indication of the way a society cares for its population in general. Consider the facts. The United States spends more money on medical care per capita than any other country in the world. Canada is second. Twenty-eight countries have lower infant mortality rates than the U.S. and two are tied with it. Clearly these countries get more for their money.

Table 21.1 Number of Infant Deaths per 1,000 Live Births

Liechtenstein	2.7	Luxembourg	7.4
San Marino	3.8	Germany	7.5
Japan	4.6	Denmark	7.5
Finland	5.8	New Zealand	7.6
Iceland	5.9	Spain	7.6
Sweden	6.0	Belgium	7.9
Taiwan	6.2	United Kingdom	7.9
Netherlands Antilles	6.3	Ireland	8.0
Singapore	6.7	Australia	8.0
Hong Kong	6.7	Italy	8.6
Netherlands	6.8	Israel	8.7
Switzerland	6.8	Slovenia	8.9
Norway	6.9	Barbados	9.0
Canada	**7.1**	Martinique	9.0
France	7.3	**United States**	**9.0**
Austria	7.4		

The Bush administration proposed that tax credits be made available, so people could purchase medical insurance. Tax credits, of course, mean little to the impoverished. Furthermore, the thousand-plus health insurance companies in the U.S. are in business to make a profit. *Their* goal is to insure healthy people and avoid insuring sick people. Health is one of the many social concerns that cannot be well-served by the profit motive. When we hear about the various ways of improving medical care, or providing social services in general, we should clearly avoid the patterns developed by the United States.

The infant mortality rate may not be the best national indicator of how well a country cares for its weakest citizens, but Table 21.1 would reflect violent crime rates rather well. Those countries with low infant mortality rates have lower crime rates. Naturally, correlation is not the same as causality. However, *caring for the weak probably reduces crime.*

Child Poverty and Crime Reduction

This is not a book about social welfare, medical care, and child poverty. It should be obvious, however, that child poverty leads to crime. Furthermore, it is much more economical for a society to take action early, rather than pay for the consequences later. Every dollar spent helping pregnant women buy nutritious food and teaching them about diet saves nearly three dollars in health-care costs in one year alone (Canadian Centre on Substance Abuse, 1992). Proper nutrition reduces the rate of low-birth-weight babies by twenty-five percent. Low birth weight contributes to mental retardation, cerebral palsy, vision and hearing loss, and impaired school performance. Doing badly in school is clearly related to delinquency and future crime. Child poverty is criminogenic. The real question is: how well have we been protecting children during the past decade or so?

Between 1974 and 1988 in the U.S., poverty among children increased from 15% to 20% (Barancik, 1989). From the late '60s to the early '80s certain trends are apparent (Adams, Duncan, and Rodgers, 1988; Duncan and Rodgers, 1991). The proportion of children, particularly Black children, in one-parent households, has risen substantially. At the same time, the average age of parents of poor children has declined three to five years. Compounding the problem is the fact that the relative earnings of young workers have declined, and this includes young working parents.

Two positive factors appear in the demographic trends, however. First, the number of children per family declined substantially. The average number of siblings of Black and White children fell by almost one half from the late 1960s to the early 1980s. Second, educational achievement rose. For example, the proportion of Black children in households in which the head has gone beyond high school doubled, from ten percent to twenty percent. These two factors should have produced a decrease in the probability of childhood poverty, but they did not. "A rare opportunity to reduce childhood poverty offered by the dramatic decrease in family size and the rapid increase in educational attainments" was squandered (Duncan and Rodgers, 1991:549).

Nurturing a Subculture of Poverty

The sources of income of families of poor children in the U.S. have changed. The contribution from fathers fell sharply from the 1960s to the 1980s, caused by the decline in the earning potential of young adults and the shift towards one-parent, mostly female-headed, households. An increased proportion of the income of poor families comes from public assistance programmes, especially the food-stamp programme (Bane and Ellwood, 1989). This contributes to a "culture of poverty." The children of such households are less likely to escape poverty as they become adults. For the selfish majority, they are now "welfare bums."

This logic could be extended to issues such as homelessness. Bill McCarthy and John Hagan (1991) found that homeless adolescents participated in more serious crimes after they left home. They also noted that changes in criminal activity did not appear to be due to the direct effects of background variables. In other words, regardless of race, education, and gender, being poor and homeless creates the potential for crime.

Space does not permit a discussion of ways to reduce poverty, but the Manitoba Basic Annual Income Experiment (Mincome) was an experimental test of guaranteed income (Hum and Simpson, 1991). Many fear that a guaranteed annual income would reduce the incentive to work. The study concludes that such fears are largely misplaced. Ideas about systematic income distribution in general should be taken seriously. Between 1974 and 1988 in the U.S., the income share of the nation's richest one-fifth increased from 41% to 44%, while the share received by the poorest one-fifth fell from 5.5% to 4.6% (Phillips, 1990). In other words, the Reagan-Bush era was criminogenic. It also influenced Canada. Social practices in North America contribute to factors that lead to crime. Such a pattern, however, can be changed.

These ideas are not original. In his book, *Confronting Crime*, Elliot Currie writes, "If we are serious about attacking the roots [of crime] ... we must build a society that is less unequal, less depriving, less insecure, less disruptive of community ties, less corrosive of cooperative values. In short, we must begin to take on the enormous task of creating the conditions of community life in which individuals can live together in compassionate and cooperative ways" (1985:225-226). Conservatives often assume that social policy initiatives cannot alter criminogenic factors. This is wrong. Other countries have adopted policies that lessen crime. Government decisions are relevant and policy-makers in the U.S. and Canada have encouraged, directly or by default, social and economic forces that undermine social cohesion. This increases crime. Then we "invoke a grossly outsized penal system to contain the predictable consequences, without notable success" (Currie, 1985:226). These patterns continue. In this chapter I focused on only two illustrations of such criminogenic features: the abuse of power by elites and social programmes for weakest members of society. Constructive suggestions by people like Currie are, unfortunately, largely unheeded by policy-makers.

A Cautionary Note on Oversimplifying Cures

Even if one were to reduce the criminogenic pressures that arise from the neglect of weaker members in a society, there would still be crime. However, the conflict theorists, along with liberal humanists, who emphasize structural variables, come closest to identifying the major sources of crime. They may not agree on specific policy strategies, but as we look around the world for societies that have done better than North America, a number of northern European countries come to mind.

Sweden, despite its recent economic problems, provides better opportunities than Canada for children to be adequately nurtured. Sweden still has delinquency and crime, and like the U.S. and Canada, a small group of serious offenders contribute disproportionately (Sarnecki, 1986).

Social policies form a *hierarchy of effectiveness*. Those societies, such as Canada, that have considerable structural inequality, would probably reduce crime the most by policies that reduce such inequality. The more socially developed countries of northern Europe have already applied the principles argued by the conflict theorists and those criminologists who emphasize structural variables. Next would be policies that strengthen the family and the quality of community life. Again, more effective models exist in Europe than in North America, although programmes in North America regarding family violence may be yielding modest results. At a lower level of effectiveness, theoretical orientations emphasizing group processes, such as control theory, become more relevant. Sarnecki (1989) notes that in Sweden the economic interdependence that links elements of families together has diminished. The opportunity for youth to interact with adults as part of meaningful jobs has been reduced. Youth are not socially integrated through work, as they were with farm work, apprenticeships, and the like. Paul Friday (1992) argues that adolescents in Sweden are more socially isolated and dependent on the peer group. "The more dependent one is on that group, the more the group's definitions prevail. ... The earlier the emancipation, the greater the group dependency" and the greater the likelihood of crime (1992:242). Having reduced the explanatory power of social class and dealt more effectively with major criminogenic conditions, more egalitarian societies may find that social psychological theories, routine activities theory, psychological orientations, and perhaps even biological factors become more relevant. However, it is silly to think that we can take a young Native man in a Canadian prison, who has grown up in criminogenic conditions, counsel him, and then release him in downtown Vancouver, assuming that he has been "cured" of criminal behaviour. The fact that we naïvely continue to "counsel" offenders to go straight is a reflection of the power of the counselling industry, rather than an intelligent approach to crime.

CONCLUSION

Few criminologists share my belief that changing corporate crime would have an impact on predatory street crime, but I feel that the morality of a society is part of a common social fabric. Powerful and wealthy people influence that morality more than others. While the courts and regulations may have little impact on corporate behaviour, publicity and exposure of their practices could help to control the subculture of power abuse.

While crime is inevitable in complex industrial societies, the level of predatory crime that exists in North America is not. The way our criminal justice system functions probably increases crime; and a range of other social policies works against social cohesiveness, destroys the institutional infrastructure of communities, and interferes with the capacity of families to socialize children into non-deviant adults. Despite the lip-service given by governments to crime prevention, while pandering to other pressures, the knowledge for reducing crime has been available and has been applied, at least moderately, in many parts of the world. Canada has a choice: it can continue to mimic the failed governmental practices of the U.S., or it can utilize the knowledge accumulated by criminologists and applied with a modest degree of success in other countries of the world.

Bibliography

Adams, Terry, Greg J. Duncan, and Willard L. Rodgers. 1988. "The Persistence of Urban Poverty." In F. Harris and R. Wilkins (eds.) Quiet Riots: Race and Poverty in the United States. New York: Pantheon.

Adams, Samuel Hopkins. 1955. "The Juke Myth." Saturday Review 38:13,48-49.

Addiction Research Foundation. 1989. Annual Report, 1988-89. Toronto: Addiction Research Foundation.

Adelberg, Ellen and Claudia Currie. 1987. Too Few Too Count: Canadian Women in Conflict with the Law. Vancouver: Press Gang.

Adlaf, Edward M. and Reginald G. Smart. 1991. "Drug Use Among Adolescent Students in Canada and Ontario: The Past, Present, and Future." The Journal of Drug Issues 21:59-72.

Adler, Freda. 1975. Sisters in Crime: The Rise of the New Female Criminal. New York: McGraw-Hill.

Adler, Jeffrey. 1989. "A Historical Analysis of the Law of Vagrancy." Criminology 27:209-229.

Ageton, Suzanne S. 1983. "The Dynamics of Female Delinquency, 1976-1980." Criminology 21:555-584.

Agnew, Robert. 1987. "On 'Testing Structural Strain Theories'." Journal of Research in Crime and Delinquency 24: 281-286.

Akers, Ronald L. 1985. Deviant Behavior: A Social Learning Approach (3rd ed.) Belmont, Calif.: Wadsworth.

Akers, Ronald. L. 1991. "Addiction: the Troublesome Concept." Journal of Drug Issues 21:777-792.

Akman, D. D. and André Normandeau. 1967. "The Measurement of Crime and Delinquency in Canada: A Replication Study." British Journal of Criminology 7:129-149.

Alexander, Bruce K., Patricia Hadaway, and Robert Coambs. 1988. "Rat Park Chronicle." In Judith C. Blackwell and Patricia G. Erickson (eds.) Illicit Drugs in Canada: A Risky Business. Scarborough, Ontario: Nelson Canada.

Allen, H. 1987a. Justice Unbalanced: Gender, Psychiatry, and Judicial Decisions. Milton Keynes, UK: Open University Press.

Allen, H. 1987b. "Rendering Them Harmless: The Professional Portrayal of Women Charged with Serious Violent Crimes." In P. Carlen and A. Worrall (eds.) Gender, Crime and Justice. Milton Keynes, UK: Open University Press.

Amir, Menachim. 1971. Patterns of Forcible Rape. Chicago: University of Chicago Press.

Andrews, Don A., Ivan Zinger, Robert D. Hoge, James Bonta, Paul Gendreau, and Francis T. Cullen. "Does Correctional Treatment Work? A Clinically and Psychologically Informed Meta-analysis." Criminology 28:369-404.

Annis, Helen M. 1979. "Group Treatment of Incarcerated Offenders with Alcohol and Drug Problems: A Controlled Evaluation." Canadian Journal of Criminology 21:3-15.

Archer, Dane and Rosemary Gartner. 1976. "Violent Acts and Violent Times: A Comparative Approach to Postwar Homicide Rates." American Sociological Review 41:937-963.

Atkins, S., and B. Hoggett. 1984. Women and the Law. Oxford: Basil Blackwell.

Bachman, Jerald G., Lloyd D. Johnston, and Patrick M. O'Malley. 1990. "Explaining the Recent Decline in Drug Use among Young Adults: Further Evidence that Perceived Risks and Disapproval Lead to Reduced Use." Journal of Health and Social Behaviour 31:173-184.

Bachman, J. G. and P. M. O'Malley. 1981. "When Four Months Equal a Year: Inconsistencies in Student Reports of Drug Use." Public Opinion Quarterly 45:536-548.

Bachman, Jerald G., Lloyd D. Johnston, Patrick M. O'Malley and Ronald H. Humphrey. 1988. "Explaining the Recent Decline in Marijuana Use: Differentiating the Effects of Perceived Risks, Disapproval, and General Lifestyle Factors." Journal of Health and Social Behaviour 29:92-112.

Backhouse, Constance. 1985. "Nineteenth Century Canadian Prostitution Law: Reflection of a Discriminatory Society." Social History 53:387-423.

Baldwin, John. 1979. "Ecological and Areal Studies in Great Britain and the United States." In Norval Morris and Michael Tonry (eds.), Crime and Justice: An Annual Review of Research, Vol. 1. Chicago: University of Chicago Press.

Ball-Rokeach, Sandra J. 1973. "Values and Violence: A Test of the Subculture of Violence Thesis." American Sociological Review 31:736-749.

Bandura, A. 1973. Aggression: A Social Learning Analysis. Englewood Cliffs, N. J.: Prentice-Hall.

Bane, Mary Jo and David Ellwood. 1989. "One Fifth of the Nation's Children: Why Are They Poor?" Science 245:1047-53.

Barak, Gregg. 1991. Crimes by the Capitalist State: An Introduction to State Criminality. Albany: State University of New York Press.

Barancik, Scott. 1989. 1989 Poverty Tables. Washington, D. C.: Center on Budget and Policy Priorities.

Barlow, Hugh D. and Lynne Schmidt. 1988. "More on the Role of Weapons in Homicidal Violence." Medicine and Law 7:347-358.

Barron, Larry and Murray A. Straus. 1989. Four Theories of Rape in American Society. New Haven, CT: Yale University Press.

Barth, Tom, Walter Watson, and Wayne Blanchard. 1966. "Parent-child Relations in Mass Society." In Jeanette R. Folta and Edith S. Deck (eds.) A Sociological Framework for Patient Care. New York: Wiley.

Bartol, Curt R. and Anne M. Bartol. 1986. Criminal Behavior: A Psychosocial Approach (2nd ed.) Englewood Cliffs, NJ: Prentice-Hall.

Beccaria, Cesare. 1963. On Crimes and Punishments. trans. Henry Paolucci. Indianapolis: Bobbs-Merrill.

Becker, Gary S. 1968. "Crime and Punishment: An Economic Approach." Journal of Political Economy 76:493-517.

Becker, Howard. 1963. Outsiders. New York: Free Press of Glencoe.

Bell, Daniel. 1978. The Cultural Contradictions of Capitalism. New York: Harper Torchbooks, Basic Books.

Bell, Laurie (ed.). 1987. Good Girls/Bad Girls: Sex Trade Workers and Feminist Face to Face. Toronto: Women's Press.

Bensman, Joseph and Israel Gerver. 1963. "Crime and Punishment in the Factory: the Function of Deviancy in Maintaining the Social System." American Sociological Review 28: 588-598.

Berk, Richard, Kenneth Lenihan, and Peter Rossi. 1980. "Crime and Poverty." American Sociological Review 45: 766-801.

Bernard, Thomas. 1987a. "Testing Structural Strain Theories." Journal of Research in Crime and Delinquency 24: 262-280.

Bernard, Thomas. 1987b. "Reply to Agnew." Journal of Research in Crime and Delinquency 24: 287-290.

Bertrand, Marie-Andrée. 1969. "Self-image and Delinquency: A Contribution to the Study of Female Criminality and Women's Image." Acta Criminologica: Etudes sur la Conduite Anitsociale 2:71-144.

Bertrand, Marie-Andrée. 1979. La femme et le crime. Montreal: L'Aurore.

Bertrand, Marie-Andrée. 1983. "Femmes et justice: problemes d'intervention." Criminologie 16:

Bertrand, Marie-Andreé. 1984. "The Drug Laws: Their Continuing Perverse Effects and Resistance to Change." Unpublished Paper, University of Montreal.

Biderman, Albert D. and James P. Lynch. 1991. Understanding Crime Incidence Statistics: Why the UCR Diverges from the NCS. New York: Springer-Verlag.

Biron, Louise L. and Carol Ladouceur. 1991. "The Boy Next Door: Local Teen-age Burglars in Montréal." Security Journal 2:200-204.

Biron, Louise and Marc LeBlanc. 1976. "La Delinquance Cachée à Montréal" (Hidden Delinquency in Montreal). Criminologie: Made in Canada 3:5-16.

Biron, Louise and Marc LeBlanc. 1977. "Family Components and Home-Based Delinquency." British Journal of Criminology 17:157-168.

Bishop, Donna M. and Charles E. Frazier. 1988. "The Influence of Race in Juvenile Justice Processing." Journal of Research in Crime and Delinquency 25:242-263.

Biswas, P. C. 1960. The Ex-Criminal Tribes of Delhi State. Delhi: University of Delhi.

Blalock, Hubert M. Jr. 1964. Causal Inferences in Nonexperimental Research. Chapel Hill, N. C.: North Carolina University Press.

Blumer, Herbert. 1951. "Collective Behaviour." In A. M. Lee (ed.), Principles of Sociology. New York: Barnes and Noble.

Boggs, Sarah Lee. 1964. "Urban Crime Patterns." American Sociological Review 30:899-908.

Boggs, Sarah. 1965. "Urban Crime Patterns." American Sociological Review 30:899-908.

Boritch, Helen. 1992. "Gender and Criminal Court Outcomes: An Historical Analysis." Criminology 30:293-325.

Boritch, Helen and John Hagan. 1990. "A Century of Crime in Toronto: Gender, Class, and Patterns of Social Control, 1859 to 1955." Criminology 28:567-599.

Bortner, M. A. and Wornie L. Reed. 1985. "The Preeminence of Process: An Example of Refocused Justice Research." Social Science Quarterly 66:413-425.

Bose, G. 1956. "Delinquency in India." In K. R. Eissler (ed.), Searchlights on Delinquency. International Universities Press.

Box, Steven. 1971. Deviance, Reality, and Society. London: Holt, Rinehart, and Winston.

Boyd, Susan B. and Elizabeth A. Sheehy. 1989. "Overview: [of Feminism and the Law in Canada]." In Tullio Caputo, et al. (eds.) Law and Society: A Critical Perspective. Toronto: Harcourt, Brace, Jovanovich, Canada.

Boyd, Neil. 1991. High Society: Legal and Illegal Drugs in Canada. Toronto: Key Porter Books.

Boyle, Christine. 1986. "Criminal Law and Procedure: Who Needs Tenure?" Osgoode Hall Law Journal 23: ??

Boyle, Christine. 1991. "Sexual Assault: A Case Study of Legal Policy Decisions." In Margaret Jackson and Curt Griffiths (eds.) Canadian Criminology: Perspectives on Crime and Criminality. Toronto: Harcourt Brace Jovanovich Canada.

Brain, Charles Kimberlin. 1981. The Hunters or the Hunted? Chicago: University of Chicago Press.

Braithwaite, John. 1989. Crime, Shame and Reintegration. Cambridge: Cambridge University Press.

Braithwaite, John and Peter Grabosky. 1985. Occupational Health and Safety Enforcement in Australia. Canberra: Australian Institute of Criminology.

Braithwaite, John. 1989. Crime, Shame, and Reintegration. Cambridge: Cambridge University Press.

Brannigan, Augustine and John Fleischman. 1989. "Juvenile Prostitution and Mental Health: Policing Delinquency or Treating Pathology." Canadian Journal of Law and Society 4:77-98.

Brantingham, Paul. 1992. Personal Correspondence.

Brantingham, Paul. 1991. "Patterns in Canadian Crime." In Margaret Jackson and Curt Griffiths (eds.) Canadian Criminology: Perspectives on Crime and Criminality. Toronto: Harcourt Brace Jovanovich Canada.

Brantingham, Patricia J. and Paul L. Brantingham. 1981. Environmental Criminology. Beverly Hills, Calif.: Sage Publications.

Brantingham, Paul and Patricia Brantingham. 1984. Patterns in Crime. New York: Macmillan.

Brantingham, Patricia L. and Paul J. Brantingham. 1981. "Notes on the Geometry of Crime." In Paul Brantingham and Patricia Brantingham (eds.), Environmental Criminology. Beverly Hills: Sage.

Brickey, Stephen and Elizabeth Comack (eds). 1986. The Social Basis of Law. Toronto: Garamond Press.

Brittan, A. 1973. Meanings and Situations. London: Routledge & Kegan Paul

Brock, Debi R. 1984. Feminist Perspectives on Prostitution: Addressing the Canadian Dilemma. M.A. thesis, Department of Sociology and Anthropology, Carleton University, Ottawa.

Brophy, Jane and Carol Smart (eds.). 1985. Women-in-Law. London: Routledge and Kegan Paul.

Brown, David and Russell Hogg. 1992. "Essentialism, Radical Criminology, and Left Realism." Australian and New Zealand Journal of Criminology 25:195-230.

Brown, Stephen, Finn-Aage Esbensen, and Gilbert Geis. 1991. Criminology: Explaining Crime and Its Context. Cincinatti: Anderson.

Brown, Lorne and Caroline Brown. 1973. An Unauthorized History of the RCMP. Toronto: James Lewis and Samuel.

Brown, Stephen E., Finn-Age Esbensen, and Gilbert Geis. 1991. Criminology: Explaining Crime and Its Context. Cincinatti: Anderson.

Brownfield, David and Kevin Thompson. 1991. "Attachment to Peers and Delinquent Behaviour." Canadian Journal of Criminology 33:45-60.

Bryan, J. H. and M. A. Test. 1967. "Models and Helping: Naturalistic Studies in Aiding Behaviour." Journal of Personality and Social Psychology 6:400-407.

Burstyn, Varda. 1987. "The Left and the Porn Wars: a Case Study in Sexual Politics." In Howard Buchbinder et al. (eds.) Who's on Top? The Politics of Heterosexuality. Toronto: Garamond Press.

Burton, R. V. 1963. "Generality of honesty reconsidered." Psychological Review 70:481-499.

Burton, R. V. 1976. "Honesty and Dishonesty." In T.

Lickona (ed.), Moral Development and Behavior. New York: Holt, Rinehart & Winston.

Byles, J. A. and A. Maurice. 1979. "The Juvenile Services Project: An Experiment in Delinquency Control." Canadian Journal of Criminology 21:155-165.

Campbell, M. 1973. Halfbreed. Toronto: McLelland and Stewart.

Canada. 1981. Second Report of the Commission of Inquiry Concerning Certain Activities of the Royal Canadian Mounted Police: Freedom and Security Under the Law (The MacDonald Report, 2 volumes). Ottawa: Minister of Supplies and Services.

Canadian Pacific Limited. 1992. Notice of Annual Meeting of Stockholders.

Canadian Centre for Justice Statistics. 1992. Just Info. Spring/Summer.

Canadian Centre for Justice Statistics. 1990. The Development of Data Quality Assessment Procedures for the Uniform Crime Reporting Survey: A Case Study of Calgary - Edmonton. Ottawa: Canadian Centre for Justice Statistics.

Canadian Centre for Justice Statistics. 1991. Adult Correctional Services in Canada. Ottawa: Publications Division, Statistics Canada.

Canadian Centre on Substance Abuse. 1992. Action News 3(3):5.

Canter, Rachelle J. 1982. "Sex Differences in Self-Report Delinquency." Criminology 20:373-393.

Caplan, Aaron and Marc LeBlanc. 1985. "A Cross-Cultural Verification of a Social Control Theory." International Journal of Comparative and Applied Criminal Justice.

Caputo, Tullio C., Mark Kennedy, Charles E. Reasons, and Augustine Brannigan (eds.). 1989. Law and Society: A Critical Perspective. Toronto: Harcourt Brace Jovanovich Canada.

Carlen, Pat. 1983. Women's Imprisonment: A Study in Social Control. London: Routledge & Kegan Paul.

Carter, Ronald L. and Kim Q. Hill. 1979. The Criminal's Image of the City. New York: Pergamon.

Cavan, Ruth Shonle and Jordan T. Cavan. 1968. Delinquency and Crime: Cross-Cultural Perspectives. Philadelphia: J. B. Lippincott.

Cernkovich, Steve A. and Peggy C. Giordano. 1979. "On Complicating the Relationship Between Liberation and Delinquency." Social Problems 26:467-481.

Cernkovich, Stephen A. and Peggy C. Giordano. 1979. "A Comparative Analysis of Male and Female Delinquency." The Sociological Quarterly 20: 131-145.

Chamberlayne, R., W. Kierans, and L. Fletcher. 1988. British Columbia Alcohol and Drug Programs Adolescent Survey: 1987: Technical Report. Victoria: B. C. Ministry of Health.

Chambliss, William. 1964. "A Sociological Analysis of the Law of Vagrancy." Social Problems 12:67-77.

Chambliss, William. 1975. "Toward a Political Economy of Crime." Theory and Society 2:149-170.

Chambliss, William. 1988. On the Take: From Petty Crooks to Presidents. Bloomington, Ind.: Indiana University Press.

Chambliss, William. 1989. "State Organized Crime." Criminology 27:183-208.

Chambliss, William J. and Robert Seidman. 1982. Law, Order and Power. (2nd ed.). Reading, MA: Addison-Wesley.

Chein, Isadore, D. L. Gerrard, R. S. Lee, and E. Rosenfeld. 1964. The Road to H. New York: Basic Books.

Chesney-Lind, Meda. 1973. "Judicial Enforcement and the Female Delinquent." Issues in Criminology 8:51-59.

Chesney-Lind, Meda. 1986. "Women and Crime: The Female Offender." Signs: Journal of Women in Culture and Society 12:78-96.

Chesney-Lind, Meda. 1988. "Girls and Status Offenses: Is Juvenile Justice Still Sexist?" Criminal Justice Abstracts 20:144-165.

Chesney-Lind, Meda. 1989. "Girls' Crime and Women's Place: Toward a Feminist Model of Female Delinquency." Crime and Delinquency 35:5-29.

Christie, Nils. 1977. "Conflicts as Property." British Journal of Criminology 17:1-26.

Chunn, Dorothy. 1992. From Punishment to Doing Good: Family Courts and Socialized Justice in Ontario 1880-1940. Toronto: U of Toronto Press.

Chunn, Dorothy E. and Shelley A. M. Gavigan. 1991. "Women and Crime in Canada." In Margaret Jackson and Curt Griffiths (eds.) Canadian Criminology: Perspectives on Crime and Criminality. Toronto: Harcourt Brace Jovanovich Canada.

Clark, Loreen and Debra Lewis. 1977. Rape: The Price of Coercive Sexuality. Toronto: The Women's Press.

Cloward, Richard and Lloyd Ohlin. 1960. Delinquency and Opportunity. Glencoe, Ill.: Free Press.

Cloward, Richard. 1959. "Illegitimate Means, Anomie, and Deviant Behaviour." American Sociological Review 24: 164-176.

Coates, B., H. E. Pusser, and I. Goodman. 1976. "The Influence of 'Sesame Street' and 'Mister Rogers' Neighborhood' on Children's Social Behavior in the Preschool." Child Development 47:138-144.

Cohen, Albert K. 1955. Delinquent Boys: The Culture of the Gang. Glencoe, Ill.: Free Press.

Cohen, Albert K. 1966. Deviance and Control. Englewood Cliffs, N. J.: Prentice Hall.

Cohen, Lawrence and Marcus Felson. 1979. "Social Change and Crime Rate Trends; A Routine Activities Approach." American Sociological Review 44:588-608.

Cohen, Lawrence and David Cantor. 1981. "Residential Burglary in the United States: Life Style and Demographic Factors Associated with the Probability of Victimization." Journal of Research in Crime and Delinquency 18:113-127.

Cohen, Lawrence. 1981. "Modeling Crime Trends: A Criminal Opportunity Perspective." Journal of Research in Crime and Delinquency 18:138-162.

Cohen, Lawrence, James R. Kluegel, and Kenneth C. Land. 1981. "Social Inequality and Predatory Criminal Victimization: An Exposition and Test of a Formal Theory." American Sociological Review 46:505-524.

Cohen, Stanley. 1985. Visions of Social Control. Cambridge: Polity Press.

Coleman, James W. 1985. The Criminal Elite: The Sociology of White Collar Crime. New York: St. Martin's Press.

Coleman, John R. 1980. "What I Learned Last Summer." Psychology Today 14(11):17-20.

Colvin, Mark and John Pauly. 1983. "A Critique of Criminology: Toward an Integrated Structural-Marxist Theory of Delinquency Production." American Journal of Sociology 89:513-551.

Comack, Elizabeth and Stephen Brickey (eds.). 1991. The Social Basis of Law (2nd. Ed.). Halifax: Garamond Press.

Comack, Elizabeth. 1993. "Women Offenders' Experiences with Physical and Sexual Abuse." Presentation at the Canadian Law and Society Meetings at Carleton University in Ottawa.

Comack, Elizabeth. 1992. "Women and Crime." In Rick Linden (ed.) Criminology: A Canadian Perspective (2d Ed.). Toronto: Harcourt Brace Jovanovich Canada.

Commission of Inquiry into the Non-Medical Use of Drugs. 1973. Final Report. Ottawa: Information Canada.

Committee on Sexual Offenses Against Children and Youth. 1984. Sexual Offenses Against Children. Ottawa: Department of Supply & Services.

Conrad, John. 1985. The Dangerous and the Endangered. Lexington, Mass.: D. C. Heath.

ad, P., and J. W. Schneider. 1980. Deviance and Medicalization: From Badness to Sickness. St. Louis: C. V. Mosby.

Corrado, Ray. 1991. "Contemporary Political Crime: National and International Terrorism." In Margaret Jackson and Curt Griffiths (eds.) Canadian Criminology. Toronto: Harcourt Brace Jovanovich, Canada.

Corrado, Ray. 1992. "Political Crime in Canada." In Rick Linden (ed.) Criminology: A Canadian Perspective (2nd Edition). Toronto: Harcourt Brace Jovanovich Canada.Cossins, Diane. 1991. Canadian Juvenile Justice Before and After the Young Offenders Act. Unpublished MA thesis, Department of Sociology, University of Alberta, Edmonton, Alberta.

Cullen, Francis. 1984. Rethinking Crime and Deviance Theory: The Emergence of a Structuring Tradition. Totowa, New Jersey: Rowman and Allanheld.

Cullen, Francis. 1988. "Were Cloward and Ohlin Strain Theorists? Delinquency and Opportunity Revisited." Journal of Research in Crime and Delinquency 25: 214-241.

Cullen, Francis T., William J. Maakestad and Gray Cavender. 1991. "The Ford Pinto Case and Beyond: Assessing Blame." In Michael C. Braswell, Belinda R. McCarthy, and Bernard J. McCarthy (eds.), Justice, Crime and Ethics. Cincinatti: Anderson

Currie, Dawn. 1990. "Battered Women and the State: From the failure of theory to a theory of failure." Journal of Human Justice 1:77-96.

Currie, Elliot. 1985. Confronting Crime. New York: Pantheon Books.

Currie, Elliott. 1987. What Kind of Future? Violence and Public Safety in the Year 2000. San Francisco: National Council on Crime and Delinquency

Curry, J. C. 1932. The Indian Police. London: Faber and Faber.

Dahrendorf, Ralf. 1959. Class and Class Conflict in Industrial Society. Stanford, Calif.: Stanford University Press.

Daly, Kathleen. 1989. "Criminal Justice Ideologies and Practices in Different Voices: Some Feminist Questions about

Daly, Kathleen. 1990. "New Feminist Definitions of Justice." Proceedings of the First Annual Women's Policy Research Conference. Washington, DC: Institute for Women's Policy Research.

Daly, Kathleen and Meda Chesney-Lind. 1988. "Feminism and Criminology." Justice Quarterly 5:497-538.

Darley, J. M. and B. Latané. 1968. "Bystander Intervention in Emergencies: Diffusion of Responsibility." Journal of Personality and Social Psychology 8:377-383.

Davies, Robertson. 1972. The Manticore. Toronto: Macmillan Company of Canada.

Davis, Kingsley. 1937. "The Sociology of Prostitution." *American Scociological Review* 2:744-755.

de Rahm, Edith. 1969. How Could She Do That? New York: Clarkson N. Potter

Dekeseredy, Walter, and Ron Hinch. 1992. Woman Abuse: Sociological Perspectives. Toronto: Thomson Educational Publishers.

Denno, Deborah. 1984. "Neuropsychological and Early Environmental Correlates of Sex Differences in Crime." International Journal of Neuroscience 23:199-214.

Denno, Deborah. 1985. "Sociological and Human Developmental Explanations of Crime." Criminology 23:711-741.

Desroches, Fred. 1991a. "Tearoom Trade: A Law Enforcement Problem." Canadian Journal of Criminology 33:1-21.

Desroches, Frederick J. 1991b. "Profiling the Modern Bank Robber." Paper presented at the Annual Meeting of the Canadian Sociology and Anthropology Association.

Dowie, Mark. 1977. "Pinto Madness." Mother Jones (Sept-Oct):18-32.

Duffala, D. C. 1976. "Convenience Stores: Armed Robbery and Physical Environmental Features." American Behavioral Scientist 20:227-246.

Duncan, Greg J. and Willard Rodgers. 1991. "Has Children's Poverty Become More Persistent?" American Sociological Review 56: 538-550.

Durkheim, Emile. 1933. The Division of Labor in Society. New York: Free Press.

Durkheim, Emile. 1951. Suicide. New York: Free Press.

Elliott, Delbert, David Huizinga, and Suzanne Ageton. 1985. Explaining Delinquency and Drug Use. Beverly Hills, CA.: Sage.

Elliott, Delbert. 1985. "The Assumption That Theories Can Be Combined with Increased Explanatory Power: Theoretical Integrations." In Robert F. Meier (ed.) Theoretical Methods in Criminology. Beverly Hills, CA.: Sage.

Engels, Frederick. 1958. The Condition of the Working Class in England. (translated and edited by W. O. Henderson and W. H. Chaloner.) Oxford: Basil Blackwell.

Erickson, Patricia G. 1992. "Recent Trends in Canadian Drug Policy: The Decline and Resurgence of Prohibitionism." Daedalus 121:239-267.

Erickson, Patricia G. and Reginald Smart. 1988. "The LeDain Commission Recommendations." In Judith C. Blackwell and Patricia G. Erickson (eds.) Illicit Drugs in Canada: A Risky Business. Scarborough, Ontario: Nelson Canada.

Erickson, Patricia G. and Tim Weber. 1992. "Cocaine, Control and Crime." Paper presented at the annual meeting of the American Society of Criminology, New Orleans.

Erickson, Patricia, Edward Adlaf, Glenn Murray, and Reginald Smart. 1987. The Steel Drug: Cocaine in Perspective. Lexington, Mass.: Lexington Books, D. C. Heath.

Ericson, Richard V. 1975. Criminal Reactions: The Labelling Perspective. Westmead, Farnborough, Hants.: Saxon House.

Ericson, Richard V. 1981. Making Crime: A Study of Detective Work. Toronto: Butterworths.

Ericson, Richard V. 1982. Reproducing Order. Toronto: University of Toronto Press.

Ericson, Richard V. 1987. "The State and Criminal Justice Reform." In R. S. Ratner and John L. McMullan (eds.) State Control: Criminal Justice Politics in Canada. Vancouver: University of British Columbia Press.

Ericson, Richard V. and Patricia M. Baranek. 1982. The Ordering of Justice: A Study of Accused Persons as Dependents in the Criminal Process. Toronto: University of Toronto Press.

Ericson, Richard V., Patricia Baranek, Janet B. L. Chan. 1987. Visualizing Deviance: A Study of News Organization. U of Toronto Press.

Ericson, Richard V., Patricia Baranek, Janet B. L. Chan. 1989. Negotiating Control: A Study of News Sources. Toronto: U of Toronto Press.

Eysenck, Hans J. 1977. Crime and Personality (2d ed.). London: Routledge & Kegan Paul.

Eysenck, Hans J. and S. B. G. Eysenck. 1976. Psychoticism as a Dimension of Personality. London: Hodder and Stoughton.

Eysenck, Hans J. 1981. A Model for Personality. New York: Springer.

Farnworth, Margaret and Michael Leiber. 1989. "Strain Theory Revisited." American Sociological Review 54:263-274.

Fattah, Ezzat. 1971. La Victime est-elle Coupable? Montréal: Les Presses de l'Université de Montréal.Fattah, Ezzat A. 1987. "Ideological Biases in the Evaluation of Criminal Justice Reform." In R. S. Ratner and John L. McMullan (eds.) State Control: Criminal Justice Politics in Canada. Vancouver: University of British Columbia Press.

Feinman, Clarice. 1980. Women in the Criminal Justice System. New York: Praeger.

Felson, Marcus and Lawrence Cohen. 1980. "Human Ecology and Crime: A Routine Activity Approach." Human Ecology 4:389-406.

Ferri, Enrico. 1901. Criminal Sociology. Boston: Little, Brown.

Festinger, Leon. 1957. A Theory of Cognitive Dissonance. New York: Harper and Row.

Figueira-McDonough, Josefina and Elaine Selo. 1980. "A Reformulation of the 'Equal Opportunity' Explanation of Female Delinquency." Crime and Delinquency 26:333-343.Finkelhor, David and Larry Baron. 1986. "Risk Factors for Child Sexual Abuse." Journal of Interpersonal Violence 1:43-71.

Fischer, Stanley I. 1979. Moving Millions: An Inside Look at Mass Transit. New York: Harper and Row.

Fleming, J. B. 1979. Stopping Wife Abuse. Anchor, New York.

Fogelman, E. and V. L Wiener. 1985. "The Few, the Brave, the Noble." Psychology Today 19:61-65.

Forbes, G.A. 1977. Street Prostitution in Vancouver's West End. Vancouver: Vancouver Police Report.

Forge, K. L. and S. Phemister. 1987. "The Effect of Prosocial Cartoons on Preschool Children." Child Study Journal 17:83-88.

Fox, John and Timothy Hartnagel. 1979. "Changing Social Roles and Female Crime in Canada: A Time Series Analysis." Canadian Review of Sociology and Anthropology 16:96-104.

Francis, Diane. 1988. Contrepreneurs. Toronto: Macmillan of Canada.

Fréchette, M. and Marc LeBlanc. 1985. Des Délinquantes: Emergence et Dévéloppment. Chicoutimi: Gaetan Morin.

Freud, Sigmund. 1965. New Introductory Lectures on Psychoanalysis. N. Y.: W. W. Norton.

Friday, Paul C. 1992. "Delinquency in Sweden: Current Trends and Theoretical Implications." International Journal of Comparative and Applied Criminal Justice 16:231-246.

Gabor, Thomas and André Normandeau. 1989. "Armed Robbery: Highlights of a Canadian Study." Canadian Police College Journal 13:273-282.

Gabor, Thomas, Micheline Baril, Maurice Cusson, Daniel Elie, Marc LeBlanc, and André Normandeau. 1987. Armed Robbery: Cops, Robbers, and Victims. Springfield, Ill: Charles C. Thomas.

Galbraith, John Kenneth. 1992. The Culture of Contentment. Boston: Houghton Mifflin Co.

Gautier, J. 1977. "Brief." Report of the Royal Commission on Violence in the Communications Industry (Vol. 1). Toronto: Publication Centre, Government of Ontario.

Gavigan, Shelley A. M. 1983. "Women's Crime and Feminist Critiques." Canadian Criminology Forum 6:75-90.

Gavigan, Shelley A. M. 1987. "Women's Crime: New Perspectives and Old Theories." In Adelberg and Currie (eds.) Too Few to Count: Canadian Women in Conflict with the Law. Vancouver: Press Gang.

Gavigan, Shelley A. M. 1986. "Women, Law, and Patriarchal Relations: Perspectives within the Sociology of Law." In Neil Boyd (ed.) Social Dimensions of Law. Scarborough, Ontario: Prentice-Hall Canada.

Gaylord, Mark S. and John F. Galliher. 1991. "Riding the Underground Dragon: Crime Control and Public Order on Hong Kong's Mass Transit Railway." British Journal of Criminology 31:15-26.

Geis, Gilbert. 1972. "Jeremy Bentham." In Herman Mannheim (ed.) Pioneers in Criminology. Montclair, NJ: Patterson Smith.

Geis, Gil. 1965. Juvenile Gangs. Washington, D. C.: President's Committee on Juvenile Delinquency and Youth Crime.

Gelles, Richard. J. and Murray Straus. 1979. "Determinants of Violence in the Family: Toward a Theoretical Integration." In W. Burr., et al. (eds.), Contemporary Theories about the Family. New York: Free Press.

Gelsthorpe, Lorraine and Allison Morris. 1988. "Feminism and Criminology in Britain." British Journal of Criminology 28:223-240.

Gibbons, Don C. 1987. Society, Crime, and Criminal Careers. 5th Ed. Englewood Cliffs, N. J.: Prentice-Hall.

Gibbs, Jack. 1985. "The Methodology of Theory Construction in Criminology." In Robert F. Meier (ed.), Theoretical Methods in Criminology. Beverly Hills, Calif.: Sage.

Gibbs, Jack. 1989. Control: Sociology's Central Notion. Urbana: University of Illinois Press.

Gibbs, Jack P. and Maynard L. Erickson. 1976. "Crime Rates of American Cities in an Ecological Context." American Journal of Sociology 82:605-620.

Giffen, P. J. 1965. "Official Rates of Crime and Delinquency." In W. T. McGrath (ed.), Crime and Its Treatment in Canada. Toronto: Macmillan.

Giffen, P. J. 1966. "The Revolving Door: a Functional Interpretation." Canadian Review of Sociology and Anthropology 3: 154-166.

Giffen, P. J. 1976. "Official Rates of Crime and Delinquency." In W.T. McGrath (ed.), Crime and Its Treatment in Canada 2d Ed. Toronto: University of Toronto Press.

Giffen, P. J. and Sylvia Lambert. 1988. "What Happened on the Way to Law Reform?" In Judith C. Blackwell and Patricia G. Erickson (eds.) Illicit Drugs in Canada: A Risky Business. Scarborough, Ontario: Nelson Canada.

Giffen, P. J., Shirley Endicott, and Sylvia Lambert. 1991. Panic and Indifference: The Politics of Canada's Drug Laws. Ottawa: Canadian Centre on Substance Abuse.

Gilligan, Carol. 1982. In a Different Voice. Cambridge, Mass.: Harvard University Press.

Gilligan, Carol. 1987. "Moral Orientation and Moral Development." In E. Kittay and D. Meyers (eds.) Women and Moral Theory. Totowa, N.J.: Rowman and Littlefield.

Gillis, A. R. 1973. "Types of Human Population Density and Social Pathology." Discussion Paper No. 7. The University of Alberta Population Research Laboratory.

Gillis, A. R. and John Hagan. 1982. "Density, Delinquency, and Design: Formal and Informal Control and the Built Environment." Criminology 19:514-529.

Gillis, A. R. and John Hagan. 1990. "Delinquent Samaritans: Network Structure, Social Conflict, and the Willingness to Intervene." Journal of Research in Crime and Delinquency 27:30-51.

Giordano, Peggy C., Sandra Kerbel, and Sandra Dudley. 1981. "The Economics of Female Criminality: An Analysis of Police Blotters, 1890-1975." In Lee H. Bowker (ed.), Women and Crime in America. New York: MacMillan.

Girault, Henriette. 1984. "La Detention Provisiore de Mineurs." Unpublished paper, Centre de Recherche Interdisciplinaire, Vaucresson.

Glueck, Sheldon and Eleanor Glueck. 1950. Unravelling Juvenile Delinquency. New York: Commonwealth Fund.

Godfrey, Ellen. 1981. By Reason of Doubt: The Belshaw Case. Vancouver: Clarke, Irwin and Co.

Goff, Colin H. and Charles E. Reasons. 1978. Corporate Crime in Canada. Scarborough, Ont.: Prentice-Hall of Canada.

Goode, Erich. 1990. "Crime Can be Fun: The Deviant Experience." Contemporary Sociology 19:5-12.

Gordon, Robert M. and Ian T. Coneybeer. 1991. "Corporate Crime." In Margaret Jackson and Curt Griffiths (eds.) Canadian Criminology. Toronto: Harcourt Brace Jovanovich, Canada.

Goring, Charles. 1913. The English Convict. London: H. M. Stationery Office.

Gould, Leroy C. 1969. "The Changing Structure of Property Crime in an Affluent Society." Social Forces 48:50-59.

Gove, Walter R., Michael L. Hughes, and Omer R. Galle. 1979. "Overcrowding in the Home." American Sociological Review 44:59-80.

Grapendaal, M. 1991. "Dutch Drug Policy and the Economics of Crime." Paper present at the American Society of Criminology Meetings, San Francisco.

Gray, Diana. 1973. "Turning Out: A Study of Teenage Prostitution." Urban Life and Culture (January): 401-425.

Greenberg, David. 1977. "Delinquency and the Age Structure of Society." Contemporary Crises 1:189-223

Greenberg, David F. 1979. Mathematical Criminology. New Brunswick, NJ: Rutgers University Press.

Greenberg, DaSvid. 1981. Crime and Capitalism. Palo Alto, CA: Mayfield.

Greenland, Cyril. 1988. Preventing CAN Deaths: An International Study of Deaths Due to Child Abuse and Neglect. London: Tavistock

Griffiths, Curt. (ed.). 1987. Northern Youth in Crisis: A Challenge for Justice, The Northern Conference. Burnaby, B. C.: Simon Fraser University.

Gurr, Ted. 1981. "Historical Forces in Violent Crime." In Michael Tonry and Norval Morris (eds.) Crime and Justice. Vol. 3. Chicago: University of Chicago Press.

Hackler, James C. 1966. "Boys, Blisters, and Behaviour: The Impact of a Work Program in an Urban Central Area." Journal of Research in Crime and Delinquency 3:155-164.

Hackler, James C. 1978a. The Great Stumble Forward: The Prevention of Youthful Crime. Toronto: Methuen.

Hackler, James C. 1978b. "The Dangers of Political Naivete and Excessive Complexity in Evaluating Delinquency Prevention Programs." Evaluation and Program Planning 1:273-283.

Hackler, James C. 1979. "Invitation to Error: The Dangers of Evaluation and Some Alternatives." Canadian Journal of Criminology 24:39-51.

Hackler, James C. 1988a. "A Developmental Theory of Delinquency." In Ronald A. Farrell and Victoria Lynn Swigert (eds.) Social Deviance (3rd edition). Belmont, Calif.: Wadsworth.

Hackler, James C. 1988b. Practising in France what Americans Have Preached: the Response of French Judges to Juveniles. Crime and Delinquency 34:467-485.

Hackler, Jim. 1991a. "The Reduction of Violent Crime Through Economic Equality for Women." Journal of Family Violence 6:199-216.

Hackler, James C. 1991b. "Good People, Dirty System: The YOA and Organizational Failure." In Alan Leschied, Peter Jaffe, and Wayne Willis (eds.) The Young Offenders Act: A Revolution in Canadian Juvenile Justice. Toronto: University of Toronto Press.

Hackler, Jim. 1991c. "Two Strategies for Defending Juveniles in Australia: Which Does the Least Damage?" In Jim Hackler (ed.) Official Responses to Problem Juveniles: Some International Reflections. Oñati, Spain: International Institute for the Sociology of Law.

Hackler, James C. 1992a. "Strain Theories." In Eric Linden (ed.) Criminology: A Canadian Perspective. (2nd ed.) Toronto: Harcourt Brace Johanovich Canada.

Hackler, James C. 1992b. "The Manifest Functions of Legal Aid." International Criminal Justice Review 2:58-75.

Hackler, Jim. 1993. "The Selfish Majority: Is Canada

also Heading for Private Riches and Public Squalor?" Policy Options 13 (10):44-45.Hackler, James C., Diane Cossins, and Kim Don. 1990."Comparing Crime Rates: When Are They Meaningful?" Edmonton: Centre for Criminological Research, Discussion Paper 24.

Hackler, James C. and Kim Don. 1989. "Screening Juveniles and the Central City Phenomenon: Using Official Statistics to Understand the Dynamics of Police Systems." Canadian Police College Journal 13:1- 17.

Hackler, James C. and Kim Don. 1990. "Estimating System Biases: Crime Indices that Permit Comparison Across Provinces." Canadian J of Criminology 32:243-264.

Hackler, James C. and Laurel Gauld. 1982. "A Comparison of sentencing strategies for violent crime in Columbus, Ohio and Edmonton, Alberta," Canadian Journal of Criminology 24:173-190.

Hackler, James C. and John Hagan. 1975. "Work and Teaching Machines as Delinquency Prevention Tools: A Four Year Follow-up." Social Service Review 49:92-106.

Hackler, James C. and Chris Janssen. 1985. "Police Killings." Canadian Journal of Criminology 27:227-232.

Hackler, James C., Kwal-ylu Ho, and Carol Urquhart-Ross. 1974. "The Willingness to Intervene: Differing Community Characteristics." Social Problems 21:328-344.

Hackler, James C. and Melanie Lautt. 1969. "Systematic Bias in Measuring Self-Reported Delinquency." Canadian Review of Sociology and Anthropology 6:92-106.

Hackler, James C. and Eric Linden. 1970. "The Response of Adults to Delinquency Prevention Programs: the Race Factor." Journal of Research in Crime and Delinquency 7: 31-45.

Hackler, James C. and Wasanti Paranjape. 1984. "Official reaction to juvenile theft: comparisons across provinces." Canadian J of Criminology 26: 179-198.

Hackler, James C. and Wasanti Paranjape. 1983. "Juvenile Justice Statistics: Mythmaking or System Response?" Canadian Journal of Criminology 25:209-226.

Hagan, Frank. 1986. Introduction to Criminology: Theories, Methods and Criminal Behaviour. Chicago: Nelson-Hall.

Hagan, John. 1973. "Labelling and Deviance: A Case Study in the 'Sociology of the Interesting'." Social Problems 20:447-458.

Hagan, John. 1974. "Extra-legal Attributes and Criminal Sentencing: An Assessment of a Sociological Viewpoint." Law and Society Review 8:357-383.

Hagan, John. 1975. "The Social and Legal Construction of Criminal Justice." Social Problems 22:620-637.

Hagan, John. 1985. Modern Criminology: Crime, Criminal Behaviour, and Its Control. New York: McGraw-Hill.

Hagan, John. 1987. "White Collar and Corporate Crime." In Rick Linden, Rick (ed.). 1987. Criminology: A Canadian Perspective. Toronto: Holt, Rinehart, and Winston of Canada.

Hagan, John. 1991. The Disreputable Pleasures: Crime and Deviance in Canada. (Third Edition). Toronto: McGraw-Hill Ryerson.

Hagan, John. 1992a. "White-Collar and Corporate Crime." In Rick Linden (ed.) Criminology: A Canadian Perspective (2nd Edition). Toronto: Harcourt Brace Jovanovich Canada.

Hagan, John. 1992b. "The Poverty of a Classless Criminology." Criminology 30:1-19.

Hagan, John and Celesta Albonettl. 1982. "Race, Class, and the Perception of Criminal Injustice in America." American Journal of Sociology 88:329-55.

Hagan, John, A. R. Glllls, and Janet B. Chan. 1978. "Explaining Official Delinquency: a Spatial Study of Class, Conflict, and Control." Sociological Quarterly 19: 386-398.

Hagan, John, A. R. Glllls, and John Simpson. 1985. "The Class Structure of Gender and Delinquency: Toward a Power-Control Theory of Common Delinquent Behaviour." American Journal of Sociology 90:1,151-1,178.

Hagan, John, A. R. Glllls, and John Simpson. 1987. "Class in the Household: A Power-Control Theory of Gender and Delinquency." American Journal of Sociology 92:788-816.

Hagan, John, Marie Huxter, and Patricia Parker. 1988. "Class Structure and Legal Practice: Inequality and Mobility Among Toronto Lawyers." Law and Society Review 22:9-55.

Hagan, John and Jeffrey Leon. 1977. "Rediscovering Delinquency: Social History, Political Ideology, and the Sociology of Law." American Sociological Review 42: 587-598.

Hagan, John and Patricia Parker. 1985. "White Collar Crime and Punishment: The Class Structure and Legal Sanctioning of Securities Violations." American Sociological Review 50:302-16.

Hancock, Linda. 1981. "The Myth that Females are Treated More Leniently than Males in the Juvenile Justice System." Australian and New Zealand Journal of Sociology 16:4-14.

Hanmer, J. and M. Maynard (eds.) 1987. Women, Violence, and Social Control. Atlantic Highlands, N.J.: Humanities Press International.

Hare, R. D. 1970. Psychopathy: Theory and Research. New York: Wiley.

Hare, R. D. 1980. "A Research Scale for the Assessment of Psychopathy in Criminal Populations." Personality and Individual Differences 1:111-119.

Hare, R. D. 1985. "A Comparison of Procedures for the Assessment of Psychopathy." Journal of Consulting and Clinical Psychology 53:7-16.

Hare, R. D. and L. McPherson. 1984. "Violent and Aggressive Behaviour by Criminal Psychopaths." International Journal of Law and Psychiatry 7:35-50.

Hartnagel, Timothy F. 1982. "Modernization, Female Social Roles, and Female Crime: A Cross-national Investigation." Sociological Quarterly 23:477-490.

Hartnagel, Timothy F., James J. Teevan Jr., and Jennie J. McIntyre. 1975. "Television Violence and Violent Behavior." Social Forces 54:341-351.

Hartshorne, H. and M. A. May. 1928-30. Studies in the Nature of Character. (3 vols.) New York: Macmillan.

Hawkins, K. 1984. Environment and Enforcement: Regulation and the Social Definition of Pollution. Oxford: Clarendon Press.

Heather, Barbara. 1993. "Clear Language: Initiation into Sociology." Society 17, No. 2:3-8.

Helfgot, Joseph. 1981. Professional Reforming: Mobilization for Youth and the Failure of Social Science. Lexington, Mass.: Heath.

Hempel, Carl G. 1952. Fundamentals of Concept Formation in Empirical Science. Chicago: University of Chicago Press.

Henshel, Richard L. 1990. Thinking About Social Problems. San Diego: Harcourt Brace Jovanovich.

Hepworth, Dorothy (ed.). 1979. Explorations in Prairie Justice Research. Regina: Canadian Plains Research Centre.

Herman, Edward S. 1991. "Drug 'Wars': Appearance and Reality." Social Justice 18:76-84.

Hinch, Ronald. 1983. "Marxist Criminology in the 1970s: Clarifying the Clutter." Crime and Social Justice (Summer):65-74.

Hinch, Ronald. 1985. "Canada's New Sexual Assault Laws: A Step Forward for Women?" Contemporary Crises 9:33-44.

Hinch, Ronald. 1987. "Cultural Deviance and Conflict Theories." In Rick Linden (ed.) Criminology: A Canadian Perspective. Toronto: Holt, Rinehart and Winston of Canada.

Hinch, Ronald. 1988. "Inconsistencies and Contradictions in Canada's Sexual Assault Law." Canadian Public Policy 14:282-294.

Hinch, Ronald. 1992. "Conflict and Marxist Theories." In Rick Linden (ed.) Criminology: A Canadian Perspective. (2nd ed.) Toronto: Harcourt Brace Johanovich Canada.

Hindelang, Michael J. 1971. "Age, Sex, and the Versatility of Delinquent Involvements." Social Problems 18:522-535.

Hindelang, Michael J., Michael R. Gottfredson, and James Garofalo. 1978. Victims of Personal Crime: An Empirical Foundation for a Theory of Personal Victimization. Cambridge, Mass.: Ballinger Publishing Co.

Hirschi, Travis. 1969. Causes of Delinquency. Berkeley: University of California Press.

Hirschi, Travis and Hanan Selvin. 1967. Delinquency Research: An Appraisal of Analytic Methods. New York: The Free Press.

Hogarth, John. 1971. Sentencing as a Human Process. Toronto: University of Toronto Press.

Holton, Gerald. 1992. "How to Think About the 'Anti-Science' Phenomenon." Current Contents 45:6-10.

Holton, Gerald. 1993. On Science and Anti-Science. Cambridge, MA.: Harvard University Press.

House, J. D. 1986. "Working Offshore: the Other Price of Newfoundland's Oil." In K. P. Lundy and B. Warme (eds.), Work in the Canadian Context. Toronto: Butterworths.

Hubbard, Ruth. 1982. "Have Only Men Evolved?" In Ruth Hubbard, M. S. Henifin, and Barbara Fried (eds.) Biological Woman—The Convenient Myth. Cambridge, MA: Schenkman.

Hudson, Diane. 1987. "You Can't Commit Violence Against an Object: Women, Psychiatry, and Psychosurgery." In Hanmer, J. and M. Maynard (eds.) Women, Violence, and Social Control. Houndsmills, Basingstoke, Hampshire: Macmillan Press.

Hum, Derek and Wayne Simpson. 1991. Income Maintenance, Work Effort, and the Canadian Mincome Experiment. Ottawa: Economic Council of Canada.

Humphreys, Laud. 1970a. Tearoom Trade: Impersonal Sex in Public Places. Chicago: Aldine.

Humphreys, Laud. 1970b. "Tearoom Trade: Impersonal Sex in Public Places." Transaction 7(3):10-25.

Irwin, John and James Austin. 1987. It's About Time: Solving America's Prison Crowding Crisis. San Francisco: National Council on Crime and Delinquency.

Jackson, Margaret, and Curt Griffiths (eds.). 1991. Canadian Criminology: Perspectives on Crime and Criminality. Toronto: Harcourt Brace Jovanovich Canada.

Jacobs, Jane. 1961. The Death and Life of Great American Cities. New York: Random House.

Jeffrey, C. R. 1965. "Criminal Behavior and Learning Theory." Journal of Criminal Law and Criminology 56:294-300.

Jennings, W. S., R. Kilkenny, L. Kohlberg. 1983. "Moral-Development Theory and Practices for Youthful and Adult Offenders." In W. S. Laufer and S.M. Day (eds.), Personality Theory, Moral Development, and Criminal Behavior. Lexington, Mass.: Lexington Books.

Jepsen, Jorgen. 1988. "Drugs, Crime and Social Control in Scandinavia: International Moral Entrepreneurism in Action and Research." Paper presented at the International Conference on Crime, Drugs, and Social Control; Research Committee for the Sociology of Deviance and Control, University of Hong Kong.

Johns, Christina. 1991. "The War on Drugs: Why the Administration Continues to Pursue a Policy of Criminalization and Enforcement." Social Justice 18:147-165.

Johns, Christina. 1992. State Power, Ideology, and the War on Drugs: Nothing Succeeds Like Failure. New York: Praeger.

Johnson, Holly. 1986. Women and Crime in Canada. Ottawa: Solicitor General of Canada.

Johnson, Holly. 1987. "Getting the Facts Straight: A Statistical Overview." In Adelberg and Currie (eds.) Too Few to Count: Canadian Women in Conflict with the Law. Vancouver: Press Gang.

Johnson, Holly and Vincent F. Sacco. 1990. Patterns of Criminal Victimization in Canada. Ottawa: Minister of Supply and Services Canada

Johnston, L. D. and P. M. O'Malley. 1985. "Issues of Validity and Population Coverage in Student Surveys of Drug Use." In B. A. Rouse, N. J. Kozel, and L. G. Richards (ed.) Self-Report Methods of Estimating Drug Use. Washington, D. C.: NIDA Research Monograph.

Joy, L. A., M. M. Kimball, and M. L. Zabrack. 1986. "Television and Aggressive Behaviour." In T. M. Williams (ed.), The Impact of Television: A Natural Experiment Involving Three Towns. New York: Academic Press.

Justice. " International Journal of the Sociology of Law 17:1-18.

Kamin, Leon. 1986. "Is Crime in the Genes? The Answer May Depend on Who Chooses What Evidence." Scientific American (Feb):22-27.

Katz, Jack. 1988. The Seductions of Crime: Moral and Sensual Attractions in Doing Evil. New York: Basic Books.

Keane, Carl, A. R. Gillis, John Hagan. 1989. "Deterrence and Amplification of Juvenile Delinquency by Police Contact." British Journal of Criminology 29:336-352.

Kelman, S. 1981. Regulating America, Regulating Sweden: A Comparative Study of Occupational Safety and Health Policy. Cambridge, MA: MIT Press.

Kincaid, P. J. 1985. The Omitted Reality: Husband-Wife Violence in Ontario and Policy Implications for Education. Concord, Ontario: Belsten.

King, Michael and Marie-Agnes Petit. 1985/6. "Thin Stick and Fat Carrot: the French Juvenile Justice System." Youth and Policy 15:26-31.

King, Harry. 1972. Box Man: A Professional Thief's Journey. New York: Harper and Row.

Klein, John F., Jim R. Webb, and J.E. DiSanto. 1978. "Experience with the Police and Attitude Towards the Police." Canadian Journal of Sociology 3:441-456.

Klein, Dorie. 1973. "The Etiology of Female Crime: A Review of the Literature." Issues in Criminology 8:3-30.

Kobrin, Sol. 1951. "The Conflict of Values in Delinquency Areas." American Sociological Review 16:653-61.

Koenig, Daniel. 1975. "Police Perceptions of Public Respect and Extra-Legal Use of Force." Canadian Journal of Sociology 1:313-24.

Koenig, Daniel J. 1991. Do Police Cause Crime? Police Activity, Police Strength and Crime Rates. Ottawa: Canadian Police College.

Kohlberg, Lawrence. 1976. "Moral Stages and Moralization: The Cognitive-Developmental Approach." In T. Lickona (ed.), Moral Development and Behaviour. New York: Holt, Rinehart & Winston.

Kornhauser, Ruth. 1978. Social Sources of Delinquency. Chicago: University of Chicago Press.

Krisberg, Barry, Ira Schwartz, Paul Litsky, and James Austin. 1986. "The Watershed of

Juvenile Justice Reform." Crime and Delinquency 32:5-38

LaFree, Gary D., Barbara F. Reskin, and Christy A. Visher. 1985. "Jurors' Responses to Victims' Behaviour and Legal Issues in Sexual Assault Trials." Social Problems 32:389-407.

Lambert, Leah and Patrick G. Madden. 1975. The Adult Female Offender before-during-after Incarceration: Summary, Conclusions and Recommendations. Vanier Research Centre Report No. 3. Toronto: Ontario Ministry of Correctional Services.

Landreville, Pierre, C. Menghile, and P. Pepin. 1974. "Description de la population de l'establisement de detention de Montréal." Montréal: Donner Foundation of the League of the Rights of Man of Quebec.

Landreville, Pierre. 1974. La Prison de Montréal (Bordeaux) 1913-1940. Montréal: Counseil des Arts.

Landreville, Pierre, V. Blankevoort, and A. Pires. 1979-80. "Les Cout Sociaux du Systeme Penal." Crime et/and Justice 7-8:180-189.

LaPrairie, Carol. 1987. "Native Women and Crime: A Theoretical Model." In Adelberg and Currie (eds.) Too Few to Count: Canadian Women in Conflict with the Law. Vancouver: Press Gang.

LaPrairie, Carol. 1990. "The Role of Sentencing in the Over-representation of Aboriginal People in Correctional Institutions." Canadian Journal of Corrections 32:429-440.

Larsen, Nick. 1992. "Time to Legalize Prostitution." Policy Options 13 (7):21-22.

Latané, Bibb and Judith Rodin. 1969. "A Lady in Distress: Inhibiting Effects of Friends and Strangers on Bystander Intervention. Journal of Experimental Social Psychology 5:189-202.

Latané, Bibb, John Darley, and J. M. Darley. 1968. "Group Inhibition of Bystander Intervention." Journal of Personality and Social Psychology 10:215-221.

Lautt, Melanie. 1984. A Report on Prostitution in the Prairie Provinces. Working Papers on Pornography and Prostitution, Report No. 9. Ottawa: Department of Justice.

LeBlanc, Marc. 1976. "Le Systeme de Justice pour mineurs au Québec: Quelques données statistiques." Criminologie: Made in Canada 3:47-66

LeBlanc, Marc. 1983. Boscoville: la rééducation évaluée. Montréal: Hurtubise HMH.

LeBlanc, Marc, Louise Biron, G. Coté, and L. Pronovost. 1978. "Le Délinquance Juvenile: Son Development en Regard du Developpement Psychosocial durant l'Adolescence." Annales de Vaucresson 15.

LeBlanc, Marc and Richard Tremblay. 1985. "An Integrative Control Theory of Delinquent Behaviour: A Validation 1976-1985." Paper presented at the American Society of Criminology annual meetings, San Diego.

Lemert, Edwin M. 1964. "Social Structure, Social Control, and Deviation." In Marshall Clinard (ed.)

Anomie and Deviant Behaviour. New York: Free Press.

Letkemann, Peter. 1973. Crime as Work. Englewood Cliffs, N. J.: Prentice-Hall.

Leuw, Ed. 1991. "Drugs and Drug Policy in the Netherlands." In Michael Tonry (ed.), Crime and Justice: A Review of Research 14. Chicago: University of Chicago Press.

Liebow, Elliot. 1967. Tally's Corner. Boston: Little, Brown.

Liker, Jeffrey. 1982. "Effects of Employment on Affective Well-being of Ex-felons." American Sociological Review 47: 264-283.

Lincoln, Alan J. and Straus, Murray. 1985. Crime and the Family. Springfield, Ill.: C. C. Thomas.

Linden, Rick. 1987. "Social Control Theory." In Rick Linden (ed.) Criminology: A Canadian Perspective. Toronto: Holt, Rinehart and Winston of Canada

Linden, Rick (ed.). 1992. Criminology: A Canadian Perspective (2d Ed.). Toronto: Harcourt Brace Jovanovich Canada.

Linden, Rick and Cathy Fillmore. 1981. "A Comparative Study of Delinquency Involvement." Canadian Review of Sociology and Anthropology 18: 343-361.

Linden, Rick and James C. Hackler. 1973. "Affective Ties and Delinquency." Pacific Sociological Review 16: 27-46.

Lindesmith, Alfred R. 1965. The Addict and the Law. Bloomington, Indiana: Indiana University Press.

Link, Bruce G. 1987. "Understanding Labeling Effects in the Area of Mental Disorders: An Empirical Assessment of the Effects of Expectations of Rejection." American Sociological Review 52:96-112.

Link, Bruce G., Francis T. Cullen, Elmer Struening, Patrick E. Shrout, and Bruce P. Dohrenwend. 1989. "A Modified Labeling Theory Approach to Mental Disorders." American Sociological Review 54:400-423.

Liska, Allen and Mark Tausig. 1979. "Theoretical Interpretations of Social Class and Racial Differentials in Legal Decision-Making for Juveniles." Sociological Quarterly 20:187-207.

Liska, Allen E. and Mark D. Reed. 1985. "Ties to Conventional Institutions and Delinquency: Estimating Reciprocal Effects." American Sociological Review 50:547-560.

Locke, Daisy. 1993. "Court Services in Canada." Juristat 13, No. 2. Canadian Centre for Justice Statistics. Ottawa: Publications Division, Statistics Canada.

Lombroso, Cesare. 1911. Crime, Its Causes and Remedies. Boston: Little, Brown.

Lombroso, Cesare. 1972. The Criminal Man. Montclair, NJ: Patterson Smith.

Lombroso, Cesare and William Ferrero. 1895. The Female Offender. London: Unwin Fisher.

Lowman, John. 1984. Vancouver Field Study of Prostitution. Working Papers on Pornography and Prostitution, Report No. 8. Ottawa: Department of Justice.

Lowman, John. 1985. "Prostitution in Canada." Resources for Feminist Research 14(4)::35-37.

Lowman, John. 1987. "Taking Young Prostitutes Seriously." The Canadian Review of Sociology and Anthropology 24:99-116.

Lowman, John. 1988. "Street Prostitution." In Vincent F. Sacco (ed.) Deviance: Conformity and Control in Canadian Society. Scarborough, Ont.: Prentice-Hall Canada.

Lowman, John. 1989. Street Prostitution: Assessing the Impact of the Law: Vancouver. Ottawa: Department of Justice.

Lowman, John. 1991. "Prostitution in Canada." In Margaret Jackson and Curt Griffiths (eds.) Canadian Criminology. Toronto: Harcourt Brace Jovanovich, Canada.

Lowman, John. 1992. Personal correspondence, November 19.

Maccoby, E. E., Joseph P. Johnson, and Russel M. Church. 1958. "Community Integration and the Social Control of Juvenile Delinquency." Journal of Social Issues 14:38-51.

Mack, John A. 1972. "The Able Criminal." British Journal of Criminology 12:44-54.

MacLean, Brian D. (ed.) 1986. The Political Economy of Crime: Readings for a Critical Criminology. Scarborough: Prentice-Hall Canada.

MacLeod, Linda. 1980. Wife Battering in Canada: The Vicious Circle. Ottawa: CAACSW.

Maestro, Marcello. 1973. Cesare Beccaria and the Origins of Penal Reform. Philadelphia: Temple University Press.

Maeve W. McMahon and Richard V. Ericson. 1987. "Reforming the Police and Policing Reform." In R. S. Ratner and John L. McMullan (eds.) State Control: Criminal Justice Politics in Canada. Vancouver: University of British Columbia Press.

Malamuth, N. M. and J. V. P. Check. 1981. "The Effects of Mass Media Exposure on Acceptance of Violence Against Women: A Field Experiment." Journal of Research in Personality 25:436-446.

Mann, Coramae Richey. 1993. Unequal Justice: A Question of Color. Bloomington: Indiana University Press.

Mann, W.E. 1967. Society Behind Bars. Toronto: Social Science Publishers.

Marris, Peter and Martin Rein. 1973. Dilemmas of Social Reform (2d. Ed.) Chicago: Aldine.

Marshall, Donald S. 1972. "Too Much in Mangaia." Change: Readings in Society and Human Behaviour. Del Mar, CA: Communications Research Machines.

Martens, Peter L. 1981. "Socioeconomic Status, Family Structure and the Socialization of Early Adolescent Children." Research Report 16, Project Metropolitan: A Longitudinal Study of a Stockholm Cohort. Stockholm: Department of Sociology, University of Stockholm.

Martin, Randy, Robert J. Mutchnick, W. Timothy Austin. 1990. Criminological Thought: Pioneers Past and Present. New York: Macmillan

Massey, James, Marvin Krohn, and Lisa Bonati.
1989. "Property Crime and the Routine Activities of Individuals." Journal of Research in Crime and Delinquency 26:378-400.

Matza, David. 1964. Delinquency and Drift. New York: Wiley and Sons.

Matza, David. 1969. Becoming Deviant. Englewood Cliffs, NJ: Prentice Hall.

Maxim, Paul S. and Carl Keane. 1992. "Gender, Age, and the Risk of Violent Death in Canada, 1950-1986." Canadian Review of Sociology and Anthropology 29:329-345.

Mayhew, Pat and Natalie Aye Maung. 1992. "Surveying Crime: Findings from the 1992 British Crime Survey." Research Findings, No. 2. Home Office Research and Statistics Department.

McCarthy, Bill and John Hagan. 1991. "Homelessness: a Criminogenic Situation?" British Journal of Criminology 31:393-410.

McDaniel, Susan A. and Ben Agger. 1982. Social Problems Through Conflict and Order. Don Mills: Addison-Wesley

McDonald, Lynn. 1976. The Sociology of Law and Order. Montreal: Book Centre.

McDonald, Lynn. 1969. "Crime and Punishment in Canada: A Statistical Test of the Conventional Wisdom." Canadian Review of Sociology and Anthropology 6:212-236.

McDonald, Lynn. 1969. "Crime and Punishment in Canada: A Statistical Test of the 'conventional Wisdom.'" Canadian Review of Sociology and Anthropology 6:212-236.

McDougall, J. Lorne. 1968. Canadian Pacific: A Brief History. Montreal: McGill University Press.

McLaren, John. 1986. "Chasing the Social Evil: Moral Fervour and the Evolution of Canada's Laws, 1867-1917." Canadian Journal of Law and Society 1:125-165.

McLaren, John and John Lowman. 1990. "Prostitution Law and Law Enforcement, 1892-1920: Unravelling Rhetoric and Practice." In Martin Friedland (ed.) Securing Compliance: Seven Case Studies. Toronto: University of Toronto Press.

McNaughton-Smith, Peter. 1976. Permission to be Slightly Free. Ottawa: Law Reform Commission of Canada.

McPhie, Paul and Francis Remedios. 1992. "Legal Aid in Canada: 1990-91." Juristat Service Bulletin, Canadian Centre for Justice Statistics 12 (23).

Mednick, S. A. and K. Christiansen (eds.). 1977. Biosocial Bases of Criminal Behaviour. New York: Gardner.

Mednick, Sarnoff. 1985. "Crime in the Family Tree." Psychology Today 19 (3):58-61.

Mednick, S. A. J. and Volavaka. 1980. "Biology and Crime." In N. Morris and M. Tonry (eds.) Crime and Justice: An Annual Review of Research Vol 2. Chicago: University of Chicago Press.

Menzies, Robert J., Dorothy E. Chunn, and Christopher D. Webster. 1992. "Female Follies: The Forensic Psychiatric Assessment of Women Defendants." International Journal of Law and Psychiatry 15:179-193.

Merry, Sally Engle. 1991. Getting Justice and Getting Even: Legal Consciousness among Working-Class Americans. Chicago: University of Chicago Press.

Merton, Robert K. 1938. "Social Structure and Anomie." American Sociological Review 3: 672-682.

Merton, Robert K. 1968. Social Theory and Social Structure. New York: Free Press.

Messerschmidt, James. 1986. Capitalism, Patriarchy, and Crime: Toward a Socialist Feminist Criminology. Totowa, NJ: Rowman and Littlefield.

Messner, Steven and Kenneth Tardiff. 1985. "The Social Ecology of Urban Homicide: An Application of the 'Routine Activities' Approach." Criminology 23:241-267.

Miethe, Terance D., Mark C. Stafford, and J. Scott Long. 1987. "Routine Activities/Lifestyle and Victimization." American Sociological Review 52:184-194.

Mihorean, Steve. 1992. "Correctional Expenditures and Personnel in Canada, 1991-92". Juristat. Vol 12, No. 22.. Canadian Centre for Justice Statistics. Ottawa: Publications Division, Statistics Canada.

Milgram, Stanley. 1974. Obedience to Authority. New York: Harper and Row.

Milgram, Stanley. 1963. "Behavioral Study of Obedience." Journal of Applied Social Psychology 67:371-378.

Miller, Eleanor M. 1986. Street Woman. Philadelphia: Temple University Press.

Mohr, J. J., A.K. Gigeroff, and R.E. Turner. 1969. "Sex Offenders on Probation: An Overview." Federal Probation 33:22-26.

Morash, Merry and Meda Chesney-Lind. 1991. "A Reformulation and Partial Test of the Power Control Theory of Delinquency." Justice Quarterly 8:347-377.

Morris, Allison. 1987. Women, Crime, and Criminal Justice. Oxford: Basil Blackwell.

Morrison, Peter. 1991. "The Future of Crime Statistics in Canada: The Revised Uniform Crime Reporting Survey." Paper presented to the Annual Meetings of the Canadian Sociology and Anthropology Association in Kingston, Ontario.

Mugford, Stephen. 1992. "Crime and the Partial Legalization of Heroin: Comments and Caveats." The Australian and New Zealand Journal of Criminology 25:27-40.

Mugford, Stephen. 1991. "Toward a Unified Policy for Legal and Illegal Drugs." In Terry Carney, et al. (eds.), An Unwinnable War against Drugs. Sydney: Pluto Press.

Naffine, Ngaire. 1987. Female Crime: The Construction of Women in Criminology. Sydney: Allen and Unwin.

Nease, Barbara. 1971. "Measuring Juvenile Delinquency in Hamilton." In W. E. Mann (ed.) Social Deviance in Canada. Vancouver: Copp Clark.

Netherlands Ministry of Justice. 1991. "Woningbraak: Motieven en Werkwijzen Vanuit

Daderperspectief. (Domestic Burglary: Motives and Modus Operandi from the Offender's Perspective.) Gravenhage, NETH.: Crime Prevention Directorate. (From Criminal Justice Abstracts 24, June 1992: #0406.)

Nettler, Gwynne. 1982. Lying, Cheating, and Stealing. Cincinatti, OH: Anderson.

Nettler, Gwynne. 1984. Explaining Crime (Third Ed.). New York: McGraw-Hill.

New York Institute of Public Administration. 1952. Crime Records in Police Management. New York: New York Institute of Public Administration.

Newman, Oscar. 1973. Architectural Design for Crime Prevention. Washington, D. C.: U. S. Government Printing Office.Nielsen, Marianne. 1979. RCMP Policing: A Question of Style. Master's Thesis, University of Alberta, Edmonton.

Nye, F. Ivan and James F. Short, Jr. 1957. "Scaling Delinquent Behaviour." American Sociological Review 22:326-331.

Nye, F. Ivan, James F. Short, Jr., and Virgil J. Olsen. 1958. "Socioeconomic Status and Delinquent Behaviour." American Journal of Sociology 53:381-389.

Nylund, Marianne. 1991. "Young Offenders and the Mediation Program in Finland." In Jim Hackler (ed.) Official Responses to Problem Juveniles: Some International Reflections. Oñati, Spain: Oñati Institute for the Sociology of Law.

O'Brien, Robert. 1989. "Relative Cohort Size and Age-Specific Crime Rates: An Age-Period-Relative-Cohort-Size Model." Criminology 27:57-78.

O'Brien, Robert M. 1985. Crime and Victimization Data. Beverly Hills: Sage.

O'Brien, C. P., E. P. Nace, J. Mintz, A. L. Meyers, and N. Ream. 1980. "Follow-up of Vietnam Veterans: I. Relapse to Drug Use After Vietnam Service." Drug and Alcohol Dependence 5:333-340.

O'Malley, Pat and Stephen Mugford. 1991. "The Demand for Intoxicating Commodities: Implications for the 'War on Drugs.'" Social Justice 18:49-74.

Pagelow, Mildred Daly. 1984. Family Violence. New York: Praeger.

Pagelow, Mildred Daly. 1989. "The Incidence and Prevalence of Criminal Abuse of Other Family Members." In Lloyd Ohlin and Michael Tonry (eds.) Family Violence, Vol. 11, Crime and Justice: A Review of Research. Chicago: University of Chicago Press.

Palys, T. S. and Stan Divorski. 1986. "Explaining Sentence Disparity." Canadian Journal of Criminology 28:347-362.

Panitch, L. 1977. The Canadian State: Political Economy and Political Power. Toronto: University of Toronto Press.

Pease, Ken and Kristiina Hukkila. 1990. Criminal Justice Systems in Europe and North America. Helsinki: Helsinki Institute for Crime Prevention and Control.

Pepinsky, Harold E. and Richard Quinney (eds). 1991. Criminology as Peacemaking. Bloomington, IN.: Indiana University Press.

Perkins, Roberta and Garry Bennett. 1985. Being a Prostitute. Winchester, MA: Allen and Unwin.

Peterson, Ruth D. and William C. Bailey. 1988. "Forcible Rape, Poverty, and Economic Inequality in U. S. Metropolitan Communities." Journal of Quantitative Criminology 4:99-119.

Phelan, G. F. 1977. "Testing Architecturally Defensible Design: How Burglars Perceive Clues of Residential Vulnerability." Paper presented at the American Society of Criminology, Atlanta, Georgia.

Phillips, Kevin. 1990. The Politics of Rich and Poor: Wealth and the American Electorate in the Reagan Aftermath. New York: Random House.

Platt, Anthony M. 1969. The Childsavers. Chicago: University of Chicago Press.

Platt, Anthony. 1974. "The Triumph of Benevolence: the Origins of the Juvenile Justice System in the United States." In Richard Quinney (ed.) Criminal Justice in America. Boston: Little, Brown.

Pollak, Otto. 1961. The Criminality of Women. New York: Barnes.

Popham, Robert E., Wolfgang Schmidt, and Jan de Lint. 1976. "The Prevention of Hazardous drinking: Implications for Research on the Effects of Government Control Measures." In J. A. Edwing and B. A. Rouse (eds.), Drinking. Chicago: Nelson-Hall.

Poulantzas, Nico. 1973. Political Power and Social Classes. London: New Left Books.

Quinney, Richard. 1975. "Crime Control in a Capitalist Society." In Ian Taylor, Paul Walton, and Jock Young (eds.) Critical Criminology. London: Routledge and Kegan Paul.

Rafter, Nicole Hahn. 1986. "Left Out by the Left." Socialist Review 16:7-23.

Rafter, Nicole Hann. 1990. Partial Justice: Women in State Prisons, 1800-1935. 2nd Edition. Boston: Northeastern University Press.

Ratner, Robert S. and John L. McMullan (eds.). 1987. State Control: Criminal Justice Politics in Canada. Vancouver: University of British Columbia Press.

Ratner, Robert. 1984. "Inside the Liberal Boot: The Criminological Enterprise in Canada." Studies in Political Economy 13: 145-164.

Ratner, Robert, and John McMullan. 1989. "State Intervention and the Control of Labour in British Columbia: A Capital-Logic Approach." In Tullio Caputo, Mark Kennedy, Charles Reasons, and Augustine Brannigan (eds.) Law and Society: A Critical Perspective. Toronto: Harcourt Brace Jovanovich, Canada.

Reasons, Charles E., Lois L. Ross, and Craig Paterson. 1981. Assault on the Worker: Occupational Health and Safety in Canada. Toronto: Butterworths.

Reasons, Charles E. (ed.). 1984. Stampede City: Power and Politics in the West. Toronto: Between the Lines.

Reckless, Walter. 1967. The Crime Problem. New York: Appleton, Century, Crofts.

Reckless, Walter C., Simon Dinitz, and Ellen Murray. 1956. "Self Concept as an Insulator Against Delinquency." American Sociological Review 21:744-746.

Redl, F. and Hans Toch. 1979. "The Psychoanalytic Perspective." In Hans Toch (ed.), Psychology of Crime and Criminal Jusice. New York: Holt, Rinehart, and Winston.

Reeg, Axel R. 1988. "Recent Developments of Western-European Criminal Drug Law Policies." Paper presented at the International Conference on Crime, Drugs, and Social Control; Research Committee for the Sociology of Deviance and Control, University of Hong Kong.

Reiman, Jeffrey. 1990. The Rich Get Richer and the Poor Get Prison (3rd. Ed.) New York: Macmillan.

Research Statistics Group, Program Branch, Solicitor General of Canada. 1986. "Reported and Unreported Crimes." In Silverman, R. A. and J. J. Teevan (eds.). Crimes in Canadian Society, 3rd Edition. Toronto: Butterworths.

Reynolds, Henry. 1981. The Other Side of the Frontier. Townsville: History Dept, James Cook University.

Robins, L. N. 1966. Deviant Children Grow Up. Baltimore: Williams and Wilkins.

Robins, Lee. 1992. "Antisocial Personality and Crime: Separable or Synonymous." Edwin H. Sutherland Award Presentation Address, American Society of Criminology, New Orleans.

Roesch, Ronald. 1978. "Does Adult Diversion Work?" Crime and Delinquency 24:72-80.

Rose, Stephen. 1972. The Betrayal of the Poor: The Transformation of Community Action. Cambridge, Mass.: Schenkmann.

Ross, Robert. 1980. "Violence in, Violence out: Child-abuse and Self-mutilation in Adolescent Offenders. Canadian Journal of Criminology 22:273-287.

Ross, I. 1980. "How Lawless Are Big Companies?" Fortune 102 (December 1):56-64.

Rossi, Peter. 1980. "The Challenge and Opportunities of Applied Social Research." American Sociological Review 45: 889-904.

Rushton, J. P. 1988. "Race Differences in Behaviour: A Review and Evolutionary Analysis." Personality and Individual Differences 9:1009-1024.

Rushton, J. P. and A. F. Bogaert. 1987. "Race Differences in Sexual Behaviour: Testing an Evolutionary Hypothesis." Journal of Research in Personality 21:529-551.

Rushton, J. P. 1988. "Race Differences in Behaviour: A Review and Evolutionary Analysis." Personality and Individual Differences 9:1009-1024.

Sacco, Vincent F. and Holly Johnson. 1990. Patterns of Criminal Victimization in Canada. Ottawa: Statistics Canada.

Sacco, Vincent. 1985. "City Size and Perceptions of Crime." Canadian Journal of Sociology 10:277-293.

Sarnecki, Jerzy. 1989. Juvenile Delinquency in Sweden: An Overview. Stockholm: The National Council for Crime Prevention Sweden.

Sarnecki, Jerzy. 1986. Delinquent Networks. Stockholm: The National Council for Crime Prevention Sweden.

Schechter, S. 1982. Women and Male Violence. Boston: South End Press.

Schmidt, Wolfgang and Robert E. Popham. 1978 "The Single Distribution Theory of Alcohol Consumption." Journal of Studies on Alcohol 39:400-419

Schrag, Clarence. 1971. Crime and Justice: American Style. Rockville, Md.: National Institute of Mental Health.

Schrag, Clarence. 1967. "Elements of Theoretical Analysis in Sociology." In Llewellyn Gross (ed.), Sociological Theory: Inquiries and Paradigms. New York: Harper and Row.

Schwartz, Michael and Sandra Tangri. 1965. "A Note on Self-Concept as an Insulator Against Delinquency." American Sociological Review 30:922-26.

Schwendinger, Herman and Julia S. Schwendinger. 1985. Adolescent Subcultures and Delinquency. New York: Praeger.

Schwendinger, Herman and Julia S. Schwendinger. 1979. "Delinquency and Social Reform: a Radical Perspective." In LaMar Empey (ed.) Juvenile Justice. Charlottesville, VA: University of Virginia Press.

Schwendinger, Herman and Julia Schendinger. 1967. "Delinquent Stereotypes of Probable Victims." In Malcolm Klein (ed.) Juvenile Gangs in Context: Theory, Research, and Action. Englewood Cliffs, N. J.: Prentice Hall.

Scully, Diana. 1990. Understanding Sexual Violence: A Study of Convicted Rapists. Boston: Unwin Hyman.

Sellin, Thorsten. 1938. Culture Conflict and Crime. New York: Social Science Research Council.

Sellin, Thorsten and Marvin E. Wolfgang. 1964. The Measurement of Delinquency. New York: John Wiley and Sons.

Shaver, Frances M. 1985. "Prostitution: A Critical Analysis of Three Policy Approaches." Canadian Public Policy 11:493-503.

Shaver, Frances M. 1988. "A Critique of the Feminist Charges Against Prostitution." Atlantis 4:82-89.

Shaver, Frances M. 1992. "The Regulation of Prostitution: Avoiding the Morality Trap." Paper presented at Canadian Law and Society Meetings, Charlottetown, PEI.

Shaw, Margaret, with Karen Rodgers, Johanne Blanchette, Tina Hattem, Lee Seto Thomas, and Lada Tamarack. 1992. Paying the Price: Federally Sentenced Women in Context. User report 1992-13. Ottawa: Corrections Branch, Solicitor General Canada.

Shaw, Margaret. 1991. The Federal Female Offender: Report on a Preliminary Study. User report 1991-3. Ottawa: Solicitor General Canada.

Shearing, Clifford D. and Jeffrey S. Leon. 1977. "Reconsidering the Police Role." Canadian Journal of Criminology 19:331-345.

Sheldon, William. 1940. The Varieties of Human Physique: An Introduction to Constitutional Psychology. New York: Harper and Row.

Shelley, Louise. 1981. Crime and Modernization. Carbondale, Ill.: Southern Illinois Press.

Short, James, Jr. 1975. "The Natural History of an Applied Theory: Differential Opportunity and Mobilization for Youth." In N. J. Demerath (ed.) Social Policy and Sociology. New York: Academic Press.

Short, James F. Jr. and Fred L. Strodtbeck. 1965. Group Process and Gang Delinquency. Chicago: University of Chicago Press.

Shrofel, Salina. 1985. "Equality Rights and Law Reform in Saskatchewan: An Anlysis of the Charter Compliance Process." Canadian Journal of Women and the Law 1:

Signorielli, N., L. Gross, and M. Morgan. 1982. "Violence in Television Programs: Ten Years Later." In D. Pearl, L. Bouthilet, and J. Lazar (eds.), Television and Behavior: Ten Years of Scientific Progress and Implications for the Eighties: Vol 2, Technical Reviews. Washington: U.S. Government Printing Office

Silverman, Robert A., James J. Teevan, Jr., and Vincent F. Sacco (eds.). 1991. Crime in Canadian Society. 4th ed. Toronto: Butterworths.

Silverman, Robert A., James J. Teevan, Jr., and Vincent F. Sacco. 1991. Crime in Canadian Society. 4th ed. Toronto: Butterworths.

Silverman, Robert A. 1977. "Criminal Statistics: A Comparison of Two Cities." Report to the Solicitor General of Alberta. Mimeographed.

Silverman, Robert and Leslie Kennedy. 1993. Deadly Deeds: Murder in Canada. Scarborough, Ont.: Nelson Canada.

Silverman, Robert A. and Leslie W. Kennedy. 1987. "The Female Perpetrator of Homicide in Canada." Discussion Paper No. 11. Edmonton, Alberta: Centre for Criminological Research.

Silverman, Robert A. 1980. "Measuring Crime: A Tale of Two Cities." In R. A. Silverman and J. J. Teevan (eds.), Crime in Canadian Society. 2nd ed. Toronto: Butterworths.

Silverman, Robert A. 1992. "Crime Rates." In Encyclopedia of Sociology I:347-353. New York: Macmillan.

Simon, Rita and Jean Landis. 1991. The Crimes Women Commit, The Punishments They Receive. Lexington, MA: Lexington Books.

Simon, Rita James. 1975a. The Contemporary Woman and Crime. Washington, D. C.: U. S. Government Printing Office.

Simon, Rita. 1975b. Women and Crime. Lexington, Mass: Lexington Books.

Singer, Simon I. and Murray Levine. 1988. "Power-Control Theory, Gender, and Delinquency: A Partial Replication with Additional Evidence on the Effects of Peers." Criminology 26:627-647.

Single, Eric. 1991. "Canadian Drug Control in the 1990s: Prospects for an Integrated Strategy Regarding Alcohol Control." Canadian Law and Society Meetings, Kingston, Ontario.

Skogan, Wesley G. 1992. Disorder and Decline: Crime and the Spiral of Decay in American Neighbourhoods. Berkeley: University of California Press.

Skogan, Wesley G. and Michael G. Maxfield. 1981. Coping with Crime: Individual and Neighbourhood Reactions. Beverly Hills: Sage.

Sloan, John Henry, Arthur L. Kellerman, and Donald T. Reay. 1988. "Handgun Regulations, Crime, Assaults, and Homicide." New England Journal of Medicine 319:1256-62.

Small, Shirley. 1978. "Canadian Narcotics Legislation, 1908-1923: A Conflict Model Interpretation." In William K. Greenaway and Stephen L. Brickey (eds.) Law and Social Control in Canada. Scarborough, Ontario: Prentice-Hall of Canada.

Smandych, Russ. 1985. "Marxism and the Creation of Law: Re-examining the Origins of Canadian Anti-Combines Legislation 1890-1910." In Thomas Fleming (ed.), The New Criminologies in Canada: Crime, State, and Control. Toronto: Oxford University Press.

Smart, Reginald G. and Edward M. Adlaf. 1992. "Recent Studies of Cocaine Use and Abuse in Canada." Canadian Journal of Criminology 34:1-13.

Smart, Reginald G. 1986. "Cocaine Use and Problems in North America." Canadian Journal of Criminology 28:109-129.

Smart, Carol. 1976. Women, Crime, and Criminology. London: Routledge and Kegan Paul.

Smart, Reginald G. and George K. Jarvis. 1981. "Do Self-Report Studies of Drug Use Really Give Dependable Results?" Canadian Journal of Criminology 23:83-92.

Smith, Douglas A. and Raymond Paternoster. 1987. "The Gender Gap in Theories of Deviance: Issues and Evidence." Journal of Research in Crime and Delinquency 24:140-172.

Snider, Laureen. 1993. Bad Business: Corporate Crime in Canada. Scarborough, Ont.: Nelson Canada.

Snider, Laureen. 1978. "Corporate Crime in Canada: A Preliminary Report." Canadian Journal of Criminology 20:142-168.

Snider, Laureen. 1992. "Commercial Crime." In Vince Sacco (ed.) Deviance: Conformity and Control in Canadian Society (2nd Edition). Scarborough, Ont.: Prentice-Hall Canada.

Solicitor General of Canada. 1986. Canadian Victimization Survey. Bulletin No. 7

Special Committee on Pornography and Prostitution (Fraser Committee). 1985. Pornography and Prostitution in Canada. Ottawa: Department of Supply and Services.

Stack, Steven. 1982. "Social Structure and Swedish Crime Rates: A Time Series Analysis, 1950-1979." Criminology 20:499-513.

Stack, Carol. 1974. All Our Kin. Strategies for

Survival in a Black Community. New York: Harper Colophon Books.

Stanko, Elizabeth Anne. 1985. Intimate Intrusions: Women's Experiences of Male Violence. Boston: Routledge and Kegan Paul.

Stanko, Elizabeth Anne. 1982. "Would You Believe this Woman? Prosecutorial Screening for 'Credible' Witnesses and a Problem of Justice." In Elizabeth Stanko and Nicole Hann Rafter (eds.) Judge, Lawyer, Victim, Thief. Boston: Northeastern University Press.

Stark, Rodney. 1987. "Deviant Places: A Theory of the Ecology of Crime." Criminology 25:893-909.

Statistics Canada. 1983. Historical Statistics of Canada. 2nd Ed. Ottawa: Statistics Canada.

Statistics Canada. 1986. Canadian Crime Statistics 1985. Ottawa: Minister of Supply and Services.

Statistics Canada. 1993. "Occupation," 1991 Census of Canada. Catalogue Number 93-327. Ottawa: Industry, Science and Technology Canada.

Steffensmeier, Darrell J. 1980. "Sex Differences in Patterns of Adult Crime, 1965-1977: A Review and Assessment." Social Forces 58:1080-1108.

Steffensmeier, Darrell J. 1981. "Crime and the Contemporary Woman: An Analysis of Changing Levels of Female Property Crime, 1960-1975." In

Steinhoff, P. G. 1991. "Political Offenders in the Japanese Criminal Justice System." Paper presented at the American Society of Criminology Meetings, San Francisco.

Steinmetz, Suzanne and Murray Straus. 1974. Violence in the Family. New York: Harper and Row.

Stephens, Richard C. 1991. The Street Addict Role: A Theory of Heroin Addiction. Albany: SUNY Press

Stephens, William. 1979. Our Children Should be Working. Springfield, Ill.: Charles C. Thomas.

Stevenson, G. H., L. P. A. Lingley, G. field. 1956. Drug Addiction in British Columbia

Straus, Murray, Richard Gelles, and Suzanne Steinmetz. 1980. Behind Closed Doors: Violence in the American Family. Garden City, N.Y.: Doubleday/Anchor.

Straus, Murray and Richard Gelles. 1986. "Societal Change and Change in Family Violence from 1975 to 1985 as Revealed by Two National Surveys." Journal of Marriage and the Family 48:465-479.

Sutherland, Edwin H. and Chic Conwell. 1937. The Professional Thief: By a Professional Thief. Chicago: University of Chicago Press.

Sutherland, Edwin H. 1949. White Collar Crime. New York: Dryden

Sutherland, Edwin H. and Donald R. Cressey. 1978. Criminology. Tenth Edition. Philadelphia: J. B. Lippincott.

Sykes, Gresham, and David Matza. 1957. "Techniques of Neutralization: A Theory of Delinquency." American Sociological Review 22:664-70.

Syndicat de la Magistrature. 1979. "Mineurs: l'Art de la Fugue." Justice 69: no pages on reprint.

Tannenbaum, Frank. 1938. Crime and Community. Boston: Ginn & Co.

Tappan, Paul. 1947. "Who Is the Criminal?" American Sociological Review 12:96-102.

Tardiff, Guy. 1974. Police et Politique au Québec. Montréal: L'Aurore.

Taylor, Ian, Paul Walton, and Jock Young. 1973. The New Criminology. London: Routledge and Kegan Paul.

The Financial Times of Canada, September 3, 1979.

The Economist, May 16, 1992. "The Tobacco Trade: The Search for Eldorado." Vol 323:21-24.

Thomas, Charles and John Hepburn. 1983. Crime, Criminal Law, and Criminology. Dubuque, Iowa: William C. Brown.

Thomas, Derrick. 1993. "The Foreign Born in the Federal Prison Population." Paper Presented to the Canadian Law and Society Association, Carleton University, Ottawa.

Thomas, William I. 1923. The Unadjusted Girl: With Cases and Standpoint for Behaviour Analysis. New York: Harper and Row.

Thornberry, Terence P., Alan J. Lizotte, Marvin D. Krohn, Margaret Farnworth, and Sung Joon Jang. 1991. "Testing Interactional Theory: An Examination of Reciprocal Causal Relationships Among Family, School, and Delinquency." Journal of Criminal Law and Criminology 82:3-35.

Thornberry, Terence P. 1987. "Toward an Interactional Theory of Delinquency." Criminology 25:863-891.

Thrasher, A. 1976. Skid Row Eskimo. Toronto: Griffin House.

Tierney, Kathleen J. 1982. "The Battered Women Movement and the Wife Beating Problem." Social Problems 29:207-220.

Tong, Rosemarie. 1984. Women, Sex, and the Law. Totowa, N. J.: Rowman and Allanheld.

Trasler, Gordon. 1962. The Explanation of Criminality. London: Routledge & Kegan Paul.

Turk, Austin T. 1969. Criminality and the Legal Order. Chicago: Rand McNally.

Twelfth Report of the Standing Committee on Justice and the Solicitor General. 1993. Crime Prevention in Canada: Toward a National Strategy. Ottawa: Queen's Printer.

U. S. Bureau of the Census. 1992. Statistical Abstract of the United States, 112th Edition. Washington, D. C.: U. S. Bureau of the Census.

U. S. Department of Justice. 1983. Report to the Nation on Crime and Justice. Washington, D.C.: Bureau of Justice Statistics.

Ursel, Jane. 1992. Private Lives and Public Policy: 100 Years of State Intervention in the Family. Toronto: Women's Press.

Ursel, Jane. 1986. "The State and the Maintenance of Patriarchy: A Case Study of the Family, Labour and Welfare Legislation in Canada." In James Dickinson and Bob Russell (eds.) Family, Economy, and State: The Social Reproduction Process Under Capitalism. Toronto: Garamond Press.

Ursel, Jane. 1991. "Considering the Impact of the Battered Women's Movement on the State: The Example of Manitoba." In Elizabeth Comack and Steve Brickey (eds.) The Social Basis of Law: Critical Readings in the Sociology of Law. (2nd Ed.) Toronto: Garamond.

Van Dine, Stephen, John Conrad, and Simon Dinitz. 1979. Restraining the Wicked. Lexington, D. C.: Heath.

Van Brunschot, Erin Elan Gibbs. 1991. "Working Girls: A Study of Youthful Involvement in Calgary Street Prostitution." MA Thesis, Department of Sociology, University of Calgary.

Veltmeyer, H. 1986. The Canadian Class Structure. Toronto: Garamond Press.

Veltmeyer, H. 1987. Canadian Corporate Power. Toronto: Garamond Press.

Vincent, Claude. 1979. Policeman. Toronto: Gage.

Visano, Livy A. 1987. This Idle Trade: the Occupational Patterns of Male Prostitution. Concord, Ont.: VitaSana Books.

Visher, Cathy. 1983. "Gender, Police Arrest Decisions, and Notions of Chivalry." Criminology 21:5-28.

Vogel, D. 1986. National Styles of Regulation: Environmental Policy in Great Britain and the United States. Ithaca, NY: Cornell University Press

Vold, George. 1958. Theoretical Criminology. New York: Oxford University Press.

Voumvakis, Sophia E. and Richard V. Ericson, 1984. News Accounts of Attacks on Women: A Comparison of Three Toronto Newspapers. Centre of Criminology, U of Tor

Wade, Andrew L. 1967. "Social Processes in the Act of Juvenile Vandalism." In Marshall B. Clinard and Richard Quinney, Criminal Behaviour Systems: A Typology. New York: Holt, Rinehart, and Winston.

Wahlsten, D. 1992. "Betwixt Gene and Behaviour." Behavior Genetics 22:11-14.

Wahlsten, D. 1990. "Insensitivity of the Analysis of Variance to Heredity-environment Interaction." Behavioral and Brain Sciences 13:109-161.

Waldo, Gordon and Simon Dinitz. 1967. "Personality Attributes of the Criminal: An Analysis of Research Studies 1950-1965." Journal of Research in Crime and Delinquency 4:185-202.

Walker, Lenore E. 1984. The Battered Woman Syndrome. New York: Springer.

Waller, Irvin. 1974. Men Released from Prison. Toronto: University of Toronto Press.

Weatherburn, Don. 1992b. "Rejoinder to Mugford." The Australian and New Zealand Journal of Criminology 25:41-43.

Weatherburn, Don. 1992a. "Crime and Partial Legislation of Heroin." The Australian and New Zealand Journal of Criminology 25:11-26.

Webber, Marlene. 1991. Street Kids: the Tragedy of Canada's Runaways. Toronto: University of Toronto Press.

Weizmann, F., N. I. Weiner, D. L. Wiesenthal, and M. Ziegler. 1990. "Differential K Theory and Racial Hierarchies." Canadian Psychology 31:1-13.

West, W. Gordon. 1984. Young Offenders and the State: A Canadian Perspective on Delinquency. Toronto: Butterworths.

West, W. Gordon. 1978. "The Short-Term Careers of Serious Thieves." Canadian Journal of Criminology 20:169-190.

West, Donald. 1969. Present Conduct and Future Delinquency. New York: International Universities Press.

West, Donald and David Farrington. 1973. Who Becomes Delinquent? London: Heinemann.

White, Susan O. and Straus, Murray. 1981. "The Implications of Family Violence for Rehabilitation Strategies." In Susan Martin, Lee Sechrest, and Robin Redner (eds.) New Directions in the Rehabilitation of Criminal Offenders. Washington, D. C.: National Academy Press.

Whitehead, Paul and Reginald Smart. 1972. "Epidemiological Aspects of Drug Use and Implications for the Prevention of Drug Abuse." In Craig Boydell, Carl Grindstaff, and Paul Whitehead (eds.), Deviant Behaviour and Societal Reaction. Toronto: Holt, Rinehart, and Winston.

Widom, Cathy S. 1989b. "The Intergenerational Transmission of Violence." In Neil Warner and Marvin Wolfgang (eds.) Pathways to Criminal Violence. Newbury Park, CA.: Sage.

Widom, Cathy Spatz. 1986. "Early Child Abuse, Neglect, and Later Violent Criminal Behaviour." Paper to the conference on "Perinatal and Early Childhood Factors in Deviant Development" Palm Springs.

Widom, Cathy S. 1989a. "Child Abuse, Neglect, and Violent Criminal Behaviour." Criminology 27:251-271.

Wilbanks, William. 1987. The Myth of a Racist Criminal Justice System. Monterey, California: Brooks-Cole.

Wilbanks, William. 1982. "Murdered Women and Women Who Murder: A Critique of the Literature." In Elizabeth Stanko and Nicole Hann Rafter (eds.) Judge, Lawyer, Victim, Thief. Boston: Northeastern University Press.

Williams III, Franklin P. 1980. "Conflict Theory and Differential Processing: An Analysis of the Research Literature." In James Inciardi (ed.) Radical Criminology: The Coming Crisis. Beverly Hills: Sage.

Wilson, James Q. and Richard J. Herrnstein. 1985. Crime and Human Nature. New York: Simon & Schuster.

Wilson, James Q. and Richard J. Herrnstein. 1985. Crime and Human Nature. New York: Simon & Schuster.

Wolf, Daniel R. 1991. The Rebels: A Brotherhood of Outlaw Bikers. Toronto: University of Toronto Press.

Wolfe, Nancy, Frank Cullen, and John Cullen. 1984. "Describing the Female Offender: A Note on the Demographics of Arrests." Journal of Criminal Justice 13:483-492.

Wolfgang, Marvin E. and Franco Ferracuti. 1967. The Subculture of Violence. London: Social Science Pap

Wolfgang, Marvin. 1972. "Cesare Lombroso." In Herman Mannheim (ed.) Pioneers in Criminology. Montclair, NJ: Patterson Smith.

Wong, S. 1984. The Criminal and Institutional Behaviours of Psychopaths. (Programs Branch User Report.) Ottawa: Ministry of the Solicitor General.

Wright, James D. 1991. "Guns and Crime." In Joseph Sheley (ed.). 1991. Criminology: A Contemporary Handbook. Belmont, CA.: Wadsworth.

Wright, Christine. 1992. "Homicide in Canada, 1991". Juristat. Vol 12, No. 18. Canadian Centre for Justice Statistics. Ottawa: Publications Division, Statistics Canada.

Yeudall, L. T. 1987. "A Neuropsychosocial Theory of Persistent Criminality: Implications for Assessment and Treatment." In R. W. Rieber (ed.), Advances in Forensic Psychology and Allied Disciplines: An International and Interdisciplinary Review, Vol 2. Norwood, N.J.: Ablex.

Yeudall, Lorne. 1977. "Neuropsychological Assessment of Forensic Disorders." Canada's Mental Health 25:7-15.

Young, Jock. 1986. "The Failure of Criminology: The Need for a Radical Realism." In Roger Matthews and Jock Young (eds.), Confronting Crime. London: Sage.

Zimbardo, Philip G. 1970. "The Human Choice. Individuation, Reason, and Order versus Deindividuation, Impulse, and Chaos." In W. J. Arnold and D. Levine (eds.), Nebraska Symposium on Motivation, 1969 Lincoln, NE: University of Nebraska Press.

Zimbardo, Philip G. 1973. "The Psychological Power and Pathology of Imprisonment." In T. R. Sarbin (ed.) Social Psychology. New York: Van Nostrand.

Zuckerman, M. and N. Brody. 1988. "Oysters, Rabbits and People: A Critique of 'Race Differences in Behaviour' by J. P. Rushton." Personality and Individual Differences 9:1025-1033.

Name Index

Subject Index